MW01195640

Too Ma.
on the Ice

Too Many Men on the Ice

The 1978–1979 Boston Bruins and the Most Famous Penalty in Hockey History

JOHN G. ROBERTSON

McFarland & Company, Inc., Publishers
Jefferson, North Carolina

All photographs are from the author's collection.

ISBN (print) 978-1-4766-7100-0
ISBN (ebook) 978-1-4766-3288-9

LIBRARY OF CONGRESS CATALOGUING DATA ARE AVAILABLE

BRITISH LIBRARY CATALOGUING DATA ARE AVAILABLE

Front cover: Boston Bruins head coach Don Cherry (center with tie)
among his players on the bench (Mecca/Hockey Hall of Fame)

Printed in the United States of America

*McFarland & Company, Inc., Publishers
Box 611, Jefferson, North Carolina 28640
www.mcfarlandpub.com*

To the 1978–79 Boston Bruins—the final installment
of Don Cherry's "Lunch Pail Athletic Club,"
as they were lovingly and accurately dubbed
by the great Francis Rosa of the *Boston Globe*.
Although you came up heartbreakingly short
in your quest to win Lord Stanley's silver cup,
you will forever be heroes in my eyes.
Rosa put it succinctly: "Never has a team
won so much in defeat."

Acknowledgments

The author thanks the following people who assisted with this project: the staff at the Dana Porter Arts Library at the University of Waterloo for their assistance in accessing their impressive newspaper microfilm collection; the staff at the Queen's Square and Preston branches of the Cambridge, Ontario, public library system for their help in obtaining valuable materials via inter-library loan; Carl Madden for his preliminary proofreading efforts; Chris Borowiec for providing DVDs of Game #4 and Game #7 of the 1979 Bruins-Habs semifinal; and the brave individuals who risked the wrath of the NHL by posting unauthorized clips and full games from the 1978 and 1979 Stanley Cup playoffs on YouTube.

Table of Contents

Preface

"May 10, 1979: Boston led Montreal 4–3, at the Forum no less, with 2:34 left in Game #7 of their Stanley Cup semifinal when linesman John D'Amico made, in conjunction with referee Bob Myers, a call as indisputable as it was ineluctable. In violation of Rule 18, the Bruins had too many skaters on the ice…"
—Michael Farber, in his 2014 *Sports Illustrated* article
"Three Little Words"

"In 1977 we were the superior team. In 1978 we were even. In 1979 I think we stole their Cup from them."
—Montreal forward Bob Gainey assessing the Bruins-Habs
rivalry from the late 1970s in the 2017 Sportsnet
documentary *The Names on the Cup*

Words can be surprisingly powerful.

In March 1982, I was thumbing through *The Book of Sports Lists*. One section featured sports historian Bill Libby's personal choices for the toughest losses in history.

Libby mentioned the 1938 Duke University football team. He recounted the formidable Blue Devils romping through their nine-game regular season undefeated, winning every game by a shutout, and earning a coveted berth in the 1939 Rose Bowl game. In that contest, Duke led Southern California 3–0 with 40 seconds to play when USC's third-string quarterback, Doyle Nave, heaved a desperation pass caught by Al Krueger, a second-string end, for the game-winning touchdown. In one single play Duke's undefeated season, shutout streak, and aspirations to win the Rose Bowl and the national championship were all shattered.

More than four decades had passed, yet Libby vividly recalled listening to Duke's devastating loss on the radio—and his emotional reaction to it. "I locked myself in the bathroom and wept," he wrote. "I was 11 years old. I don't know why Duke was my team, but it was. Its loss was mine and typified all the losses suffered by all the boys who never again will root as hard for their teams."[1]

Full disclosure here: I am a Boston Bruins fan. I candidly admit it. I have been since the age of three when I started collecting hockey cards and watching games from the six-team National Hockey League on a black-and-white television in the family living room. I am also a Canadian, born and raised above the 49th parallel. I really don't know with any absolute certainty why I support a team that plays its home games in a foreign country.

Whatever the origin of my fandom may be, I have stayed loyal to my team through both good times and bad. Like Libby, I cannot rationally explain my allegiance. The Bruins are my team, they have always been my team, and they always will be my team.

1

As a six-year-old, I witnessed the incomparable Bobby Orr's Stanley Cup-winning goal in the aforementioned living room on May 10, 1970. Two years and one day later, Orr scored a lesser-known but prettier championship-clinching goal versus the New York Rangers at Madison Square Garden to make it two Cups in three seasons for my heroes in black and gold. I was certain that more Stanley Cup championships for the Bruins—my Bruins—would follow in the near future. Such is the optimistic naivety of children. The Bruins indeed made three more Cup-final appearances before the 1970s concluded. Alas, there were no further hockey championship parades in Boston until 2011, just varying degrees of disappointment—overshadowed by one moment of absolute infamy.

Despite the Stanley Cup pinnacles of 1970 and 1972, my passion for the Bruins reached its zenith as I entered my teenage years. Therefore the Bruin teams I most closely associate with are those from the Don Cherry-coached era, a truly fun five-season span from 1974–75 to 1978–79. I discovered, with a bit of luck, that I could listen to every Bruin game on WBZ-AM (*"The spirit of New England.... All the good sports are on ... WBZ!"*). Those radio broadcasts seemed magical and otherworldly. The reception was not always great; the signal tended to fade in and out as the night progressed—especially if the weather happened to be rotten. Nevertheless, I listened to many Bruin games, enjoying the deep, assuring voice of Bob Wilson describing the action from venerable Boston Garden and other NHL buildings where my Bruins ventured.

Broadcasts from the cozy Garden seemed especially vivid. I could sometimes hear the shouts of individual fans. John Kiley's excellent work on the organ came through loud and clear, as did the pleasant New England accent of public-address announcer M. Weldon Haire. Many nights I drifted off into peaceful slumber after a Bruins victory safe in the knowledge that all was right with the world. That was usually the case as the Bruins won far more often than they lost in those five seasons. Colorful Don Cherry was the coach of the Boston Bruins for precisely 400 regular-season games. He compiled a very solid 231–105–64 record. That's an impressive .658 winning percentage. In Cherry's final four seasons at the helm, his Bruins finished atop the Adams Division every year and advanced to at least the Stanley Cup semifinals. I think I was particularly drawn to these Bruins by their sheer grittiness. They seemingly battled and clawed their way to every one of those 231 victories. It was an endearing trait.

When I read Libby's sad words about Duke's football team in 1982, I knew exactly how he felt. In 1979, my Boston Bruins suffered a similarly heartbreaking fate when their dream victory was moments away from being realized. The Montreal Canadiens—it was always the Montreal Canadiens—struck the fatal dagger blow in Game #7 of a Stanley Cup semifinal. I was 15 years old. I thought I was beyond experiencing severe emotional disappointment for a team that played its home games 600 miles from where I lived. I was wrong.

That awful loss weighed heavily on my mind for a long, long time. On some level, I still haven't gotten over it—especially how it happened when sweet victory seemed so tantalizingly near. For years, I loathed seeing the video snippets from Game #7 that always seemed to crop up on *Hockey Night in Canada* retrospectives. To my dismay, two Montreal goals would always be shown: Guy Lafleur's booming slap shot to tie the game with 1:14 left in the third period, and Yvon Lambert's redirection of Mario Tremblay's pass for the win at 9:33 of overtime. They were always accompanied by Danny Gallivan's original calls for *HNIC*, which somehow made them worse. Never once would Jean Ratelle's lovely overtime goal in Game #4 be shown nor any of the Bruins' four goals in Game #7. This irked me to no end. I commonly complained to anyone within earshot, "The Bruins won a lot of games in those days. It would be nice to see a Boston goal once in a while! Is that asking too much?"

In writing this book, I had the unpleasant task of re-watching Game #7 in its entirety for the first time in more than 37 years. The source was a DVD I acquired from a collector in North Carolina who had recorded it from the NHL Network in 2008. It was a slightly edited version of the original *HNIC* feed I had watched in the family rec room on May 10, 1979. Even after the passage of all those years, I dreaded the inevitable outcome. I stopped the DVD at the end of the second period (with Boston holding a 3–1 lead and clearly outplaying the favored Habs) and postponed watching the sad conclusion as long as I possibly could. Finally, after two days had passed, I forced myself to re-insert the disc and watch everything agonizingly unravel in the third period and in the frantic overtime. The passage of time had somewhat cushioned the blow, but not entirely. Irrationally I was hoping that history had somehow changed and the Bruins would win the game and the series.

In researching this book my memory was refreshed regarding several aspects of the 1978–79 NHL season and playoffs. I had forgotten how injuries had ravaged the Bruins' roster all season; I had forgotten that Montreal had inexplicably lost their last regular-season game in Detroit and thus unexpectedly handed the number-one playoff seed to the New York Islanders; I had forgotten about goaltender Gilles Gilbert's untimely attack of hives before Game #3 of Boston's quarterfinal series versus Pittsburgh; I had forgotten about the contentious penalty that Bob Myers had assessed to Toronto's Tiger Williams in Game #4 of the Maple Leafs-Habs quarterfinal; I had forgotten about Dave Newell's strange refusal to award Boston an obvious penalty shot in Game #1 of the semifinal; I had forgotten how remarkably similar Guy Lafleur's slap shot goal in Game #4 was to his famous game-tying goal a week later in Game #7; and I had forgotten that Scotty Bowman's coaching future in Montreal was about as uncertain as Don Cherry's was in Boston. I had also forgotten the irony of ironies: Stan Jonathan's hat-trick in Game #6 that made him the toast of Boston for about 48 hours. All glory is fleeting.

Mostly, however, I had forgotten what a wonderful team those 1978–79 Boston Bruins were! They were an everyman's outfit of aging stars, young hopefuls, and seasoned pros nearing their peaks. They combined to play terrific hockey and came within 74 seconds of pulling off a staggering upset. Most of all they were coach Don Cherry's "Lunch Pail Athletic Club," a collection of characters with a terrific work ethic who valued teamwork over individual glory; a team that reveled in their scrappy identity; a team that took pride in being the Boston Bruins. They also had the most flamboyant coach in all of professional hockey, the most colorful in NHL history. Don Cherry never won a Stanley Cup but he won thousands of hearts and the respect of the vast majority of his players in his five years at the Bruins' helm. After hundreds of hours of reading newspaper accounts of that season's odyssey from the archives of the *Boston Globe* and other newspapers, I believe if Cherry had ordered his Bruins to march single-file into machine-gun fire they would have obliged. He was that popular with his players. The Boston media, of course, loved Cherry and his antics and reported them with great gusto. As a result, Bruin fans were treated to both bread *and* circuses. It was no coincidence that the gritty, hard-working Bruins of that era routinely had the best road attendance in the NHL. Rick Middleton recalled years later that few Bruins games from the late 1970s were stinkers. No, they certainly were not.

This project opened my eyes to how good this Bruin team was and how many obstacles it overcame to get as far as it did. The fact that the 1978–79 Boston Bruins came up a teensy bit short in the most important game of the season did not diminish my admiration for this bunch in the slightest. The Bruins had battled and clawed their way to within reach of professional hockey's grandest prize only to succumb to a dreadful mistake, a gaffe that Dick Irvin of *Hockey Night in Canada* accurately labeled "the most famous penalty in hockey history."[2] My team truly deserved a better fate than the toughest of losses.

On Thursday, May 10, 1979, a tension-packed Stanley Cup playoff game that night at the Montreal Forum provided two brutally harsh life lessons. One was that faith, dedication and hard work are not always fruitfully rewarded. Secondly, one's hopes and dreams can be dashed in a manner most cruel. The disastrous result of a single game—one firmly entrenched in NHL lore—converted me from an optimist to a cynic, a pessimist, and a realist. I was terribly stunned and embittered. I secretly vowed I would never again permit myself to become so thoroughly emotionally attached to the fortunes of any one sports team. The promise was kept for 25 years until the 2004 Boston Red Sox proved utterly irresistible.

Brian Cazeneuve accurately noted in a video feature about that historic contest, "There's no greater or worse moment—depending on your perspective—than what happened in Game #7 of 1979."[3] To fully understand why this one playoff game and why that one unfortunate blunder packed such a crushing blow, one must fully grasp the circumstances and the history behind it. That is what this book will attempt to do.

Introduction
Those Unbeatable Habs

"I watch the Canadiens skate through their warm-ups in grand, wonderful loops. The same as always. They fire those low slap shots at their goaltender. They stride and glide. Around and around. Familiar and awful. Beautiful and lethal. Isn't that Jacques Plante, the old Snake, in the net? No, couldn't be. He passed away a couple of years ago. Must be Ken Dryden, tall and correct, the Ivy League man. No, he's a lawyer now in Toronto. Must be the Gumper. Gump Worsley. No, must be Steve Penney. No, must be Patrick Roy. No … must be … must be … spring again."
—Leigh Montville, *Sports Illustrated*, April 25, 1988

"If you hate anyone, hate the Habs."
—Matt Kalman, author of *100 Things Bruins Fans Should Know & Do Before They Die*

In simplest terms, the Montreal Canadiens were the Boston Bruins' bugaboo going into the 1978–79 season. The jinx—as some cynics referred to it—went back a long, long way.

When the Bruins entered the National Hockey League in 1924 as its first expansion team outside of Canada, the defending Stanley Cup champions were the Montreal Canadiens. For historical purposes, it would have been wonderful had Boston's first opponent had been the Habs. Unfortunately, it was the Montreal Maroons—the other expansion team that began play in 1924—who faced off against the Bruins on December 1 at old Boston Arena. Boston won 2–1. Fred (Smokey) Harris scored the first goal in Bruins history. Glory was fleeting for Harris; he was traded after playing a mere six games for Boston. John J. Hallahan of the *Boston Globe* declared the Bruins' Opening Night win to be an auspicious start and "every one of the fairly good sized crowd was pleased."[1] Nevertheless, in a sidebar article, Hallahan wondered if professional hockey would ever truly be embraced by Bostonians.

The first time the Canadiens faced the Bruins, on December 8, 1924, the Canadiens were 4–3 winners. (Boston's first win against the Habs occurred in the teams' third matchup, on January 10, 1925. It was a 3–2 overtime triumph.)

After playing their first four seasons at undersized Boston Arena—a facility that still exists today as Matthews Arena, home of the NCAA's Northeastern Huskies—the famous Boston Garden opened its doors for Bruins hockey on Tuesday, November 20, 1928. That night the home team disappointingly lost 1–0 to … the Montreal Canadiens. On January 8, 2016, the Bruins recorded their 3,000th regular-season victory, a considerable total eclipsed by only one other NHL club … the Montreal Canadiens. Among Boston's five rivals from the Original Six NHL teams, both the Habs and Detroit Red Wings hold an edge in all-time wins versus Boston—but only Montreal has a truly significant win difference (360–275 with 103 ties at the end of the 2016–17 NHL season). As hard as it might be for a Bruin or Hab fan to grasp, the Bruins held an edge in their all-time head-to-head record versus Montreal as late as 1959–60. Consider this mathematical reality: Beginning with the 2017–18 season, if the Bruins somehow average two more wins than the Habs in their head-to-head meetings each season for the foreseeable future, it will take Boston 43 years to erase Montreal's lead in the all-time series.

> "Forty-five years. Eighteen playoff series. Finals. Semifinals. Quarterfinals. Preliminaries. Best of seven. Best of five. Sweeps. Thrillers. The results have always been the same. The Montreal Canadiens have won. They have been favored and won. They have been underdogs and won. They have won hard and won easy, and won and won."
> —Leigh Montville, *Sports Illustrated*, April 25, 1988

The Stanley Cup playoffs were where Boston especially struggled to topple the illustrious Habs. The Canadiens had been an utterly immovable obstacle for the Bruins since the Second World War ended. One could argue that Boston's playoff jinx at the hands of Montreal dates as far back as 1930. That season a superb and clearly superior Bruins team that had compiled a fantastic 38–5–1 record in the 44-game regular season unexpectedly faltered in two straight games in the best-of-three Cup final versus the Habs. Nobody saw it coming. "So confident are the Bruins of winning tonight," declared the *Globe*'s John J. Hallahan prior to Game #1 on April 1, "they will be ordered to pack all their belongings, take them to Montreal, and be ready for their exhibition tour of the Pacific Coast after the second game at the Forum."[2] That same day, the *Globe* ran a cartoon by Gene Nair featuring a flattering illustration of Montreal's Howie Morenz, dubbing him "the speed boy of hockey."[3] The cartoonist cockily noted, however, "They'll need six Morenzes to win."[4] Montreal won 3–0 at Boston Garden and 4–3 at the Montreal Forum to take the Cup. (Controversy engulfed the end of Game #2. Boston had an apparent game-tying goal disallowed as Cooney Weiland was ruled to have illegally kicked the puck into the Montreal net.) During the 1929–30 regular season, Boston had won all four meetings versus the Canadiens— which, of course, meant absolutely nothing when the Stanley Cup was on the line. "The collapse of the Bruins on Tuesday and the defeat tonight followed the usual course of hockey history," Hallahan duly noted in his *Globe* report following Game #2. "Teams that have gone great guns during the course of a season usually have petered out when the big tests came."[5] It would become a recurring and maddening trend for the Bruins and their fans that has extended into the 21st century.

From 1929 to 1978, the Boston Bruins faced the Montreal Canadiens 17 times in the Stanley Cup playoffs. The Bruins won just two of those series: a semifinal round in 1929 and again in 1943. In none of the four seasons that fell between 1929 and 2011 when Boston won the Stanley Cup did they have to face the Habs in the playoffs. Beginning with the

Opposite page, top: This is an exterior shot of Boston Garden, the famous home of the Boston Bruins from 1928 to 1995. The Montreal Canadiens were the first and last visiting team to play the Bruins at the Garden. **Bottom:** Built in 1924 as the home of the Montreal Maroons, the Montreal Forum became a fortress for the Canadiens who seldom lost there during their dynasty periods of the 1950s and 1970s. It closed in 1996.

huge surprise of 1930, Montreal again rolled to postseason triumphs over Boston in 1931, 1946, 1947, 1952, 1953, 1954, 1955, 1957, 1958, 1968, 1969, 1971, 1977, and 1978. Most of those series were not even close; Montreal typically won with ease.

Even early in the rivalry there were complaints that the Bruins seemed to get the short end of the stick when it came to referees' decisions in playoff games versus the Habs. In recalling the seldom-discussed 1931 semifinal 40 years later, Harold Kaese of the *Boston Globe* wrote, "The officiating was so anti–Boston that one of the ice cops lost his job."[6] [Author's note: This statement appears to be inaccurate. A two-man officiating system was used in the NHL in 1931 in which both officials combined the same duties as today's linesmen and referees. The duo of Mickey Ion and Bobby Hewitson, remarkably, officiated all five games of the series—an utterly unthinkable arrangement by modern standards. Both referees worked NHL games long after 1931—and both have been enshrined in the Hockey Hall of Fame.]

Covering the best-of-five series for the *Globe* was Victor O. Jones. The Bruins won 5–4 in Game #1 at Boston Garden on a thrilling Cooney Weiland overtime goal after Montreal blew a 4–1 third-period advantage. Describing Montreal's seemingly insurmountable lead, Jones wrote, "The crowd was cast in the deepest gloom."[7] After the Boston comeback, however, Jones was decidedly upbeat. He tempted fate by writing, "The result of last night's game forecasts a straight three-game win for the team of [Boston coach] Art Ross, for Howie Morenz and his mates will hardly again enjoy a three-goal advantage with 17 minutes to play."[8]

Late during Montreal's 1–0 win at Boston Garden in Game #2, referee Mickey Ion made an egregious mistake—he sent the wrong Bruin to the penalty box! Jones described the scene:

> [Boston defenseman Eddie] Shore knocked [Howie] Morenz cold with a desperate dive, and then, as a sad anticlimax, referee Mickey Ion ruled George Owen off the ice for five minutes, presumably for inflicting upon Morenz a cut which Howie actually sustained in at the hands of Shore.
> This penalty so aroused the populace that play had to be halted for 15 minutes while the ice was three times littered with every imaginable sort of refuse. The rafters shook with boos.[9]

Owen's phantom major penalty put the Bruins in a shorthanded situation for the rest of the game, effectively eliminating any real chance of a comeback. Boston attempted to offset the penalty with a heretofore-unknown tactic: Art Ross pulled goaltender Cecil (Tiny) Thompson late in the game for an extra attacker, a maneuver that startled the Boston Garden crowd and probably the Canadiens too. It did not pay dividends. Montreal held on to its tenuous 1–0 advantage until the final horn to level the series at one game apiece. The remaining games would be played at the Montreal Forum.

After Boston lost by a 4–3 score in overtime in Game #3, Bruins coach Art Ross deemed the officiating to be very suspicious and contacted Charles Adams back in Boston to inquire about filing a formal protest. Jones reported that NHL president Frank Calder had comically admitted the referees "were wrong on *only* two goals and one penalty,"[10] but cautioned the Bruins about making any sort of protest unless they possessed irrefutable evidence that one or both of the referees were on the take. The Bruins' chief complaint was that two of Montreal's four goals had clearly been illegally kicked into the net but were allowed to stand.

Boston was at their best in Game #4 and comfortably won 3–1. For the first time in the series, Boston scored the game's opening goal. Entering the third period the Bruins nursed a secure 3–0 lead and, according to the *Globe*'s Victor O. Jones, "played tight defensive hockey, waiting for breaks and covering the red shirts like leeches."[11]

Ion and Hewitson were the focal points of the Habs' 3–2 overtime win in Game #5, especially among the Boston newspapermen and the hundreds of Bruins fans who had traveled by special train to Montreal to witness the deciding game. Jones disgustedly wrote in the *Globe*, "As has been the case in almost every one of these fiercely fought battles this week and last, the referees, misters Ion and Hewitson, played too prominent a part in deciding the fortunes of the battle."[12] Perhaps it was appropriate that the game was contested on April Fool's Day.

Calling the game "a farce," Jones reported, "The Bruins were being sent off every time they frowned on a Canadien." Howie Morenz did not score a goal or record an assist. Nevertheless, he may have been the Habs' most valuable asset for his ability to draw penalties—a few of them of the specious variety. "He kept the Bruins almost chronically shorthanded by getting them exiled," Jones declared. "On at least one or two of these penalties, Howie proved himself a fine actor, playing on the sympathies of the referees with contortions which would have done credit to a professional wrestler."[13]

Jones did not bluntly say that the fix had been in, but he certainly suggested there had been something akin to blatant corruption, favoritism, or both on the part of Ion and Hewitson. He noted,

> Those who have held that professional hockey has been the one moneyed game which needed no legislative investigations and was above the manipulations of both the gamblers and the owners are now wondering [about its honesty], if not entirely disillusioned.
>
> Nine penalties [were] called against the Bruins, all but one of them by Mickey Ion as against three against Les Canucks, all called by Bobby Hewitson, with seven of the nine Bruins penalties called against Eddie Shore and George Owen, four of them so spaced that the Bruins were left two men short on two occasions.
>
> If somebody in hockey doesn't do something about the refereeing and rules situations, the game is going to suffer for it.[14]

The *Montreal Gazette*'s report by L.S.B. Shapiro barely mentioned the officiating, only noting that "Eddie Shore was the strength and the driving power of the Bruins, but what he did on the ice was lost when he made four trips to the penalty box. Shore and Owen proceeded to step into the Frenchmen from the start, but the referees were on their toes and the two defensemen were closely watched. Their charges invariably brought penalties in their wake."[15]

After the fiasco of 1931, 12 years would pass before the Bruins and Habs met again in the playoffs. A dominant Boston team won the Stanley Cup twice (1939 and 1941), and probably should have won a couple more. In 1943, the Bruins ousted the Canadiens in five games in a semifinal. It was not especially noteworthy at the time, but it marked the last Bruins victory over Montreal in a Stanley Cup playoff series for 45 years as Montreal proceeded to remarkably compile 13 consecutive series wins versus the Bruins.

Most of the 13 Habs-Bruins playoff series that all went Montreal's way between 1946 and 1978 were not even close. Montreal usually won quite comfortably. The 1952 semifinal was one exception. "We should have beaten them in '52," recalled Boston's Ed Sandford in a 1988 interview. "That was the year we had our chance."[16]

The underdog Bruins were leading the series three games to two but lost the sixth game at home in double overtime, forcing a seventh game back at the Forum. (The winning goal in Game #6 was notched by Paul Masnick, a 20-year-old rookie who deftly batted the puck out of the air and into the Bruins' net. Masnick had scored a grand total of one regular-season goal in 1951–52.) Game #7 featured a Hollywood-type ending: Maurice (Rocket) Richard, sporting two black eyes and a bloody bandage across his forehead, returned from being knocked senseless to score the winning goal for the Habs late in the third period. "The 14,508 rabid Montreal partisans staged a hysterical demonstration of several minutes," declared *Boston Globe* writer Tom Fitzgerald, "littering the ice with programs and millinery following the great individual feat of their hero."[17] An empty-net goal by Billy Reay (who would later coach the Chicago Blackhawks for 14 years) sealed Montreal's 3–1 win. A terrific postgame news photograph of Richard shaking hands with the equally battle-scarred Boston goalie Sugar Jim Henry is an iconic image in Canada.

"After we lost the final game, everyone seemed to disappear," remembered Sandford. "I didn't know where they went. Hal Laycoe and I were left. We went to some restaurant in Montreal. We ordered some food. Neither of us was saying much. Finally Laycoe says, 'The hell with this!' He stands up, turns the table upside down, and walks out the door. Stuff was everywhere on the floor. It's a mess. I'm sitting there and I have to pay for it all."[18]

After Montreal routinely ousted the Bruins in a 1955 semifinal in five games, Tom Fitzgerald outlined the Bruins' recent playoff woes against the Habs. "This was the fourth straight year the B's have been eliminated from the post-season tournament by the Canadiens," he wrote in the *Globe*. "In that stretch they have been able to win only five out of 21 games. In the last three series it has been two out of 14."[19] Two years later, after the Bruins lost the 1957 Stanley Cup final in five games to the Canadiens, Fitzgerald echoed the familiar refrain of the defeated. He wrote, "[Boston] can look back on a season that was generally successful, even though it fell short of complete fulfillment Tuesday night in Montreal. Not long after the Canadiens had drained the champagne from Lord Stanley's old vase, many hockey people were talking of the Bruins as prime challengers for next season."[20]

Only twice in the seven Bruins-Habs series contested from 1953 and 1969 did the Bruins threaten to win. In 1958, Boston was a substantial underdog because they had finished the regular season in fourth place, one game under .500. But they surprisingly knocked off the second-place New York Rangers in the semifinals and gallantly took vastly superior Montreal to six games in the final. The tipping point was a tough 3–2 overtime loss in Game #5 at the Forum on April 17. In the extra period, 36-year-old Rocket Richard— arguably the greatest clutch scorer in Stanley Cup history—beat Boston goalie Don (Dippy) Simmons on a long, waist-high wrist shot on which Simmons was partially screened by defenseman Allan Stanley. It was only the second shot on goal Richard had managed all game. Simmons, a journeyman netminder, was named the game's first star. In Boston Garden for Game #6 three nights later, the disheartened Bruins mustered another decent fight. They were down 2–0 after two minutes, and 4–1 after 40 minutes, but mounted a third-period rally to get to within 4–3. Alas, an empty-net goal by Montreal's Doug Harvey clinched the game and the third consecutive Stanley Cup for the Habs by a 5–3 score. "You could almost hear hearts breaking all over the place,"[21] declared Tom Fitzgerald in the *Globe*. The two teams would not meet in the playoffs again until after the NHL had doubled in size with its historic 1967 expansion.

In 1959, Boston lost in the Stanley Cup semifinals to Toronto in an upset and then descended into the team's lowest period—an awful run of eight straight seasons in which they failed to make the playoffs. (Johnny Bucyk uniquely endured that entire demoralizing postseason drought as a Bruin player.) In six of those eight campaigns, the Bruins finished dead last in the six-team NHL.

Bobby Orr's arrival in 1966 provided obvious hope for a much-needed Bruins revival, but even he could not prevent another last-place finish in the final year of the so-called Original Six era. Boston finished the season with a dismal 17–43–10 record. At Boston's final home game of the 1966–67 campaign on April 2, frustrated Bruin fans began a derisive chant: "We're number six! We're number six!" A creative bunch added, "Next year we're number twelve!" Tom Fitzgerald's report in the *Boston Globe* tersely said, "The Bruins concluded their seasonal activities Sunday night in the steamy Garden in characteristic fashion. They lost to the Toronto Maple Leafs, 5–2. A gathering of 12,056 [fans], coatless and shirt-sleeved, offered the customary disparagements of a general and personal nature...."[22]

Ending the annoying playoff jinx against Montreal seemed like a far-off goal when any postseason action whatsoever was proving so elusive. However, Boston's fortunes were about to take a dramatic swing upward in the NHL's expansion era. In the first year of the 12-team NHL, the 1967–68 Bruins at least qualified for the playoffs by finishing a strong third in the newly created Eastern Division—comprised of the familiar six teams that made up the league from 1942 to 1967—with a 37–27–10 record. Harold Kaese of the *Globe* optimistically declared, "There is no powerhouse in the NHL this season. The Bruins look good enough to stay in there with any of the other three [Eastern division] qualifiers."[23] Kaese was wrong. Boston, still in an inchoate stage, promptly dropped four games to the Habs who outscored them 15–8. "I didn't think we'd lose four straight," said a dejected Phil Esposito. "Worsley was excellent."[24] Indeed, Montreal got superb goaltending from Lorne (Gump) Worsley and some surprising offensive punch from an unexpected source. Claude Larose equaled his regular-season output of two goals with two scores in Game #4. Nevertheless, the Bruins were obviously a team to be reckoned with in the near future. "We learned something in this playoff series," coach Harry Sinden admitted to the *Globe*'s Kevin Walsh after the last game. "We learned we have to strengthen ourselves. The club made one step this year. We can't afford to stand still."[25]

Boston got a rematch with Montreal the following spring. The 1969 Eastern Division final between the Habs and the Bruins was basically a toss-up. Montreal had ended the 1968–69 season with 103 points in 76 games. Boston came in second place with exactly 100 points. The Bruins had demolished overmatched Toronto in four games in the first round of the playoffs, outscoring the Leafs 24–5 in the process and prompting Toronto to fire coach George (Punch) Imlach who had been with the team since 1958 and still had a year left on his contract.

The Bruins-Maple Leafs series—Boston's first playoff series victory in 11 years—is mostly remembered for an incident in the second period of Boston's 10–0 Game #1 win in Boston. Toronto's Pat Quinn knocked Bobby Orr unconscious with a hard elbow to the head delivered just inside the Bruins' blue line. Tom Fitzgerald of the *Globe* was seething. He wrote, "It is obvious that the Maple Leafs were a parody of a major league club. Since they were outplayed in such essentials as shooting, passing and skating, the Leafs resorted to the last refuge of the humiliated. They gave a pretty good impression of a vengeful gang, dedicated to any consolation to be derived by provoking violence." Fitzgerald also declared that Quinn and Leafs enforcer Forbes Kennedy were sent onto the ice "to chop down their superiors in talent."[26] Quinn was attacked in the penalty box by several irate Orr fans and had to be escorted to the visitors' dressing room by a cordon of Boston policemen for his own safety. Orr spent the night in Massachusetts General Hospital as a precaution, but returned the next night to play in Boston's 7–0 win in Game #2. Obviously, concussion protocols were unheard of in 1969.

The Habs-Bruins Eastern Division final was generally perceived by knowledgeable fans to be the "real Stanley Cup final" because one of the six inferior 1967 expansion teams that comprised the Western Division was guaranteed a berth in the actual final. As in 1958, Boston lost to Montreal in six games. Three of Montreal's four wins required overtime. Youthful Montreal goalie Rogie Vachon, replacing the injured Gump Worsley, was especially good.

Game #6 at Boston Garden was an agonizing double-overtime thriller in which Phil Esposito twice missed an open net in the extra periods. In regulation time, Boston failed to capitalize on a two-man advantage in the second period. Jean Béliveau scored the only overtime goal in his storied NHL career on a pass from Claude Provost at the 11:28 mark of the second extra period to seal the series for Montreal with a 2–1 win. It was the first overtime game played at Boston Garden in 14 years. (The Bruins lost that one to the Habs too, on Donnie Marshall's goal in Game #3 of the 1955 semifinals.) It was only the fourth home game in 43 that Boston had lost all season. It was Montreal's first win in Boston since the fourth game of their 1968 quarterfinal series.

The double-overtime game extended past midnight; it was the second longest Boston-Montreal playoff game in history. (Not surprisingly, the Habs also won the longest one back in 1947. Johnny Quilty, the Calder Trophy winner from 1940–41, got the winner that night. Immediately after the 1946–47 season ended, the Bruins acquired Quilty in a trade with the Habs. Quilty scored three goals in his first five games with Boston, but he gruesomely broke his leg in his sixth game and never played another second in the NHL.) In 1969 Montreal was still the better team—but just by a smidgen, although former Bruin great Milt Schmidt, who was now the team's general-manager, did not agree and was more than happy to say so publicly. The day after the tough loss in Game #6, Schmidt bitterly told Tom Fitzgerald, "Nobody can come into this office and tell me that the best team is in the Stanley Cup final."[27] Fitzgerald only partially agreed with Schmidt. He editorialized in the *Boston Globe*, "Possibly more objectively, it might be better to present the finding that Montreal and Boston are the two best hockey teams in the world, barring dissent from Moscow."[28]

Despite the disappointing ouster, Boston was clearly a team on the rise. Bobby Orr and Phil Esposito were approaching their heydays and they had a very solid core of supporting players to bolster the roster. "The present may belong to the Canadiens. The future definitely belongs to the Bruins,"[29] Tom Fitzgerald optimistically wrote in the *Globe*. For the first time since the glory years of the famed Kraut Line in the early 1940s, the Bruins were genuine Stanley Cup threats. "This is a very good Boston team,"[30] the victorious Béliveau concurred. Bruins coach Harry Sinden agreed. "I'm stunned," he told Fitzgerald. "We have such a great team. We really deserved to win so often in this series."[31]

In fact, Phil Esposito, upon arriving in Boston's training camp in London, Ontario, in September 1967 as part of one of the most lopsided trades in sports history, uncannily predicted the Bruins' short-term future. "This is a team that will learn how to win," Espo accurately prophesized. "The first year [1967–68] we'll make the playoffs for sure. The next year we'll come in second or third. The third year we'll win the whole thing—the Stanley Cup."[32] That was quite a bold statement considering the Bruins had become the NHL's doormats once the 1950s had ended and had embarrassingly missed qualifying for the Stanley Cup playoffs for a record eight consecutive seasons. (That dubious mark was later equaled by the Washington Capitals and surpassed by the Edmonton Oilers when the NHL was a much larger circuit.)

Nevertheless, just as Esposito called it, the Cup came to Boston at the conclusion of the 1969–70 season as Montreal failed to make the playoffs for the first time since 1948. The Eastern Division race was incredibly tight with the top five teams only separated by seven points. Montreal finished fifth, tied with the New York Rangers on both points and wins, but lost narrowly on the NHL's second tie-breaker rule: goals scored. Toronto finished in last place, marking the first time in NHL history that no Canadian-based teams qualified for the postseason. Forty-six years would pass before the Stanley Cup playoffs would again be without Canadian teams.

Boston, who had finished in second place with 99 points, dispatched the Rangers in six games in a quarterfinal series. It was the sternest test the Bruins would face in the 1970 postseason. Horribly uncivil behavior by the New York fans at Madison Square Garden sullied the series. They threw eggs and ball bearings at the Bruins and set the arena's mezzanine on fire when the result of Game #6 was no longer in doubt. Boston then surprisingly blew away the Chicago Blackhawks in four straight games in the semis to reach the Stanley Cup final for the first time in 12 years. Considering Boston had compiled a poor road record against their divisional rivals in 1969–70, the triumph over Chicago was stunningly easy— and Bobby Orr was at the forefront. Gary Ronberg of *Sports Illustrated* gushed, "There was Orr, gliding along as if shielded by an invisible barrier as the Hawks sleep-skated sheeplike in his wake. One of the most amazing moments of any Cup series came in the third game when Orr skated behind the Chicago net with three Hawks chasing after him and then leisurely set up the easiest kind of goal."[33]

Unstoppable, the Bruins dominated the St. Louis Blues in another four-game sweep in the final to win the Stanley Cup for the first time since 1941. The Blues were coached by highly-regarded Scotty Bowman. By winning their last ten playoff games, Boston set a new NHL record for consecutive postseason wins. In the May 11 issue of the *Globe & Mail*, Dick Beddoes acknowledged that the Bruins had been progressively getting stronger over the past three NHL seasons, but concluded they had truly begun their re-building process in 1948. "That's the year Bobby Orr was born," he coyly noted.

Scotty Bowman coached the Montreal Canadiens to four consecutive Stanley Cups in the late 1970s. A tough taskmaster whom his players respected but did not necessarily like, Bowman was once rated as the greatest pro sports coach of all time by *Sports Illustrated*.

The Stanley Cup win in 1970 dramatically and forever changed everyone's perception of the Bruins. "It's easy to forget," wrote Jerry Nason in a *Globe* piece titled "None Laughing at Bruins Now," "that [not too long go] they weren't hockey's Big Bad Bruins at all, but the Sitting Ducks of the NHL and annual candidates for last place."[34] On the Bruins' radio postgame show, Johnny McKenzie, in the champagne-splashed victorious dressing room, figured the new champions had begun an unbeatable dynasty. Indeed, the days of the Bruins being perceived as pushovers were long gone. One unnamed Bruin insider comically told Gary Ronberg of *Sports Illustrated* after Boston's semifinal sweep of Chicago, "People read that the Bruins are coming to town and they think we're going to rob all the banks and rape all their daughters."[35]

"It must be great to be 22 years of age, and wear the colors of the Boston Bruins, and be the man who scored the [Stanley Cup-winning] overtime goal," noted CBS' Dan Kelly as the Bruins joyfully celebrated their first championship in 29 years. Orr picked up a mind-boggling collection of awards at season's end. Besides the team achievement of the Stanley Cup, the humble Orr's individual honors included the NHL's Conn Smythe Trophy (playoff MVP), Hart Trophy (regular season MVP), Art Ross Trophy (scoring champion), and Norris Trophy (best defenseman), *Sports Illustrated*'s Sportsman of the Year, the Lou Marsh Memorial Award for Canada's most outstanding athlete—and the undying love of Boston's sports fans. Bud Collins, best known as a tennis writer and commentator, declared in his *Boston Globe* column, "It is generally agreed that Bobby Orr is the greatest thing since The Pill."[36]

One interesting statistic from 1969–70: Despite missing the playoffs for the first time in a generation—an utter calamity for Montreal—the Habs still fared better than the Bruins in their eight regular-season contests. Montreal won three times, Boston won twice, and three games ended in ties.

To this day Boston's playoff loss to Montreal in 1971 remains especially galling to Bruin fans. In 1970–71, Boston was a true powerhouse, bludgeoning opponents en route to one lopsided victory after another. It was the year when Phil Esposito famously scored a record-shattering 76 goals. Bill Hewitt of *Hockey Night in Canada* often referred to Boston as "the high-flying Bruins"—and for good reason. Four NHL players attained at least 100 points that season. All four were Boston Bruins: Phil Esposito, Bobby Orr, Johnny Bucyk and Ken Hodge. Seven of the top nine scorers in the NHL were Bruins. Bobby Orr's plus/minus figure was a stratospheric plus-124—a record that has never been broken and perhaps never will. No one has come close to it in 40 years. (For purposes of comparison, Ryan Sutter and Jason Zucker tied for the NHL lead in 2016–17 with a more human-like plus-34.) Such was the 23-year-old Orr's overall dominance in 1970–71 that his usual defense partner, Dallas Smith—hardly an all-time great despite having a solid 15-year NHL career—was plus-94. That's the fourth-highest plus/minus ever attained in one season since the statistic was kept.

Boston routinely scored goals in bunches in 1970–71. Four times that season the Bruins scored more than eight goals in a single game. On March 16 versus Detroit—at the Olympia, no less—they scored 11 times. (Boston averaged a stunning 5.1 goals per game in 1970–71 in notching a record 399 goals—an NHL record that stood until the Wayne Gretzky-era Oilers broke it four times.) Montreal had the second most goals in the NHL that year—a comparatively paltry 291. The Bruins were shut out only once during the entire campaign (by the St. Louis Blues in the tenth game of the season), had a 13-game winning streak, another run where they were undefeated in 14 games, and finished the 78-game regular season with 121 points to easily top the NHL's Eastern Division—the first time in 30 years the Bruins had finished atop the standings. Four of the team's 14 losses that season came in succession late in March when they lacked motivation because they already had first-place clinched. The Bruins lost only four of their 39 home games that season. Boston won five out of the six games versus Montreal during the regular season in which they outscored the Habs 29–14. Even though the Canadiens had solidly accrued 97 points in 1970–71, heading into the postseason they were widely perceived to be cannon fodder for Boston.

In a playoff-preview article, Harold Kease of the *Globe* practically invited disaster. He arrogantly wrote, "It will not happen this year of course, but many times in the last 50 years the team finishing with the best record in the National Hockey League's regular season has failed to win the Stanley Cup."[37] Hall-of-Famer Dit Clapper agreed that the Bruins were shoo-ins to win it all. Commenting from his home in Peterborough, Ontario, the 64-year-old ex-Bruin captain and coach declared, "They've got the best [roster] and I can't see them being stopped."[38] Clapper, the only man to play on three Bruin Stanley Cup-winning teams, told Kaese he planned to attend some games at the Garden during the 1971 Cup final as he had the previous year.

In the first round of the playoffs—the last year the NHL used its illogical first-versus-third and second-versus-fourth playoff pairings—the third-place Canadiens lost the first game of the best-of-seven quarterfinal 3–1 in Boston on April 7. Gerry Cheevers was excellent, stymying the Canadiens on numerous scoring opportunities. Referee John Ashley came under heavy criticism by the Bruins for some iffy calls. Montreal's lone goal came on a power play. Bobby Orr was assessed a misconduct for arguing a holding penalty in the third period, which prompted a boisterous chant of "Ashley is a bum!" by the irate home fans. Montreal was unable to capitalize. "Bobby himself was being tripped and hooked and held all night," insisted Bruins first-year coach Tom Johnson. "I couldn't blame him for being upset."[39] (Despite the Bruins' displeasure with the referee, Ashley was highly regarded by the NHL. During the 1971 Stanley Cup playoffs, he would achieve a first by officiating three seventh games: a quarterfinal, a semifinal, and the final.) Boston had now won 11 consecutive playoff games over the past two postseasons, but the closeness of Game #1 should have been a warning. Despite Cheevers' outstanding work in the Boston net, Tom Johnson insisted that he would continue to rotate his two goalies throughout the playoff games just as he had done for most of the regular season. Veteran Ed Johnston, who had been with the Bruins since 1962, would be Boston's goaltender in Game #2.

In Game #2 at Boston Garden the very next night, the Bruins romped to a 5–1 lead before the halfway point in the second period. Bobby Orr figured in four of the Bruin scoring plays with a goal and three assists. The home team seemed to have the game well in hand; it looked like another typical Bruins rout. With 25 minutes to play, the score was still 5–1 for Boston. The Canadiens appeared badly overmatched. Longtime Bruins broadcaster Fred Cusick recalled in a 1988 *Sports Illustrated* interview, "The year we [the Bruins] should have won was 1971. We were better [than Montreal]. Much better. I remember doing interviews between periods about possible opponents in the next round. That's how certain it was."[40]

Somehow Montreal rallied to score six unanswered goals—five in the third period—to win that contest 7–5, severely rattling the Bruins' collective psyche in the process. Veterans Henri Richard and Jean Béliveau led the Habs' offensive push with two goals apiece. It was the first time in team history that Boston had scored five goals in a Stanley Cup playoff game and lost. Phil Esposito had not scored a goal in either of the first two games of the series, although he did notch three assists.

"We just had a total defensive collapse in the last period—a total collapse,"[41] Boston coach Tom Johnson glumly told the media after the game. (Johnson had replaced Harry Sinden behind the Boston bench in 1970–71. Sinden had surprisingly walked away from the club in a contract dispute after the 1969–70 Cup-winning season.) "The Bruins didn't merely collapse. They evaporated," wrote a disgusted Harold Kaese in the *Globe*. "The Canadiens didn't become merely inspired. They became ethereal—out of this world."[42] Boston goaltender Ed Johnston was not especially good once the Habs' onslaught began, but often he was left to fend for himself. (Cheevers would return to the Boston goal for Game #3; Johnston did not play another minute of the series.) Kaese, a veteran scribe who had been covering Boston sports since 1933, declared the Bruins' gasp-inducing reversal of fortune in Game #2 to be the single most startling thing he had ever witnessed. Nevertheless, he believed Montreal's comeback win in Game #2 was "nothing more than a grandiose fluke."[43] Tom Fitzgerald wrote in the *Globe* that the setback was a "calamity" and, in a wonderful bit of understatement, noted, "There will be at least a slight delay in the progress of the Bruins to another Stanley Cup. That much was assured last night."[44]

Aside from the epic Boston cave-in in Game #2, the 1971 Habs-Bruins quarterfinal series is mostly remembered for a gutsy personnel change made by interim Montreal coach Al MacNeil who had taken over the Habs' bench 23 games into the season: Montreal's two veteran regular goalies, Rogie Vachon and Phil Myre, were bypassed in favor of a lanky rookie named Ken Dryden. Dryden, a Cornell University law student, had played just six games for the Habs during the regular season. He won all six, allowing just nine goals. Dryden had spent the majority of the 1970–71 season with the Montreal Voyageurs of the American Hockey League. At times in the series, Dryden was absolutely brilliant. After one especially spectacular glove save against Boston's top sniper, frustrated Phil Esposito angrily called Dryden a "thieving giraffe."[45] Espo had launched 11 shots at Dryden in Game #1 without finding a weak spot in his armor.

With momentum suddenly on their side, the Canadiens took Game #3 at the Forum 3–1, but Boston temporarily righted their ship to win Game #4, 5–2. Boston forward Derek Sanderson noted afterward that although the Bruins had apparently regained the momentum in the series, the Habs were no pushovers. He even created a fictitious team to make his point. "What you have to remember is that the team we're playing is not the Motortown Rockets," he said. "These are the Montreal Canadiens. These guys are good hockey players."[46] Even though Boston played well and evened the series, Leigh Montville noted after Game #4, "If there were any overconfident thoughts by the Bruins, they have to be gone now."[47]

The series' first four games were played in a frantic space of just five days to accommodate both American and Canadian television interests. The tight schedule took its toll on both teams. Things indeed seemed to be returning to regular-season form for the Bruins after they comfortably won Game #5 at Boston Garden, 7–3, but Montreal easily thumped Boston 8–3 in Game #6 at the Forum to force a climactic seventh game. The *Globe* called Boston's lopsided loss "their most humiliating defeat of the season" and declared that Ken Dryden, who was studying for final exams between games, "looked anything but a rookie in the net."[48]

In front of a North American Sunday afternoon television audience, a 4–2 Montreal win in Game #7 completed one of hockey's greatest upsets. Boston got off to an early 1–0 lead on a Ken Hodge goal, but the Bruins were "never in command again,"[49] according to the *Globe's* front-page story. Despite being prohibitive favorites when the quarterfinal began, it was the 11th time in succession dating back to 1946 that the Bruins had failed to win a playoff series versus Montreal. Dan Kelly, calling the game for CBS, declared Montreal's series win to be "a tremendous upset." The cover of the April 26, 1971, issue of *Sports Illustrated* went a bit further, proclaiming "Catastrophe in Boston." Few Bruin fans considered it hyperbole.

Harold Kaese, in his post-mortem for the *Globe*, lamented the superb regular season the Bruins had wasted. He wrote, "The Bruins set 41 scoring records this season—or was it 141?—and that plus 15 cents will buy them a cup of coffee at any lunch counter today." But Kaese also focused on the Canadiens' achievement. Kaese noted, "In beating the Bruins, the Canadiens walked across the Atlantic, climbed Everest in track suits, and trumped from one end of the Sahara to another without taking a drink."[50]

Many of the Canadiens quietly reveled in upending the Bruins, whom some hockey writers had prematurely called the greatest team of all time. Others were more vocal. "That's one dynasty that didn't last very long,"[51] cackled John Ferguson to Mark Mulvoy of *Sports*

Illustrated. Mulvoy assessed what had happened: "When the Canadiens were able to stymie Orr by harassing him with two forecheckers or by ganging up on him at their blue line…. Boston sputtered like any machine suddenly deprived of its horsepower."[52]

Mulvoy described the Bruins in defeat. "Cocky and brash during their romp through the league during the regular schedule, they were now morose," he wrote. "Most of them expected Montreal to die in four straight games."[53] Only goaltender Gerry Cheevers was able to retain his sense of humor. When told that Ken Dryden liked to spend his spare time perusing law school libraries, the horse-playing Cheevers quipped, "At least I'll never run into him off the ice. I start every day the same way, with the Lord's Prayer: 'Our Father, who art in heaven, give us this day our daily double.'"[54]

On some level, the residue from the 1971 quarterfinal defeat still lingers in the minds of Bruin fans who are always fearful that some horrible disaster is waiting just around the corner in a red, white and blue uniform. "It's all been so sad," Cusick lamented in 1988. "I've been the voice of the undertaker for so long on these things. It all seems to be one blur."[55]

The purposeful Bruins were again the NHL's powerhouse in 1971–72, but they still retained the dangerous habit of taking victories for granted. On February 23, Boston was losing 6–1 on the road to the lowly California Seals in the second period, but rallied to win the game 8–6. The Bruins rebounded to win the Stanley Cup in 1972 but Montreal was not a playoff obstacle for Boston that spring. The Bruins ousted Toronto in five surprisingly tough games in a quarterfinal and utterly crushed St. Louis in four games in a laughably one-sided semifinal in which they outscored the overmatched Blues 28–8. After a 10–2 Boston triumph in Game #2, Blues coach Al Arbour said, "I think our young team is awed by the Bruins. We're playing in a trance. We're mesmerized. We see Orr and Esposito and Bucyk and the rest of them out there and we wonder what we're doing playing on the same ice with them."[56] The youthful Blues, a team with eight rookies it its lineup, had a right to feel overwhelmed and outgunned. St. Louis had finished 11 games under .500 in the regular season, yet that was still good enough for third place in the decidedly weaker Western Division. Their 67 points were 52 fewer than Boston's 119.

Boston was pushed to six games by the tough and talented New York Rangers in a hard-fought final. The two teams and their fan bases had grown to dislike each other intensely. After the series concluded, Ranger coach Emile Francis said, "I wouldn't pay $15 to see anything … except if you put all the Boston hockey fans and all the New York hockey fans into Shea Stadium and let them fight. I'd pay 15 bucks to see that!"[57] Ted Blackman of the *Montreal Gazette* held Ranger fans in especially low esteem. He wrote in his May 13 column, "New York fans toss batteries, ball bearings and shaving-cream cans on the ice. Their average IQ is six. It takes eight to bark, you know."[58]

In Game #1 at Boston Garden, the Bruins rolled out to an early big lead—including scoring two shorthanded goals on the same Rangers power play while Don Awrey was in the penalty box. The score prompted one fan to heckle the Rangers with "Bring back St. Louis! We want some competition!" However, Boston shockingly allowed the Rangers to rally from a 5–1 second-period deficit in a span of 17 minutes to tie the score, incredibly duplicating the epic disaster against Montreal from the previous spring. It must have been a nightmarish feeling of déjà vu for coach Tom Johnson. However, Garnet (Ace) Bailey's goal late in the third period gave Boston a 6–5 victory, thus averting another monumental collapse. Ken Hodge said, "Let's face it. We got lucky. There's too much at stake now. We can't afford any more letdowns."[59] Bobby Orr had a subpar game. Ted Blackman's *Gazette* report said, "When Orr can't crack the three-star circle, the Bruins are … well, they're the Swedish Nationals with elbows."[60]

In Game #2, the Bruins needed a timely third-period goal by Hodge to win 2–1 when New York was two men shorthanded. Referee Art Skov was heavily criticized by the visitors after the game for the iffy penalty call on Walt Tkaczuk that gave the Bruins the five-on-three advantage that proved so critical. Don Awrey figured the Rangers were in big trouble, stating he doubted they could play any better than they had in Game #2. Nevertheless, the Rangers roared back for a 5–2 win in Game #3 on their home ice, but Boston took Game #4 by a 3–2 score to take a 3–1 series lead. New York spoiled the Bruins' victory plans in Game #5 at Boston Garden with a come-from-behind 3–2 win on two goals by ex-Hab Bobby Rousseau. Tim Burke of the *Montreal Gazette* declared that the Rangers "had caught everyone's fancy outside of Boston for their refusal to lie down."[61]

The clinching game of the series occurred at Madison Square Garden on May 11, and was a solid 3–0 triumph for Boston. As in 1970, Bobby Orr got the winning goal and assisted on Wayne Cashman's deflection in the third period that sealed the victory. He also won the Conn Smythe Trophy for a second time. Thirty-nine years would pass before another Bruin would win it.

Gerry Cheevers thoroughly enjoyed recording the shutout in New York City. "I felt like [Kentucky Derby winner] Riva Ridge tonight," he said. "I just couldn't lose." When the Bruins lost Game #3 at the same locale, Cheevers was struck on the head with a bag of garbage tossed from a balcony. It was reported that Cheevers displayed "the peace sign" to the Ranger fans in that general area once Game #6 had concluded—but it may have actually been a far different and less friendly gesture. When asked if he got an extra charge from winning the Cup in front of his tormenters, Cheevers probably wanted to respond in the affirmative, but he diplomatically replied, "I wouldn't have cared if we had won it in Hong Kong."[62]

Another Bruin was even less subtle in his contempt for the Rangers and their fans. Forward John McKenzie skated to center ice. He conspicuously mimicked a Statue of Liberty pose with one arm while placing his other hand around his neck in a "choke" gesture. He then jumped up and down several times.

Tom Fitzgerald basked in the Bruins' triumph. He wrote in the next day's *Globe*, "After that regrettable one-year absence, the Stanley Cup went back home to Boston early this morning in the custody of the exuberant but pride-filled Bruins."[63] Some 10,000 fans sacrificed a decent night's sleep to greet the champions at 2:30 a.m. at Logan Airport.

Under new coach Scotty Bowman, Montreal accrued 108 points in 1971–72 yet only managed to finish third in the tough Eastern Division. The Habs were basically a non-factor in the 1972 playoffs, having fallen to the Rangers in a six-game quarterfinal. The Bruins and many members of the hockey media considered their 1972 Stanley Cup victory—the fifth in the 48-year history of the club—retribution for the disastrous 1971 playoffs and a reaffirmation of the team's overall excellence, but they still had not shaken their frustrating postseason jinx versus the Montreal Canadiens. It hardly mattered to most Bruin fans, though, as Boston reasserted its supremacy over all other NHL teams. Kevin Walsh, in his summary of the Stanley Cup final for the *Globe*, wrote, "The tools are there. The Bruins just have to put them to proper use and there isn't a team in professional hockey their equal. Any doubters would only have to ask the players from Toronto, St. Louis and New York who fell along the way."[64]

It was a good time to admire how good the Bruins of the early 1970s were because the team would endure major changes before the 1972–73 season. The rival new World Hockey Association would lure away Derek Sanderson, Ted Green, John McKenzie, and Gerry Cheevers with more lucrative contracts than the Bruins were prepared to offer. (Cheevers quipped that the biggest difference between playing for Boston and the WHA's Cleveland Crusaders was that his teammate wearing #4 with the Bruins was Bobby Orr. In Cleveland, #4 was Ralph Hopiavuori. Apparently, Hopiavuori's mother saw no humor in Cheevers' comment.) The NHL was also broadening from 14 to 16 teams, and Ed Westfall would be lost in the expansion draft to the New York Islanders. Similarly, promising minor-league goalie Dan Bouchard would be snatched by the Atlanta Flames. Bobby Orr remained a Bruin, but he would undergo another intrusive knee surgery. He was only 24, but he was a fragile commodity. In an article that appeared in the *Boston Globe* on the day the team opened its 1972–73 season, Tom Fitzgerald wrote, "You can look for things to be a little different for the Bruins this season—not necessarily worse or necessarily better—just different."[65]

Despite the substantial personnel turnover, the Bruins were still a force in 1972–73. They began the season poorly, but by New Year's Day, they had the best record in the NHL. However, Boston faltered in the final half of the season, finishing in second place in the Eastern Division with 107 points. (Montreal finished ahead of Boston, losing just 10 games all season.) Substandard goaltending hurt the Bruins badly when it mattered most. Forty-four-year-old Jacques Plante—the Habs' superstar goalie from the late 1950s who was at least a decade past his prime—was acquired in early March to bolster the team's shaky netminding. Plante won seven of eight games and recorded two shutouts for Boston as the regular season wound down. Plante was glaringly weak in the quarterfinal versus the New York Rangers, however, allowing 10 goals in two starts. With Phil Esposito sidelined with a leg injury he suffered in Game #2, there was no successful Stanley Cup defense. Boston tepidly bowed out in five lackluster games to a hungrier opponent, uncharacteristically losing all three games at Boston Garden. "This wasn't the same Bruins team as last year,"[66] new coach Bep Guidolin admitted.

Boston and Montreal did not meet in the playoffs again until the 1977 Stanley Cup final. That year Montreal was overwhelmingly dominant during the regular season. Unlike the 1971 Bruins, they kept their form throughout the playoffs and romped to the Stanley Cup without too much resistance from their three postseason opponents. Consistency—always a Montreal trademark—seemed to be an elusive trait whose absence constantly plagued Boston teams in playoff rounds versus the hated Habs.

1

The Arrival of Don Cherry
and the "Lunch Pail A.C."

Perhaps the most famous Bruin of the late 1970s era was the coach rather than any of his players. Don (Grapes) Cherry was a well-traveled career minor-league defenseman who managed to play in just one NHL game—a Stanley Cup playoff game for Boston versus Montreal in 1955 at the Montreal Forum. He did not record a point. (Is it even necessary to say the Canadiens won that night?) According to Cherry's autobiography, he uprooted his family 53 times during his 16-year playing career and nearly a decade of subsequent coaching gigs. "Nobody has played in or coached in as many cities as I have. I played in every professional league that existed,"[1] Cherry declared in another book titled *Straight Up & Personal.*

When Cherry was a child, his father frequently read to him from Horatio Alger novels as a means of illustrating the virtues of honesty, diligence and hard work. Every Alger plot was seemingly the same: A poor boy rises from humble beginnings by being righteous and fighting the good fight. Those values stayed with Cherry into adulthood. "In one way, it worked; in another it didn't," Cherry stated. "In the books, the heroes were always at odds with their bosses and authority. I think after a while it got to me. Every job I had and every general-manager I had, I was at odds with them."[2]

After coaching the Rochester Americans in the American Hockey League—and winning that league's Coach of the Year Award twice—Cherry was promoted to the NHL. On June 13, 1974, he replaced Bep Guidolin as the coach of the Boston Bruins—a team that had lost to Philadelphia in the Stanley Cup final a month earlier in a minor upset. Guidolin resigned in late May over a contract dispute. Guidolin had demanded nothing less than a five-year pact. Harry Sinden, who had returned to the Bruins in 1972 as their general-manager, countered with a one-year offer. Unwilling to budge, Guidolin telephoned his resignation to Sinden from his home in Barrie, Ontario. Cherry and Guidolin were friends, having crossed paths during Cherry's extensive minor-league odyssey.

Someone with almost no experience in the NHL being installed as coach of the mighty Bruins worried some Boston media folks. Cherry sensed he was under scrutiny before he held his first practice. "I wouldn't have taken the job if I didn't think I could do it,"[3] Cherry confidently assured Bob Kinsley of the *Boston Globe*, one of the doubters.

Cherry was, of course, an unknown quantity in the NHL when he debuted as the new Bruins bench boss—Ernie Roberts of the *Globe* wrongly reported that Cherry's surname was pronounced "sherry"—but he did not remain anonymous very long. His press conferences and blustery tirades against all and sundry who conspired to sidetrack him and his beloved Bruins made him something of a folk hero to New Englanders. Cherry exuded confidence from Day One, but he knew he had been dealt a strong hand. "You're not much of a coach if you can't win with the Bruins,"[4] he told the *Globe*'s Francis Rosa.

Cherry became particularly well known for his sartorial splendor—especially on game nights. In a *Globe* feature about him penned by Ernie Roberts in January 1978 titled "Boston's Own Dandy Don," Cherry explained he had altruistic reasons for being well outfitted. "I think the players like to be proud of their coach, the way he is dressed. [People] ridiculed Bep Guidolin's clothes when he was [coaching] here. Maybe I overdo it a bit behind the bench, with the pins and cufflinks and chains, but hockey players are basically the best-dressed athletes in sports and they like to see their coach look good."[5] Eddie MacCabe of the *Ottawa Citizen* declared, "Cherry is the paragon of NHL chic. His thinning hair is Krazy-Glued over the naked spot, shoes always highly buffed."[6] In George Plimpton's book *Open Net*, Cherry revealed that his collection of dapper game-day suits were designed entirely for show—not practicality. His trousers were so form-fitting he could not sit down in them.

In the same *Globe* article, Roberts described Cherry as a self-educated individual. "Like many Canadians who get wrapped up in junior hockey and then the minor leagues," Roberts wrote, "Cherry never graduated from high school. But he is an intelligent, well-read man, not self-conscious about his lack of formal education."[7] Volumes on military history—especially famous naval commanders—dominated his personal library. His wife Rose concurred. "Don has read every book ever written on Lord Nelson. He reads every night before he goes to sleep,"[8] she noted.

The result of Cherry's very first NHL game as Boston's coach, on October 10, 1974, was a humbling 9–5 loss to the Sabres in Buffalo. The Bruins fell behind 1–0 after just 18 seconds and never recovered. The *Globe* bluntly described the contest as "a debacle."[9] Displaying the moxie and straightforwardness that would largely characterize his five-year run with the Bruins, the rookie coach accepted the blame for the embarrassing setback. Cherry stated, "We were all in this together. There will be no back-stabbing. Everybody was to blame and I blame myself as much as anybody else."[10] His honesty and no-buck-passing quickly won the respect of his players. The straight-shooting, down-to-earth Cherry earned the loyalty and trust of his Bruins because he acted like one of them instead of management, much to general-manager Harry Sinden's chagrin. The Bruins only managed only a tie and two losses in Cherry's first three games at the helm. His first NHL win came on October 17, 1974, against the Flyers in Philadelphia—the team that briefly usurped the Habs in the mid–1970s as Boston's biggest rival. "That's just the beginning," Bobby Orr told Cherry after the game. "It will be like this all the time."[11] Orr was correct. After that initial win came, the Bruins won consistently thereafter.

In the years between 1971 and 1977, the Bruins changed their "identity." After post-season disappointments in 1974 (losing in the Stanley Cup final to Philadelphia in a series they were favored to win) and 1975 (a shocking first-round collapse in a preliminary series versus Chicago), the Bruins transformed themselves from the offensive-minded team that typically won games 7–3 and 6–2 to a grinding team that outworked opponents and were more likely to be involved in 3–1 and 4–2 games. Coach Don Cherry remembered how that change of philosophy occurred. The Bruins had just been ousted from the 1975 playoffs. Cherry met Harry Sinden at a restaurant to discuss strategy to restore the Bruins to contender status. Sinden candidly told Cherry, "You've got to find a way to make this team win or we're both going to be fired. Do whatever you have to do. Turn the players against me, if necessary."[12]

"I took that comment to heart and took it to the extreme," Cherry admitted. "We were against the world. We thought Harry was against us. We thought the league was against us, everyone was against us."[13] With Orr on his last legs, and Esposito about to be traded to the New York Rangers, two months into the 1975–76 season the formerly high-flying Boston Bruins were quickly transformed into the "Lunch Pail A.C."—an apt term coined by *Boston Globe* writer Francis (Fran) Rosa to describe how the Bruins would approach each game for the remainder of Cherry's tenure in Boston and for years afterward.

The term originated in a casual conversation. "I recall talking to someone about the Bruins," Rosa remembered. "I said, 'They're like working stiffs—[they] get up and go to work and then go home.' The other person said, 'Like a lunch-pail guy.' I agreed and started using the term Lunch Pail Gang or Lunch Pail A.C. [short for Athletic Club] to describe the team. Some of the players initially resented the nickname because they thought it implied they had no talent—that they were just a bunch of working stiffs. That wasn't true. They had talent on those Cherry teams. The nickname just described the work they did."[14] The nickname Rosa created stuck and became well known across the NHL. Tim Burke of the *Montreal Gazette* thought it was an apt description. "The Bruins are rightly called a 'lunch-pail team' cast in the mold of their irrepressible coach, Don Cherry, as delightful a blue-collar guy as you'll ever run into."[15]

"You couldn't find a more relentless, courageous, determined bunch of players in the entire NHL,"[16] according to hockey historian Matt Kalman. One player especially stood out. "Terry O'Reilly became the poster child for the Bruin teams of the late 1970s because of his all-out effort every night."[17] The work of O'Reilly and his teammates endeared the Bruins to the fans at Boston Garden. They also became the NHL's top-drawing road team. Most importantly, the lunch-pail attitude fostered tremendous camaraderie among the Bruin players, turning them into a tight-knit brotherhood that consistently played winning hockey and dutifully watched out for each other.

"There was nothing better in the history of hockey than sitting with those players after a game," said Peter McNab, who was acquired by the Bruins in the summer of 1976. "It could be the greatest moment of your life or the worst moment. If you didn't play well it could be an embarrassing or humbling moment. On the other hand, Wayne Cashman or Terry O'Reilly might come by and say, 'Good game!' [After hearing that simple compliment] you could not be higher."[18]

"We had such a good team, a hard-working team, a team that cared," said Rick Middleton, a highly talented goal scorer whose promising career was stagnating with the New York Rangers until a 1976 trade to Boston revitalized it. "Errors by one guy never really stood out. They were always covered up by the success of others. If one line had a bad game, the other lines usually picked it up. Not often did we ever really throw a stinker out there."[19]

Heaven help any Bruin who did not play Cherry's system precisely as he wanted it. Veteran blueliner Dallas Smith found this out the hard way. He repeatedly refused to follow Cherry's specific order that defensemen were to move the puck up the ice along the boards—and only along the boards. With the exception of Brad Park—who was a special case and allowed to use his good judgment and puck-moving skills at all times—they were not to engage in solo rushes up the ice or make dangerous passes through the middle. During the 1976–77 season Cherry berated the 35-year-old Smith intensely for constantly defying his edict and reduced Smith's ice time so dramatically that he abruptly quit the team in March. He had first played with Boston as an 18-year-old in 1959.

Brad Park believed that because the Cherry-era Bruins were labeled a "lunch pail" outfit they are often underrated by hockey historians. "We had a lot of good talent. Jean

Ratelle was among the best ever to play the game. Cash [Wayne Cashman] was near the top with Rick Middleton, Peter McNab and Terry O'Reilly. Dick Redmond was underrated and Stan Jonathan was a hard worker. And who had two better goalies than Gerry Cheevers and Gilles Gilbert? You don't stay near the top just by digging. You have to have something extra—a thing called talent."[20]

As a players' coach, Don Cherry would go the extra mile for his troops and erect windmills to be slayed. It was all part of Cherry's master plan to foster a cohesive unit. "Cherry was always seeking causes for his men to unite behind him," wrote Francis Rosa in the *Boston Globe* shortly after Cherry parted ways with the Bruins in 1979. "One year it would be the [NHL's] officials; the next year it would be management."[21] Cherry's us-versus-the-world fixation sometimes took on comically absurd aspects. The crazier Cherry's antics were, the more his players and the Boston fans seemed to love him. Rival coach Fred Shero claimed the secret to Cherry's unquestioned success was that he had the players believe he was one of them rather than an extension of the team's management. The section of Cherry's Wikipedia biography describing his tenure behind the Bruins' bench accurately notes, "Cherry quickly developed a reputation for being an eccentric, flamboyant coach who strongly encouraged physical play among his players...."[22] Here are a few examples of Cherry's "eccentricity":

- Before a game in Toronto in 1978, the Bruins followed the Leafs onto the ice at Toronto's suburban practice facility. Cherry immediately became enraged, accusing Maple Leafs coach Roger Neilson of deliberately roughing up the ice in front of the two goals to gain some sort of obscure tactical edge for that night's game at Maple Leaf Gardens.
- Cherry once blew his top when a Bruins practice at Boston Garden ran 15 minutes beyond its scheduled time—and the arena's maintenance crew began moving parts of the basketball court onto the ice to prepare for an upcoming Boston Celtics home game. Cherry bellowed to all and sundry, "Would this happen to Scotty Bowman at the Montreal Forum?"[23]
- The Bruins were playing the Detroit Red Wings at home in a nationally televised Saturday afternoon contest on January 21, 1978. Cherry was interviewed immediately after the game and wasted no time in lambasting referee Ron Wicks for calling two late penalties against the Bruins. To Cherry it was completely irrelevant that Boston played a nearly flawless Bruin-esque game and won in a rout, 7–1, and the two penalties had absolutely no bearing on the game's outcome. He was determined to foster the idea that the brotherhood of NHL officials (and by extension the entire NHL brass) were deliberately out to sabotage his team.

For the rest of the 1970s whenever the NHL's two best teams met, it was the contrasting styles of Lunch Pail A.C. versus the glamorous and elegant Habs. It made for some interesting, excellent and exciting hockey.

2

No Contest
The 1977 Stanley Cup Final

"Tonight the Boston Bruins begin their challenge to take the Stanley Cup away from the Montreal Canadiens: the gang from the boiler room against the penthouse set."

—Francis Rosa, *Boston Globe*, May 7, 1977

The 1976–77 Montreal Canadiens were one of the strongest NHL teams ever assembled. Some hockey historians maintain they were *the* greatest NHL team of all time. The squad's stats make a compelling argument for it. Throughout the 80-game regular season, the Canadiens lost just eight times in accumulating the staggering total of 132 points—49 points ahead of their closest pursuers in the Norris Division. During one stretch the Habs lost just once in 41 games. However, three of Montreal's losses in 1976–77 came at the hands of the Boston Bruins. One was a sound 7–3 thumping, giving Boston's fans at least a glimmer of hope that their team could pull off a monumental upset in the Stanley Cup final that spring—or at least be reasonably competitive.

The 1976–77 Bruins were vastly different than the juggernaut Boston squad that had won Cups in both 1970 and 1972. Bobby Orr, exiled to Chicago, was all but retired due to a crippled knee. Phil Esposito was playing for the New York Rangers. The Bruins, led by colorful and quotable third-year coach Don Cherry, now had to outwork teams for their victories. But those victories still came in large quantities, not all that far from the 51 wins the 1973–74 Bruins had attained in last season they appeared in the Cup final. (Boston lost to Philadelphia in six games with Bep Guidolin as coach.) In 1976–77, the Bruins compiled a solid 49–23–8 record for 106 points and claimed the Adams Division title. It took a while for the patrons in Boston to get used to having no Bobby Orr or Phil Esposito to cheer. Fans were so miffed that Orr was acquired by the Chicago Blackhawks in June for virtually nothing that something akin to a boycott of the team kept attendance at Boston Garden down all season long. Fewer than 10,000 fans attended the home opener versus Minnesota. Even some playoff games did not sell out.

Boston struggled to beat the Los Angeles Kings in the quarterfinals in six games after winning the first three games fairly easily. After falling behind 0–3 in the series, the Kings surprisingly won the next two games to fleetingly seize the momentum. That Bruins-Kings series is best remembered for an audacious prank perpetrated by Boston's Wayne Cashman and trainer Frosty Forristal prior to Game #6 at the Los Angeles Forum. The Kings' management proudly announced they were going to present the greatest pregame ceremony ever, culminating with anthem singer Frank Mahoney warbling "God Bless America." If Kate

Smith could derail the Bruins in 1974 with the Irving Berlin standard, why shouldn't Mahoney have the same success? Alas, nobody heard a note Mahoney sang. Cashman and Forristal had cut the singer's microphone cord just before show time. Whatever momentum the Kings had built up was lost. Boston scored three goals in the game's first eight minutes to win the game and the series.

In the semifinals Boston surprisingly ripped through the favored Philadelphia Flyers in four straight games—although the first two games at the Spectrum both required overtime to settle matters. (In one game, the Bruins' uncharacteristically squandered a three-goal lead.) Cherry simply outcoached the Flyers' Fred Shero. Cherry liberally mixed up his line combinations to befuddle the team that had beaten the Bruins in the Stanley Cup final in 1974 and in a 1976 semifinal. Cherry did a bit of gloating. "A year ago some people were knocking me because we tried so many different line combinations," he said. "They didn't like the way I kept moving guys around. The first thing I wanted was Gregg Sheppard playing against Rick MacLeish at all times. Every time MacLeish was on the ice, I wanted Shep out there with him. When Philadelphia beat Toronto [in a quarterfinal series], it seemed that MacLeish scored every key goal."[1] Cherry's containment strategy worked. MacLeish failed to score even once in the four games versus the Bruins. The series also saw Jean Ratelle consistently beat Bobby Clarke in draws despite Clarke being widely considered the NHL's best faceoff man.

Gerry Cheevers received overwhelming praise from his teammates. Brad Park was the leading spokesman. "I played against him [when I was] with the Rangers," he said. "I don't think I truly appreciated how great he is. He's the complete professional. He never panics. He's always talking to us out there."[2] Jean Ratelle agreed. "Cheevers is such a team man. Just as long as we score more goals than the other team he is happy. He doesn't think of his [goals-against] average, and I've never heard him blame anyone for any goal scored against him."[3] In Boston's 2–1 win in Game #3, Cheevers was especially clutch when it counted the most. Don Cherry noted, "Philadelphia seemed to be lying back, waiting for a break, and when they got it, Cheesey stoned them."[4]

Cheevers downplayed his accomplishments and the plaudits he was receiving from the media and his Bruin teammates. He said he preferred to concentrate on the task ahead. "I started to watch Game #5 on TV between the Canadiens and the Islanders," he amusingly told Tom Fitzgerald of the *Globe*. "But when I saw Steve Shutt's shot hit [Isles goalie] Billy Smith on the coconut, I switched right over to *Starsky & Hutch*."[5]

At the conclusion of the Bruins' 3–0 triumph in Game #4 at Boston Garden, longtime organist John Kiley, who was something of a showboat, serenaded the departing Flyers with his own rendition of "God Bless America"—which was a little bit over the top. Flyer coach Fred Shero was very complimentary toward the Bruins. "More than anything else, the Bruins had togetherness," Shero stated, implying it was a key attribute the Flyers lacked. "They had a group of hard-working forwards like Terry O'Reilly, and I never remember seeing Jean Ratelle play so hard and so physically as he did in this series."[6] Philadelphia's Jimmy Watson concurred. "It seems funny not being in the finals. We had planned to be playing until about May 18. What it came down to was that one good team can make another good team look bad."[7] The Stanley Cup final and the Habs were next on the Bruins' agenda.

To many people's surprise it had taken Montreal six games to dispose of the ascending New York Islanders. The sixth game of that semifinal was a controversial 2–1 Montreal win; TV replays showed that both Montreal goals had been offside. Islander goalie Glenn (Chico) Resch gave the Bruins a good chance at defeating the vaunted Habs. "They're not as awesome as people think," he declared. "They're overrated and they probably overrate themselves."[8] Islander coach Al Arbour noted, "We softened them up for Boston."[9]

The Bruins entered the Stanley Cup final knowing they were outclassed. Montreal had nine future Hall of Famers on their roster: Ken Dryden, Guy Lafleur, Jacques Lemaire, Guy Lapointe, Yvan Cournoyer, Serge Savard, Larry Robinson, Bob Gainey and Steve Shutt. Each was in his prime. "We had three: Cheevers, Ratelle and me," recalled Brad Park in his autobiography. "So you can see we were the underdogs. We knew that Lafleur was a great player and [we] would try to have Don Marcotte, our best checker, with him as much as possible. If Guy went for a pee, Donny was there to put up the seat."[10]

Montreal's Guy Lapointe predicted the Bruins would be tougher foes than the Islanders were. "They've been working hard all season and they have those unnoticed players," he said. "Terry O'Reilly—there is a man. There is a real man. I'll take him on my team. I'd want him on my team. There will not be one easy game in this series. The Bruins are very impressive."[11]

Despite Boston's positive regular-season results in five games versus Montreal, the heady endorsements of Mr. Arbour and Mr. Resch, and the respect shown by Guy Lapointe, the playoff upset was not to be. There was little drama. Montreal won the series in four straight games, precisely the same fate that had befallen Philadelphia in 1976.

The Canadiens attempted to have Game #1 of the final moved from Saturday night to Sunday night, but the idea was vetoed by Clarence Campbell, who was about to end his tenure as the president of the NHL after 31 seasons. The Bruins found Montreal's request to be amusing and took it as a compliment. Boston general-manager Harry Sinden sarcastically noted, "Saturday or Sunday? What difference would it make playing against the greatest hockey team ever assembled? It just would have been difficult rearranging all our travel plans."[12] The horse racing-loving Gerry Cheevers was pleased that Game #1 would be played on the same Saturday as the Kentucky Derby. "That's two great events on one day!"[13] he noted.

Boston entered the Stanley Cup finals as the better-rested team, having finished off the Flyers six days previously. Before the opening game of the series, Brad Park cautioned Tom Fitzgerald of the *Boston Globe* that the Bruins' extended rest, though welcome, may have dulled the team's edge. He may have been right. In Game #1 at the Forum—played on Saturday, May 7, as scheduled—the Habs jumped out to a fast 4–1 lead. Boston doggedly whittled it down to 4–3 by the end of the second period to provide a measure of hope for their fans. Three goals by Montreal in the third period, however, emphatically sealed a 7–3 win for the home team.

Three nights later Game #2 was an easy 3–0 shutout win for Montreal. Coach Don Cherry felt his Bruins had being treated unfairly by the referees in the two games at the Forum. It was a common refrain by Cherry, but referee Andy van Hellemond certainly did Boston no favors in Game #1. When the game was scoreless, Montreal was given four consecutive power-play opportunities. The home team took the lead on the fourth man-advantage situation. Cherry told the *Globe* after Game #2, "For the last three years that I've been here, they [the refs] stiff you at the start of the game, and then give us condescending [power plays], little pats on the head, at the end of the game. I hate that even worse than the penalties the call against us."[14]

Late in Game #1 Cherry, as a form of protest against the way the game had been officiated, creatively tried to decline a penalty handed to Guy Lafleur, but the Bruins' coach was told by van Hellemond that hockey's rules provided no such option. In an amusing column about Cherry's methods of protesting the officiating, Alan Richman of the *Globe* suggested the Bruins ought to embrace the protest culture of the 1960s and hire Joan Baez to sing the national anthem before Game #3.

In Game #2, a disgusted Cherry heaved a towel onto the ice in the general direction of referee Ron Wicks. (Wicks generously chose not to give the Bruins a bench penalty for the transgression.) "There's no sense in us even playing this series," continued Cherry. "They should just award the Stanley Cup to Montreal and get it over with. These officials are not going to give us a chance in this series."[15] Harry Sinden was also irate about the officiating. He chased Frank Udvari, the NHL's supervisor of officials, down a corridor to protest a late misconduct call that went against Mike Milbury.

Embarrassed by the two decisive losses in the Forum, before Game #3 at Boston Garden Bruins tough guy John Wensink—who had been scratched from Boston's Game #2 lineup—promised to slow down Guy Lafleur's offensive prowess by whatever means necessary. Wensink predicted that Lafleur would be "lucky to get out of Boston alive."[16] Whatever malice Wensink had planned for Montreal's best player failed miserably. Montreal's 4–2 win was powered by two Lafleur goals. Lafleur safely left the premises unharmed. Meanwhile, the Bruins' bushy-haired enforcer, whose admirers hoisted a huge banner declaring "John Wensink Eats Frogs," became the object of derision in the Habs' dressing room and in the Montreal media. (What the Bruins' three French-Canadian players—Jean Ratelle, Don Marcotte, and Gilles Gilbert—thought of the disparaging sign is not known.)

Montreal jumped out to a 3–0 lead in the first period of Game #3, but Boston carried the play most of the way as the Habs were content to sit on their lead with stifling defensive play. Ken Dryden was especially good in the Habs' net when he had to be. "I've heard that Ken Dryden can play some bad games," said Boston captain Wayne Cashman. "But in the six or seven years I've played against him, I've never seen him play a bad one."[17] Still Cashman remained defiant as he tiredly sat in the home team's dressing room. "Montreal still hasn't got the Cup yet," he insisted. "You only get that by winning four games, and they haven't got the fourth one yet. I guarantee there will be 22 guys who come out of this room ready to play hockey on Saturday night. There's no way we want to give up the Cup in our own building."[18]

Boston did play inspired hockey in Game #4. Ultimately it was not enough. Throughout the short, one-sided series, Boston only held one lead in any of the four games—a 1–0 edge in Game #4 that was erased in the second period by a Jacques Lemaire goal. Lemaire won the Cup for the Habs with an overtime tally largely due to an egregious giveaway by Boston defenseman Al Sims who had spent a considerable part of his pro hockey career shuttling to and from the minor leagues. (After Game #3, Sims, thoroughly impressed by his opponents, sincerely told the Boston media, "Wow! Those Canadiens are even faster than their Nova Scotia farm team!"[19])

The Habs' Cup-winning goal was remarkably reminiscent of a similar overtime blunder committed by Bruin captain Milt Schmidt 24 years earlier in the deciding game of the 1953 Stanley Cup final. Sims tried to freeze the in the corner to Gerry Cheevers' left. With no Hab player very close to him, Sims had to move the puck. Move it he did: Sims carelessly kicked the rubber disc directly to Guy Lafleur. Lafleur quickly passed it to Jacques Lemaire who was conveniently stationed in the slot. Lemaire beat Cheevers with a rising, 15-foot shot. When the red light flashed behind the beaten Cheevers, the Canadiens had won their 20th Stanley Cup. Cheevers had been superb in the Boston goal all game, but he could not keep the surging Canadiens at bay indefinitely. Tom Fitzgerald wrote in the *Globe*, "Jacques Lemaire whipped in the overtime goal Saturday night to shatter another Bruins' Stanley Cup dream."[20]

"Winning the Stanley Cup is never routine for Montreal," wrote Francis Rosa in another *Globe* article. "The Canadiens regard it as their special property and they came out shooting and forechecking in that overtime period."[21] It was the second time Habs had been awarded the Cup at Boston Garden, the previous time was in 1958. Guy Lafleur won the Conn Smythe Trophy as the playoffs' MVP. In the final two games Lafleur had either scored or assisted on every Montreal goal.

The Canadiens had one major regret, however. In a postgame television interview Serge Savard said: "To the Canadiens watching on TV, I'm sorry we did not win it in Montreal."[22] Writing in the *Globe*, Alan Richman mocked Savard's remark. "A Canadien should not have to carry the Stanley Cup in the Boston Garden, a foreign arena smelling of stale pizza and fouled with the aroma of decaying Celtics programs. He should not have to share his greatest moment with ladies who wear tee-shirts in the loge."[23]

The clearly better team had won handily. Montreal scored more goals in the first game than the Bruins did in the entire series. Boston sportswriter Peter Gammons covered the Stanley Cup final for *Sports Illustrated*. In the May 23 edition of *SI*, Gammons, in a story aptly titled "They Ruined the Bruins," conceded that Montreal totally dominated the four-game series. Wayne Cashman offered a brutally honest assessment: "Any excuses we could come up with would be bull," he candidly said. "It all came down to one thing: The Canadiens are too good."[24]

"You cannot lose when you play for Montreal," insisted Guy Lapointe. "There's so much pressure. Win, win, win. They let you know that the first day you come to training camp."[25]

Red Storey, a former NHL referee turned broadcaster, was in the minority when he opined that other Montreal teams had been better. "I'm afraid [the 1977 Habs] don't compare to the Canadiens of, say, 1958," Storey said to Ted Blackman of the *Montreal Gazette*. In fact, Storey did not think the '77 Canadiens would be able to beat the Detroit Red Wings of the early 1950s. Storey conceded that it would be difficult for many young fans to fathom that some past teams might rival the almighty Habs of 1976–77. How difficult? Storey said it would be "like trying to appreciate Raquel Welch from her chest x-rays."[26]

Writing in the *Boston Globe*, Fran Rosa summarized, "It was, after all, an impossible dream. But it was worth dreaming out—the Stanley Cup. And now it looks like it's going to stay in Montreal … forever? It looks that way when you check this team's youth and its talent. The Bruins went down—to a superior team—but they went down with their heads up, playing as though this was the seventh game of the finals, not the fourth. Tip your hat to them. They went as far as they could in pursuit of a dream."[27]

Indeed, in 94 regular-season and playoff games in 1976–77, Montreal had outscored its opponents by a phenomenal 440:194 ratio and had lost just 10 times. In retaining the Stanley Cup they had seized from Philadelphia in 1976, Montreal had compiled a 24–3 playoff record over two seasons. Gammons rightly wondered if this Canadiens team, with two straight Stanley Cups on their résumé—and presumably more on the way because of their overall youth—could perhaps surpass the feat of the Habs dynasty of the late 1950s that won five consecutive Cups when the NHL was a mere six-team loop. Wayne Cashman had nailed it: The Montreal Canadiens were that dominant in 1976–77.

Still, Don Cherry commended his underdog troops for getting as far as they did. "I just told them something I've told them before," Cherry said to the media. "I was a player for 16 years and I've been a coach for five years. I've never been associated with any team that made me prouder than this year's Boston Bruins."[28]

Francis Rosa reported that members of each team casually dropped in on the other's dressing room following the final game's conclusion. "After Saturday night's game, Bruins goalie Gerry Cheevers, clad in a bathrobe and sandals, went to the Montreal Canadiens' dressing room to visit. Guy Lapointe, Serge Savard, Larry Robinson and Peter Mahovlich went to the Bruins' room and chatted with coach Don Cherry. Cherry, they said, was a man they'd enjoy playing for. They admire and respect him."[29]

Cheevers, whose career experienced something of a renaissance after his return to the Bruins from the World Hockey Association's Cleveland Crusaders in 1976, was disappointed by the result of the Stanley Cup final but was realistic about the quality of Boston's opponents. "[The Canadiens] just have so many ways to beat you. The rest of us just have to rely on our regular games. They can do it just about any way they choose." Cheevers added, "I am proud to have played on this team and helped in some way to get us this far. You can be sure it was a wonderfully reviving thing for me to come back here from Cleveland."[30]

General-manager Harry Sinden promised some broad off-season changes to strengthen the Boston defense and especially the power play which he considered a major weakness in the Bruins' arsenal. "And very definitely we want Don Cherry to remain as our coach,"[31] Sinden told Tom Fitzgerald.

To a man, the Bruins expected to be back in the Stanley Cup final in 1978.

3

A Valiant Effort
The 1978 Stanley Cup Final

"I predict only that we will witness a memorable series, whether it be four or seven games. The Canadiens are no myth. But be assured also that this Bruin team has not been manufactured deceptively, either. They are as fine a combination of enthusiasm and professionalism as I've ever seen."
—Bob Ryan, *Boston Globe*, May 13, 1978

In the spring of 1978 the Bruins and Canadiens staged a return match in the Stanley Cup final just as they had done 20 years earlier in 1957 and 1958. Montreal was not quite as dominant as they had been in 1977—the Habs *only* won 59 games in accruing 129 points during the 80-game regular season—while the Bruins had improved. Boston's offense may have been the most balanced attack in NHL history. The Bruins' 333 goals—the third-highest output in the NHL that season—equaled an average of 4.16 per game, but the truly startling stat was that a record 11 different Bruins managed to score at least 20 goals that season. (The 1970–71 Bruins and the 1974–75 Canadiens had shared the NHL mark; each had 10 players who scored 20 goals.) John Wensink came within four goals of making it a dozen Bruins with a score of scores. Yet only one Bruin—Terry O'Reilly—finished among the league's top 13 point-scorers. The rewards of such diversity are obvious: If one frequent goal-scorer slumped, there were plenty of Bruins to pick up the slack. Boston's longest losing streak all year was a mere two games. Only twice did they absorb shutouts.

Boston cruised past Chicago in a playoff quarterfinal in four straight games. Philadelphia only fared marginally better. They managed just one win against Boston in the semifinal, going out rather quietly in five games in Fred Shero's last season behind the Flyers' bench and what also turned out to be Bernie Parent's final playoff game. In the last game, a 6–3 win at Boston Garden, Peter McNab figured in the first five Bruins goals. McNab had only played "so-so" in Philadelphia, according to Cherry, so he shuffled lines and flanked his big center with Bobby Schmautz and Don Marcotte—a strategic decision that obviously paid off. Altogether the line accounted for eight scoring points. "Cherry is like Steve Cauthen, the jockey," McNab said afterward. "He knows when to tighten the reins."[1]

The Garden crowd, of course, was jubilant from the moment that Jean Ratelle put the game away with an empty net goal with just 64 seconds to play. Their roars continued as the final seconds wound down. "The crowd sang 'God Bless America' until the roof trembled,"[2] wrote Francis Rosa in the *Globe*. Commenting on *Hockey Night in Canada*, Brian McFarlane opined, "I haven't heard this place rock like this since the glory days of Orr and Esposito."[3]

31

Meeting with the media before Game #5, Cherry continued to defend his underappreciated players. Citing a poll of hockey writers that listed the best NHLers in certain skills, Cherry was aghast that not one Bruin was atop any of the 24 categories. "We don't have the best forechecker, the best shooter, the best defenseman. We must have done something right to get to where we are,"[4] Cherry sarcastically said. Ex-Flyer Bill Clement agreed during the *HNIC* telecast's waning moments, "That's all right. They've got one of the best teams. That's all that counts."[5] The defeated Flyers concurred. "They [Boston] have a helluva shot at Montreal,"[6] one said.

Montreal hardly broke a sweat in pummeling Detroit in a five-game quarterfinal and Toronto in a four-game sweep of their semifinal to reach the Stanley Cup final for the third consecutive season. As in the previous spring, the Bruins were again underdogs in 1978 versus Montreal, but Boston's strong playoff showing in the first two rounds was cause for optimism. Unlike in 1977, this time the prognosticators gave Boston some chance of upending Montreal's quest for three Stanley Cups in succession—even though they had compiled a dismal 0–4–1 record versus the Habs in the regular season and were badly outscored 21–8 in those five games. Montreal was the only opponent in the 18-team NHL the Bruins failed to beat at least once in 1977–78.

Still, the Bruins entered the 1978 Stanley Cup finals with a far different and more positive outlook than they had in 1977. "The Bruins will admit to having had a we're-just-happy-to-be-here attitude in last year's final, which, you may recall, ended in a four-game Montreal sweep," wrote Bob Ryan in his series preview for the *Globe*. "The Bruins say it's different this time, that instead of having their noses pressed against the glass window of a fine restaurant, they are going to barge in and demand service, buddy, and make it snappy."[7]

Boston's superb forechecker, Don Marcotte, concurred. "We're hungry. Not many guys on this team have ever won the Stanley Cup."[8] There were, in fact, five: Marcotte, Wayne Cashman, Gary Doak, Gerry Cheevers, and Rick Smith. All five were veterans of Boston's 1970 Cup win. Cashman, Marcotte and Cheevers were two-time champions, having been on the 1972 team as well. Philadelphia coach Fred Shero also believed Boston appearance in the Cup final was more than "a kamikaze mission." He said, "The Bruins have a good chance—better than they had last year. Gerry Cheevers did not have a good series last year. I think he'll do better. I believe the Bruins are very strong in the middle—they've got three damn good centers—and enough strength on the wings to make things interesting."[9]

In Game #1 at the Forum on May 13, Boston got off to a fast 1–0 lead on a Brad Park goal, but that was all the offense the visitors could muster. Montreal comfortably won 4–1. Game #2, played three nights later, was a tightly contested affair. Again Boston scored the first goal.

The booming baritone voice of Bob Wilson thrilled and comforted Bruins' radio listeners for nearly three decades. In 1987 Wilson was awarded the Foster Hewitt Memorial Award for excellence in broadcasting.

Again it was notched by Brad Park—but it did not come until the fourth minute of the second period. Steve Shutt quickly tied the score at the 7:00 mark. Montreal edged into the lead at 12:12 of the third period on a goal by Bob Gainey. However Rick Smith leveled the score for Boston at with a clutch goal at 15:48. The third period ended with the score tied, 2–2. During the overtime session, Montreal controlled much of the play, but Boston had a couple of chances—including one where Ken Dryden awkwardly juggled a Wayne Cashman shot, but managed to keep the puck out of the Habs' net. In the visitors' radio booth, Bruins analyst Bob Lobel, putting all neutrality aside, bluntly told his WBZ broadcast partner Bob Wilson and the fans listening in Boston, "If there is any such thing as justice in the world, the Bruins deserve a break."[10] It was not to be. Guy Lafleur, the best player in hockey, broke the Bruins' hearts with the game-winner at 13:09 of the extra session. It was a long, low blast that beat Gerry Cheevers on the short side. It was the 20th Stanley Cup playoff game between Montreal and Boston that had gone into overtime. Montreal had won 15 of them.

When the series shifted to Boston on May 18, an international broadcasting controversy arose: Danny Gallivan, the familiar English-language TV voice of the Montreal Canadiens since 1952, was not calling the game on CBC's *Hockey Night in Canada*. Instead it was the equally capable Dan Kelly at the microphone. Kelly had done pregame, postgame and between-period commentary for *HNIC* during the first two games at the Forum. "This is the first time in my 26 years that the Canadiens have been involved in a playoff game that I have not worked when I was physically able," the 61-year-old Gallivan sadly told the *Montreal Gazette*. "Yes, I'm disappointed."[11]

As the English-language television voice of the Montreal Canadiens from 1952 to 1984, Danny Gallivan became an iconic figure in Canadian sports broadcasting. Fans of the Habs' opponents often accused Gallivan of being overly zealous when he announced Montreal goals.

Through no fault of his own, Gallivan fell victim to the complicated broadcasting rights to the Stanley Cup final shared by the American-based NHL Network and Canadian Sports Network which managed *HNIC*. The American TV interests wanted their guy—Kelly—to call half the games, so it was decided that Kelly would call the games from Boston Garden and Gallivan would call the games from the Montreal Forum. Gallivan rejected the idea of splitting each game with Kelly, an option he was offered. Apparently having two separate feeds was out of the question. Gallivan, dressed in a suit, watched the game from a chair in his apartment "while taking an occasional sip of scotch and water,"[12] according to the *Gazette* which deemed Gallivan's exclusion so startling that it merited a front-page story. "Kelly is a good friend of mine and is terribly proficient," Gallivan diplomatically said about the awkward situation. "It's the principle that annoys me. I'm against this network in the States being able to exert such pressure."[13] Among Bruin fans and other Hab-haters in Canada, Kelly's voice was a welcome and unexpected treat as Gallivan's commentary was strongly perceived to be more than a wee bit biased toward Montreal.

The Bruins, back in cozy Boston Garden, seemed revitalized despite the disappointing loss in Game #2. Gary Doak scored just 59 second into Game #3 and Rick Middleton added a highlight reel-caliber goal as the Bruins rolled to a fairly easy 4–0 win. The result shocked the headline writer at the *Montreal Gazette*. "Canadiens Trounced? Yes. That's the Name of the Game"[14] it said. Gerry Cheevers notched the shutout for the home team and was not required to make a difficult save throughout the entire game. Montreal's defeat ended their remarkable streak of 11 straight victories in Stanley Cup finals dating back to 1973. "We haven't had to come from behind in many games this season," Scotty Bowman said to reporters afterward. "They got ahead early. It was a bad goal in more ways than one. It was in the first minute. It came on a lost faceoff in our own end, and it came on a screen."[15] Larry Robinson admitted, "We were badly outplayed, but it's not the first time [it's happened] in these playoffs. We were badly outplayed in the second game versus Detroit as well."[16] The way in which Boston won surprised the Montreal media. Many had wrongly predicted that Boston would use "goon tactics" to try to get back into the series.

Boston should have won Game #4 just as comfortably three nights later as they seemed far the better team for the second straight game. Again the Bruins were ahead 1–0 before a minute had expired, but they only held a slight 3–2 edge late in the third period. Ken Dryden was pulled from the Montreal goal with 1:13 left on the clock in favor of a sixth attacker. With under a minute to play, Steve Shutt skillfully knocked a puck out of mid-air from behind the Boston net. It bounced in front of Cheevers' crease where both Guy Laflskillfullyerge Savard were stationed. Lafleur was credited with knocking the bouncing puck into the Boston net for the tying goal, although television replays seem to indicate that Savard's name should have been the one added to the score sheet. (Inexplicably, Shutt was not credited with an assist.) As in Game #2, Game #4 would be decided in overtime.

With the momentum of the entire series on the line, Gregg Sheppard fed Bobby Schmautz a perfect cross-ice pass on a Bruins counterattack. Schmautz won the game for Boston 6:22 into a free-flowing overtime period on a low shot to Dryden's glove side. Dryden had been partially screened by sliding defenseman Larry Robinson. "I never saw anything,"[17] the Montreal goalie said afterward. When the red goal light went on, all six Canadiens on the ice were future Hall of Famers: Dryden, Robinson, Shutt, Lafleur, Guy Lapointe and Jacques Lemaire.

Schmautz's dramatic goal marked the first time Boston had beaten Montreal in overtime in a playoff game since Terry Reardon—a former Hab—had been the hero of Game #4 of the 1946 finals. Bedlam overtook Boston Garden. Schmautz leapt into the arms of Brad Park beside the Montreal net. (A photo of Schmautz celebrating his goal would adorn the cover of the Bruins' yearbook in 1978–79.) "I'm so wound up. I'm ecstatic. I think I bit Schmautz on the neck," Park told reporters afterward. "This is the third time I've been in the finals, but it's the first time [my team] has been even going into Game Five."[18]

The elated Bruins, thrilled with their gutty 4–3 victory, practically skipped off the ice as the partisan crowd loudly roared its approval for their tenacious home team. The deafening clamor of the cheering throng nearly drowned out organist John Kiley's happy signature tune *Paree* that wafted merrily through Boston Garden. In stark contrast, the Habs trudged to their dressing room sporting decidedly worried looks on their faces. Robinson looked especially downtrodden.

In the Boston dressing room the Bruins strongly began to believe an upset was imminent. "This is a victory toast," Park said as he lifted a beer. "I can taste victory; I can smell it. Nobody gave us a chance to beat Montreal in the finals. No one. But now, if we've done nothing else, we have destroyed the myth of the Canadiens' invincibility."[19] Covering the series for *Sports Illustrated*, Mark Mulvoy was decidedly impressed by the terrific effort put forth by the Bruins. "The series was not supposed to be this tough for Montreal," he wrote. "The Canadiens had expected to dispose of Boston in less time than it takes Roger Doucet to polish off *O Canada* before games at the Forum."[20] With the finals now whittled down to a best-of-three, the unthinkable was within the realm of possibility: the almighty Montreal Canadiens—losers of just 29 of 240 regular-season games in the past three seasons—might not win the Stanley Cup after all in 1978. "Suddenly the Habs are on the run,"[21] blared an accurate headline in the *Kitchener-Waterloo* [Ontario] *Record*.

Alas, the upset was not to be. Montreal rebounded admirably following the two disheartening losses in Boston and handily won Game #5 at the Forum two nights later, a game in which the Bruins played surprisingly tentatively. Larry Robinson, perhaps to atone for screening Dryden on Schmautz's winning goal in the previous game, scored on a marvelous one-man rush to give Montreal a 1–0 advantage in the first period when each team was a man short. (Robinson's picturesque goal would be included in the opening montage for *HNIC* in 1978–79.) Montreal's grasp on the game never looked threatened in an unexpectedly easy 4–1 victory. Another Habs Stanley Cup was on the horizon.

The Bruins, although well beaten, were less than thrilled by Dave Newell's refereeing in Game #5. Late in the second period, with Boston trailing 4–0, Bob Gainey roughly grabbed Wayne Cashman and threw him to the ice without being penalized. Instead, Cashman was given an unsportsmanlike conduct penalty for questioning Newell's non-call. "This was the most important game of my career and I feel that it was taken away from me. It's a shame and a joke," insisted Brad Park, the most quotable of the Boston players. "We might just as well have turned our hockey sticks around and played with the knobs on the handles. We played tough and deserved some penalties, of course, but I couldn't believe some of the things the Canadiens got away with."[22] Gerry Cheevers, who was lifted from the Boston net in the third period for Ron Grahame, said, "I'm very disappointed in the officiating. I'm not a sour grapes guy, but Bruce Hood is the #1 official in the league and John McCauley's got everyone's respect—but where are they when you need them?"[23]

In Game #6 in Boston two nights later, the gutsy Bruins rushed out to quick a 1–0 lead—again on a Brad Park goal—but the Montreal tide was unstoppable. Steve Shutt equalized three minutes later. Mario Tremblay scored once in the first period for the Habs and again in the second period. Réjean Houle also tallied a second-period goal. The deflated Bruins had no reply. The third period produced no further scoring; Montreal was ahead 4–1 as the final buzzer echoed through a largely silent Boston Garden. The Bruins did not have any complaints about the officiating in Game #6. "The officials didn't beat us tonight," said captain Wayne Cashman. "The Montreal Canadiens did. They just played a super hockey game."[24] Mike Milbury concurred, "[The Habs] just outplayed us, plain and simple, in every aspect of the game."[25]

For the second consecutive spring Montreal was awarded the Stanley Cup on Boston ice—never a fun experience for any home team or their fans to endure. Apart from the Cup disappointment, many Boston fans and media personnel firmly believed that 29-year-old Brad Park—who had scored nine postseason goals and added 11 assists—should have been awarded the Conn Smythe Trophy as playoff MVP for his overall excellent play despite being on the losing team. It would hardly have been unprecedented. Three times in the trophy's 13-year history, a player from a losing team had been named the Conn Smythe recipient, the most recent example being Reggie Leach of the Philadelphia Flyers in 1976. But Boston was even denied that consolation prize; it was instead awarded to Montreal's

Larry Robinson. Years later Gerry Cheevers said, "If the Bruins had won the Cup, I'd have bet my life on Brad winning the Conn Smythe Trophy."[26]

Robinson knew his team had been soundly tested by Boston's valiant effort. He felt a small pang of sympathy for the vanquished. He noted, "They will have to spend their summer vacations answering the most depressing question of all: 'Why didn't you win?'"[27]

For the second straight postseason, the Boston Bruins had to settle for being the NHL's runner-up team. It was not a badge that many of the feisty Bruins took solace in wearing. "You can't go around pretending to be happy about being second-best," said a dejected Peter McNab. "We played this series feeling that we could win—and that's why losing hurts so much. A year ago they just blew us out in four games. We knew they were better then, even though we tried our hardest. But this year we really thought we had a chance."[28]

Don Cherry was gracious in defeat, explaining to *SI's* Mark Mulvoy,

You know what really bothers me about the damned Canadiens? [They] are a bunch of good guys. I couldn't even work up a good hate against them if I tried for a month. It's easy to work up a hate for a club like Philadelphia. And I suppose—well, I know—it's pretty easy for teams to work up a good hate against the Bruins. But hating the Canadiens is like hating your mother.

[Three] of my best friends in hockey are ... Robinson, Savard and Lapointe. I got to know them when I was one of Team Canada's coaches. All three like to have the odd beer, just like me, and we spent a lot of time together sweating it off in the sauna. Believe me, there aren't three nicer gentlemen anywhere.[29]

Thirty-seven-year-old Gerry Cheevers, who showed no signs of age in his brilliant play throughout the playoffs, was eager to take another crack at upending the Habs. "I'm looking forward to playing next year with this team," he said. "This season was fun. We're getting closer to being on par with Montreal all the time. I think we're only one player away from being as good as they are. If we get that player you'll see a helluva finals next year—and we'll be there with them. I'll tell you one thing: I'm going to be buying a lot of tickets for next year's finals because we're going to be in it with them. It's going to be a great series if we just improve as much over the next year as we have over the last year."[30]

"They beat us in our own building. They're the champs," Don Cherry said to a scrum of reporters. He smiled and added, "That's what Harry told me to say."[31] Cherry echoed Cheevers' sentiments and made a bold prediction to the scribes: "Starting this series I said we'd win more games than we did a year ago. Now I'm telling you that we'll win more games in next year's final than we did in this year's. Remember that!"[32]

• • •

In Greek mythology there is an earthly king named Sisyphus whose hubristic behavior draws the ire of the gods on Mount Olympus. As punishment for his arrogant thoughts and actions, Sisyphus is eternally doomed to push an enormous boulder up a steep hill. With tremendous effort, he seems to have the goal within his grasp. As soon as Sisyphus is within sight of the summit, however, the boulder cruelly rolls away from him and back down the hill, forcing the king to begin the laborious task anew. At the end of the 1977–78 season, the Boston Bruins began to look more and more like hockey's version of Sisyphus—although the acts of hubris that the hockey gods were making them atone for were difficult to pinpoint. Others preferred to evoke a closer and apt comparison with baseball's Brooklyn Dodgers, a talented, gritty and lovable bunch of endearing characters who seemingly always came up just a little bit short versus the glamorous and haughty New York

Yankees in the World Series. Brooklyn fans annually took solace in the somewhat pitiful mantra of "Wait 'til next year!" The Dodgers eventually defeated their powerful nemesis in 1955. The Bruins and their fans could only hope that the 1978–79 NHL season would be their "next year" and would finally put an end to their ongoing postseason disappointments versus the Montreal Canadiens.

4

High Hopes and
Cautious Optimism
for 1978–79

"We're not much better [than we were last year]. I mean basically we're the same team. We're more experienced and we've acquired more confidence, but [we're] much the same."
> —Don Cherry's comment to Francis Rosa of the *Boston Globe*,
> before the first regular-season game of the 1978–79 season

"Montreal, the most cosmopolitan city in North America, is still up there in Quebec, near Mount Royal. It still has a hockey team called the Canadiens. They are still the champions of all hockey, the Stanley Cup champions. They'll fly through the winter with an effect as chilling as the Montreal Express. And the National Hockey League shudders."
> —Francis Rosa, from that same seasonal preview piece,
> in the October 6, 1978, *Globe*

In its preview of the 1978–79 NHL season, the 1979 edition of *The Complete Handbook of Pro Hockey* described the Boston Bruins thusly: "Coach Don Cherry likes to boast that the qualities which most distinguish the Bruins are togetherness and unselfishness. Certainly there is no other team where so many players rely so deeply on each other."

The preview continued,

Consider that 11 players scored 20 or more goals last season (no other team had more than seven), and only one Peter McNab, notched as many as 30 goals. It is further significant in Cherry's scheme of things that McNab, despite the fact that he went on to score 41 goals, first had to play his way out of the doghouse.

Even without a single super scorer, Boston registered 333 goals, making for the third most potent offense in the NHL.[1]

Boston made only one significant personnel move in the offseason. Gregg Sheppard was dealt to Pittsburgh in a three-way deal that saw the Bruins acquire Dick Redmond from Atlanta. Redmond, a solid blueliner, would bolster the Boston defensive unit. The only other trades Boston made were purely money deals in which they gave up four late-round draft choices to the St. Louis Blues in exchange for cash. Rookie Al Secord made the team and would appear in 71 games. Secord was the only true rookie who would play any sort of truly substantial role on the team, although Tom Songin and Bill Bennett would provide occasional help. (Dwight Foster had played 14 games for Boston in 1977–78;

statistically he was still considered a rookie by the NHL in 1978–79.) Johnny Bucyk, who had been with the Bruins since 1956 but had seen reduced action in the past two seasons, called it quits at age 43. Third-string goalie Ron Grahame had been traded. Fringe players Mike Forbes and Matti Hagman each opted to sign with World Hockey Association clubs. (Hagman, a Finn, was not exactly a Don Cherry favorite. He ran afoul of the coach so often that he was nicknamed Doghouse Hagman. When Hagman died in 2016, one obituary claimed that Cherry talked to him exactly twice during the 1976–77 season: He said hello at training camp and goodbye when the season ended.) Thus the 1978–79 Bruins, with a few exceptions, remained relatively unchanged from the team that had taken Montreal to a sixth game in the 1978 Stanley Cup final. Boston was definitely one of the NHL's top-notch teams, but they were a year older, and time was catching up to Jean Ratelle, Wayne Cashman, Don Marcotte and Gerry Cheevers. All four had careers that had begun in the six-team NHL. The general but unspoken feeling going into the season was that this core of veteran Bruin players had maybe one last truly good shot at winning it all.

Sports Illustrated's 1978–79 NHL preview article strangely appeared in the October 23, 1978, issue—nearly two full weeks after the hockey season began. Nevertheless, the Bruins, perceived as serious threats to the Canadiens, merited a full paragraph in *SI*—a luxury only granted to a few of the league's elite teams. Here's what America's premier sports magazine had to say about the Bruins and their chances to topple the Habs:

> Boston awarded Terry O'Reilly a fat new contract. [He] prefers the company of the Bruins' hard-nosed operatives like Don Marcotte and Stan Jonathan. They have rookie Al Secord, a checking specialist whose taste for the corners makes him a Boston-style player. To help Brad Park, the Bruins traded for veteran Dick Redmond, and with Park now out until December following knee surgery last week, Redmond will have to quarterback Boston's power play. The Bruins hope for speed from young Dwight Foster. If Foster gets into gear, if aging center Jean Ratelle has another good season, if center Peter McNab can match his 41-goal season, and if Park and goalie Gerry Cheevers come back strong from their operations, Boston [could face] Montreal in the Stanley Cup finals for a third straight year.[2]

The 1978–79 hockey season was the last year that the NHL had to compete with the World Hockey Association for talent. The WHA, entering its seventh season, was slowly but inevitably dying. The Houston Aeros, once one of the league's marquee teams, folded before the season began, dropping the number of WHA teams to a mere seven. Only six would survive the season. The Indianapolis Racers folded 25 games into the schedule, but not before owner Nelson Skalbania had signed 17-year-old Wayne Gretzky to a contract. (Gretzky, obviously possessing immense talent, was ineligible to be drafted by the NHL because he was not yet 18 years old. The WHA had no such age restriction.) After eight games in Indianapolis, Gretzky was dealt to the Edmonton Oilers for much-needed cash. With no major television contract to generate revenue to the financially-strapped WHA, and hockey fans generally perceiving it as a less-skilled league than the NHL, its days were numbered. (Bill Friday, a former NHL official who became the WHA's referee-in-chief, said years later that the best WHA teams would only finish in the middle of the pack in the NHL.) Four WHA teams would be absorbed into the NHL for 1979–80—three of them located in Canada: the Oilers, Quebec Nordiques, and Winnipeg Jets. The New England Whalers were the lone American-based team to gain admission. The Cincinnati Stingers and Birmingham Bulls faded into oblivion.

Not everywhere in the NHL was there financial bliss, however. As inconceivable as it was to hockey fans in Montreal, Boston and other traditional NHL cities, in some American locales the world's foremost professional hockey league was not a major attraction. For the first time since 1942 when the Brooklyn American ceased operations, the NHL contracted its membership by one team. The struggling Cleveland Barons and Minnesota North Stars—both on the verge of folding—were permitted to merge in the offseason. The combined team would retain the Minnesota North Stars' name but play in the Adams Division along-side the Bruins, Buffalo Sabres and Toronto Maple Leafs. That was the division where the unfashionable Barons—formerly the Oakland/California Seals—had largely resided in anonymity for their two forgettable seasons, playing before puny crowds in suburban Rich-field, OH in what was then the NHL's largest building. Not once did they come even close to filling the 18,700 available seats. The highlight of the year for Cleveland in 1977–78 must have been their 2–1 home victory over the mighty Habs on November 23, 1977. They also beat Boston once and tied them twice in six meetings that year. In the end, an uncompetitive team, a distant arena, and overwhelming fan apathy doomed the Barons. Crowds numbering fewer than 6,000 paying customers were commonplace in the vast Richfield Coliseum. In the March 26, 1978, edition of the *Boston Globe*, Francis Rosa incorrectly but humorously reported, "Cleveland is said to be ready to go one more year in its Big House on the Prairie. It would be nice if they built a city around it."[3]

With the Cleveland Barons rele-gated to the history books, for the 1978–79 season alone, the NHL operated as an ungainly 17-team circuit. Given that the NHL opted to retain its 80-game-per-team schedule, and further given that the league's playoff system at the time ren-dered its divisional standings almost meaningless, a balanced schedule of each team playing the other 16 teams five times each would have made plenty of sense. However, the NHL wanted to foster divi-sional rivalries, so mathematical sim-plicity was shelved. Boston would play their three Adams Division rivals eight times apiece in 1978–79, the Rangers, Islanders, Blackhawks, and Flyers five times each, and the nine other teams—including Montreal—four times each.

A balanced schedule it was not. Don Cherry figured the new setup hurt the Bruins' chances of finishing first over-all. "Our objective is the win the [Adams] Division," Cherry told Fran Rosa in a *Boston Globe* interview just before the season began, diplomatically declaring all the Adams Division teams to be tough. "First overall? Forget it."[4] Cherry figured Montreal would be the beneficiaries of a much softer schedule, playing 32 games

Francis (Fran) Rosa was Boston's most beloved hockey writer. Along with other sports, Rosa elo-quently covered the Bruins and the rest of the NHL for the *Boston Globe* for decades until his retirement in 1991. His courtly manner of engaging interview subjects earned him the moniker "The Gentleman from the *Globe*."

versus perceived lightweights Detroit, Washington, Los Angeles and Pittsburgh. "Does anything ever change?" asked Rosa rhetorically. "Must every team forever chase Montreal?"[5]

Despite the Habs being in a different division and the Bruins only encountering them four times in 1978–79, they were never too far from the Boston players' thoughts. "Just give us another shot [at them]," Brad Park told Rosa. "That's all we want."[6] Terry O'Reilly, on the other hand, took a more pragmatic approach to the Canadiens. "Montreal is always there in your head whatever time of the year it is," he stated. "What we have to do is put it in the back of our minds and keep it there until the spring. There are a lot of steps before we get there."[7]

This would also be the fifth year that the NHL would use a variation of its creative "double seeding" method to determine its playoff matchups. It was first introduced in the 1974–75 season when the league expanded from 14 to 16 teams with the addition of the Washington Capitals and Kansas City Scouts. The Eastern and Western Divisions, which had been the norm since the 1967–68 season, were scrapped. Instead the league was split into four divisions, each bearing the name of an NHL builder: (Jack) Adams, (Lester) Patrick, (James) Norris, and (Conn) Smythe. Since 18 teams could not be evenly split into four groups, two of the divisions had five teams while two had four. There was no geographical sense to the divisions. The California Golden Seals were slotted into the Adams Division with Boston, Buffalo and Toronto. The Los Angeles Kings played in the Patrick Division alongside Montreal, Pittsburgh, Detroit and Washington. Twelve teams qualified for the Stanley Cup playoffs. The four divisional champions all received first-round byes regardless of how many points each had accrued during the 80-game regular season. The second- and third-place teams were also guaranteed playoff berths to round out the field. The eight non-divisional winners faced a perilous best-of-three opening round where they were seeded according to their point totals. Divisional standings meant nothing beyond the champions getting first-round byes. Brackets were scrapped. After the first round was played, the four teams that survived the first round were combined with the four teams that received byes and re-seeded based on the regular-season standings from one to eight.

The newfangled playoff system had many strong points: It made all regular-season games more relevant as it better rewarded sustained excellence, and it meant that any two teams could face each other at any time in the Stanley Cup playoffs. (Contrast that system to today's NHL playoffs where Boston and Montreal cannot possibly meet in the Stanley Cup final because they play in the same conference.) But the double-seeding mechanism had one glaring flaw: The champion of a weak division would get a bye while many also-rans in tougher divisions would have to endure the risk of playing a short first-round series. For example, in the 1974–75 season, the Vancouver Canucks finished atop the decidedly weak Smythe Division with just 86 points. Five teams in other divisions with greater point totals had to battle for survival in a rushed first-round playoff series—typically contesting three games in just four nights—while the Canucks got a generous free pass into the quarterfinals.

The first year this playoff system was employed, there were two huge upsets in the first round: The Los Angeles Kings, who finished the season with 105 points but behind Montreal in the Patrick Division, were the top seed among the also-rans. They were surprisingly ousted by eighth-seeded Toronto—who had finished two games below .500—in three games all decided by one goal. Before the Leafs-Kings series, many Canadian hockey writers mocked the idea of Toronto even qualifying for the playoffs, having done so only by achieving the not-too-difficult feat of finishing ahead of the pitiful California Golden Seals who won just 19 of their 80 games.

In the NHL, however, the playoffs often render the regular season meaningless. Second-seeded Boston, in Don Cherry's first year behind the Bruins' bench, suffered a surprise loss to seventh-seeded Chicago somewhat reminiscent of 1971 debacle versus Montreal. Even though the two teams had split their four regular-season games, the Blackhawks were considered huge underdogs. Boston easily won the first game at home 8–2. They then lost 4–3 in Game #2 in Chicago on Ivan Boldirev's overtime goal (which Don Cherry always maintained was offside), a game in which Bruins general-manager Harry Sinden labeled referee Bruce Hood as gutless for refusing to call obvious penalties in a playoff game. Boston then surprisingly lost 6–4 in Game #3 back in Boston despite outshooting the Blackhawks by an enormous margin. Nobody knew it at the time, but it was Bobby Orr's final Stanley Cup playoff game.

In Game #1 Chicago goalie Tony Esposito—the younger brother of Boston sniper Phil who scored a hat-trick—was yanked from the Chicago net when Boston's lead reached an unassailable and embarrassing 7–0. He was mocked by the Boston media, likened to both Swiss cheese and a sieve. Phil joined in the chorus of critics, declaring his brother looked gaunt and undernourished from overwork during the regular season. John Ahern of the *Boston Globe*, in a piece titled "You Can't Put All the Blame on Tony O," said the Hawks' goalie was only to blame on two of the seven goals he permitted because Chicago's defensemen had been thoroughly horrendous.

But Tony O was clearly the star of Game #3, making one brilliant stop after another to thwart the Boston offense. Afterward, Boston goaltender Gilles Gilbert did not endear himself to Cherry by telling the media that the six Chicago shots that eluded him—from a total of just 19 he faced—were "tough." Meanwhile Tony Esposito had been deluged with 56 Boston shots. ("How many tough saves did *he* have to make?" an angry Cherry reasonably retorted.) Also residing in Cherry's doghouse for his ill-advised comments was Phil Esposito. During an NBC hockey telecast of a quarterfinal game, Esposito, a studio guest, opined that the Bruins had been upset by the weaker Blackhawks because they had not been "mentally prepared" for the series—a thinly veiled criticism at how Cherry had coached his team. Esposito promised brighter things were in store for the Bruins, however. "It's going to be a whole new deal next season," he told Jim Proudfoot of the *Toronto Star*. "Now we've got something to prove for our own satisfaction."[8] In the following four years, Cherry's Bruins avoided the minefield of the dreaded short first-round series by winning the Adams Division each season and thus securing a precious first-round playoff bye and its accompanying week's rest.

Phil Esposito—who never saw eye to eye with Cherry—was traded in November 1975 to the New York Rangers as part of the huge deal that brought Jean Ratelle and Brad Park to the Bruins. The Rangers had suffered a minor upset in the first round of the 1975 playoffs too—losing in three games to their upstart neighbors the New York Islanders. The result of that series largely—but not entirely—set the directions of those two teams for the next decade: The Islanders were ascending to contender status while the Rangers were mostly in decline. Both Boston and the Rangers were in need of a shakeup when their two general-managers organized the blockbuster deal. At the time, the much-discussed trade was generally seen as a win-win situation for both teams.

The Bruins had a lackluster 1978–79 exhibition season, winning just three of ten games. Coach Don Cherry did not put too much stock in preseason results, however. "Last year we lost one of ten [in the preseason] and had a horrendous start to the regular season. The year before we won one of ten games [in the preseason] and then started the regular season with just two losses in our first 18 games." In the final Bruins practice before the first game of the regular season, Cherry showed his team video highlights of their fine 1977–78 campaign—including a clip of Stan Jonathan pummeling Philadelphia's André (Moose) Dupont. "I want to get them revved up," Cherry declared. "They've been down, down, down."[9]

Boston started the 1978–79 campaign on October 12 with a home game versus the Pittsburgh Penguins—and they were indeed as revved up as Cherry had hoped. Boston got out of the gate in fine fashion, blasting the Penguins 8–2. The eight goals established a new Bruin record for team scoring in the first game of any season. It was also the highest one-game goal output Boston would attain during the entire 1978–79 season. "This was opening night for the Bruins and they played as though they wanted rave notices," wrote Francis Rosa in the *Globe*. "They got them. It was a footlight parade on Causeway Street. It was a star-studded cast."[10]

A less-than-capacity crowd of 11,168 saw the Bruins forecheck and attack the out-gunned Penguins without relent. It was a very one-sided affair. Bob Whitley, of the *Pittsburgh Post-Gazette*, declared, "[The] Penguins were slow off the mark, miserable with the puck, and timid in the corners. In short, overmatched." It was Pittsburgh's 30th game in Boston since entering the NHL in 1967. The Pens had lost 27 of them. Whitley concluded, "The Penguins are little more than stuffed birds at the Garden."[11]

"That's the way to play the game,"[12] crowed an injured Wayne Cashman who restlessly watched the game in street clothes "from a dozen different places,"[13] according to Rosa. Stan Jonathan got the first Boston goal of the season on a delayed penalty at 17:40 of the first period. At one point Pittsburgh was trailing just 2–1, but the Bruins seemed to accelerate at will on this night. Peter McNab scored two goals from the slot just 31 seconds apart to put the game out of reach for the visitors. Don Marcotte, the Bruins' best penalty killer, even added a shorthanded goal to emphasize Boston's dominance. The team's uninspired play in their meaningless preseason games was quickly forgotten.

The satisfaction the Bruins had experienced after their opening night win was short-lived. The following morning, all-star defenseman Brad Park—who had scored a goal and added two assists in the Boston victory—complained about pain and swelling in his right knee. It was the same knee he had had a cartilage operation on 13 years earlier while playing junior hockey. It would require another surgery. Park was expected to sidelined anywhere from five to eight weeks.

"I'm sick—I'm physically sick over this [news]," declared Don Cherry when apprised of the situation. "No team in any sport—any team, any sport—depends on one guy like we depend upon Brad Park."[14] Park, 30, had slightly injured the knee in a preseason game in Halifax on October 2 but initially did not think it was anything serious. "It gave me a little bit of pain for about 20 seconds and after that it didn't really bother me," he said. "Then it started getting stiffer and sorer every game. I gave it a good test in the opener against Pittsburgh and when I woke up the next morning it was all swollen up."[15] Although Park expressed confidence that the Bruins would be able to roll along nicely without him, *Globe* writer Steve Marantz was not so optimistic. "The Bruins will be struggling without their one indispensable cog,"[16] he wrote. As it turned out, the estimated recovery time was correct. Park would not return to the Bruins' lineup until November 21.

Park's injury indirectly led to more tension between Cherry and Harry Sinden. With Park unavailable and Dick Redmond enduring a painful bad back, the Bruins were critically short of defensemen. Al Sims was called up from the Bruins' minor league affiliate in Rochester to fill the void. In Boston's 7–2 victory in St. Louis on October 24, Sims was clearly the outstanding Bruin on the ice. "That was one of the best performances I've seen by a defenseman since I've been in the league,"[17] Cherry proudly told the *Globe*. Remarkably,

Sinden thought little of Sims. Scuttlebutt circulated that Sims would be sent back to Rochester—a rumor that angered his fellow Bruins.

Shortly thereafter, the Bruins had a chance to pick up the steady and reliable Dennis Kearns from the Vancouver Canucks to bolster their defense. Instead, Sinden signed 29-year-old journeyman Ab DeMarco who was nearing the end of a mediocre career. In fact, DeMarco thought his career had ended. He had been invited to Boston's training camp and had been so unimpressive that he had been released without even being sent to Boston's AHL affiliate in Rochester. Sinden managed to track down DeMarco on a moose-hunting vacation in northern Ontario and told him to report to the team. DeMarco had not been on skates in three weeks. Cherry was not pleased. "Another reclamation job," he disgustedly told Fran Rosa of the *Boston Globe*. "How many miracles do they think I have in me?"[18] DeMarco lasted all of three games. When DeMarco was released, Cherry archly quipped, "I hear the moose are still running."[19] Sims did stay with Boston for most of the 1978–79 campaign, but he would be left unprotected by the Bruins at the end of the season. From the DeMarco fiasco onward, Cherry's relationship with Bruins upper management was seldom a happy one.

The Penguins, who featured ex-Bruin Gregg Sheppard, rebounded in a return match in Pittsburgh two nights later and battled Park-less Boston to a 4–4 tie. Orest Kindrachuk's goal that leveled the game for the home team was an ugly one. It pinballed off several Bruins before trickling past goalie Gilles Gilbert with only 30 seconds remaining. Pittsburgh's Dale Tallon absorbed a severe thrashing in a third-period scuffle with Bobby Schmautz. According to Bob Whitley of the *Pittsburgh Post-Gazette*, Tallon sustained multiple injuries, including 14 stitches, a separated shoulder and a damaged wrist.

Francis Rosa of the *Globe* wrote the disappointing tie result occurred "on a night when morale was low" because of Park's knee injury. "The Bruins without a doubt missed Park," Rosa noted. "The approach without Park must now be to play their system of hockey without considering who will do the things he did. Every Bruin must pick up the slack."[20]

The following night at Boston Garden, the gritty Bruins somehow managed to beat the Toronto Maple Leafs 4–2 in a game which Jean Ratelle played with a left wrist so banged up he couldn't take faceoffs, Gary Doak could not grip his stick before the game, Dick Redmond was enduring the agony of a sore back, and Bobby Schmautz played with a tender hand from battling Pittsburgh's Dale Tallon the night before. "Imagine all these guys hurt and the team goes out and plays a game like that!"[21] marveled Don Cherry. Cherry was even more surprised at Rick Middleton who decisively pummeled Darryl Sittler in a third-period display of fisticuffs. No Bruin could remember that last time Middleton had fought anybody—because he had not. It was the first fighting major that Middleton was assessed as a Bruin. (In the previous two seasons combined, Middleton had only accrued five minor penalties. For the rest of the 1978–79 season, Middleton would get just one minor penalty.) Cherry joked, "Middleton is going to be known as the goon. He's kept his fighting ability from me all this time. Now I'm going to expect it."[22]

After the plucky victory over Toronto, the Bruins embarked on their annual early-season road trip as a circus occupied Boston Garden. How the Bruins managed on this extensive absence from the Garden was often a harbinger of how the entire regular season would unfold. Boston proved up to the task, going a very respectable 4–1–1 in six games, their only loss being a 6–5 defeat to the Blackhawks in Chicago. Thirteen games into the 1978–79 campaign the Bruins were 8–2–3 and sitting atop the Adams Division. They seemed to be in good stead to challenge for the Stanley Cup despite Brad Park's frequent absences from Boston's lineup.

Park, eager to return to the team, unwisely shortened his recuperation time and reinjured the bad knee. He would only play in 40 of the Bruins' 80 games in 1978–79, but he would be well rested for the playoffs. After a Bruins gutsy 3–2 win over Los Angeles on October 18 on Boston's first westward swing of the year, Cherry praised how well his team was coping without Park and Mike Milbury. "Half the other guys looked like they staggered out of Wounded Knee," declared Cherry, showing his fondness for military history. "I don't know how we do it, but we just do it."[23] Recently retired Johnny Bucyk was also impressed by his former mates' resilience. "Most teams would fold," Bucyk opined. "This is remarkable. It's seems that there's almost too much to overcome—and still these guys overcome it. What a team! What a bunch of guys!"[24]

In another valiant effort, on October 24 the Bruins handily thumped the woebegone St. Louis Blues 7–2 on the road, despite being undermanned due to injuries. The game featured Bob Miller and Rick Middleton scoring two goals apiece and Terry O'Reilly getting his 200th career assist. It was also the first glimpse the Bruins and the Boston media had of the Blue Angels, a cheerleading troupe comprised of eight comely, pompom-shaking lasses whom the Blues unveiled as a new attraction for 1978–79. Francis Rosa of the *Globe* saw the sideshow as irrefutable evidence of the decline of hockey in St. Louis. He wrote:

> The Blues took four rows of seats out of their stands to give the Blue Angels a platform. They stand there and shake their gold and blue pompoms together, maybe trying to distract the fans from what's going on on the ice. It is also a sad commentary about what has happened to hockey in this city, taking out seats in an arena that once rocked to the cheers of 20,000 people per game.
> The Blue Angels had better legs than the Blues.[25]

The November 1 issue of the *Globe* contained a surprising endorsement for the Bruins from an unlikely source: the Toronto Maple Leafs' maverick owner, Harold Ballard, emphatically predicted Boston would win the Stanley Cup! The Bruins had only played nine regular-season games and had a 6–1–2 record, but that small sample was enough to convince the 75-year-old Ballard there would be a Stanley Cup parade in Boston in May. The *Globe*'s John Ahern took Ballard's vote of confidence with a grain of salt. "That's like giving the Red Sox the pennant because George Scott was hitting big in Winter Haven,"[26] he wrote.

5

Looking Like Contenders

There was always some bizarre, amusing, peripheral incident surrounding the 1978–79 Boston Bruins. Case in point: On November 2, the Bruins handily thumped the New York Islanders 4–1 at Boston Garden. When the game was no longer in doubt, Cherry got into a verbal sparring match with mild-mannered Islander Ed Westfall. Westfall, nearing the end of a lengthy NHL career, had been a Bruin for more than a decade until he was scooped up by the Islanders in the 1972 expansion draft. Cherry explained what the heated discussion was all about. "For years [Westfall has] been coming here and saying how much he enjoys playing in front of his old friends in Boston Garden, scoring and beating us. So I just said to him, 'Are you enjoying the game? Are you happy in front of all your friends?'"[1]

Westfall was both miffed and puzzled. "Why is [Cherry] trying to build a reputation against a 38-year-old man?"[2] he asked. Westfall also accused Cherry of using foul language.

"I don't swear," Cherry insisted. "But if I used profanity against the Reverend Westfall and offended him, I apologize."[3]

In the first Bruins-Canadiens matchup of the season, the teams played to a tenacious and cautious 1–1 tie at Boston Garden on Sunday, November 5. Neither team was at their sharpest that night. Fatigue was a factor: Montreal was playing their fourth game in five nights while Boston was playing their third in four nights. Gilles Gilbert played well in goal for Boston. It was a solid comeback game for him after surrendering five goals to the Philadelphia in the first period the night before in the Flyers' easy 7–3 win at Boston Garden.

Prior to the game, Montreal coach Scotty Bowman stated, "We don't have a divine right to any hockey game."[4] Writer Francis Rosa commented, "A few hours later the entire Bruins team would have challenged that statement. The Bruins can wonder about Montreal's divine right to any hockey game, even a tie."[5]

Boston thought they had gotten the short end of the sick on a decisive and controversial penalty call by referee Ron Wicks. "If I say anything I'll live to regret it," said coach Don Cherry who was struggling to contain his fiery emotions. "It would be a $5,000 to $10,000 fine, so I have nothing to say."[6] Here is what irked Cherry, his team, and the sell-out crowd at Boston Garden: With Boston leading 1–0 in the third period, Terry O'Reilly was battling Doug Risebrough for a loose puck near the end of a Bruins power play. "Risebrough came up with his stick and hit me just below the mouth," O'Reilly said after the game. "We fell down and I gave his head a shove. There was blood on my face. I got two minutes—and he got nothing."[7] Montreal scored on their ensuing power play.

"It's frustrating to get a bad call like that," opined the stately Jean Ratelle. "A team like Montreal just needs one power play."[8] Rick Middleton, easily the best player on the ice for either team that night, concurred. "We should have won the game," he said. "We deserved it. If they didn't get the power play, they wouldn't have scored."[9]

Glenn Cole of the *Montreal Gazette* noted, "Cherry gave some indication during the game that he was upset with the work of referee Ron Wicks who was good at times and bad at others during the contest."[10]

Despite their inability to defeat the Habs, a dozen games into the 1978–79 season the Bruins were once again looking like a legitimate Stanley Cup threat. Cherry praised his entire team's performance despite injuries taking a substantial toll. "You know this is remarkable," a prideful Cherry told John Ahern of the *Globe*. "These guys have only lost twice in 12 games and all the time we looked like the survivors at Bataan."[11] After a 7–3 home victory over Vancouver on December 12 (in which rugged John Wensink scored a hat-trick), the battered Bruins surprisingly led the NHL's overall standings with 42 points after 29 games.

On November 23, in Boston's 5–2 home win over the Buffalo Sabres, Brad Park returned to Boston's lineup for the first time since Opening Night. He made little impact on the game as one of the NHL's new rules for the 1978–79 season—one that both goalies and coaches universally despised—came into play. Buffalo goalie Don Edwards suffered an ankle injury after Terry O'Reilly fell over him in the third period. According to the very strict rule, Edwards' replacement, a rookie named Randy Ireland who was forced off the Buffalo bench to make his NHL debut, was not permitted any warm-up shots whatsoever.

The rule was designed to prevent coaches making frivolous, temporary goaltending changes to buy a few minutes of rest time for their starting goalie or their team in general—which became a common tactical play during the previous NHL season. Most coaches saw the rule as overkill, though. "It's absolutely ridiculous," said Toronto coach Roger Neilson when asked about it by Francis Rosa of the *Globe*. "It's like putting a pitcher into a baseball game without letting him warm up. They say the idea is to speed up the game, but how much time would it take to let him have eight shots?"[12] Gerry Cheevers concurred. "It's tough to come into a game like that," he said. "A goalie likes to get a few shots to get a feel for the game. It's not fair—not fair at all—to make a goalie come in cold. Me? I'd be worthless under those conditions."[13] (Ireland, however, was likely thrilled for the opportunity to play regardless of the circumstances. His whole NHL career consisted of just 30 minutes spread over two games. Ireland surrendered two goals to Boston.)

On Saturday, November 25, the Bruins were hit with another injury in a game at Washington. Rick Middleton jammed his hand. Cherry was unsure about how long Middleton would be lost to the team. "He can't grip the stick."[14] A rare but costly Brad Park blunder allowed the Capitals to get a 5–5 tie in a game Don Cherry figured was in the bag. Afterward, Cherry criticized Park in front of his teammates in the visitors' dressing room. Park glared at him. Cherry blew his stack, throwing water bottles and towels at Park. According to Park's autobiography, he and Cherry did not speak for two weeks. Park eventually requested a private meeting to patch things up where he demanded a public apology from his coach. Cherry initially refused, but eventually relented. At the end of a practice Cherry told his Bruins he was an emotional person "who sometimes says things he shouldn't and sometimes throws things he shouldn't."[15] That was the extent of Cherry's apology, but Park accepted it. He and Cherry got along splendidly from that point onward.

The night after the tie in Washington, Cherry attained a personal milestone without being aware of it when the Bruins beat the Atlanta Flames 4–2 at Boston Garden. It was Cherry's 200th regular season win as the Bruins' coach. Only Art Ross and Milt Schmidt had accrued more coaching victories for Boston. When informed about the feat, Cherry pooh-poohed his achievement. "Aw, what's the difference: 200, 150 or what?"[16] he asked.

The game also featured Terry O'Reilly leveling Atlanta's enormous Harold Phillipoff with a thunderous third-period check. "It was a good clean check at center ice, with O'Reilly taking Phillipoff's legs out from under him and upending him," declared Francis Rosa in the next day's *Globe*. Rosa cheekily added, "It was coincidental the two had fought in the second period."[17] Thirty years later Don Cherry recalled it as "one of the hardest checks I've ever seen. It was like an explosion. [Phillipoff] goes down on his back and he's flopping like a chicken on the ice." With medical personnel on the ice to tend to the flattened Flame, Cherry saw O'Reilly standing near the Bruins' bench pensively leaning on his stick. Cherry mistook O'Reilly's posture for concern about Phillipoff's well-being. "Terry, don't worry," Cherry assured him. "He's going to be all right." Without changing his expression, O'Reilly quickly corrected his coach's misperception. "Oh, no, Grapes," he said. "I really don't care if the [expletive] dies."[18] A headline in the *Globe*'s on November 28 declared, "Phillipoff out for five weeks."[19]

With Boston playing surprisingly well despite injuries and other setbacks, other coaches and executives from around the league tried to figure out how the Bruins were leading the overall NHL standings in early December. "They beat you with consistency," Detroit coach Bobby Kromm said. "They play at the same pace no matter what the score. They don't play in spurts and then let down. They play the same way all the time."[20] General-manager Max McNab of the Washington Capitals (the father of Boston center Peter McNab) believed the Bruins' excellence trickled down from the top. "It's a combination of good management and good coaching," he stated. "The Bruins are winners, and when players are out with injuries, the other guys on the club don't go around looking for crutches."[21]

The Bruins were in top form in early December. A victory over 6–5 home triumph over Detroit on December 7 gave them a six-game winning streak, the longest string of consecutive victories they would enjoy all season. On December 17, Boston beat the New York Rangers 4–1 at Madison Square Garden in which the team's grinding, hard-work style was plainly evident and thoroughly successful. Afterward a reporter asked Phil Esposito why the Bruins always seemed to play so hard every game. The ex-Bruin superstar generously replied, "Because Boston is such a great place to play, you work your tail off to stay there."[22] Along those same lines, Don Cherry was irked that not one of his Bruins was anywhere near the top of the fan voting at any position on the NHL's all-star squad. "If I were the coach, I'd bring up my whole team,"[23] he said, undoubtedly ingratiating himself further with his Bruins.

The Bruins held their annual Christmas party at Boston Garden on December 18 for the players' children. Everyone was all smiles—except for Don Cherry. He had been shown more early returns in fan voting for the NHL's all-star team that would play a best-of-three series versus the Soviet Union's national team in February at Madison Square Garden. Cherry's Bruins were far from the lead at any position. Cherry was more than a little bit miffed. He vented, "Here we are leading the National Hockey League [in overall points]; we have two 20-goal scorers [Peter McNab and John Wensink]; we've scored more goals than anyone else; we have two undefeated goaltenders [Gerry Cheevers and Jim Pettie]; we were finalists for the Stanley Cup last season—and the best we've done in the balloting is a distant fifth place. Brad Park got that, and he's a guy who should be an automatic selection."[24] John Ahern of the *Boston Globe* blamed the Bruins' poor showing in the polls on a general lack of knowledge about the voting process and a general malaise in the Hub. While there was an ongoing heavy drive for votes in New York, Toronto, and Montreal, curiously no announcements had yet been made at Boston Garden to instruct fans how to cast votes.

In his December 24 hockey roundup column in the *Globe*, Francis Rosa wrote, "This is why Don Cherry is unhappy with the voting: There are only two Bruins in the top 25 vote-getters, according to the latest tabulation. They are Terry O'Reilly, fifth among right wingers; and Brad Park, fifth among defensemen. Can you believe that Bob Sirois of Washington is running ahead of the Islanders' Mike Bossy as well as O'Reilly on right wing?"[25]

Rosa also used the space to suggest various Christmas gifts for prominent NHL figures that Santa Claus ought to bring. Some of them were comical. For the Minnesota North Stars, Rosa asked for "another team to merge with and another 10 players to sell." For the St. Louis Blues, Rosa wanted "a new owner so the players wouldn't have to eat Ralston-Purina dog food," a reference to the team's new corporate owners. For bombastic Toronto owner Harold Ballard, Rosa thoughtfully requested "a different pair of shoes for each day of the week so he'll get a different taste when he opens his mouth to change feet." Others suggestions were more heartfelt. "For Jean Ratelle," Rosa wrote, "a Stanley Cup, for once."[26]

By December 23, the Bruins had only lost one of their last 17 games. Incredibly, they also hit the 100 mark for games lost by players due to injuries and illnesses. It did not seem to matter. "At this point, today's opponent at the Garden, the Buffalo Sabres, seem to be no threat,"[27] wrote an impressed Francis Rosa in the *Globe*. Rosa was right: Boston beat Buffalo 6–4 that Saturday afternoon despite falling behind by two goals within the first three minutes of play. Everything was clicking for the Bruins heading into Christmas.

Boston was hit with another injury setback: Brad Park reinjured his knee in a 1–1 tie versus Toronto at Maple Leaf Gardens on December 27. He would be out of the Bruins' lineup until the middle of February. Naysayers predicted Park might retire.

The Habs were never far from the Bruins' radar—even if Don Cherry's squad tried to pretend it was not the case. Before the Bruins played the Canadiens at the Forum on December 30, the *Boston Globe* was predictably hyping the importance of the marquee matchup. Cherry tried to downplay the second Bruins-Habs encounter of the season, saying his club's primary goal was to finish atop the Adams Division and a win over Montreal would only be as helpful to the cause as a victory over any other NHL team. The *Globe*'s Francis Rosa was having none of it. He stated decisively, "Everybody sees the game as a midseason preview of the Stanley Cup final."[28] Asked if he agreed, Cherry light-heartedly responded, "I hope Montreal gets there."[29] After what occurred, Cherry may have wanted to revise his post–Christmas wish list.

Boston outplayed Montreal for about 15 minutes, but Ken Dryden held the fort in the Canadiens' net. Boston then surrendered four goals in a span of 3:28 as Gerry Cheevers had a rare bad night guarding the Boston cage. (Entering the contest, Cheevers was riding a personal 16-game unbeaten streak.) The Habs won easily, 6–1, before 18,001 excited spectators—the largest crowd of the year at the Forum. Boston, however, rebounded the following night with a decisive 7–3 road victory over Buffalo on New Year's Eve to finish 1978 on a high note. "We forget yesterday," said captain Wayne Cashman, who scored a hat-trick in the rout. "We seem to tighten up in Montreal."[30]

As the year 1978 drew to a close, the *Globe*'s Peter Gammons gave the Bruins very high praise, saying they were Boston's most successful yet underappreciated team of the past 12 months. He glowingly wrote in a piece titled "Bruins Don't Capture Headlines—Just Victories":

All they have become is the team Boston should be proudest of. They won more than the Red Sox, more than the Patriots, more than the Celtics. But it wasn't only the winning, because in the past the Bruins have won more and distinguished themselves less. They've had as many injuries as the Red Sox and have kept on winning.

I'm told the Bruins are dull because they don't have an Orr. Dull? They only lead the league in goals. Dull? Any group of athletes that tries as hard as this one does can't be dull.

As 1978 ends, the Bruins can pride themselves on having given Boston more than any of their brothers. They are New England's team of the year.[31]

6

The New Year
Brings Troubles—
and a Tribute

Perhaps the most remarkable game the Bruins played during all of the 1978–79 season was a January 3 contest in Chicago Stadium against the Blackhawks. It was remarkable that they got to Chicago at all and remarkable they were able to play a winning game. Francis Rosa of the *Globe* charitably called the Bruins' journey to the Windy City a "fiasco." A heavy snowstorm—one of the worst on record to hit Chicago—had made air travel into Illinois extremely difficult as the chronicle of Bruins adventures and misadventures clearly showed:

- The Bruins are booked on a commercial flight out of Boston's Logan Airport bound for San Francisco with a stopover in Chicago where they would disembark.
- The flight is supposed to leave at 6:30 p.m. eastern time on Tuesday, January 2. Word reaches Logan Airport that the worst blizzard to hit Chicago in a decade has made O'Hare Airport a nightmare. Only one runway is operable. The flight leaves Boston 160 minutes late to avoid a backlog of arrivals that already exists.
- Nevertheless, the Bruins' flight is caught in a holding pattern over O'Hare. A long delay ensues. An even longer one occurs on the ground before the passengers can deplane at 3:30 a.m. Chicago time. The pilot informs everyone over the intercom that this is the worst mess he has ever seen at O'Hare. There is a three-hour delay at the baggage claim.
- Players scramble for the few limos and taxis that are providing ground transportation to the Bruins' hotel. The typical $13 fare has been jacked up to anywhere from $60 to $100.
- The Bruins learn their equipment has wrongly continued on to San Francisco. Airline officials tell the team they can expect their equipment to be at O'Hare Airport by 3 p.m. Chicago time. It arrives at 6 p.m.
- NHL vice-president Brian O'Neill is apprised of the situation. Not wanting to postpone the game, O'Neill tells the Bruins, "If your equipment is at O'Hare Airport, play the game no matter how late you have to start."
- Gerry Cheevers tells Francis Rosa, "I'm not sure if I'm playing goal tonight, but I'm not playing without equipment."
- At 7:10 p.m. (25 minutes before the game is supposed to begin), the P.A. announcer at Chicago Stadium informs the crowd of 12,672 fans that the Bruins'

equipment is on its way and the game will begin as soon as the visitors can get dressed.

- The Bruins' personal luggage, also thought to have been erroneously forwarded to San Francisco, is found strewn around O'Hare Airport among an estimated pile of 10,000 bags from dozens of flights.
- The Bruins' equipment arrives at Chicago Stadium at 7:47 p.m. The game starts exactly one hour later.
- Boston comes from two goals behind to win the game, 6–3. "Just another night in the life of the Bruins," declares Rosa in his game report. "When things go wrong, they play better."[1]

With the Bruins in cruise control by early January, and the clear favorites to finish first in the Adams Division for the fourth straight season, for one night the organization could fondly look back and honor the most beloved Bruin of them all: Bobby Orr. Orr had his #4 jersey retired in a memorable ceremony before an exhibition game versus the Wings of the Soviet (the USSR's Air Force team) on January 9. Orr, not quite 31, was forced into premature retirement due to knees badly damaged by on-ice collisions and further wrecked by the primitive surgical techniques of the day. "Orr was a perishable civic asset … doomed by a ravaged left knee to retire at 30 when he should have been ripening and mellowing like a fine Bordeaux,"[2] wrote John Powers in the following day's *Boston Globe*. (Powers would win a Pulitzer Prize in 1983.)

Earlier in the day Orr was feted by the Massachusetts state legislature and by civic officials in Boston who formally proclaimed January 9, 1979, to be "Bobby Orr Day" in the Hub. House Speaker Thomas W. McGee gave Orr a ceremonial wooden gavel. Orr grasped it firmly and said, "I hope you don't mind if I hold this. I feel a little more comfortable with a piece of lumber in my hand."[3]

The organizers of the tribute at Boston Garden naively envisioned a quick, efficient, and tidy retirement ceremony climaxing with Orr's number being hoisted to the rafters. But the sell-out Boston Garden crowd had other ideas. They were not going to let Orr slip quietly into the night without a clear display of how highly they thought of him. He received a thundering seven-minute standing ovation that totally disrupted the wonderfully disjointed and chaotic ceremony. Emcee Tom Fitzgerald utterly lost control of the goings-on. The Garden crowd lovingly hijacked the proceedings and the deafening applause for Orr continued unabated. The 66-year-old Fitzgerald was a crusty but lovable hockey writer who covered the Bruins for the *Boston Globe* from 1940 until his retirement in 1977. He won a Lester Patrick Award in 1978 for his contributions toward the growth of hockey in the United States. He had covered Orr's debut game—October 19, 1966—in which he referred to Orr as "the 18-year-old super-boy who more than fulfilled the demanding assignment by living up to all of his extravagant notices."[4] (Boston won that game 6–2. Orr got an assist that night on a second-period power play when Wayne Connelly deflected his shot from the right point past Detroit's Roger Crozier. Typical of the extreme modesty that he would display throughout his career, Orr claimed the goal he created was entirely lucky and that he had partially whiffed on the shot.) Fitzgerald was at a complete loss at how to quiet Orr's noisy admirers. With the boisterous crowd unwilling to stop cheering Orr despite repeated pleas, the flummoxed Fitzgerald helplessly muttered, "I don't know what to do"[5] to the assembled dignitaries on the ice. It was a remarkable display of admiration and respect by fans to a beloved athlete. It may not have been equaled anywhere in sports in all the years since. Bruins captain Wayne Cashman summed up most everyone's feelings about Orr: "He was the greatest athlete in any sport," he said. "He could do anything out there."[6]

Orr had last played for Boston on November 26, 1975, at Madison Square Garden. It was Boston's first visit to the Rangers' home building since the Phil Esposito trade. (Esposito sat out the game due to a bad ankle. Jean Ratelle was heartily cheered by the New York crowd after scoring a goal for Boston. Bark Park, on the other hand, was inexplicably booed.) Francis Rosa of the *Globe* noticed that Orr was "limping somewhat and looking as if games on consecutive nights had taken a toll." Nevertheless, Orr starred in the 6–4 Bruins win. (Orr's final goal for Boston came on a powerful 40-foot slapshot that ripped through the webbing of goalie John Davidson's glove!) For a mere 10 games he and Park were teammates. The Bruins lost just one of them. In those games Boston's power play featured both men on the blue line and scored at a stellar 31 percent rate. Don Cherry giddily but prematurely told his wife that the Stanley Cup was in the bag. Then Orr's left knee locked up as he was walking across a parking lot to board a bus that was taking the Bruins to Logan Airport for their next game in Chicago. Not long afterward he was under the knife for the fifth time since 1968. Writing in the *Globe* on November 30, 1975, columnist Ray Fitzgerald feared the worst: "Hockey is a game of pivoting, of sudden stops and starts, and unexpected hits. It is a difficult enough occupation for a man with sound knees. For Bobby Orr, recovering from a fifth operation, the task may be too much."[7]

It was the beginning of the end for hockey's biggest superstar, although Orr did muster one last truly heroic effort ten months later. Never having played international hockey except for one exhibition game as a junior, Orr willed himself to play for Canada in the 1976 Canada Cup tournament—and was named the event's MVP. "You'd see him the morning before a game and he could barely walk, but he was the best player on the ice once the game started. I don't know how he did it. It took a tremendous amount of courage,"[8] marveled Team Canada teammate Bobby Clarke. Bobby Hull concurred. "He was better on one leg than the rest of us were on two. That's how great he was."[9] Brad Park agreed. "[Orr] was two steps ahead of everyone," he said. "After his knee injury he was one step ahead. [There's] no one like him. Players like Gilbert Perrault and Guy Lafleur are fun to watch … but they can't control a game the way Orr did."[10]

Under unhappy circumstances, Orr ended up in Chicago where he played a mere 26 games over parts of two seasons for the Blackhawks. He allegedly never cashed a Blackhawk paycheck because he felt he had not earned it. Orr played no games from January 1977 until October 1978. A few games into the 1978–79 season, reality set in and retirement was forced upon Orr at the young age of 30. It was a tragedy by any measure, the NHL's version of Sandy Koufax. To a great many fans, Bobby Orr will always be the greatest hockey player of all time—bar none.

The actual game versus the Soviet Wings was a sore spot for the Bruins. They did not want it on their schedule, but the NHL insisted upon it. (Francis Rosa wrote it had been "shoved down the Bruins' throats by the NHL brass."[11]) It was one of five exhibition games the touring Soviet team played in North America in the space of ten days, part of a reciprocal deal that allowed the February's Challenge Cup series between the Soviet National Team and the NHL's All-Stars to take place. Especially irksome to the Bruins was that the Soviet Wings were permitted to play the Montreal Canadiens' top farm team, the Nova Scotia Voyageurs, instead of the Habs.

Boston took the meaningless game lightly, reducing most of their star players' ice time and playing all three goalies for a period apiece. Boston lost 4–1 in a contest where the crowd's emotion was largely spent on the pregame ceremony. Although the game did not count in the standings, the Bruins were enraged at what they thought was underhanded, dirty play by the Soviets. Peter McNab had his legs taken out from under him by winger Yuri Turin, yet somehow McNab was assessed an interference penalty by referee Wally Harris. McNab told Rosa after the game, "I felt it was completely unnecessary. I don't get upset very often, but [Turin] was out to injure me on that play in the first period. He faked hitting me in the chest and hit me under the knees. I only have one career to play and I don't want some clown finishing it off in a game that doesn't mean anything. He's just a dirty player. They're much more subtle than we are. They kick you in the back of the legs. They spear. They're a dirty crew."[12]

On January 15, Don Cherry got star treatment as a feature article about him and his Bruins—but mostly about him—appeared in *Sports Illustrated*. It was a rare honor for an NHL coach. In 1979 *SI* still largely considered NHL hockey to be a regional passion and seldom carried feature- length articles about hockey figures. Written by Jerry Kirshenbaum, the story was cleverly titled "The Wrath of Grapes." The piece included a photo montage of Cherry modeling three of his favorite suits and another shot of him snuggling with his beloved bull terrier Blue. Kirshenbaum referred to Cherry as "the NHL's most vocal and visible coach … [who] directs the Bruins with a studied mixture of sternness and malarkey."[13] The author described Cherry's coaching philosophy and over-the-top personality thusly:

> Cherry … expects his players to go into the corners, never to back away from fights, and to be fresher in the third period than in the first. "We don't win, my family doesn't eat," he growls.
> But Cherry is not just another hockey tough guy. He claims, "Nobody in this game has more fun than I do." He has been known to yell "Gong!" when removing errant players from games, and he incessantly carries on about Blue.
> Cherry sports a handsome and expensive assortment of mix-and-match ensembles that he tops off with stickpins, cufflinks and chains. In hopes of looking thinner, Cherry squeezes into jackets at least a size too small. Thus girdled, he has the uncomfortable appearance of an urchin forced to dress for church when he could be stealing hubcaps.[14]

Writer Kirshenbaum then provided the Bruins with something to post on the team's bulletin board whenever they needed inspiration or motivation for the remainder of the 1978–79 season: "The Bruins succeed even though they have few players anywhere near as colorful as Cherry. Unlike the dazzling Canadiens, the Bruins boast only two certified NHL stars: Brad Park, who recently reinjured his knee, and goalie Gerry Cheevers. The rest of the roster is largely filled with retreads."[15]

The same week that Cherry was profiled in *SI*, Harry Sinden discussed the negotiations to retain his services for the 1979–80 season and beyond. It did not sound very promising. Writing in the *Boston Globe*, Francis Rosa summarized what Sinden had already told the Toronto *Globe & Mail* in a lengthy interview: "The implication of his words are (1) if Cherry can get a better offer somewhere else maybe he should take it. (2) There is a recognition that Cherry is both a successful coach and the game's #1 personality. (3) It is indicated that the Bruins may be willing to go higher."[16]

Sinden had told the *Globe & Mail*, "The offer to Cherry is well thought out … and the salary is in line with other top coaches in the league. A lot of people are missing a point, a very valid point: Our coaches of the past ten years have accomplished much the same thing [getting the Bruins to the Stanley Cup finals]."[17] Rosa pointed out a couple of key differences that were just as valid: "Those coaches did it with the best hockey player of all time, Bobby Orr, and with the greatest scoring center in history, Phil Esposito, both in their primes—and the Stanley Cup champions of 1970 and 1972 did not have to play Montreal in the finals."[18]

Not only was the Boston sports media overwhelmingly on the side of Cherry in his contract battle with the Bruins, so were the city's newspaper cartoonists. Cherry stated his personal favorite from 1978–79 was a cartoon that showed Blue in the general-manager's office. The caption read, "Yeah, Grapes. I'll be right there. I just want to leave a little something something for Harry!"[19]

Cherry won extraordinary favor with the Boston hockey writers because he granted them availability on a personal level well beyond the call of duty. He said in one of his books, "One of the reasons [the Boston media liked me] was that if the sportswriters needed a column, they could call my house. Even if it was 11 o'clock at night, if they didn't have anything, they could phone. I'd be up watching Johnny Carson and I'd do a column for them. So they'd protect me."[20]

In mid–January a flu bug cruelly struck the Bruins, taking its toll on a roster already depleted by injuries. "We picked it up in Chicago," Cherry theorized on January 11. "Nobody is down with it yet, but the whole club is weakened. I'm worried about that."[21] Jean Ratelle was sidelined with his own medical issue: strep throat. Despite Cherry's concerns, the resilient Bruins beat Minnesota 6–4 at Boston Garden that night without Ratelle, Brad Park, Rick Smith or Bobby Schmautz in the lineup. The Bruins then lost three straight games From January 13 to 16—equaling their longest streak of regular-season defeats during Cherry's tenure in Boston—to teams that were not among the NHL's powerhouses. The Penguins beat them 5–3 in Pittsburgh; the Los Angeles Kings surprised the Bruins 6–3 in Boston; and the Blues knocked off Cherry's squad 5–2 in St. Louis.

On Saturday, January 27 the Bruins and Habs met for the third time in 1978–79. The Forum was the venue. Montreal won 3–1 by scoring three third-period goals. Scotty Bowman called Montreal's win "nice." Don Cherry called the loss "maddening."[22] Francis Rosa of the *Boston Globe* seemed equally frustrated. He wrote, "It has become worse than *Mission: Impossible*. At least in the old TV series the impossible mission was always accomplished. In the hockey series between the Bruins and Montreal Canadiens, winning a game in the Forum is impossible for Boston."[23]

"It was the most entertaining game of the season,"[24] declared Glenn Cole of the *Montreal Gazette*.

Trying something completely different, Don Cherry started seldom-used Jim Pettie in goal—and the ploy very nearly paid dividends. The third-string netminder, making his tenth start of the season, was excellent for more than 40 minutes. Before the game he had been coached by Gerry Cheevers about what to expect from the various Montreal shooters. Pettie's style was similar to Cheevers, a fact not lost on Scotty Bowman or the Montreal hockey writers. "On seeing him the first time, one would swear he's a carbon copy of Cheevers," said Dave Carter in his report for the *Gazette*. "Pettie likes to challenge the shooters, make sweeping pad saves, roam out of his cage, and also distract the opposition by swinging his stick in their faces."[25]

Boston took a 1–0 lead on a second-period goal by Dwight Foster—his first of the season. As usual in this rivalry, something peculiar happened at the Forum to thwart Boston. An apparent second Bruins goal was oddly waved off by Bryan Lewis on a quick whistle. Positioned behind the Montreal goal on the play, Lewis somehow missed that a scoring attempt by Bob Miller slid across the crease to Rick Middleton who banged the puck past Ken Dryden. The red light flashed, but Lewis maintained he had blown the play dead because he had lost sight of the puck. "When Lewis blew the whistle, the puck was in the goal," Middleton insisted after the game. Miller concurred. "That was the key play," he stated. "We get that one and we're two goals upon them."[26]

Instead, the score remained only 1–0 in Boston's favor until the second minute of the third period. Yvon Lambert tied the game for Montreal at 1:49. Guy Lafleur put the Habs ahead 2–1 at 3:52. Mario Tremblay added a power-play goal at 7:59. Pettie's excellent work until the third period went for naught in a little over six minutes. "Without Pettie, we would have won 10–0,"[27] Tremblay cockily noted. The loss extended a slump for the Bruins, who had lost six of their last eight games. Cherry was optimistic, though. "We've lost a few battles, but the war isn't over. The troops will be back,"[28] he declared.

Carter praised Pettie in defeat. "Pettie's goaltending performance Saturday night at the Forum was nothing less than outstanding,"[29] he wrote. Pettie was named the game's third star.

Cherry found something unique to complain about: He thought his team was being shortchanged in the tabulation of shots on goal at the Forum. "They don't even count shots on goal here," he roared. "I looked up at the shot clock [sic] and it said we had seven shots. We took three more shots on goal and it still said seven. They didn't even count our goal as a shot. That must make [Ken] Dryden feel good."[30]

On January 31 Boston returned to Chicago for the first time since the awful blizzard of January 2–3. This time Boston only managed a 2–2 tie at Chicago Stadium, but it was not for a lack of trying. The Bruins outshot the Blackhawks 17–4 in the third period, but Tony Esposito held the fort for the home team magnificently. "We should have won this game," declared Dwight Foster, "but [getting] a point is not bad on the road in front of a crowd that doesn't like us."[31] The Bruins were unanimous in their praise for the veteran Chicago netminder, but they were also unanimous in blasting referee Bob Myers for a few calls he made and a handful of calls he did not make. Terry O'Reilly made the sweeping statement, "The refereeing is inconsistent, from man to man, from game to game. It's a joke."[32] The Bruins were primarily upset that Myers called, in their opinion, several minor infractions but ignored more flagrant fouls for both teams. Myers was fast becoming Boston's least favorite NHL referee. In a 1982 *Sports Illustrated* feature story about NHL officiating, an unnamed general-manager said of Myers, "He could be the top official, but he's a bit of a show-off, among other things. He thinks the people paid to see him referee. They didn't."[33]

Even after a mediocre January, Cherry's retreads entered February with a 30–13–8 mark after 51 games. A few rough spots emerged as obstacles. Rugged Stan Jonathan broke his thumb and would miss more than half the season. His goal total dropped from 27 in 1977–78 to just six in 1978–79 because of the hand injury. In retrospect, Brad Park probably came back too early from knee surgery and was not nearly as effective as he had been during the 1978 playoffs.

Boston, in effect, got a mid-season week off while Montreal did not. In February, the NHL temporarily ditched its lackluster All-Star Game format (Campbell Conference versus Wales Conference) in favor of something far more substantial: a matchup of the league's best players against the Soviet Union's national team in a three-game series at Madison Square Garden for a trophy called the Challenge Cup. Team NHL consisted of an almost entirely Canadian roster with the exception of three Swedes. (Bobby Orr performed the ceremonial faceoff—which was a nice touch. While doing TV commentary, however, Orr repeatedly called the NHL players "Canada" or "Team Canada" out of habit—which probably did not go over well with the league brass.) Seven of the NHL's reps were Habs. Only two Bruins made the final cut: Don Marcotte and Gerry Cheevers. Neither appeared in the first game.

Team NHL took the opener 4–2 on February 8. Don Cherry remarked to Ernie Roberts of the *Boston Globe*, "Blue fell asleep in the second period. There were no Bruins in the game."[34] Team NHL lost the second game, 5–4, two days later despite holding a two-goal lead with three minutes left in the second period. The following night the Soviets won 6–0 in a blowout with all the goals coming in the second and third periods. Cheevers was the netminder for Team NHL in the embarrassing loss. He looked bad on five of the goals. Back in his North Andover home, Cherry worried about how the poor game versus the Soviets would weigh on Cheevers' psyche.

On February 17, the *Toronto Star* published the results of a poll conducted by hockey journalist Frank Orr. All 17 NHL coaches submitted their selections in 28 different categories from "most underrated player" to "best goalie" to "best referee." A Bruin finished atop four categories: best fighter (Stan Jonathan); most improved player (John Wensink); toughest player (Terry O'Reilly); and best coach (Don Cherry). Several Bruins finished as runner-up or close to the top in other categories. Montreal's Guy Lafleur finished in the number-one spot in eight categories, confirming what everyone already knew: The Flower was the NHL's best player in 1978–79.

In mid–February the Bruins fared poorly on a road trip, losing to the Rangers and Flyers and only managing a tie versus a weak Minnesota team. John Ahern of the *Globe* thought Cherry's uncertain future with the Bruins was negatively impacting his troops' performance. He sought confirmation for a story in the February 19 edition of the newspaper. He got it. "Of course it has to affect us," said one player who demanded anonymity. "We like this guy. It's great playing for him. He treats us like men and he's showed us how to win. If he goes I know at least five of our guys want to go too. It doesn't do our morale any good thinking about it. We like Boston. All of us want to stay here. If Grapes goes, many of us will be traded. It's not a comfortable feeling."[35]

Perhaps the most memorable regular-season game at Boston Garden during the 1978–79 season occurred on Saturday, March 3. The Bruins were hosting the lowly Minnesota North Stars—easily the worst team in the tough Adams Division. With Gilles Gilbert occupying Cherry's doghouse again, the Boston coach felt it would be a good time to give third-string goaltender Jim (Seaweed) Pettie some work, even though Boston was languishing in one of its mini-slumps. Pettie was uncharacteristically excellent, recording a 5–0 shutout in front of a less-than-capacity crowd. It was the second (and last) time in 1978–79 that a Bruins goalie would blank their opponents. Gerry Cheevers had shut out the St. Louis Blues, 4–0, on January 18. Despite it being Pettie's first and last NHL shutout, the game is remembered, however, for Don Cherry being ejected by referee Gregg Madill. Madill's officiating had been more than a little bit questionable, according to all accounts. Cherry, as usual, thought his Bruins were getting the short end of the stick. This seemed to be the general consensus of the Garden's patrons too.

"Referee Greg [sic] Madill had his game in the spotlight yesterday," wrote Francis Rosa in the next day's *Globe*. "His refereeing turned the crowd of 13,300 into the noisiest of the year. Madill succeeded in making a routine 5–0 game a very exciting hockey game—especially from the crowd's standpoint."[36]

When asked if Madill's officiating had brought the crowd to life, Wayne Cashman said, "Yeah, but I wouldn't pay $11 to see him referee."[37]

With the Bruins leading 4–0, Madill whistled rookie Dwight Foster—who was playing his first shift of the game—for a dubious charging penalty that had the entire Boston bench in an uproar. Boston captain Wayne Cashman got a 10-minute misconduct penalty and a gross misconduct for arguing with Madill. "I just told my teammates to step aside and let the referee have the whole television spotlight," Cashman explained. "He [Madill] said I was making fun of him and so I got the gross misconduct."[38]

Cherry continued with the complaining, hollering at Madill while conspicuously standing on the boards in front of his players. ("Cherry is really giving it to Madill!"[39] bellowed an excited Fred Cusick in the TV38 broadcast booth.) Cherry received a bench penalty and was ejected when his beefs got a little too loud and personal for the referee. The Bruins, like most other NHL teams in 1978–79, had no assistant coaches, so Gerry Cheevers stepped in to replace Cherry for the game's final 16 minutes. "It was easy and fun," Cheevers told the *Boston Globe*. "I let the defensemen change themselves." After the game Cheevers extended his fun. The Boston media found him leisurely sitting behind the desk in Cherry's office. "I better get out of here," he told the surprised reporters. "My dog has an ulcer."[40]

Boston successfully killed off the two-man disadvantage—it was the second time the Bruins had been two players short during the game—as the crowd stood and roared every time a North Stars attack was thwarted. Even when a Minnesota shot was routinely deflected over the glass by Al Sims, the home fans gave the Bruins a standing ovation. As a team, the Bruins were never more united as a result of the "Madill game"—and Cherry was probably at the peak of his popularity in Boston. (The much-maligned Madill made history a month later in Moscow when he became the first NHL referee to work a game at the International Ice Hockey Federation world championship tournament. He could not escape criticism, however, even behind the Iron Curtain. The Czechs were extremely unhappy with Madill's officiating in a nightmarish 11–1 loss to the Soviet Union.)

Eight days later, on March 11, the Bruins played to a 4–4 tie at Boston Garden versus the ascending New York Islanders who were also showing themselves to be Stanley Cup contenders. They were consistently giving the Bruins loads of trouble in 1978–79. "It is becoming a frustrating experience whenever the Bruins play the Islanders," wrote Francis Rosa in the next day's *Globe*. "They outplay them, they outhit them, they outshoot them, but they don't outscore them. Three times this season they have done all those things, and the count shows one loss and two ties."[41] [Note: Rosa was incorrect. Boston's record versus the Islanders at that point in the season was actually 1–1–2.] All four Islander goals came on power plays in a game where Boston outshot the visitors 34–16. Two of them came on a five-minute man-advantage in the first period. Bobby Schmautz bluntly called his team's penalty killing, usually a Bruin strong point, "disgusting."[42] During one stretch of the game the Islanders did not record a shot on goal for 27 minutes. Don Cherry declared the final result to be "a crime. We deserved better than that."[43] The Bruins benefited from man-advantage situations too, scoring two of their

As someone who served as both the radio and television voice for the Boston Bruins from 1952 to 1997, Fred Cusick witnessed Boston's playoff futility streak versus Montreal more than any other "Bruin." He and broadcast partner John Peirson came under fire from Boston's TV critics for abandoning objectivity during the decisive moments of Game #7 of the Bruins-Habs semifinal series.

four goals on power plays and a third on a delayed penalty when they had six attackers on the ice. One hooking penalty called by referee Bruce Hood against Dwight Foster was clearly wrong. Television replays clearly showed that Lorne Henning had grabbed Foster's stick, and the Bruin was merely trying to yank it from the Islander's grasp. Rosa reported that "Cherry did a highland fling upon the Bruins' bench"[44] when Hood assessed a minor penalty to Foster instead of Henning. Thirty-three seconds later the visitors scored on their power play.

By mid–March the Bruins' inconsistent play was worrying the local scribes. After an embarrassing 7–4 home loss to the New York Rangers on March 15 (in which Phil Esposito scored four goals), Francis Rosa pointed out in the *Globe* that Boston had accrued 61 points in the first 40 games of the season, but had only mustered 25 points in the 29 games since that time. It was the second consecutive game in which Boston had allowed seven goals. "Is this any way to get ready for the playoffs?"[45] Rosa asked rhetorically. The Bruins rebounded two nights later with a more solid effort. On March 17, Brad Park equaled an NHL record by notching four assists in one period in Boston's 4–2 home victory over the Chicago Blackhawks.

Still, despite their spotty play after January, winning the Adams Division and attaining a first-round bye was already a clear likelihood for the Bruins. Qualifying for the playoffs was a virtual certainty. (In fact, Bruins radio announcer Bob Wilson had booked a tropical cruise for the one-week break he expected to get while the Bruins were enjoying their bye.) Getting the highest possible playoff seed was the real order of business in the last two months of the regular season. The higher the seed they attained, the more home games they would get throughout the postseason. Theoretically, they would also face easier opponents. Boston had been the third seed in 1977 and the second seed in 1978, but it was going to be difficult for the Bruins to improve beyond the number-three spot in 1979. Montreal and the nouveau-riche New York Islanders were just playing too well too consistently for the Bruins—or anybody else—to finish higher than third place. It was widely assumed that Montreal would outdistance the Isles and be the top-seeded team for the fourth year in a row when the regular season ended on the second Sunday in April.

Boston did wrap up the Adams Division title for the fourth consecutive season in their 76th game of the season with a 4–1 win in Washington on Saturday, March 31. Terry O'Reilly (with two second-period goals) and the penalty killers were the Bruins' stars of the night. At one point the Bruins successfully killed off a seven-minute Capitals power play. With the victory, the Bruins needed just two more points to outdistance the Philadelphia Flyers to clinch third place overall. "We've got a good hold on third," Wayne Cashman told Francis Rosa. "We've got five points on Philadelphia and four games to play."[46]

Don Cherry was proud of his charges, calling the win "the most important of the season." Cherry seemed perplexed at why Boston's fans were worried heading into the postseason. "We've got 96 points," he said. "We'll get 100. And people are asking what's wrong with the Bruins?"[47]

The fourth and final regular-season meeting between Montreal and the Bruins occurred at Boston Garden on Sunday, April 1. As in their only other clash on Boston ice back in November, there was no winner, so Boston only got one of the two points necessary to clinch the number-three seed. The teams fought to a 3–3 tie in which Montreal rallied from a 3–1 deficit entering the third period. Rod Langway, who was raised in the Boston area, scored the tying goal for the Habs.

"I thought we could have won the game if we had forced the play in the third period the way we did in the first two,"[48] lamented Cherry. Larry Robinson disagreed. He thought

Montreal deserved a win and was only deprived of it because of the "fine goaltending of Gerry Cheevers."[49] John Ahern of the *Boston Globe* said it was the Bruins' best effort in three months and that Montreal was mighty happy to get a point from the encounter. "Things have changed," said optimistic captain Wayne Cashman. "We're twice the team we were two weeks ago. We're ready to go now."[50]

As was becoming the norm in all Boston-Montreal clashes, there was complaining aplenty about the officiating. This night Bruce Hood was in charge of the game. Cherry took exception to a double-minor penalty that Hood issued to Terry O'Reilly after a scuffle in the second period. (Boston successfully managed to kill it.) Glenn Cole of the *Montreal Gazette* commented, "It was an excellent hockey game, despite the efforts of referee Bruce Hood to make it otherwise."[51]

The game indeed featured excellent goaltending by 38-year-old Gerry Cheevers, who put together two good games in a row for the first time since being embarrassed in the Challenge Cup in February. (He had been outstanding in a 4–1 Boston win in Washington the previous night.) Fans in other NHL cities had been riding Cheevers about the "Russian flu." There was even a negative banner displayed at Boston Garden asking, "Where has the goaltending gone?" Employing 20/20 hindsight, Don Cherry said, "I warned him not to go to that series—him and Marcotte. Donnie hasn't been the same since, either." Cherry was confident that Cheevers would return to normal, reliable self and predicted, "Gerry is absolutely the key to how far we'll go in the playoffs."[52]

Late in the season the simmering Cherry-Sinden feud got worse. Sinden publicly belittled the team after Boston played horribly in a 9–2 loss to Buffalo on March 28—a game where the Bruins could have clinched the Adams Division title and a first-round playoff bye with a victory. The general-manager opined that Boston would not get past the Stanley Cup quarterfinals if they played that badly in the playoffs. Sinden was obviously correct, of course, but Cherry was outraged. He replied that his team needed a confidence boost from its GM, not a kick when they were down. The Bruins did eventually clinch the division, and Cherry was pleased about securing the bye. He believed it was a requirement if the Bruins were to advance very far in the postseason. "We need that week off for healing purposes," he declared. "We have 11 players carrying injuries of one type or another and we have to have that week off. If we don't get it … see you later!"[53]

On April 8, the final night of the regular season, the Bruins beat the Toronto Maple Leafs 6–3 before a raucous gathering at Boston Garden despite falling behind 2–0 early in the contest. The win gave Boston exactly 100 points in the standings, precisely the total Don Cherry had predicted eight days earlier. It was the fourth straight year they had achieved triple digits in points and the ninth time in club history. "For the Bruins, the regular season ended last night just about the way they wanted it to," declared Francis Rosa in the *Globe*. "The big news was [goaltender Gilles] Gilbert. He played better than anyone would have expected—good enough to be voted the #1 star. He hadn't played since March 8 and spent most of the year—whether he was injured or not—on the bench or out of uniform."[54]

"I've sort have been disappointed all season," Gilbert told Rosa. "It's been like this for three years so why should I get myself down? But I felt no pressure and I'm glad I came up with a big game. I was relaxed and I think I proved I'm ready for the playoffs."[55]

"When things got straightened out [with Gilbert], there's none better," insisted Don Cherry. "He stopped three shots tonight that were labeled as goals. We have to consider him for sure. He has to be in my playoff plans the way he played tonight."[56]

Cherry also helped complete a secondary achievement for one of his personal favorites.

Bobby Schmautz had 18 goals heading into the regular season's finale. He got his 19th nine minutes into the third period. A 20-goal season would earn him a bonus—and Cherry and the rest of the Bruins knew it. Cherry began giving Schmautz extra shifts to give him every opportunity to notch the milestone goal. With Boston on a late power play, Cherry instructed the Bruins to pass the puck to Schmautz whenever possible. Schmautz netted his 20th goal with just six seconds left on the clock. Don Marcotte also recorded his 20th goal of the season in the Bruins' last game. The team had eight 20-goal scorers in 1978–79—not quite the 11 the Bruins had the previous season, but it still indicated a well-balanced offense.

Having earned a first-round playoff bye and the third seed in the playoffs, the Bruins now had eight days off to become fully healthy. Rosa called it "the pause that heals."[57] Their quarterfinal opponent was anyone's guess because of the NHL's complex double-seeding arrangement. Rosa figured the most likely scenario was a matchup versus the Atlanta Flames.

In their final 29 games the Bruins were a spotty 13–10–6. It was a decent set of results but not particularly impressive. The team never got especially hot after January nor did it suffer through a bad losing streak. However, late in the season Boston did suffer two embarrassing setbacks to Buffalo—their closest pursuers in the Adams Division—in which the Sabres scored nine goals in each game. Boston managed to go through the entire regular season without suffering a shutout for the first time since 1973–74 and for only the third time in the team's 55-year history. Boston, for the second straight season, failed to register a single win versus Montreal, managing just two ties in their four games against the Habs. They had also been outscored by a cumulative 13–6 margin in those games.

In a truly unexpected development, the New York Islanders finished ahead of Montreal in the overall standings! The Islanders topped the Habs by a single point, 116–115. The Isles won their last four games to make a successful last-ditch run at Montreal. The Habs stunningly lost 1–0 in Detroit on Sunday, April 8—the final day of the regular season. The shocking result was front-page news in the *Montreal Gazette*.

The lone goal of the game at the ancient Olympia—an arena soon to be demolished—was a fluky one. It came at 14:34 of the third period. Detroit's Dan Labraaten's pass bounced into the Montreal net off teammate Dale McCourt's knee. Jim Rutherford stopped 22 Montreal shots—including Guy Lafleur on a breakaway—to earn a surprising shutout. Four days earlier, the Habs had beaten the Red Wings 4–1 at the Forum without too much trouble. The previous night at the Forum, Montreal had mercilessly stomped on the pitiful Washington Capitals 10–3. The defeat in Detroit was Montreal's first loss in ten games and the only shutout defeat they suffered all season. Guy Lafleur, gunning for a fourth straight NHL scoring title, probably anticipated a big offensive night versus the Red Wings who had nothing to play for. With zero points in his final game, however, Lafleur ended up in third place in the NHL scoring race with 129. Bryan Trottier (134) and Marcel Dionne (130) both finished ahead of Lafleur, who would not win another Art Ross Trophy. As of 2017, no Montreal Canadien has won an NHL scoring championship since Lafleur's in 1977–78.

Detroit was one of the five NHL teams that did not qualify for the playoffs in 1978–79, so the curtain-closer versus the Habs was the Red Wings' chance to prove something. What they proved was that there was no such thing as a sure victory in the NHL. Had the Habs even managed a tie against the lowly Red Wings, they would have mathematically clinched the number one-seed as they had more wins than the Islanders. "There is no excuse for us not being ready for this one," Larry Robinson angrily told the media at the end of the game. "We certainly didn't look like a team that was fighting for first place.

Embarrassed is a very mild word to describe this. We have nobody to blame but ourselves, nobody."[58] The Habs could look back on a few surprisingly poor performances against weak NHL teams over the course of the season where they blew leads and squandered points, and therefore lost the top seed in the playoffs.

Montreal's loss to Detroit had enormous implications on three teams. The upshot of the Red Wings' win was that the Canadiens were only the second seed in the 1979 Stanley Cup playoffs—not the first seed as they had been each spring since 1976. The up-and-coming Islanders would get home ice throughout the playoffs for finishing first overall. The Isles, whose history only dated back to 1972, celebrated with champagne after their 5–2 win against the New York Rangers secured them the number-one seed. "This is it," proclaimed joyous Isles coach Al Arbour to journalist Ed Simon. "We've won the first season. Now let's go after the second season—the playoffs."[59] Furthermore, as long as Boston, Montreal, and the Islanders all advanced to the semifinals, it meant that the Bruins and Habs would meet in the semis—not in the Cup finals as they had in both 1977 and 1978.

Throughout the long season, Don Cherry's tenuous relationship with the Bruins' front office steadily got worse. Cherry complained about everything from training camp onward. He loathed the Bruins' arduous preseason schedule that forced his team to make trips far afield for meaningless games. Cherry, to the chagrin of Harry Sinden, negatively dubbed it "a safari." (Indeed, if one counts exhibition games, the Bruins played 17 of their first 19 games away from Boston Garden.) He was also embarrassed by the fact that Boston was the only team in the league to have neither its logo nor the NHL's crest embossed on the pucks used at home games. This fact had somehow escaped his attention until rookie Al Secord scored his first NHL goal and Bobby Schmautz netted his 200th—both at Boston Garden—and were given the bland, nondescript pucks as souvenirs. Cherry fumed. "These pucks looked like they were on loan from a local street hockey league,"[60] he stated in his autobiography. Cherry accused the Bruins management of extreme miserliness for using "practice pucks" during games instead of paying the estimated ten cents per unit to get game pucks professionally crested as the other 16 NHL teams did without a second thought.

Cherry, a staunch traditionalist, was also one of the few noteworthy members of the NHL who was publicly opposing the mandatory helmet rule that was going to apply to all rookies entering the league starting in the 1979–80 season. He claimed that players were losing their identities by wearing the protective headgear. Cherry was also a strong advocate of retaining fighting as part of the game. Both opinions ran contrary to what the NHL wanted to promote as the end of the rollicking 1970s approached.

By the end of the regular season, Harry Sinden and Cherry had not spoken to one another face-to-face in more than a month, resorting to awkwardly communicating by notes—and only then when absolutely necessary. With Cherry's contract expiring on June 1, 1979, his chances of getting the substantial raise he felt he deserved were becoming slimmer by the week. It was quite likely hockey's most colorful coach would leave the Bruins for parts unknown after the 1978–79 season regardless of how the Stanley Cup playoffs unfolded.

7

Only Three Contenders
The 1979 Stanley Cup Playoffs

> Every once in a while—not too often, just once in a while—something goes awry … and the Stanley Cup is taken away from the Montreal Canadiens. In the 1970s it's happened four times: Twice Boston won it; twice Philadelphia won it. Montreal held it for the other five years. Now for the last year of the decade: The Canadiens can make it four straight. Will they? No, say the Islanders. No, say the Bruins. We hope not, say nine other teams.
> —Fran Rosa from his April 8 playoff preview in the *Boston Globe*

April 8 was the last day of regular-season play in the 1978–79 NHL campaign that began in early October. By the end of the day's action, all 17 NHL teams had played their 8-game schedules. The playoff matchups and final seedings of the dozen teams that had qualified had not quite been set, but five of the league's 17 clubs definitely knew their hockey seasons would be over at the end of that Sunday: Washington, Detroit, St. Louis, Colorado and Minnesota.

The North Stars felt aggrieved by the playoff format, with some justification. It had been slightly modified in 1977 to only guarantee playoff berths to the top two teams in each division instead of the top three. Minnesota finished last in the strong, four-team Adams Division but had more points (68) than the Vancouver Canucks (63) who finished second in the embarrassingly weak Smythe Division despite being 17 games under .500. Despite being an NHL weakling, the Canucks still managed to finish well ahead of both St. Louis and Colorado—two teams that combined for only 33 victories in 1978–79—and six of those wins came in games the Blues and Rockies played against each other. (To put things in perspective, the Toronto Maple Leafs, who finished third in the Admans division, won 34 games.) The Canucks were accordingly rewarded with a playoff berth for this unimpressive feat. The NHL, always fine-tuning its playoff format, would again tweak the postseason qualification requirements for 1979–80 to eliminate that type of injustice from being repeated.

That Sunday's edition of the *Boston Globe* contained a feature article by Francis Rosa. In it he appointed himself both swami and oddsmaker as to which team would likely capture the Stanley Cup in 1979. He examined the merits and shortcomings of all 12 NHL playoff teams and came to the conclusion that Boston was only the third-best choice to win Lord Stanley's silver trophy—which exactly matched their playoff seeding.

Rosa, who had been covering the NHL for the *Globe* since 1960, placed the three-time defending Cup champion Montreal Canadiens and New York Islanders ahead of the hometown

Bruins in that order. The only team to which Rosa did not assign specific odds was Montreal. He simply labeled the Habs as "the favorites" even though they had failed to secure the top seed for the playoffs for the first time since 1975. The 11 playoff-bound challengers' respective chances were ranked based on Rosa's arbitrary handicapping from the Islanders ("rate them a 2–1 choice") to Vancouver ("at 1000–1 don't even risk a penny").

In his assessment of Montreal, Rosa heaped praise on the three-time defending titlists. "The only fear the Canadiens have is [an] upset," he wrote. "Some defensive shortcomings that showed up have been overcome. All it took was the return to action of Larry Robinson. No, they weren't bored with winning, and anyway the playoffs are their special season. And, of course, they can be had, but who's to take them? The Islanders? Possibly. The Bruins? Maybe."

As for Rosa's third choice, he declared, "The Bruins suffered through the late-season blahs but came down to the end of the regular season pretty well organized again. Injuries are the key, for they pose these questions: Will Brad Park be at 80 percent efficiency? Will Gerry Cheevers be the goalie all Boston loved in last year's playoffs? And will the week off be enough to cure the ailments of Stan Jonathan, Rick Middleton, Bobby Schmautz, et al? Make the Bruins 5–1—a good bet."

Apart from the Bruins and the Islanders, Rosa listed the other nine playoff teams as long shots in varying degrees. He was brutally harsh in some of his assessments. Consider Rosa's critique of the low-flying Chicago Blackhawks, listed at 999–1 no-hopers, who greatly benefited by the league's flawed system of awarding byes to the regular-season divisional winners regardless of how poor their records were. (The Hawks had finished seven games below .500.) "It's an NHL sin that Chicago should draw a first-round bye in the playoffs," Rosa stated. "But that's automatic for the division champions, and Chicago just as automatically wins the Smythe Division." Vancouver was skewered by the acerbic Rosa too: "Well, if the Smythe Division champion gets into the playoffs automatically, you might as well compound the felony and put the second-place team into the field. Enter Vancouver."[1]

In short, Rosa outlined what most serious fans already knew by the spring of 1979: There were only three teams that had a truly legitimate chance to parade with Lord Stanley's silverware at the end of May: Montreal, the New York Islanders, and Boston. Any other outcome would be nothing short of startling. Be that as it may, it did not stop the *Pittsburgh Post-Gazette* from running a highly optimistic banner headline in its April 10 sports section: "Pens' Stanley Cup Chase to Start Tonight."

The New York Islanders were becoming sentimental favorites among fans who recalled how pitiful they were when they entered the NHL as expansion dregs in 1972–73. (They went 12–60–6 in their debut campaign, but one of those dozen wins was a wild 9–7 victory at Boston Garden on January 18—a humiliating game for the defending Cup champs in which the flummoxed Bruins changed goalies twice. It was one of only two wins the Isles posted that January.) Since their awful debut season, the Islanders had steadily built up their squad through shrewd draft choices. The Islanders had earned the serious attention of NHL fans two years earlier when they had taken the powerful 1977 Canadiens to six games in the Cup semifinals, handing the Habs their only two losses in that spring's playoffs. The following year, 1978, the Isles unexpectedly stumbled in a seven-game quarterfinal defeat to Toronto in what was generally considered a shocking result. During the 1978–79 season, the Isles were out to prove that their playoff disappointment of 1978 was a fluke. Throughout the regular season they were undoubtedly on par with both Boston and Montreal. Accordingly, many people with no allegiance to any team gravitated toward the Isles and fancied them to seize the Cup from the Habs' grasp.

William Nack of *Sports Illustrated* was one such person on the Isles' crowded bandwagon. Even though Bryan Trottier had just won the NHL scoring championship, Nack saw the emergence of 25-year-old defenseman Denis Potvin as a key factor as to why he liked the Islanders' postseason chances. Potvin was pictured on *SI*'s April 16, 1979, cover—an infrequent honor for a hockey player in the 1970s—alongside the caption, "The Great Defender." Potvin had concluded a sensational season in which he scored 31 goals and added 70 assists for 101 points, good enough to rank seventh in the league. Those numbers put the 6-foot, 205-pound Potvin into rarefied territory: Only the recently retired Bobby Orr had ever managed to accrue 100 points in an NHL season as a defenseman, a feat the fabulous Bruin blueliner accomplished six consecutive times.

Nack wrote, "[Potvin's] dominating and controlling play, imposing himself upon the flow of the game at both ends of the ice, is the reason why the Islanders beat the Canadiens in three of the four games this year and finished the regular season last Sunday as the number-one team in the NHL." Nack cited Potvin's superb performance in the Islanders' 5–3 victory over Montreal at the Forum on March 22 as evidence that the Isles had a legitimate shot "to put an end to the Canadiens' three-year stranglehold on the Cup."[2] The Islanders' elder statesman, Ed Westfall, who had been a teammate of Orr's for five seasons in Boston, concurred. "When Denis makes up his mind to be the best player on the ice, he *is* the best player on the ice," he told Nack.[3] Since the age of 14, Potvin had been hyped—and burdened—as the second coming of Bobby Orr. To no one's surprise, Potvin was taken first overall in the 1973 amateur draft. He was perceived as a savior who could make the New York Islanders winners in a very short time. In his sixth season as a pro, Potvin was living up to his billing.

Despite his obvious skills, Potvin was not especially popular among his peers because of his outspoken personality and his utter lack of tact. This was never more evident than shortly after the Canada Cup tournament—a much awaited six-team international event in September 1976 where, for the first time, all the best players in the world would compete for their respective countries regardless of the leagues they played in or their status as pros or amateurs. After the tournament concluded, Potvin wrote a first-person article for *The Canadian*, a Saturday supplement to the *Toronto Star* that was reproduced for many weekend newspapers across Canada. In it, Potvin conceded that Bobby Orr—who was obviously on his last legs—had certainly starred in Canada's critical 3–1 round-robin victory over the Soviet Union. Nevertheless, Potvin immodestly opined that he himself had been Canada's most outstanding player that night and really deserved the award for the game's MVP rather than Orr.

Goaltender Chico Resch and other Islander teammates were horrified by Potvin's imprudent comments. "There was no reason on earth to say the things Denis said about Orr," Resch said. "I was so mad at him I could hardly talk to him. It was Orr's last hurrah and all the players knew it. Denny was going to have many more chances."[4]

Potvin's feckless words about Orr were bad enough, but his frequent public criticisms of fellow Islanders created so much dissension on the club that Potvin felt obligated to make an impromptu dressing-room apology to his teammates just before the 1976–77 season began. His speech, though awkwardly delivered, cleared the air—and the Islanders became a united force and a terrific team from that point onward. Their results versus both the Habs and the Bruins during the 1978–79 regular season seemed to give them a fairly decent chance to win it all in the upcoming Stanley Cup playoffs. Would they be a postseason force as they were in 1977, or would they again surprisingly crumble as they did in 1978? That was the lingering question facing the Islanders and their growing number of fans as they awaited a quarterfinal opponent to emerge in April 1979.

The Bruins happily entered the 1979 playoffs surprisingly healthy after a season in which they lost a staggering 186 man-games to injury, absence or illness. Stan Jonathan (who missed 47 games) and Brad Park (40 games) were the most prominent of Boston's sick and lame, but they were far from the exception. Other Bruins were shelved for considerable periods too. Here is the complete list: Bobby Schmautz was sidelined for 15 games as was Gary Doak. Dick Redmond was not far behind with 14 games missed. Rick Middleton was absent from the Boston roster nine times, Mike Milbury six times, and Wayne Cashman five times. Rick Smith, Don Marcotte, Bob Miller, Peter McNab, Al Secord and John Wensink were all injured for at least one game at some point during the 1978–79 regular season. However, heading into their quarterfinal, Boston was surprisingly healthy and rested. Seeing a fully loaded Bruins roster for the first time since early October, Francis Rosa opined in the *Globe* that Cherry was something akin to the Old Lady in the Shoe from the children's nursery rhyme in that he had so many players he did not know what to do.

On April 12, with the Bruins' quarterfinal opponent still undetermined—it could have been Toronto, Atlanta, Buffalo, or Pittsburgh—Cherry insisted he would stick with his best players regardless of who Boston's opponent might be, even though he had the luxury of a sizable pool of healthy bodies to choose from for the first time since Opening Night six months earlier. "The rule is that in the playoffs you always go with your best players," Cherry insisted. He quickly issued this disclaimer with a smile, though: "Of course, I go against the rules frequently."[5]

When the first-round pairings had been settled, on April 10 the two most prominent hockey writers for the *Montreal Gazette* made their choices as to which teams would win the four best-of-three preliminary series. Both Glenn Cole and Al Strachan foresaw a swift Philadelphia Flyers two-game sweep over the unfashionable Vancouver Canucks, but their opinions widely differed for all the other matchups.

Strachan figured the Buffalo Sabres would easily blast by Pittsburgh in two straight games while Cole predicted a three-game upset for the Penguins. (Apparently, the fact that Buffalo had not beaten Pittsburgh in their last 14 games—losing six times and playing to eight ties!—did not carry any weight with Strachan.) Cole's crystal ball told him the Atlanta Flames would oust the Toronto Maple Leafs in three games whereas Strachan thought the Leafs would take that series in three. (Atlanta, coached by the low-key tactician Fred Creighton, was certainly the most unpredictable team in the entire NHL. To everyone's surprise, the Flames had lost just one of their first 15 games to start the season fabulously—including an outright 10-game winning streak. However, they sputtered after mid–November and actually finished last in the tough, four-team Patrick Division with 90 points despite having two of the NHL's top seven scorers on their roster.) To finish his prognostications, Cole boldly picked the Los Angeles Kings to knock off the New York Rangers in the maximum three games. Strachan disagreed. He liked the Rangers to triumph in three.

In prefacing his predictions, Cole did state something that absolutely all passionate NHL fans could wholeheartedly agree with: "Now that 680 regular-season games are out of the way, and we have heard the last for a while of the Colorado Rockies and St. Louis Blues, let the real season begin!"[6]

The 53rd edition of the modern Stanley Cup playoffs would begin that night—Tuesday, April 10—in Atlanta, Buffalo, New York City, and Philadelphia. The players on Boston, Montreal, the New York Islanders and Chicago would be resting with their byes. They would, however, be watching eagerly to see which team each would be meeting in the quarterfinals.

8

The Quarterfinal

Boston Sweeps Pittsburgh

They aren't called the big, bad Bruins for nothing. Besides their obvious physical attributes and surly demeanor, the Boston Bruins possess a wealth of talent. [It's] a combination so … good that only the supreme talent of the Montreal Canadiens kept the Bruins from [winning] the Stanley Cup the last two years.
—Bob Whitley of the *Pittsburgh-Post Gazette* in his April 16 preview of the Boston-Pittsburgh quarterfinal

As a reward for finishing atop the Adams Division for the fourth straight season, the Boston Bruins got a first-round bye and more than a week off while the eight divisional also-rans suffered through nerve-wracking best-of-three series. In the four previous years the NHL had used this format, upsets were almost the norm. In 1979, two of the four preliminary series ended with the underdog on top. The Toronto Maple Leafs swept the Atlanta Flames and the Pittsburgh Penguins beat the Buffalo Sabres in three games—the deciding contest settled on a dramatic breakaway goal 47 seconds into overtime by George Ferguson. Those losses got both Atlanta coach Fred Creighton and Buffalo coach Billy Inglis fired from their respective teams. (Inglis was the third coach the underachieving Sabres had employed since 1977.) The unexpected result of the Pens-Sabres series undoubtedly pleased the Bruins as the Sabres had given them fits toward the end of the regular season. Buffalo had scored a whopping 18 goals in their last two games versus Boston.

In more predictable results, the Philadelphia Flyers ousted Vancouver in three games—the lowly Canucks won the first game at the Spectrum!—and the New York Rangers topped the Los Angeles Kings in two. Had everything gone according to form, Boston would have played Atlanta in the quarterfinals, but the two upsets shuffled the teams and, of course, their seeding order. Boston instead was slotted against the Pittsburgh Penguins for the first time ever in a postseason series. The other quarterfinals were Montreal versus Toronto, the New York Islanders versus Chicago, and the New York Rangers versus Philadelphia.

Based on their vast edge in playoff experience, Boston was expected to blow away the Pittsburgh Penguins in the best-of-seven quarterfinal without too much difficulty—even taking into account the Pens' 2–1–1 record versus Boston in their four regular-season clashes. It was the first time Pittsburgh had ever gotten the edge on Boston over the course of a whole season. Moreover, the Penguins had strung together a 10-game undefeated streak (comprised of six victories and four ties) late in March. Pittsburgh was in unfamiliar waters, however. They were making their first appearance in a Stanley Cup quarterfinal since 1975.

In contrast, the Bruins were making their twelfth consecutive playoff appearance. Only once in that stretch (1975) had Boston not gotten to the final eight.

The Bruins would face a former teammate, the popular Gregg Sheppard, who had been dealt to the Penguins in the off-season in a three-way trade that brought the valuable Dick Redmond to Boston from Atlanta. (To complete the deal, Pittsburgh's all-time leading scorer, Jean Pronovost, was sent to Atlanta.) According to an anecdote in Don Cherry's autobiography, Sheppard became persona not grata in Boston as far as general-manager Harry Sinden was concerned when he and Bobby Schmautz creatively performed a parody of the song *Onward Christian Soldiers*—titled *Onward Sinden Soldiers*—in the Bruins' dressing room near the end of the previous season. Sinden overheard the comical number and saw no humor in it. Sheppard's offensive numbers had dropped since being traded from Boston. Despite playing in six more games with the Penguins than he had with the Bruins in 1977–78, the 30-year-old Sheppard scored only 15 goals compared to the 23 he had netted in his final season as a Bruin. He did, however, set up Ferguson's series winning goal versus Buffalo. On the eve of the Boston-Pittsburgh quarterfinal, Sheppard, speaking form experience, told Bob Whitley of the *Pittsburgh Post-Gazette* that the Bruins had a simple recipe for success: hard work.

Francis Rosa of the *Boston Globe* warned Bruins fans that the Pens were peaking just at the right time. "These are the upstart Pittsburgh Penguins who play the Bruins tonight at Boston Garden," he wrote. "[They are] a team comprised of equal parts, strangers that Boston fans hardly know [and] familiar faces that Boston fans remember from other teams."[1] Indeed, Pittsburgh's lineup included George Ferguson and Randy Carlyle, both former Toronto Maple Leafs, and Ross Lonsberry, Orest Kindrachuk and Tom Bladon who all played for the Philadelphia Flyers versus Boston in the 1978 semifinal. Kindrachuk had been appointed the Penguins' team captain. (Lonsberry was a onetime Boston prospect who played just 33 games for the Bruins over three seasons in the late 1960s. He never came close to living up to expectations and was traded to the Los Angeles Kings in 1969 with Eddie Shack for Ken Turlik and two future first-round draft picks. Turlik never played a game in the NHL.)

Most importantly, Pittsburgh goalie Denis Herron was riding a crest of confidence after starring in the Pens' dramatic preliminary-round win over Buffalo. In the third period of the deciding game, Pittsburgh had been outshot 18–3 by the Sabres, but Herron's heroics kept the underdogs in the game. "They do not intend to be brushed out of the playoffs without a fight,"[2] warned Rosa. Steve Marantz, however, did not fancy the Penguins' chances. He wrote in the *Globe*, "The underlying assumption is that the Pittsburgh Penguins have come this far in the NHL playoffs to meet a swift dismissal by the Bruins."[3] One glaring weakness in Pittsburgh's recent outings was their anemic power play. It had failed to score a goal in 14 attempts in the three games versus Buffalo.

Boston entered the Pittsburgh series with great confidence—a sentiment that was not shared by general-manager Harry Sinden. Perhaps Sinden was edgy because the Penguins had beaten the Bruins 3–1 at the Garden in their most recent meeting on March 22. (It was Pittsburgh's first win on Boston ice since 1968.) Pittsburgh had also showed unexpected grit in defeating Buffalo. Whatever the reasoning, following Boston's final practice before Game #1 on April 16, Sinden called an impromptu team meeting. He posted Pittsburgh's roster on a bulletin board and discussed every Penguin's strengths. For some reason, Sinden was especially obsessed with a 22-year-old rookie named Jim Hamilton who had recently been elevated to the Penguins from the minor leagues. Hamilton had scored two goals in the deciding game of the Pens' preliminary-round victory over Buffalo. Sinden made the inexperienced Hamilton sound like a clone of Guy Lafleur. As soon as Sinden left, the Bruin players erupted in laughter. Cherry restored order and addressed them. "We're the Boston Bruins," he affirmed. "We don't worry about any other teams; they worry about us. If we're executing the way we should, they won't win a game." Cherry paused for a moment and then cheekily added, "But keep an eye on Hamilton."[4] The players roared.

Francis Rosa succinctly summed up the Bruins medical report: "The Bruins are just about at full strength. Wayne Cashman has a sore back and he is doubtful."[5] Don Cherry noted that rust could be a factor. "We have a lot of ifs," he said. "Guys like Stan Jonathan and Rick Middleton haven't played in two weeks. Bobby Schmautz hasn't played much. Pittsburgh has the momentum going. They won two games in Buffalo to get to play us. They've got a red-hot goalie—that's the most important thing in the playoffs." Rosa stated the Bruins "will not take the Penguins lightly."[6]

Well rested and well prepared, Boston won the series in four straight games, outscoring Pittsburgh 16–7. Boston's wins were by scores of 6–2, 4–3, 2–1, and 4–1. Jim Hamilton, so feared by Harry Sinden, scored one power-play goal in Game #2. That was the extent of the rookie's scoring exploits versus Boston. Remembered only by die-hard hockey fans, Hamilton played 95 NHL games over the span of nine seasons and scored just 13 regular-season goals. The exiled Gregg Sheppard, likely wishing he was still playing for Boston, scored one playoff goal that spring for the Pens.

Prior to Game #1 on April 16, Don Cherry told the Boston media, "We've had a week off. It may take us a few shifts to get out timing back."[7] Cherry was mistaken; Boston looked absolutely terrific from the get-go. "These were the Bruins of the early season," declared Francis Rosa in the *Globe*, "establishing their game early and skating away from the Pittsburgh Penguins." Rosa firmly believed the bye had assisted the Bruins in their preparations for the quarterfinal. "The one-week layoff had cured more than the Bruins' physical ailments," he opined. "It brought back their concentration and they played such a strong forechecking game that Gerry Cheevers had an easy night in the Boston goal."[8] Rosa wrote that the Bruins' 3–0 lead at the end of the first period flattered the Penguins as the visitors hardly touched the puck.

With 12 of the NHL's 17 teams qualifying for the playoffs, many regular-season games lacked spirit. The Stanley Cup playoffs, however, inspired a more dedicated mindset. Cherry cited the different circumstances as a motivating factor. He told Bob Whitley of the *Pittsburgh Post-Gazette*, "When you think about it, this was really the first game in about two months that has meant something. We had the [Adams] Division wrapped up early. It was hard for me to get the guys going [late in the regular season]. Tonight's game was the kind that really didn't need anything from me. The guys were really pumped up."

For many media folks and the Bruins themselves, the victory in Game #1 had been too easy—which was worrisome. John Ahern wrote in the *Globe* between the first two games, "[The] consensus is the Penguins are definitely better than their Monday performance indicated, and the team will be much better, much more powerful, and much more efficient for tonight's second game at Boston Garden." Wayne Cashman agreed. "There's no way they'll play the way they did on Monday," said the Boston captain. "They were tired and flat after beating Buffalo in the first round. They'll be better, much better. We have to be better than we were, too. None of us is thinking of a four-game sweep or even an easy series. This could be tough."[9] Cherry concurred, "[Pittsburgh] had a tough series with Buffalo. They were obviously down a little from that high, but they're going to get revved up again."[10]

In Game #2, the Bruins played more tactical, cautious hockey. Pittsburgh held a brief

1–0 lead but Boston was up 3–1 for most of the contest. When Pittsburgh got to within 3–2, the tenacious forechecking of the Bruins produced a Bob Miller goal and a safe 4–2 lead. Pittsburgh got to within one goal of the Bruins with just six second left on the Boston Garden clock. It was not a masterpiece of a game to be sure, but it was effective toward attaining the Bruins' desired result. When asked if he thought Game #2 had been dull, Cherry defended his tactics. "I'm not going to have my team open up the game and wind up losing," he said. "I'm not putting on the Ice Follies. We'll grind it out. That's how we win."[11]

The Penguins were unhappy with referee Dave Newell. Goalie Denis Herron blamed Newell for two of Boston's four goals. He felt the play should have been blown dead on Dwight Foster's goal. In Herron's opinion, he had the puck adequately covered before Stan Jonathan poked it loose and Foster banged it into the net. Although the red light came on, Herron also thought Peter McNab's score never actually entered the net. Bob Whitley of the *Pittsburgh Post-Gazette* called it a "phantom goal." Pittsburgh winger Gary McAdam said, "The rebound came out too far. The net isn't strung that tightly and McNab didn't shoot [the puck] that hard. It hit something else beside the net, maybe the crossbar."[12] McAdam was vexed that Newell accepted the goal judge's ruling without consulting his linesmen. Herron accused Newell of being intimidated by the partisan crowd.

Despite losing the first two games in Boston, Pittsburgh coach Johnny Wilson remained optimistic. "There's no reason why we can't turn this series around,"[13] he said. His message rang hollow with at least one Penguin. Defenseman Ron Stackhouse dejectedly said, "We did what we wanted and it produced the same result. What more can we do?"[14]

Cherry had hoped to split the Bruins' goaltending work in the series between Cheevers and 30-year-old Gilles Gilbert. Moreover, Cheevers had looked shaky on a couple of Pittsburgh goals in the first two games. "I didn't want to play Cheevers in every game versus the Penguins," Cherry declared in his 1982 autobiography *Grapes: A Vintage View of Hockey*. "Gilbert was younger than Cheevers but he didn't have Gerry's heart. I had hoped to start Gilbert in Game #3 of the Pittsburgh series, but he became so nervous he came down with a case of hives and I had to throw Cheevers into the breach."[15]

Cheevers had been planning for a relaxing Saturday afternoon, merely watching Game #3 from the press box at Pittsburgh's Civic Arena. However, about an hour before the game, it became apparent that Gilbert was in no condition to play. After he was apprised of the situation, Cheevers descended to the visitors' dressing room with alacrity.

Cheevers said afterward, "I had no idea I'd play. But as soon as I saw Gillie, I knew he wasn't going to play. His eyes were swollen and discolored. There was a rash all over his face and he was throwing up. He was one sick kid and there was no question what I had to do."[16] Cheevers switched from spectator mode to playoff goaltender instantly. "I was okay mentally," Cheevers noted. "As soon as I got the call, I got psyched up. I was ready. I was even looking forward to playing." He confidently added, "The way this team is going, anybody could play in goal and win."[17] Play well he did in the Bruins' 2–1 victory. "The old fire horse heard the alarm and came storming to the scene and the rescue,"[18] wrote Francis Rosa.

Pittsburgh's Civic Arena had no air conditioning and a warm spell had descended upon the city, resulting in sticky playing conditions for the afternoon game. Cheevers was unfazed. He was especially sharp in thwarting a late Pittsburgh offensive thrust. Cheevers made two big saves to preserve Boston's win. Boston had to rally from an early 1–0 deficit for the victory. Peter McNab and Rick Middleton supplied the two Boston goals. Cheevers admitted he was aching having played in three consecutive playoff games at his age. Nevertheless, he insisted he could play in Game #4 the following night.

In keeping with his longstanding philosophy that it did not matter how many goals he allowed as long as Boston won, Cheevers gave credit to Pittsburgh's Gary McAdam for scoring a "nice goal" in the game's opening moments. "I guess they can have one as long as we have two," Cheevers said. "I won't begrudge them that."

With the Penguins down a goal, Pittsburgh coach Johnny Wilson pulled Denis Herron for a sixth attacker late in the game. The Pens put considerable pressure on the Bruins—and Cheevers in particular. "I got lucky a couple of times," Cheevers claimed. "Gregg Sheppard's shot hit me and bounced away. Randy Carlyle's shot bounced right back to him and I was able to get the rebound. But our guys were playing great hockey. We won—and we should have."[19]

Gilbert's status for Game #4 was iffy at best. The prospect of 38-year-old Cheevers playing four intense playoff games within six days did not faze Don Cherry who proclaimed Cheevers to be the world's greatest goaltender.

Cherry was his irrepressible self during the game's final moments. When the Pittsburgh fans—described as "partisan and nutty" by the *Globe*'s John Ahern—started to insult the Bruins, the Boston coach gleefully used hand signals to remind them that his club had three wins in the series to Pittsburgh's zero. "Cherry, in his usual fashion, antagonized the crowd,"[20] reported Ahern. Debris came flying into the Boston bench from all directions. "I got drenched with beer, which I liked," Cherry chuckled afterward, "but it's going to cost me six bucks to get this suit cleaned."[21]

Before working the Pittsburgh crowd into a frenzy, Cherry kept himself occupied by liberally mixing up his lines throughout the entire game, almost from shift to shift. It was a tactic that Cherry felt kept the opposition off balance and his own players sharp and refreshed. Fran Rosa claimed Cherry was as fully involved in the game as the Bruin players.

Game #4 went according to Boston's plans entirely in their 4–1 dominating victory over the outclassed Penguins. "There's a beautiful simplicity to hockey as played by the Bruins when they are on their game," wrote Rosa in his story announcing Boston's four-game sweep. "Their fans should sleep well as the Bruins may be at the very peak of their simply beautiful hockey."[22]

Bob Whitley of the *Pittsburgh Post-Gazette* sourly summarized, "Boston did what Boston does, running interference, planting burly forwards in front of the net, clutching and grabbing, and best of all, winning."[23]

Brad Park summarized the Bruins' typical game plan: "We get the lead and we shut them down."[24] Similar to Game #3, Pittsburgh took a 1–0 lead 15:20 into the first period before a sellout crowd. A 50-foot Rod Schutt slap shot somehow sailed past Gerry Cheevers. However, the Bruins quickly rallied to lead 2–1 after the first 20 minutes—and were never seriously challenged thereafter. [Note: Schutt was a disappointing Montreal first-round draft choice in 1976. Selected 13th overall, he played just two games for the Canadiens. Schutt was dealt to the Penguins in October 1978 for Pittsburgh's first-round draft choice in 1981. According to Penguin lore, general-manager Baz Bastien blundered: He mistakenly believed he had acquired Steve Shutt!]

Jean Ratelle was superb for the Bruins. He got the game-winner as well as Boston's third goal which basically sealed the victory. Don Marcotte fortuitously banked an empty-net goal off the boards with 41 seconds remaining to ensure Boston's win. Excluding Schutt's goal, Cheevers was again excellent between the pipes for the visitors. In fact, Cherry deemed Cheevers to be fantastic. The ageless Boston netminder had played brilliantly in allowing just two goals on Pittsburgh ice. The Pittsburgh series further cemented Cheevers' reputation as a "money goaltender." In retrospect, it may have been Cheevers' last great goaltending feat.

With Boston's quarterfinal triumph, Francis Rosa wrote what everyone who followed the Bruins was thinking. "[The Bruins] have wiped out the Pittsburgh Penguins in four straight games and now get that 'one more shot' they have wanted at Montreal since last May."[25] An unnamed Associated Press scribe noted, "Boston faces a far-sterner semifinal test against the Canadiens who dominated the Bruins in the last two Stanley Cup finals"[26]— a sweeping statement that was only half right, given the closeness of the 1978 championship series.

Three of the four 1979 Stanley Cup quarterfinals went completely according to form and generally lacked drama. Boston swept aside Pittsburgh. The top-seeded New York Islanders efficiently thrashed the Chicago Blackhawks. Chicago scored just three goals in the four games.

Montreal, seeded second, swept their series versus Toronto too, although the final two games at Maple Leaf Gardens each required overtime before the Canadiens prevailed. In Game #4, Toronto remarkably rallied from a daunting four-goal deficit to tie the Habs 4–4 and force overtime. Early in the extra period, Toronto's Dave (Tiger) Williams was assessed a debatable high sticking penalty by referee Bob Myers—even though penalties were seldom called in overtime in the 1970s. Neilson, who would not return to Toronto, told the Canadian Press that Williams had simply thrown a body check on Montreal's Larry Robinson. Robinson attempted to duck under the hit, and in doing so, was clipped by Williams' stick. Montreal scored on the subsequent power play to win the game and the series. As it turned out, Robinson was the overtime goal scorer, firing a low screen shot past Leaf goalie Paul Harrison from the blue line. Williams stormed out of the penalty box in a rage and had to be restrained from going after Myers.

Toronto coach Roger Neilson was furious that the Leafs' season came to an end while playing shorthanded. "That was an unbelievable call for that time of game," Neilson moaned. "We felt we had momentum going for us. It was a bad call."[27] Leafs owner Harold Ballard agreed; he figured his team had been "screwed." Robinson thought Williams' penalty was completely justified, however. "[The Leafs] can't finish their checks without getting their sticks up," he claimed. "For a change they paid for it."[28]

Glenn Cole of the *Montreal Gazette* was appalled at Williams' behavior. "Wasn't that cute of Williams to charge after referee Myers once the goal was scored?" he asked. "It was not a class act by any means and Williams is lucky he never reached the referee because it would have cost him badly."[29]

Don Cherry noted the Williams penalty, filing it away as an example of how Montreal's games sometimes seemed to be officiated under a different set of rules.

The one outlier quarterfinal featured the upstart fifth-seeded New York Rangers surprisingly ousting the fourth-seeded Philadelphia Flyers in five games in a minor upset. After losing the first game in overtime, the Rangers easily rattled off four lopsided wins, outscoring the favorite Flyers, 26–5 in those games. The last game was an 8–3 blowout at the Philadelphia Spectrum. The Rangers' coach was Fred Shero who happily got revenge on the team that had initially refused to accept his resignation following the 1978 playoffs. A reporter cheekily asked Shero what it was like to hear "God Bless America" again in his old stomping grounds. Shero, famous for his stone-faced expression, quipped without cracking a smile, "It's a beautiful song."[30]

Regardless of which team had advanced from the Rangers-Flyers quarterfinal, the New York Islanders would tangle with the winner. Boston would confront Montreal for the third straight postseason and the sixth time in 12 years. Thus, the Habs' shocking 1–0 loss to Detroit in the regular-season finale had prevented a wholly different set of semifinal matchups: Canadiens versus Rangers and Bruins versus Islanders. Those pairings probably would have been preferred the entire rosters of both Boston and Montreal. (Boston had fared only marginally better versus the Islanders compared to Montreal. In five regular-season games versus the Isles, Boston was 1–2–2.) The Bruins, Habs and Isles all wrapped up their respective quarterfinals on April 22. Once the results were final that Sunday night, the 18th postseason series between the Boston Bruins and Montreal Canadiens was guaranteed. It would begin at the Montreal Forum on Thursday, April 26. It would prove to be more memorable than any of the 17 series that had preceded it.

9

An Old Nemesis Awaits

"The Bruins are not a team of misfits. They are a good, sound squad. What Cherry has done is bring out the best in them. He has prospered on helping a player find himself. He has created controversy—and his team has thrived on his crusades. Cherry's team wears its name, The Lunch Pail A.C., as a badge of honor. He likes it that way."

—Francis Rosa, *Boston Globe*

"It will be a tough series like this one, but the Bruins do not resort to goon-like tactics which the Leafs have apparently perfected."

—Glenn Cole of the *Montreal Gazette*, commenting on the Canadiens' four-game quarterfinal sweep over Toronto

In the April 26 edition of the *Toronto Star*, television critic Bruce Blackadar listed what he considered to be the highlights of that Thursday night's local programming schedule. After hyping *Time Express*, a four-episode mini-series on CBS starring Vincent Price (along with two of the actor's old horror flicks that would follow the premier broadcast), Blackadar noted, almost as an afterthought, "Another thriller happens at 8 p.m. on [CBC] Channel 5 when the very mighty Montreal Canadiens take on the mighty Boston Bruins in the first game of their Stanley Cup semifinal series."

Hockey fans, however, needed no prompting from a television critic or anyone else to tune in to Game #1 from the Montreal Forum. It was a given; it was at the forefront of their viewing choices. The NHL officially called the Boston-Montreal semifinal "Series J of the 1979 Stanley Cup playoffs." Having met in finals in the previous two years, Boston versus Montreal, even as a semifinal, was undoubtedly the NHL's marquee postseason matchup of 1979. It was the series every hockey fan had wanted to see since the conclusion of the previous season's hard-fought Stanley Cup final. Yes, it was coming a round earlier than most fans had anticipated when the 1978–79 season began, but who was to quibble? The Habs and Bruins always put on a good show in the playoffs regardless of which round it occurred.

Although both teams had come through fairly easy quarterfinal sweeps following first-round byes, Montreal was in worse physical shape than Boston—which gave Boston a bit more hope of pulling off an upset. A handful of key injuries suffered in the Toronto series plus two long overtime games versus the Leafs had tested the Canadiens' stamina considerably.

Montreal's Game #3 win over the Maple Leafs was an especially grueling ordeal. It required a double-overtime goal by seldom-used Cam Connor to settle matters. It was the only playoff goal Connor would ever score as a member of the Habs, matching the one goal he had scored for Montreal in 23 regular-season games. (Connor actually whiffed on his first attempt to shoot the puck. The amateurish miss turned out to be a fortuitous break for the Habs. It pulled Toronto goalie Mike Palmateer out of position, which gave Connor a bigger target for his successful second attempt at a game-winning tally.) The quirkiness of Connor's goal greatly irked Palmateer. He furiously slammed his stick on the ice as he made his way to the Leafs' dressing room.

Montreal's Doug Jarvis told the *Montreal Gazette* what kind of a challenge his team was expecting from the Bruins in the semifinals: "Boston is certainly a better hockey team than Toronto," he said. "Boston has good size. They can bodycheck well. They also have a lot of players who can handle the puck well, finesse type of players. They usually play the man a lot, but they usually keep their sticks on the ice."[1] Glenn Cole of the *Gazette* felt obligated to add, "That makes the Bruins unlike the Maple Leafs who, as been duly noted several times, used their sticks more for creating mayhem than for firing the puck at Ken Dryden."[2]

In that same edition of the newspaper, Al Strachan boldly predicted the Habs would win the semifinal series in five games. He explained his reasoning:

> The Bruins want this one badly, if only because they realize they may not get another chance.
> Some, like Gerry Cheevers, are getting on in years. Others, like Brad Park, are suffering an alarming amount of injuries.
> In this series, as was the case in the Montreal-Toronto matchup, the officials will play a key role.
> The Bruins scratch, claw and grab their way past the opposition. Many of the things they do are illegal. If the officials enforce the rules, the Canadiens' power play should be effective enough to guarantee a victory. If the officials let the Bruins get away with the kind of hockey they prefer, the Montreal attack will be badly hampered and the Bruins will be in good shape.
> Assuming average officiating, the Canadiens have to win on talent. Montreal in five.[3]

As the 1978–79 season progressed in Boston, the Bruins were beginning to put more of a welcome burden on defenseman Dick Redmond who had joined the club in the offseason in the Gregg Sheppard trade. He was being counted on to keep things under tight control when the Bruins were on the power play, were a man short, or were in a four-on-four situation.

In a *Boston Globe* piece published on the day of Game #1, Francis Rosa wrote, "It is a basic fact of playoff hockey versus the Montreal Canadiens that you first must control them on the manpower situations—power plays, your and theirs—to defeat them. Enter Dick Redmond, specialist. He specializes as a point man on the power play, as a picket (forward) when killing penalties, and tonight he may be thrown into a third role, a forward when the teams are playing four skaters a side."[4]

The way Montreal skates, four on four is almost like a power play for them," said coach Don Cherry. "We've had trouble with them on that situation in the past." Redmond emerged in March and early April as the man who could most capably hand the triple task. "The last month of the season was the time to get ready for the playoffs. I experimented on the power play and penalty killing," Cherry explained. "He [Redmond] was the one I came up with. Why? Because he can handle the puck and has developed great confidence doing those two jobs. He's a specialist, sort of like [former Bruin] Eddie Westfall, but he does more than Westfall because Redmond plays on the power plays. Redmond's jobs on this team are just as important as anyone else's. I tell him that—and he believes me."[5]

Redmond, 29, went from a Bruins part-time player who sometimes went ten to 12 minutes without a getting shift to a regular mainstay. Redmond had gotten into Cherry's doghouse early in the 1978–79 season with what the coach saw as ambivalent play. "I don't think he was [originally] very happy about being a Bruin," Cherry theorized. "He got off the team bus one day in Washington with an instructional book about computers in his hand. I said to him, 'Why don't you get a book that will teach you how to play defense?' For three months everything he did aggravated me."[6] Redmond was reputedly the best guitarist among all NHL players. Redmond's musical talent meant absolutely zilch to Cherry. In fact, it was another non-hockey hobby that irked Cherry who thought that Redmond was not totally focused on the team or the game. Cherry sternly told the *Globe* that he "would wrap the guitar around Redmond's head"[7] if he ever brought it onto the team bus.

Sometime in the last quarter of the schedule, however, Redmond adjusted his attitude. He became a true Bruin during a game in Washington where he stepped in to protect a teammate. "Now I think he has been accepted [by his teammates] and he's accepted his role—which could be one of the most important on the team,"[8] Cherry opined.

John Ahern, in an April 25 *Globe* piece titled "History Hardly on Bruins' Side," recapped Boston's past frustrations versus Montreal, in the unlikely event that any knowledgeable Bruins fans were unaware of the weighty task facing their team. He wrote, in part,

> The Bruins will meet the Montreal Canadiens tomorrow night at the Forum in the opener of their semifinal series—and talk about flying into the teeth of tradition.
>
> Not since 1943—when only two Bruins, Jean Ratelle and Gerry Cheevers had been born—have the Bruins beaten Les Canadiens in the playoffs. The last time the Bruins won a playoff game in the Forum was 1971.
>
> And to make it even more drab, the two teams have gone against each other in 17 playoff series and Montreal has won 15. So there are two ways to look at the upcoming party: either the law of averages is due to start working or it's going to be a grim week.
>
> Cheevers … admits it's going to be awfully tough.
>
> "But it's possible to accomplish," Cheevers insists.[9]

Glenn Cole prudently prefaced his prediction of the Boston-Habs series in his *Montreal Gazette* column. He wrote, "There's a voice saying 'take Boston.' Logic says Montreal should win this series. Joan of Arc heard voices and we all know what happened to her. Montreal in six."[10]

10

Game 1
No Penalty Shot?

"Hockey fans are more likely to recognize a Wally Harris or a Bruce Hood than they are the starting center of the visiting team. Indeed, in no other sport are spectators so conscious of the officials and their respective reputations. One of the first questions asked in the stands at any NHL game is, 'Who's the ref?'"
—E.M. Swift in an October 11, 1982, *Sports Illustrated* article on NHL referees titled "Earning Their Stripes"

Following Game #1 at the Forum, the Boston Bruins were a disgruntled and frustrated bunch. They felt they had gotten the short end of the stick from referee Dave Newell. Many of the media covering the series concurred.

Reporting on the series for the *Boston Globe*, Francis Rosa noted, "Just once the Bruins must win a playoff game in Montreal. Just once there must be no break that goes against them. Just once the puck must bounce for them. Says who?"[1]

Rosa was not alone. Guy Lapointe honestly chimed in, "I thought we were lucky. We should just take the win and not say too much about it."[2]

Frank Orr of the *Toronto Star* thought Boston had gotten the short end of the stick too. He wrote,

> The Bruins view the Forum as their snake pit, a spot where if it were raining soup, they'd have forks. They feel the fates, the bounces, and especially the referees work against them. Of course, the fact that they always play the Montreal Canadiens has something to do with it, too.
>
> The Bruins felt they outplayed the Canadiens last evening in the opening match of the Stanley Cup semifinal, but Montreal won the game 4–2. There's some validity to the Bruins' claim that the fortunes seem to smile upon the Canadiens.
>
> During the past two Stanley Cup finals, the Boston club, led by Don Cherry, has insisted that visitors to the Forum never receive a fair shake from the referees. Although Cherry showed uncharacteristic restraint when discussing the work of referee Dave Newell last night, he left no doubt that he figured Newell hadn't taken the view that all teams are equal.[3]

"We expected to get exactly what we got,"[4] said Cherry, who had stated earlier this week that he planned to keep quiet about the work of the officials. Nobody who was the slightest bit familiar with Boston's coach expected Cherry to keep that promise. Even before the series began Bruins general-manager Harry Sinden snidely commented, "There are three certainties in life: death, taxes, and the visiting team getting the first penalty at the Forum."[5]

Orr agreed that the Bruins had a definite right to squawk. He wrote, "The Bruins' shorts were in a knot over two plays. One was Newell's disallowing a Boston goal that would have tied the game in the third period when he ruled that Rick Middleton had directed the puck into the net with his hand. The other play—and the Bruins were more worked up about it than the disallowed goal—came late in the match when Canadien defenseman Serge Savard pulled the puck off the goal line and under his body while in the goal crease. That calls for a penalty shot."[6] "I expected Newell to call a penalty shot," said Cherry. "The least I expected was a penalty." Cherry reiterated the point with an interesting coda. "We figured they should get at least a penalty, *but it was too late in the game*. They should have had something, though."[7]

"The referee had signalled a goal on the Middleton play, then he waved it off after talking with a linesman [Leon Stickle]," said incredulous Bruin defenseman Brad Park, clearly believing his team had been jobbed. "Why didn't he talk to the linesmen on the Savard play? I just wish that when we played here we didn't always leave the building with a bad taste in our mouths."[8]

"The puck was on the line, two inches from being a goal, when Savard grabbed it with his hand and pulled it under his body," concurred veteran Bruin captain Wayne Cashman. It should have been a penalty shot—or at least a penalty."[9] When asked if he thought there was a double-standard regarding how hockey's rules are applied to the home team at the Montreal Forum, Cashman scornfully said, "This is the other set of rules."[10] Cashman took a more sarcastic view of the play when talking to Leigh Montville of the *Globe* about it. "That was my shot that Savard picked out of the crease," he said. "But I guess he didn't touch the puck because the referee said he didn't touch the puck. He couldn't have touched the puck if the referee said he didn't touch the puck, could he?"[11]

"We make an effort like that and come away empty-handed," declared an embittered Cherry. "The referee has his hand up to signal a goal and the linesman calls it back. Then we don't even get a power play when Savard smothers the puck in the crease. That's what it's come to."[12]

The Bruins lacked a solid argument to support Rick Middleton's disallowed goal; television replays showed that Newell and Stickle's decision to wave off the goal seemed proper. Middleton did indeed take his hand off his stick to deflect a Bobby Schmautz pass behind Canadiens goalie Ken Dryden. Nevertheless, Middleton pled his case to the media. "The shot was coming high and I was trying to knock it down to the ice to get my stick on it," the 25-year-old Boston center alibied. "I wasn't trying to bat it into the net. I was only standing in front of the net and the puck hit my arm."[13]

Despite half-hearted complaints from some Bruins, most journalists thought Newell's decision to disallow Middleton's goal was correct. Eddie MacCabe of the *Ottawa Citizen* wrote, "Middleton did steer it into the net with his hand. Linesman Leon Stickle was right there and he saw it."[14] Interestingly, in the Bruins' quarterfinal sweep win over Pittsburgh, Newell had refereed Game #2 and he had allowed two controversial Boston goals to stand in that contest. Schmautz thought Middleton's disallowed goal was completely legitimate. After the game Schmautz disparagingly referred to Stickle as "Stinkle."

Montreal had a goal disallowed too, but it was utterly non-controversial. Rick Chartraw put a long shot past Cheevers well after the whistle had sounded. Knowing it would not count, Cheevers did not attempt to stop the puck. Nobody disputed the no-goal call, but Chartraw's act did violate hockey's unwritten protocol prohibiting shots toward the opposing goal well after play has been stopped.

As for the non-controversial parts of the action, Frank Orr stated, "The teams staged a fairly conservative game, both in offense and aggressiveness. Each team had 21 shots on goal."[15]

"Both teams checked much better than they attacked," said Canadiens coach Scotty Bowman, whose team had just won its ninth postseason contest against Boston in 11 outings dating back three seasons. "We've just finished a very tiring series against Toronto with long overtime games and the injury factor is a big thing with us. [Forwards Steve Shutt, Réjean Houle and Mark Napier were missing.] But that's where our depth helps. We were able to use four lines in the third period and six defensemen quite a bit."[16]

Guy Lafleur was clearly Montreal's best player in Game #1, scoring one goal and assisting on two others. Jacques Lemaire, Pierre Larouche and Doug Jarvis (into an empty net) scored the others. Jean Ratelle and Don Marcotte notched the Bruin goals.

Lemaire's goal was the only tally in the first period. It was an easy tap in set up by Lafleur. Boston's two goals came within a span of 2:03 early in the second period to give the visitors a well-deserved lead. However, a bad break resulted in Montreal's tying goal early in the third period. A Lafleur pass from the corner deflected of Mike Milbury's stick and into the Boston net.

Gerry Cheevers was convinced there was some sort of jinx that affected the Bruins at the Forum. "Things just happen to us [here]," he said. "The goal that went off Milbury's stick? That goes through, doesn't touch anything when we play in Colorado. Here it hits the stick and goes in. Every time."[17]

The little-used Pierre Larouche supplied the winner, finishing off a play started by Doug Risebrough. Cherry lamented it was the only two-on-one Montreal had all night— and it produced a goal.

Lafleur, like Lapointe, conceded that the Canadiens were fortunate to win Game #1. "We had problems getting started," he said. "We were a little lucky to win. They checked us very well and kept the pace of the game very slow. That's not our style."[18]

"There was gnashing of teeth and about 10 minutes of yelling in the dressing room. Then we calmed down," Cherry said afterward about the Bruins' reaction to the loss. "We know we played a good game. We're not down. We know we can win."[19]

Brad Park showed frustration at the lack of results the Bruins were constantly getting on Forum ice during the playoffs dating back to 1977. He recapped, "Two years ago we came in here and we gooned it up and we lost four straight. Last year we came in here and didn't goon it up as much and we lost, four games to two. This time we didn't do anything and we still lost. What's the answer? Maybe we should goon it up again. Start fights all over. What's the difference?"[20] Despite the loss that put the Bruins in an oh-so-familiar 0–1 hole versus Montreal after the first game of a playoff series, Wayne Cashman took an optimistic point of view on his team's prospects. "We proved we can play with them [here]. We could have won this game. We had the chances. If we keep working, keep getting the chances… "[21]

Similarly, Terry O'Reilly was encouraged over how the Bruins played and fought hard throughout the full contest. At one point Boston was shorthanded for nearly four consecutive minutes. The visitors' defensive play was so strong, however, that the Habs failed to muster a significant scoring chance during the extended man advantage. Montreal's inability to generate any offense prompted an uncharacteristic chorus of boos for the home each time the Bruins gained control of the puck and fired it the length of the ice. Nevertheless, the outcome was another Habs victory over Boston at the Forum. Since Boston's last win in Montreal in October 1976, they had lost 12 straight games at the Forum (both regular season and playoffs) and been outscored 59–20.

Hockey fans in Montreal were accused of becoming blasé in 1978–79. It was said that the Habs' run of championships had started to bore the locals. Winning was becoming monotonous. Perhaps there was some truth to the statement as Game #1 strangely did not sell out. Glenn Cole dutifully reported in the next day's *Montreal Gazette*, "Only 16,252 fans were on hand for the game, a surprise considering the Boston-Montreal rivalry."[22]

During the 1979 Stanley Cup playoffs it had become all the rage for teams to celebrate a goal by having everyone come onto the ice to congratulate the scorer. After Jacques Lemaire put the Habs up 1–0, the Canadiens emptied their bench. Not to be outdone, Cherry sent his entire team onto the ice to console goalie Gerry Cheevers—much to the displeasure of the home fans at the Forum who loudly jeered the stunt. "It's intimidating to see [the Habs] all come onto the ice like that after a goal,"[23] Cherry insisted. Referee Newell quickly held an impromptu powwow with both teams' acting captains and declared

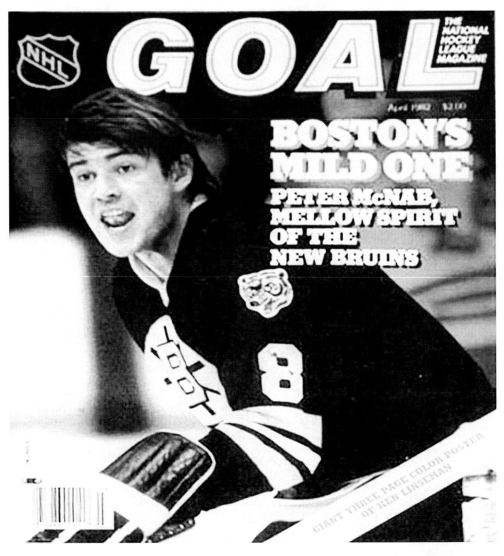

Acquired by the Bruins before the 1976–77 season, Peter McNab capably replaced Phil Esposito as Boston's clutch scorer from the slot. Although he led the Bruins in goals in 1977–78, McNab was often ridden hard by coach Don Cherry and general-manager Harry Sinden who both thought McNab could improve upon his skills.

a temporary moratorium on whole-team goal celebrations, informing everyone that if they continued "the game will last forever."[24] Starting in the 1979–80 season the NHL banned all group-hug celebrations and consolations during regulation time.

Proving how tough hockey players are, Glenn Cole wrote in his report, "[There were] no serious injuries of note, although Serge Savard lost two front teeth and his dental plate when struck by a puck in the third period."[25]

In a sidebar column, the *Globe*'s Francis Rosa reported an interesting rumor that was circulating through press row: Scotty Bowman would replace Don Cherry as the Bruins' coach in 1979–80! Bowman himself scoffed at the notion. "I have a contract here [in Montreal] that has a long time to run," Bowman accurately noted. "I also think the Bruins will work out their differences and have the same man [behind their bench] next year."[26]

While Bruins president Paul A. Mooney denied the Bowman-to-Boston rumor outright, general-manager Harry Sinden's comments were tantalizingly vague and actually gave the story more credibility than it probably deserved. "I'll deny the report this way," he authoritatively said. "If Don Cherry isn't the coach of the Boston Bruins next year, we'll go after the best available man."[27]

It had been an entertaining start to a much-awaited Stanley Cup playoff series. It was typical Habs-Bruins fare. Although defeated, the Bruins left the ice confident that they could beat the Canadiens—even at the dreaded Forum. "This is the best opening game [of a playoff series] we've ever played here," said Peter McNab, who was taking his third postseason crack at the Habs. "We'll look at it positively: Gerry Cheevers was great. The forwards were great and the defense was too. We just have to penetrate more and score more."[28]

Wayne Cashman remained optimistic. "We know there's a win here someplace," Boston's captain insisted. "We just have to find it. Maybe it's like dominoes: knock one over and who knows what will happen? Maybe…"[29]

Though cautiously contested, Game #1 had featured skillful play, plot twists, dramatic changes in momentum, and enough controversy to generate even greater interest in Game #2. The return match was scheduled for 8 o'clock Saturday, April 28 at the Montreal Forum where the Bruins had not won a game since Gerald Ford's presidency.

Game #1

First Period
1. Montreal—Lemaire (Lafleur, Gainey) 13:52.

Second Period
2. Boston—Ratelle (Middleton, Park) 3:37 (ppg);
3. Boston—Marcotte (O'Reilly) 5:34.

Third Period
4. Montreal—Lafleur (Risebrough) 3:44;
5. Montreal—Larouche (Risebrough, Lafleur) 12:17;
6. Montreal—Jarvis (Robinson, Gainey) 19:33 (en).

11

Game 2
A Two-Goal Lead Vanishes

"If the Boston Bruins entertain any hopes of winning their best-of-seven Stanley
Cup semifinal series, they are going to have to win a game here at some point."
—Glenn Cole, *Montreal Gazette*

It was another game at the Montreal Forum—and another one that slipped from the grasp of the Boston Bruins who failed to hold a two-goal lead. Once the momentum shifted to the Montreal Canadiens, they were an unstoppable force. Once again, as in 1977 and 1978, Don Cherry's Bruins began a best-of-seven playoff series with two games at the Forum and returned to Boston with a daunting 0–2 deficit to overcome.

A *Montreal Gazette* headline blared, "'Lucky' Canadiens storm back to take 2–0 series lead to Boston."[1]

"The Montreal Canadiens would make a terrific pack of door-to-door salesmen," declared Frank Orr in his extensive coverage for the *Toronto Star*. "Give them the chance to get their foot in the door and you'll be in big trouble."

Orr elaborated,

> The Boston Bruins discovered the Canadiens' ability to exploit any little edge last night, any small crack in an opponent's armor. The Bruins were in a comfortable 2–0 lead in last night's second game of the Stanley Cup semifinal when they granted the Canadiens that chance. The Montrealers pounced on it and continued to pounce for a 5–2 victory and a 2–0 lead in the series.
>
> The break the Canadiens needed was an unnecessary tripping penalty to the Bruins' Bobby Schmautz when the teams were already a man short each. The Canadiens scored on that power play and 1:24 later were into a 3–2 lead.

"We have a team that can play with great patience when a club is checking us as well as the Bruins were for the first 25 minutes," said Canadien center Doug Jarvis afterward. "We don't panic and we don't change our approach. We just plug away and try to make a break for ourselves. Then when we get it, we have the ability to take advantage of it."[2]

Take advantage of it they did. Jacques Lemaire, Bob Gainey, Mario Tremblay, Guy Lafleur and Rick Chartraw scored for the Canadiens. Rick Middleton and Peter McNab had the two Bruin goals.

"They [the Canadiens] didn't play a good game tonight," said a disappointed Don Cherry to Glenn Cole of the *Montreal Gazette*. "I'm sure they will tell you they played about five minutes well, but that was all they needed."[3]

"But the Canadiens don't need many scoring chances to produce the goals they need,"

Orr insisted. "They had 20 shots against Bruin goalie Gerry Cheevers while the Boston club had 23 on Ken Dryden."[4]

Francis Rosa of the *Globe* wrote that the Bruins were doing well when the referee put his whistle away. "Referee Bryan Lewis had gone 34 minutes and 14 seconds without calling a penalty. By that time the Bruins had taken a 2–0 lead. Then the penalties came, and in a space of 84 seconds the Canadiens went from being two goals behind to one goal ahead, 3–2, in a blitz that should have demoralized the Bruins."[5]

"I feel that our skating and passing ability is a big reason why we can grab a chance when it comes along," said Canadien defenseman Serge Savard. "When we force the other team into a little defensive error, we have the speed to get a man into the hole and the passing ability to get the puck to him."[6]

Orr thought the Bruins might not be able to recover from the loss. "It was a crushing defeat for the Bruins who played valiantly and checked the Canadiens with thoroughness until the second-period outburst."[7]

"You could see it: We just can't get a break of any kind in this building," Don Cherry said ruefully in his postgame press conference, trying not to chide the officials too much. "The Canadiens' second goal was offside and the linesmen missed it. Why don't the Canadiens get the occasional cheap penalty the way we do? Maybe we'll get a break or two in our own rink."[8]

The Canadiens' Guy Lafleur, who had a big hand in the offensive onslaught in the second period, claimed the first goal was all-important. "The Bruins were doing a big job of checking us, giving us no room at all to move, and we were tightening up, not playing loose and relaxed," Lafleur said. "As soon as we got that one goal, a big load was taken off our shoulders and we started to move better. We'll have a tough time in Boston where the ice surface is smaller and there's not much room to move."[9] Constructed when the NHL had no absolute standards for rink size, the ice surface at Boston Garden was only 191 feet long (nine feet shorter) by 83 feet (and two feet narrower) than most NHL arenas. The loss of 18 square feet of open ice was helpful to the tight-checking style of hockey the Bruins employed.

Despite the low shot total of nine—just five by the Bruins—the first period was conducted at a swift pace with some robust hitting. Both clubs concentrated on checking and avoiding penalties.

In a play resembling Serge Savard's dubious save in Game #1, once again Ken Dryden needed the aid of one of his defenders to prevent a Boston goal. This time Larry Robinson stepped into the crease to deflect a bounced puck out of danger when it appeared to be headed into the top of the net. Unlike Savard's maneuver in the first game, there was no doubt about the legality of Robinson's play. The best scoring chance of the period came in the concluding minute when a Don Marcotte pass sent Jean Ratelle in on Dryden off the wing. But the Canadien goalie stood his ground and Ratelle's shot bounced off his pad.

Orr reported, "Cheevers made his made big saves on Lemaire and Lafleur early in the second period. The force of Lafleur's shot from the blue line drilled the puck into the opening in Cheevers' skate blade."[10]

The Bruins finally broke the scoreless tie at 7:42. Canadien defenseman Brian Engblom lost control of the puck in his zone. Rick Middleton pounced on the error and drove a 25-foot slap shot off Dryden's upper arm into the net. Three minutes later McNab won a faceoff from Pierre Mondou in the Canadiens' zone and slid the puck back to Rick Smith. Marcotte and McNab both deflected Smith's shot behind Dryden. Boston enjoyed a 2–0 lead until late in the second period.

However, the undisciplined Bobby Schmautz penalty allowed the Canadiens to get started—and they did. The Habs produced three goals in just 84 seconds to take the lead. On the power play Larry Robinson deflected in a Jacques Lemaire shot at 17:41. Just 30 seconds later, Gainey drilled in a 40-foot slap shot. (There was some doubt about the legality of Gainey's goal. Glenn Cole of the *Gazette* agreed with Cherry. He declared that linesman Ray Scapinello missed the offside call because he was screened.) At 19:05, Tremblay made it 3–2 for Montreal, deflecting a shot by Doug Risebrough past Cheevers. Boston's hard-fought lead had swiftly evaporated.

Orr continued, "[In the third period] after the Bruins had three shots in rapid succession at Dryden, including one over a gaping net, the Canadiens embarked on a scoring rush. Lafleur and Lemaire exchanged passes which pulled Cheevers out of position and Lafleur had an easy tap-in. Jarvis wrapped up the win at 15:43 when his soft backhand shot beat Cheevers who was screened on the play."[11] The loss was Boston's 13th straight at the Forum—including both regular-season and playoff games—dating back to October 30, 1976.

Leigh Montville, covering the series for the *Boston Globe*, declared Guy Lafleur to be the overriding reason why the Habs were up two games to none in the series. He wrote, "Lafleur has been everywhere. He has never left the ice, playing on one side, playing on the other side, playing so much that you would think there are at least two guys wearing #10 on their shirts. Give Lafleur to the Bruins and [they] would have a 2–0 lead in this series. Simple as that."[12] Montville had high praise for Boston's efforts, despite their having no wins. "The Bruins have never played the Canadiens better," Montville claimed. "They have played absolutely shrewd hockey. The Bruins have been able to create more opportunities against this team. They simply have not been able to covert on those opportunities."[13]

Cheevers' allowing five Montreal goals, a stat largely excused by Orr and other journalists covering the series, planted a seed in Don Cherry's mind to consider a goaltending change when the series resumed in Boston on Tuesday, May 1. Cherry did not take long to make up his mind about what could have been a contentious issue. After all, Cheevers was the goaltender for the Bruins' Cup-winning teams in 1970 and 1972, a task he had split with Ed Johnston, five years his senior. The team's fortunes took a discernable tumble when Cheevers jumped to the WHA after the 1972 Cup parade. Not surprisingly, Cheevers was welcomed back to the Bruins in February 1976 as a good-humored and valued veteran. He was immediately restored as the team's number-one goalie. He was a large reason why the Bruins got to the 1977 and 1978 Cup finals and were competitive when they got there. Cheevers, at age 38 during the 1979 Stanley Cup playoffs, was still among the elite goalies in the NHL. In contrast, Gilbert was considered a little bit flaky and typically had more bad nights guarding the Boston cage than Cheevers did. Gilbert also got off to a self-inflicted rocky start with Cherry shortly after Don's disastrous coaching debut with the Bruins—October 10, 1974—a game where Buffalo soundly trounced Boston 9–5. On the team bus after the humiliating loss, Gilbert bluntly said to a teammate that he was more interested in his goals-against average than the result of the game. Cherry overheard the remark and never really liked Gilbert from that point onward.

In a sidebar story, Frank Orr reported the Canadiens were optimistic that two injured players, Steve Shutt and Mark Napier, could be back in their lineup for Game #3 in Boston. Shutt was nursing a badly bruised thigh. Napier had a bruised kneecap. Both had been sidelined during Montreal's third quarterfinal game versus Toronto. Napier had been acquired by the Habs from the Birmingham Bulls of the soon-to-be-defunct WHA. He had played well versus the Leafs and was expected to pull "heavy duty" versus Boston.

The Canadiens, however, were considerably less optimistic about Réjean Houle's prospects of returning anytime soon. He was suffering the lingering effects of a groin injury, described by Montreal's medical staff as the worst they had ever seen. It extended to his stomach area and had already kept him out of action for two months. He was not expected to play for the rest of the season.

Also ailing was Boston captain Wayne Cashman, who was battling a recurring malady—a painfully bad back. Orr wrote, "There are countless people in North America who could offer sympathy but no solution [to Cashman]. His back gave out this week and [he] was forced to miss last night's game versus Montreal.

"Cashman … tried skating yesterday morning and it turned out to be agony. Back problems have plagued Cashman for several years but have been in recession for the past two seasons."

"I guess I'm like the hundreds of people who have back troubles," Cashman said philosophically. "The doctors can't tell me exactly what's wrong. There's no schedule for it flaring up. I wish somebody would tell me why it has to be now when we're in the biggest series of the season. Why couldn't it happen in July and only interfere with golfing or fishing?"[14]

Leigh Montville sensed an unsettling blasé attitude among Montrealers during the first two games—and it surprised him. In the *Globe* he wrote, "Hockey in Montreal might still be the closest that sport can come to organized religion, but there are signs [it] is becoming less fervent. Baseball bounced the series to strange places in some of the Montreal papers. There were seats available for the opening game. The trappings are still in evidence at the Forum—Roget Doucet and the big voice, the big spenders in their St. Laurent style, the hockey idols of the past returning with their season tickets—but there is a decided lack of passion."[15]

After a side trip to Olympic Stadium to watch quotable ex-Red Sox starter Bill Lee pitch for the Montreal Expos—Lee was Don Cherry's only serious rival as the best interview subject in New England sports—the Boston media could return to the more serious business of covering the Bruins-Habs semifinal series. Cherry defiantly promised them his team would turn the series around in the happier and more comfortable confines of Boston Garden. "[The Canadiens] did what they had to do," Cherry commented. "They won their two games here. Now we're going back home to win our two games there. We'll be back here on Saturday. I've already ordered the steaks."[16]

Brad Park strongly echoed Cherry's sentiments. "We played well [in Montreal] and we're far from finished," he said confidently. "They're going into our building now. It's a lot smaller. There's no place to go, no place to hide. Nobody likes to come to Boston Garden—except us."[17]

In an odd postgame incident, an intruder somehow accessed Don Cherry's press conference without possessing media credentials. He asked Cherry about perhaps changing goalies for Game #3. Cherry said he'd consider it. The man then lambasted Cherry for being unfair to Gilles Gilbert all season. Cherry then realized the man was not a reporter at all. He identified himself as a fan from North Andover, Massachusetts—the Boston suburb where Cherry resided. Cherry asked for security to remove the interloper. When no one quickly responded to Cherry's request, Boston's coach took matters into his own hands: He shoved the interloper out of the press room into the hallway—much to the delight of the legitimate members of the media. Cherry returned to the reporters and huffed, "Gee, that felt great," Cherry noted, "I wish he'd taken a swing at me. North Andover, indeed! I'll get Blue after him."[18]

Game #2

First Period

No scoring.

Second Period

1. Boston—Middleton (unassisted) 7:42;
2. Boston–McNab (Smith, Marcotte) 10:54;
3. Montreal—Lemaire (Lafleur) 17:41 ppg;
4. Montreal–Gainey (Savard) 18:11;
5. Montreal—Tremblay (Risebrough, Lemaire) 19:05.

Third Period

6. Montreal—Lafleur (Lemaire, Mondou) 4:50;
7. Montreal—Chartraw (Jarvis, Gainey) 15:43.

12

Game 3

Gilbert Gets the Nod

"For some reason, in hockey, more than any other sport, players play no matter what happens to them. Stitched together, bandaged together, cut by the surgeon's knife on Thursday, they play on Friday. For some reason hockey players just play and it never is anything special."

—Leigh Montville, *Boston Globe*

"Few teams have won the Stanley Cup, or even gotten as far as the finals, without a dominant defenseman who can take charge and govern the tempo of a game. If not for Brad Park, the Bruins would not have made it to the finals the past two years."

—William Nack in the April 16, 1979, issue of *Sports Illustrated*

"It was the whole sport of hockey crowded into seven seconds," according to Francis Rosa of the *Boston Globe*. "It was like a broken-field run in a football game, seen in slow motion and instant replay."[1] Rosa was referring to Brad Park's spectacular tie-breaking goal with a little more than three minutes left in the third period that gave Boston its first win in the semifinal series and restored the Bruins' hope that they could recover from dropping the first two games at the Montreal Forum.

The gushing Rosa further claimed that Park's marker was "the winning goal in a hockey game that belongs among the classics of this sport." With both teams a man short, a faceoff in the Boston end produced no clear winner between Jean Ratelle and Jacques Lemaire. Park swooped in and corralled the loose puck and began to move up the ice with it. He skated down the middle as the Montreal defensemen retreated. Park was joined in the attack by Don Marcotte and Mike Milbury. Park blew by Rick Chartraw and only had Larry Robinson to deal with. Robinson expected Park to make a pass to one of his Bruin teammates. He guessed wrong. "I was waiting to see what he would do," Park said of Robinson. "His move eliminated the pass, so I took a quick look and saw a foot or so on the stick side and shot."[2] The puck whizzed past Ken Dryden and the Bruins had a 2–1 lead. The Boston bench poured onto the ice to join in goal celebration. Even Gilles Gilbert skated the length of the ice to be part of the enthusiastic back-slapping.

Park's weapon to beat Dryden was an unusual weapon for him—a wrist shot. "I very seldom use a wrist shot," Park happily said after the game. "Usually it's just the slap shot. But this was one of the best wrist shots I have ever made."[3] Park's goal broke Bobby Orr's NHL record for career playoff goals by a defenseman. A banner hanging from the upper reaches of Boston Garden appropriately read "Boston's Favorite Park … Brad Park." Park had only scored seven goals during his injury-plagued regular-season.

Frank Orr of the *Toronto Star* definitely concurred that Park was worthy of bouquets. He wrote,

> All praise went to Boston's stalwart blueliner Brad Park after the Bruins recorded their first win of the series on Tuesday, May 1 on home ice.
>
> Last night Park scored the winning goal on a rink-long rush at 16:48 of the third period after he'd assisted on the Bruins' first score. He also played 40 minutes of superb two-way hockey and controlled the pace of the match in a way few other players can.

Orr then discussed the circumstances behind Cherry's decision to throw Gilbert into the fray. "Often in coach Don Cherry's doghouse, Gilbert played only 23 matches this season and even lost the backup job to Cheevers for a while to Jim [Seaweed] Pettie. The only game Gilbert had played in the past two months was the [regular] season's finale against the Maple Leafs. But after the Bruins lost Saturday's second game at Montreal, Cherry told Gilbert he'd be the starter in Game #3. Cheevers was the only other Bruin who knew Gilbert would be playing last night until just before the game."

"I was in favor of a change because maybe the team needed something to shake it up," Cheevers somewhat surprisingly said. "We'd played two good games in Montreal—and lost—and changing goalies seemed to be a good idea. It turned out that it was a great idea."

Gilbert was sworn to secrecy about the assignment. It was only his fifth start in the past three months. He didn't even tell his wife he would begin Game #3 in the Boston goal. "I looked up and saw a full house and said to myself, 'Well, you've got your chance. Gillie, you've got to come up big.'"[4]

Gilbert admitted that once he learned he would be Boston's goalie for Game #3, "I did everything I could to keep my mind off hockey. I went for walks with my [three-year-old] son Terry and tried to forget about it. I didn't tell my wife because she's a nervous girl, especially against Montreal."[5]

Orr added, "Aided by the excellent checking and clearing of his mates, Gilbert had to face only 18 shots from the Canadiens, but he made a half dozen excellent saves, and his puck-handling was an asset too."[6] Gilbert stopped breakaways by Doug Risebrough and Yvon Lambert and was generally "superb" in Cherry's judgment.

"I didn't think I'd get a chance to play in the playoffs because Cheevers is such a great goalie when the pressure is on," Gilbert said.

> I'd been working really hard in practice to be ready in case I was needed and it felt good that the team had enough confidence in me to use me in such a big game. Gerry had a talk to me before the game. He told me to be sure to come out and challenge their shooters and not to fall to the ice very much.
>
> It was a tough sort of a game. We had a 1–0 lead for such a long time and a goalie doesn't want to make a mistake in that situation. Then the Canadiens tied it and things got really hot. But the guys on our team just checked all the harder and Park made the big play to get us the win.[7]

Glenn Cole of the *Montreal Gazette* reported, "It was tough sledding from start to finish [for the Canadiens]."[8] This time it was Montreal complaining about the refereeing of Andy van Hellemond, making it three consecutive games in the series that the visiting team had felt short-changed by the head official.

"I can't believe we just got one power play," moaned Larry Robinson after the game. Robinson was especially irked regarding a sequence where Brad Park was playing with a broken stick—a fact that apparently went unnoticed by van Hellemond. "I don't know what [the referee] was looking at. He had the gall to say he didn't see it. If he was following the play he is going to see it. Bob Gainey got called for the same thing in Colorado on our last trip there. Is it different rules for different referees?"[9]

Cole, however, thought the officiating was just fine. "Van Hellemond, who is the NHL's best referee, did not lose the game for Montreal," he wrote. "The fact they did not force the play the way they should have cost them a victory here."[10]

Brad Park felt the goaltending switch had upset the Canadiens' style of attack, at least slightly. "I think Cherry made the change more to throw the Canadiens off the pattern they use when Cheevers plays than to shake up our team," Park said. "It did that. Their shooting and passing has been geared to Cheevers and they had to change it a little because Gilbert is a different type of goalie."[11]

More than 30 years later Park said in his autobiography, "Grapes had ridden Gillie for a couple of years and was convinced that he was not dedicated. Gillie was a terrific goalie. We all knew it and had no problem playing for him. He stood on his head for us in the playoffs."[12]

Ken Dryden gave Boston full credit for their win. "We didn't pressure them," he said. "They kept the pressure on us. We have to be more consistent. We can't expect to hit a big flurry and hope that will carry us to a victory. You just can't play that way."[13] Larry Robinson agreed, saying the Habs' lack of aggressive forechecking was their doom. "We're giving them too much room,"[14] he said.

Frank Orr commented on the Habs' injury situation: "The Canadiens were missing injured defenseman Guy Lapointe, whose infected hand was swollen so badly that he could not get a glove on it. That threw the ultra-heavy load to their other two [defensemen] Larry Robinson and Serge Savard, each of whom played more than Park. They were tiring noticeably in the late stages of a grinding, fast-paced game."[15]

"They also had a great deal of ice time in the overtime games against Toronto [in their quarterfinal series] and they had to be on the ice for 45 minutes tonight," Cherry declared. "That has to be taking a toll on those guys. Park handles the heavy ice load extremely well because he can play with such economy. He never wastes a move and he passes the puck more than he rushes it."[16]

"While elated with the win, Cherry still wants his team to generate more offense," Orr wrote. "The Bruins had 31 shots at Canadien goalie Ken Dryden, who played a standout game."[17]

"I figured we might be able to generate more than two goals, because if you don't get more than that against the Canadiens you are asking for trouble," Cherry said. "But we cut down on our mistakes and didn't give them the crack in the door to get their foot into it. Even when we gave up the lead I didn't feel the way I did when we lost our leads in the two games in Montreal. This time it was sort of a desperation goal that tied the game. In Montreal [in Game #2] they just took charge of the game and wiped out our lead."[18]

The Bruins scored first at 12:19 of the opening period when Dwight Foster won the draw on a faceoff in the Canadiens' zone and slid the puck back to Park at the point. Park's hard, low shot produced a rebound that Stan Jonathan flipped over Dryden's shoulder.

Strong Bruin checking held the Canadiens to four shots on goal in the second period. In the third, the Canadiens pressed hard but the Bruins moved the puck slickly from their own zone. Gilbert made three saves on Pierre Larouche, Pierre Mondou and Cam Connor during one scramble. He made two more on Mario Tremblay and Larouche before Robinson flipped in the tying goal.

When Jonathan and Dryden were penalized for a slashing exchange at 15:11, it appeared to be the Canadiens' big chance to grab the lead because they operate strongly in four-skaters-each situations. This time, though, it was the Bruins who made the most of the wide open spaces. The play started innocently enough when Jean Ratelle won the draw in the Bruins' zone and got the puck to Park. Park moved slowly out of his zone. The Canadiens, anticipating a pass, headed for the other Bruins and supplied Park with plenty of room. When Park moved across the Canadiens' line, his defense partner, Mike Milbury, roared in ahead of him taking Robinson out of position. Park skated on and beat Dryden with a 20-foot shot to the stick side.

"When I started out, I guess the Canadiens thought I'd pass it," Park said. "Space just opened up in front of me and I kept on going. When Milbury moved in, Robinson had to play it as a two-on-one so I took the shot."[19]

"Last night's game was a superior demonstration of NHL hockey at its entertaining best—fast, with plenty of good, clean hitting," Orr opined. "Referee Andy van Hellemond ruled it leniently, handing out nine minor penalties, five to the Canadiens." Boston general-manager Harry Sinden concurred. "When everyone keeps their sticks on the ice, it cuts out so much of the baloney," Sinden said. "Then the players can body-check without running into sticks in the head. Stick fouls create most of the troubles in our game."[20]

Toronto Maple Leaf owner Harold Ballard congratulated Don Cherry after the game and said in no uncertain terms that the Leafs would be interested in acquiring Brad Park in the unlikely event the Bruins were willing to trade him. "I knew he was good when I had him as a junior," Ballard recalled. "I knew how good he was with the Rangers. "I watched him the other night and now he's outstanding, a superstar."[21] Ballard was also likely trolling for Cherry too, knowing full well about the Boston coach's very public contract squabble with the Bruins.

Frank Orr also covered peripheral parts of the engrossing Habs-Bruins series for the *Toronto Star*, including Wayne Cashman's ongoing back pain and his laudable and heroic efforts to play through it.

Orr wrote in a sidebar piece,

> When the Boston Bruins had a pregame meal in Montreal last Saturday, their captain Wayne Cashman was in such agony from the recurrence of a chronic back problem that he had to hold a chair to get across the dining room. When the team returned to Boston after the game in which they fell behind 0–2 in the Stanley Cup semifinal to the Montreal Canadiens, Cashman was hospitalized, placed in traction, and constant heat and wire-sound treatment was applied to his back to ease the pain. The Bruins had written him out of their plans for the third game. He was discharged from the hospital late Tuesday afternoon but had problems moving easily.[22]

Nevertheless, Cashman arrived quite unexpectedly at the Bruins' noon practice. He took two laps around the ice and had to quit due to the pain in his back. Incredibly he played that night. "Fifteen minutes before the game, Cash told me to put him in the lineup because he was ready to go," said coach Don Cherry. "I couldn't believe it."[23]

"Cashman played almost a regular shift for the Bruins in their 2–1 win—then reported back to the hospital where he will stay until just before tomorrow's fourth game,"[24] reported Orr.

"When we got back to Boston I could barely walk," Cashman declared. "The doctors figured that I had to have constant treatment, so that's why I went to the hospital. I had the traction and the heat all the time. By Tuesday afternoon the back had loosened up a bit and I was able to walk. The pain had gone down a great deal. By game time it felt pretty good. I didn't do much in the game, but at least I was able to be part of a great win."[25]

Commenting about Cashman's grit, Leigh Montville wrote in the *Globe*, "Cashman looked as if he had a 2 × 4 taped to his back. He is Exhibit A in this year's Stanley Cup peek into the world of hockey macho."[26]

Orr reported that the injury bug had struck the Canadiens once more. "Another Hab was injured," wrote Orr. "Brian Engblom was lost for part of the game with a mild concussion. The Habs knew Engblom was wonky when he claimed that Dave Hutchison had checked him to the ice. Hutchison plays for Toronto."[27]

Guy Lapointe was missing from the Montreal lineup in Game #3. He was suffering from an infected hand that was injured in a mishap far from the ice. Orr wrote, "[Lapointe] scraped it adjusting a seat in his car. It became infected from his glove in Game #2. He is doubtful for Game #4."[28]

Orr further reported both good and bad news regarding old Hab injuries: "[Mark] Napier is ready to return. [Steve] Shutt's injury is worse than originally thought. Knee damage may keep him out of the rest of the series."[29]

Game #3

First Period
1. Boston—Jonathan (Park, Foster) 12:19.

Second Period
No scoring

Third Period
2. Montreal—Robinson (Larouche, Tremblay) 13:23;
3. Boston—Park (Ratelle) 16:48.

13

Game 4

Ratelle to the Rescue

"You have to be good to beat the Montreal Canadiens, very good. But it does not hurt to have Lady Luck strolling past the bench either. In the two losses at Montreal, the Bruins had some—all bad."

—Ray Fitzgerald, *Boston Globe*, May 4, 1979

"Tremblay on the right side … takes a look. He lost it to Rick Smith … ahead to Middleton. Ratelle is coming up on the play. Over to Ratelle … going in…. They score!"

—Danny Gallivan's seldom-heard *Hockey Night in Canada* call of Jean Ratelle's Game #4 overtime goal

In 1979 one generally associated French-Canadian hockey players with the Montreal Canadiens. For most of the years of the Original Six era, each team held the exclusive territorial rights to any and all players who lived within 50 miles of their home arenas. This obviously favored the Canadian teams—and to some extent Detroit whose territory overlapped into southern Ontario. It is not a coincidence that in the 25 seasons of the Original Six NHL, every Stanley Cup but one was won by Toronto, Montreal or Detroit. Teams were free to sign whomever they pleased beyond those territorial boundaries. Montreal also had an undeniable cultural advantage in Quebec; it was a given that the Canadiens were overwhelmingly the team of preference for most French-Canadians.

However, not all French-Canadians were ensnared by the Habs' large, sweeping recruitment net. Apart from Gilles Gilbert, Boston had two other prominent French-Canadians on their roster in 1978–79: Jean Ratelle and Don Marcotte. The latter did an excellent job acting as Guy Lafleur's omnipresent shadow. The former was a truly outstanding hockey player admired for both his skill and classy deportment on and off the ice. Born in Lac St. Jean, Quebec, on October 3, 1940, Jean Ratelle was the perennial scoring leader of the New York Rangers. He teamed with Vic Hadfield and Rod Gilbert to form the potent GAG Line. GAG was an acronym for "goal a game." A member of Team Canada '72, Ratelle was 38 years old in the spring of 1979. He had broken into the NHL in 1960. He routinely scored 30 goals a season and twice exceeded the 40-goal mark in the early 1970s. Clearly Ratelle's best days were behind him. He was in top form when he was one of the driving forces behind the Rangers when they were legitimate Stanley Cup contenders in the early 1970s. Seemingly immune from injuries, Ratelle played all 80 games for the Bruins in both 1977–78 and 1978–79. To endure the long season, Ratelle was given special privileges by Don

Cherry—such as the option to skip occasional practices and morning skates to conserve his energy. In Game #4 Ratelle proved that with the extra rest he could still be a major offensive force if the opportunity presented itself.

"It was a grand night for the fine old French-Canadian gentleman," wrote Frank Orr in his coverage of Game #4 for the *Toronto Star*. "Boston Bruin center Jean Ratelle, 38, one of the most admired and respected men among his peers in the NHL, scored three goals, including the winner after 3:46 of overtime, as the Bruins downed the Montreal Canadiens 4–3 to even their Stanley Cup semifinal 2–2. Now the series heads for the pivotal match, Game #5 [Saturday] evening at the Forum where the Bruins feel they have a serious chance of snapping the 'homer' pattern of the series."[1] It was Ratelle's first playoff hat-trick.

"We played well in the first two games there, even though we lost," Ratelle said. "If we play that well on Saturday we think we have a good chance to win—and that would give us a big boost towards taking the series."[2]

Orr continued,

> Ratelle gave the Bruins what they needed most—a player to break out in an offensive binge. In two exceptional hockey games here, the Bruins have checked the Canadiens' powerhouse extremely well, holding the Montrealers to only 42 shots in the two matches. Goalie Gilles Gilbert … played soundly and so did the entire Boston team, working with an intensity that will be difficult to maintain minus their roaring faithful [at Boston Garden]. But the evening belonged to Ratelle, that elegant, classy man.[3]

"If I'd scored three goals myself, I probably wouldn't be as happy as I am because Jean scored them," declared Boston captain Wayne Cashman. "He's a very special player in this league because he brings so much dignity to hockey. He's the man we'd all like to be—quiet and peaceful."[4]

Orr reminded the *Star*'s readers of the trade that brought him to Boston in 1975, and continued, "Since then, he's been one of the anchors of the Bruins' strong performances, although his output did slip to 72 points this season. At 38, Ratelle is in remarkable condition, a reward for all those nights on the road he's watched the 10 o'clock news and gone to sleep."[5]

Gilles Gilbert came up with the funniest postgame quip: "To think," he said, "the winning goal was scored by a guy my father went to school with!"[6]

The Habs opened the game with a flurry of offensive activity. They got more than half their shots—13—in the opening period. Gilbert made four splendid saves in the Boston net to thwart the Canadiens who were intent on taking a stranglehold on the series before it returned to the Forum for Saturday night's fifth game. One notable Gilbert save was on a Pierre Mondou breakaway. His most spectacular save, however, was an acrobatic stop on Mario Tremblay from just outside the goal crease.

The Boston crowd was boisterous throughout the game. Offside calls against the Bruins were loudly booed, even if they were obvious. Some of the closer blue-line infractions whistled by linesman Claude Béchard were questioned by the home team.

Despite carrying the play, Montreal fell behind 1–0 three-quarters of the way through the opening stanza. Montreal succeeded in playing an aggressive style of dump-and-chase similar to the Bruins' typical routine at Boston Garden. Jean Ratelle was heavily bounced around three different times. The Bruins opened the scoring at 15:15 when Ratelle poked home a rebound produced by what Frank Orr described as "the energetic digging of Terry O'Reilly."[7] O'Reilly had disrupted a play behind the Montreal net when Ken Dryden vacated the goal to make a short pass to Gilles Lupien. O'Reilly snatched the loose puck and tried a wraparound. Dryden recovered in time to make a sliding save, but Ratelle alertly banged home the rebound amongst a huddle of players around the goal crease.

Montreal tied the game at 18:59. It was a power-play goal. Pierre Mondou flipped in a rebound originating from Guy Lapointe's hard shot from the blue line. Terry O'Reilly had been sent off for roughing by referee Wally Harris—a call heartily disputed by both O'Reilly and Don Cherry. Cherry gave Harris a dirty look after Mondou's tying goal.

Montreal surged into a 2–1 lead at 7:58 of the second period, worrying the tense home crowd. Guy Lafleur was the marksman of record. In a harbinger of things to come, he moved along the right boards and fired a blazing slapshot past Gilbert's right pad. The Boston goalie later commented, "For once a shot can be called a bullet with no exaggeration."[8] Dick Irvin, awestruck in the *HNIC* booth, concurred. "We're sitting 50 feet away from where Lafleur took that shot. I did not see it."[9]

Many veteran hockey scribes in the press box wrongly sensed that Lafleur's goal would open the floodgates and the Bruins would fall apart as they had in Game #2 at the Forum. Red Fisher of the *Montreal Star* told his colleagues, "The Bruins are all done."[10] Montreal tried to capitalize on the momentum shift. "The Canadiens were hungry. You could see it in their eyes," Mike Milbury said afterward. "They were hungry and going after the meat."[11] Ray Fitzgerald of the *Globe* likened the Canadiens to "fighter planes around a bomber"[12] as they swarmed around Gilbert looking for a third goal.

However, Boston leveled the affair at 13:21 on Ratelle's second tally of the game. He deftly finished off a passing play that garnered assists by both Don Marcotte and Bobby Schmautz. To a man the Bruins insisted it was the most important goal of the night. It stemmed the rising Montreal tide and got the Boston Garden faithful back into the game. "When the Canadiens went ahead, we went into a little sag, a sort of natural letdown," said Rick Middleton. "Then we were tied again and it was a big lift."[13] Ratelle was quick to praise his linemate on the play. "Bobby Schamutz gave me just a perfect pass," he insisted. Fitzgerald noted, "After [Ratelle's second goal], the fighter planes didn't seem to buzz around quite so much."[14]

Boston seized the momentum and played a strong third period, outshooting Montreal 15–5 and putting Ken Dryden to the test several times. Peter McNab put the home team ahead 3–2 at the 16:18 mark. He tried to work his way around defenseman Brian Engblom, whiffed on his initial attempt on goal, but corralled the puck. Dryden was off balance after the missed shot and McNab beat Dryden on his second attempt with a low shot to the short side. (The Bruins' snipers had determined that the lanky Dryden was beatable on low shots to his glove side. In Don Cherry's 1982 autobiography, he recalled telling his shooters to fire high on Dryden on long shots "to straighten him out" but to aim low to Dryden's left side on close-in shots.) The Boston crowd was roaring with delight. They were so loud that Boston Garden public-address man M. Weldon Haire smartly delayed his official announcement of the Bruins' goal for several minutes so he had a decent chance to be heard.

Montreal leveled the score at three goals apiece at the 17:54 mark of the third period to temporarily quiet the raucous Boston crowd. The goal was scored by Guy Lapointe whose swollen and infected hand was considerably better than it had been earlier that week. Allowed to advance the puck to the top of the left faceoff circle in the Boston zone, Lapointe drilled Mark Napier's pass through Gilbert's pads. Napier was making his return to the Montreal lineup for the first time since Game #3 of the Habs' quarterfinal series versus Toronto. (He had been nursing a bruised kneecap he suffered in that game's overtime period when he violently crashed into the Leafs' net.) After a few moments of concerned silence at the turn of events, the home crowd gave Gilbert a long round of applause for keeping the Habs at bay for as long as he did. "You can't appreciate what they did for me," Boston's goalie told the *Globe*'s Ernie Roberts after the game. "They've been behind me 150 percent."[15]

Ray Fitzgerald of the *Globe* described the emotional roller coaster the home fans endured in the third period. "Peter McNab's go-ahead goal sent the old barn into fantasy land," he wrote. "Guy Lapointe's equalizer with only 2:06 remaining turned the place into a wake. The buzzer that began the overtime brought on severe palpitations, not to mention acute trepidation."[16]

Heading into the overtime period, the Bruins' philosophy was to go on the attack and try to win the game within the first five minutes. "I told the guys to go right after them," said coach Cherry. "The longer an overtime game goes against a team with the Canadiens' scoring power, the better chance they have of winning it. I'm glad now I've given Ratelle all those days off from practices. I can't remember the last time he was at one of our workouts."[17] Indeed, the only Boston drills in which Ratelle had participated in since the playoffs started had been lightly paced morning skates.

Despite allowing the Habs to tie the score late in regulation time, the Bruins were surprisingly upbeat heading into overtime. Mike Milbury said, "We were exuding confidence in the dressing room. Grapes [Cherry] came in and said, 'Most of these overtime things are won in the first five minutes, so take it right to them.' And that's what the guys did."[18]

"The Bruins produced the winning goal when they caught the Canadiens in a rare technical mistake—a sloppy line change," wrote Orr. Mario Tremblay was dispossessed of the puck by Rick Smith in the Bruins' zone as the Canadiens were changing. Smith sent a quick pass to swift Rick Middleton near center. Ratelle headed for the open ice into the Canadien zone. Before the Montreal's troops, who had jumped on the switch, could catch up, Middleton had fed a deft backhand pass beyond sprawling Larry Robinson to Ratelle as he approached the slot. Ratelle swung the puck from his backhand to his forehand and beat goalie Ken Dryden on the far side "to set off five minutes of total delirium in the Garden."[19] It was Ratelle's first career playoff hat-trick. Organist John Kiley's celebratory music was barely audible amidst all the clamor.

"Thank God for Rattie [Ratelle's nickname]!" declared Wayne Cashman afterward, who blamed himself for Montreal's game-tying goal late in the third period. "He saved my scalp. What class he has as a player, a man, and a human being. I just watched *The Legends of Golf* on TV. Now I've seen the Legend of Hockey tonight."[20]

"I was just in the right place at the right time," Ratelle modestly said. "It won't mean a thing unless we win two more games versus Montreal."[21] Although Ratelle downplayed his clutch heroics, Ray Fitzgerald did not, categorizing him among other notable Boston athletes who performed at their best when their best was needed: John Havlicek and Carl Yastrzemski."

"Don Cherry has been really good [to me] because he's given me a great deal of time off," Ratelle said amid the celebrations in the happy Boston dressing room. "After a game it's usually four o'clock before I can get to sleep—and getting up to be at practice for 10:30 is very tough when you are my age. I'm not the only player who gets time off. Brad Park, Wayne Cashman, and Gerry Cheevers don't work out every day, either. Cherry says he wants to save our energy for the games."[22]

As was becoming the predictable custom in this series, the losing team had gripes with the officiating. This time it was the leniency of referee Wally Harris that upset the Canadiens. There were no penalties called in the third period or in the overtime. Serge Savard commented, "It's funny that whenever there's a big brawl in the league, he always happens to be the referee."[23] Al Strachan of the *Montreal Gazette* thought Harris went out of his way not to call penalties. "The Bruins cross-checked, grabbed, and tripped at random." he wrote. "Don Cherry even kicked a towel onto the ice that floated down in front of linesman Claude Béchard without any infraction being called. Béchard meekly picked up the towel and returned it to the Boston bench."[24]

Despite the two losses in Boston, Montreal remained confident that home-ice advantage would be the deciding factor in the series. Accordingly, they insisted they were still in the proverbial driver's seat heading back to the Forum for Game #5. Bob Gainey was especially philosophical about the situation. "'We played an 80-game season to get that home ice advantage in the playoffs—and now it appears we may need it,' he said. 'The Bruins played extremely well here because they know how to use their own ice surface—which is a little smaller than ours—so well. But they still have to win a game in our building.'"[25]

Little-used Habs forward Pat Hughes said Montreal simply needed to read Boston's plays better. "We're not reacting quickly enough to the things the Bruins have been doing," he noted. "We have to get on them more quickly."[26]

Frank Orr attributed Boston's two wins to stifling Montreal's attack from the blue line. He wrote, "A key to the Bruins' success was cutting down the offensive contribution of the Canadiens' defensemen. Last night neither Larry Robinson nor Serge Savard had a shot on goal. Guy Lapointe, who had four shots plus a goal and an assist, helped the cause after missing Tuesday's third game with an infected hand. Robinson's puck-carrying is a big factor for the Canadiens, but he did not play with his usual effectiveness last night."[27]

Brad Park viewed both Boston wins as a just reward for the Bruins staying out of the penalty box. "The Canadiens like to play you even when the teams are at full strength, then use their power play to get the edge," he explained. "We've concentrated on not taking penalties of any kind, especially the silly ones. It means turning the other cheek and skating away from things, but it's been important to us."[28]

Orr also reported that the Canadiens were hopeful that high-scoring winger Steve Shutt, who had missed the entire series so far with a severely bruised thigh, could be available for Game #5.

Scotty Bowman deliberately snubbed the hordes of media personnel covering the series for the second straight game. After both Hab losses, Bowman did not appear at the formal postgame press conference, irking the reporters who wished to ask him questions. Orr reported that Bowman avoided any interviews by retreating into the hospitality room off the team's dressing room—which was off-limits to the media.

The Canadiens seemed to pack up their belongings and exit Boston Garden in record time to catch their charter flight back to Montreal's Dorval Airport. No Habs were in a particularly talkative mood. However, Larry Robinson said it was "a hell of a relief" to be heading back home after losing two games in Boston. When asked what the difference was between this year and the two teams' 1978 playoff encounter, Robinson brusquely said, "Three hundred sixty-five days have passed. That's the difference." When asked if he thought the pressure was now squarely on the Canadiens, Robinson answered the question with one of his own: "When hasn't it been?"[29]

After the game, Boston's Rick Smith gave a wonderful, old-school reply to a journalist who asked him what he thought about the Bruins returning to Montreal for Game #5. Smith said, "A hockey game is won by playing it, not by thinking about it."[30]

Serge Savard managed a joke about how the series was progressing and specifically how it compared to the 1978 Stanley Cup finals. He said, "I figure we're ahead of last year. Last year we lost the third game 4–0."[31]

Frank Orr also reported a pleasant surprise that Rene Rancourt—the Bruins' national anthem singer since 1976—received from his renowned Montreal counterpart, Roger Doucet, whom Orr tabbed "the Babe Ruth of anthem warblers."[32] Doucet, the Forum's operatic baritone since 1970, commended Rancourt for using his unique *O Canada* lyrics where the phrase "we stand on guard for rights and liberty" is substituted for the traditional "we stand on guard, we stand on guard for thee." However, Doucet's personalized version of *O Canada* was getting decidedly negative reactions from many English-speaking Canadians who suspiciously interpreted his tampering with the national anthem as an unwanted intrusion of Quebec separatist politics into a major sporting event. (Doucet, who came under fire from fans and prominent conservative politicians during the 1978 Stanley Cup finals for doing the same thing, speciously claimed that since Canada did not officially have a national anthem as passed by parliament he was free to improve *O Canada* any way he saw fit. Canada's federal government corrected that oversight in 1981.) Be that as it may, Doucet's telegram to Rancourt read: "Inspirational singing. You helped win for the Bruins."[33] The *Globe*'s Ernie Roberts said Rancourt was beaming after receiving Doucet's kind wire.

Roberts also reported that Toronto Maple Leafs owner, 75-year-old Harold Ballard, who was very interested in acquiring Don Cherry's services for the 1979–80 season, had attended both games in Boston. Roberts opined, "Ballard may be aging and feisty, but he's one owner with more interest in the game than the dollar."[34]

John Ahern of the *Globe* noted that Montreal's Rod Langway, an American defenseman hailing from nearby Randolph, Massachusetts, was bumped out of Montreal's Game #4 roster by the return of Guy Lapointe. It happened to be Langway's 22nd birthday. Ahern joked, "It's in Rod's contract. He gets his birthday off."[35]

With the series level at two games apiece, Al Strachan of the *Montreal Gazette* penned a marvelous pro–Don Cherry column for the May 4 edition of that English-language newspaper. He could not fathom why the Bruins' upper management would even consider parting ways with their colorful, quotable coach who had revived stagnating hockey interest in Boston with both his personality and success. Strachan believed that Cherry was masterful in constantly getting optimum use out of less-than-marquee players. "Look at Cherry's defense," he wrote. "Admittedly Brad Park can play on any team in the league. But then what? Gary Doak! Mike Milbury! Rick Smith! Dick Redmond! Even Dennis O'Brien is playing well for Cherry. Three other teams—including Colorado—gave up on him last year."[36]

Cherry would have appreciated the personal praise on many levels had he seen Strachan's column—an unlikely situation in the pre–Internet days. Strachan sounded very much like a Bruins beat reporter in noting, "The Bruins' management, led by the redoubtable Harry Sinden (who once played for the Whitby Dunlops but has been in over his head ever since), has decided Cherry isn't worth keeping. Sinden's attitude seems incomprehensible, but after years of dealing with NHL executives, we are no longer surprised by decisions, which are, to say the least, bizarre."

On the other hand, Cherry likely would have strongly disapproved of Strachan's bluntly negative characterizations of two of his favorite grinders, even though the writer's remark was intended as a compliment to the Boston coach. "Who else could turn stiffs like John Wensink and Stan Jonathan into 20-goal scorers?" asked the Montreal newspaperman.

Strachan concluded that Sinden and assistant general-manager, Tom Johnson, simply resented the enormous personal publicity that Cherry was getting in Boston. "Cherry would be welcome in many other hockey venues," Strachan declared, "but not in Boston."[37]

Game #4

First Period

1. Boston—Ratelle (O'Reilly) 15:15;
2. Montreal—Mondou (Lapointe) 18:59 (ppg).

Second Period

3. Montreal—Lafleur (Engblom) 7:58;
4. Boston—Ratelle (Schmautz, Marcotte) 13:21.

Third Period

5. Boston—McNab (O'Reilly) 16:18;
6. Montreal—Lapointe (Napier, Gainey) 17:54.

Overtime

7. Boston—Ratelle (Smith, Middleton) 3:46.

14

Game 5

Montreal Reasserts Its Dominance

The Boston Bruins have already captured a kind of moral Stanley Cup with their play in the first four games [versus Montreal].

Few expected the home team to play on such even terms with the champions, with their great speed, and finesse, and superior talent. After [they dropped] the first two games, even the blind optimists began turning to baseball....

But when the money is on the table, Don Cherry's teams play with an inordinate determination. True grit is a match for pure talent. Now, after the Bruins' stirring win in overtime Thursday night, anything can happen. The Bruins have a reasonable chance to win it all."

—"True Grit vs. Pure Talent," *Boston Globe* editorial, May 5, 1979

The previous spring, after four games of the 1978 Stanley Cup final had been contested, Boston and Montreal were tied at two games apiece. Boston had won the fourth game in overtime after a late third-period goal by Montreal had erased a slim Bruins one-goal lead. In Game #5 Montreal blew out Boston 4–1 at the Forum to retake control of the series and put themselves one game away from eliminating the upstart Bruins. Proving that history can occasionally repeat itself, the same scenario unfolded after four games of the two team's 1979 semifinal series. Everyone saw the parallels.

Prior to Game #5 Don Cherry acknowledged the script was unfolding almost exactly as it had in the 1978 Stanley Cup finals, but he insisted there would be a different outcome in 1979. "This year we're playing them better. I think last year we went into the fifth game thinking we couldn't win. This year we've played them so well in the Forum we know we can beat them. We know we can play well enough to win."[1]

"The Canadiens are a little apprehensive," opined Francis Rosa in the May 5 edition of the *Boston Globe* based on some conversations he had with a few Montreal players. "Boston is playing harder than last year," said Guy Lafleur. "Maybe last year they didn't have the same confidence. Maybe this year they have too much this time. We have to win the next game."[2]

Boston's Wayne Cashman said the fact that Boston should have won one—if not both—of the first two games at the Forum, combined with the two Bruin wins at Boston Garden, had his team's confidence soaring.

"Imagine where that confidence would go with a victory tonight!"[3] Rosa proposed.

It was not to be. This time Montreal's win in Game #5 was even more lopsided than the previous spring's triumph had been under remarkably similar circumstances. The Habs won in a romp, 5–1.

Frank Orr reported, "When the teams went to Montreal for Game #5 on Saturday, the Bruins honestly believed they had a chance to end a 13-game losing streak at the Forum. It turned out they had no chance at all. The Canadiens wiped them out about as thoroughly as it's possible to be wiped out."[4] Orr predicted, "If history [last year's] repeats itself, the Montreal Canadiens will qualify for the Stanley Cup finals [Tuesday] evening at Boston Garden."[5]

Brad Park said the Canadiens exploited the Forum's larger ice surface to their advantage. "It very difficult to contain the Canadiens as well as we have, but here in the Forum you have to watch them in the center zone. They have that extra skating room to get up speed. It's maybe just a couple of extra strides, but it makes them that much harder for us to handle when they get into our end."[6]

Orr declared the Bruins to be all but dead. He wrote, "All indications are that the Canadiens will finish off the Boston Bruins in the sixth game of their semifinal series, a set that has taken on precisely the same pattern as the Cup final the two clubs played in 1978. In both series the Canadiens won the first two games in Montreal, then talked themselves into believing they couldn't play a skating game, by far their most efficient approach, on the smaller ice surface at Boston Garden. They promptly lost Games #3 and #4, both times to a plucky Bruins team."[7]

"What the Canadiens wanted was the first goal," wrote Rosa in the *Globe*. "What they got was the first, and the second, and the third—all in the first period. It was the biggest early-game lead in the series. Montreal's game plan was so apparent, so inevitable: Float like a butterfly, sting like a bee. They buzzed for nearly the full first period in the Boston zone, getting faceoffs, winning faceoffs, and forcing Gilbert to make save after save."[8]

Boston coach Don Cherry readily admitted the Bruins were badly outplayed in Game #5. "The Canadiens just didn't let us do anything," he lamented. "They caught us flat at the start and played a great game. There's no other word for us [than 'flat']. But we'll be back. This series is going to go seven games. No doubt about it."[9]

During his tenure as Bruins coach, Don Cherry frequently referred to his beloved bull terrier Blue, sometimes kidding that the pooch made the decision on which goalie the Bruins ought to use for big games. Cherry considered Blue to be one of his Bruins. In one official team photo, Blue is contentedly seated on Cherry's lap. When the Bruins returned home from a road trip, Cherry's first priority usually was to take Blue for a walk regardless of what hour it was. After the bad 5–1 loss in Game #5, Cherry joked that even his famous pooch would not want to be seen with him in public after the lopsided defeat.

Frank Orr conceded that the Bruins will put up a fight on Tuesday night at Boston Garden, but still foresaw a six-game Montreal triumph. He wrote, "Of course Cherry isn't likely to wave any white flags, and although his team isn't one to give up, it's possible the Canadiens will discover they can play their skating game in the Garden, just as they did a year ago. In that decisive match, their 4–1 win gave them a third consecutive Stanley Cup."[10]

"Sure, we have to make some adjustments in our style from the Forum to the Boston Garden, but there's no reason why we can't skate there,"[11] Montreal's Doug Risebrough said. Orr noted that Risebrough's nose "was slightly flatter and wider after a fight with Terry O'Reilly. He suffered a broken nose, underwent surgery [on Monday], and will be sidelined for ten days."[12] (In fact, O'Reilly had administered a fairly severe beating on Risebrough. O'Reilly became enraged when Risebrough brought his stick down across his wrist. "It was the dirtiest thing that's ever happened to me in hockey," O'Reilly insisted. "He could have broken my wrist."[13])

Risebrough continued with his assessment of Boston Garden, "The short neutral zone and smaller corners there seem to fit right in with the Bruins' tight-checking style. But in the two games in the series [played in Boston Garden], we slowed down and played their game. We have to open it up and skate, because speed is our biggest edge on them."[14]

Orr credited the insertion of Steve Shutt, who had been absent from the first four games of the semifinal series with a thigh injury, with sparking the Canadiens to their most decisive win so far. "[Shutt] gave the Canadiens a major boost on Saturday," Orr declared. "He's one of their quickest skaters. Although he claimed to have lost a little conditioning during his absence, he hadn't lost any hunger on the attack. His zip seemed to rub off on line-mates Guy Lafleur and Jacques Lemaire—and they made life miserable for the Bruin defenders."[15]

Cherry acknowledged Shutt's importance to Montreal's overall skill level. "It's a great boost for a team heading into a key game to suddenly have a guy who's been a 50-goal scorer dropped into their lineup for the first time in the series," admitted the Boston coach. "They didn't really need him. We didn't play that badly. It was more a case of the Canadiens just playing a terrific game."[16]

Plaudits were plentiful for the returning Shutt, who picked up an assist. "Steve was rushing their defensemen and [Boston] had to throw the puck around the boards," said Lafleur. Shutt said his presence bolstered Lafleur's game. "I think he has a little more confidence. He knows he's going to get the puck, so he starts skating through holes. Once he starts skating, everybody on the whole team starts skating."[17]

Serge Savard believed that had Shutt played in Games #3 and #4, the Canadiens might be in total command of the series. "I think [Shutt] is the type of player who could have made a big difference in those two games in Boston because he's got so much speed on the outside. He's a strong skater. He gets open and can shoot the puck well. When you're only one shot away from winning a game [in Boston], it's got to make a difference."[18]

The Canadiens romped out to a big lead in Game #5 in which they fired 12 shots at Gilles Gilbert in the first 20 minutes scored three times. Guy Lafleur scored two goals himself in the space of just 25 seconds and Larry Robinson recorded the third Montreal goal. Montreal outshot Boston 18–6 in the first period. That stat accurately indicated how one-sided the play was.

There were no goals in the second period, but the Habs notched two more from the sticks of Serge Savard and Mario Tremblay in the third period to assume an unassailable 5–0 advantage. Montreal's fourth goal came on a delayed penalty. Wayne Cashman's power-play goal with 1:28 left foiled Ken Dryden's bid for a shutout. The Bruins, for what little consolation it was worth, at least maintained their admirable record of not being shut out during the entire 1978–79 season, including the playoffs.

Boston defenseman Mike Milbury figured his team was due for a bad game. He optimistically said the Bruins had gotten it out of their system.

Again, the officiating came under criticism from the media. Francis Rosa was not impressed with referee Ron Wicks' handling of the game, describing it in his report for the *Boston Globe* as "the poorest officiating of the series." Rosa continued, "Wicks turned the game into the chippiest of the series. Wicks didn't win the game for Montreal, but he also didn't lose it for Boston. He was completely inconsistent. For short times he'd call marginal infractions; for others he would call nothing."[19]

Rosa pointed out that during an on-ice scuffle eight minutes into the third period, a few agitated Hab fans began flinging dangerous objects in the general direction of the Bruins' bench. Two cigarette lighters struck Don Cherry on his shoulder. Cherry was appalled at the goings-on. "I expect that in other places, but never in Montreal,"[20] he said. After the game, Cherry produced as evidence the lighters from his pocket that had been thrown at him by a spectator seated four rows behind the visitors' bench. Jim Coleman of the *Calgary Herald* described the culprit as "a middle-aged Montreal spectator who must have been dipping his beak in the grog between periods."[21]

"Imagine that bum throwing two cigarette lighters at me. It's common knowledge that I don't smoke!" Cherry said with a grin. He continued, "They complain that the Boston hockey spectators are animals. What about the fans at the Forum?"[22] The man was efficiently hustled out of the building by security personnel when several aggravated Bruins threatened to go into the stands and mete out frontier justice.

Coleman quoted an unnamed official from one of the teams who had some general thoughts on the refereeing through the first five games: "This series has become a survival of the fittest. It looks as if [NHL referee-in-chief] Scotty Morrison has instructed his officials to keep their whistles in their pockets. This is show-biz entertainment. The spectators are certainly getting their money's worth of action. No one can complain that these games are being slowed down by the ice officials."[23]

Frank Orr noted that Cherry now had a critical decision to make going into Game #6: Which goalie should guard the net for the Bruins? Should he stick with Gilles Gilbert or go back to Gerry Cheevers? "Cherry must now make a major decision—to stick with Gilles Gilbert in goal, where he has played superbly in the past three games, including Saturday's—or return to Gerry Cheevers, the veteran who's been an excellent 'big game' goalie in the past,"[24] he wrote. Although Gilbert did not produce any heroics in Game #5, Cherry opted to continue with him for Game #6 back in Boston. Gilbert had been named the first star of both games at Boston Garden.

Jim Coleman opined that everyone on the Canadiens' payroll was outstanding in Game #5, even anthem singer Roger Doucet who nailed both "The Star-Spangled Banner" and "O Canada" with his traditional flair and competence. "I felt good," Doucet told the hockey writer between the first and second period. "As soon as I felt my first notes coming up out of my chest, I knew that I was in top form."[25]

Game #5

First Period
1. Montreal—Lafleur (Lapointe, Shutt) 8:35;
2. Montreal—Lafleur (Robinson, Mondou) 9:00;
3. Montreal—Robinson (Lemaire) 19:02.

Second Period
No Scoring

Third Period
4. Montreal—Savard (Robinson, Lemaire) 10:03;
5. Montreal—Tremblay (Mondou) 12:00;
6. Boston—Cashman (O'Reilly, Milbury) 18:32 (ppg).

15

Game 6

The Bruins' Big Win Forces a Decider

"I want this game more than any other in my whole career. I can't stand having them beat us at home. If we can just get this one, anything can happen up there in Montreal on Thursday night."

—Don Cherry's comment to Ernie Roberts
of the *Boston Globe* prior to Game #6

"It's everything you want from a hockey series—and a little bit more," declared Francis Rosa in the *Boston Globe* following Game #6. "The little bit more? Why, getting to see how the Montreal Canadiens will play in a seventh game in their own building. That will happen tomorrow night because the Bruins played another unforgettable game at the Garden last night."[1]

Don Cherry enjoyed playing head games with everyone he encountered. So it was really no surprise that he would use the Bruins' dire situation and the likelihood that his days as the Bruins' coach were numbered as motivating tools for his team as they entered Game #6 at Boston Garden on Tuesday, May 8. The ploy worked. Boston played their best game of the series, decisively winning 5–2 and sending the series back to Montreal for a winner-take-all seventh game.

The *Canadian Press* reported, "Coach Don Cherry asked his Boston Bruins for one more effort—with feeling—and the result is a seventh game in their NHL semifinal against the Montreal Canadiens."[2]

"I told them it could be my last game here," said Cherry before sending the Bruins out to smother the Canadiens 5–2 on Tuesday night and set up a deciding game in the best-of-seven series Thursday night at Montreal. "I said it possibly would be the last game for quite a few of us in the Stanley Cup semifinals because maybe we'll go through the whole remainder of our careers from now on and never get this far again. I said, 'If you've got anything to give. Don't lay back and don't have anything left after the game because we might not all be together next year.'"[3]

Ernie Roberts wrote in his coverage for the *Boston Globe*—which appeared on the font page—"Whatever happens, Don Cherry is riding high this morning. His hard-working squad has surprised the experts by getting a third trip to Montreal."[4]

Stan Jonathan heard the call from his beleaguered coach loud and clear, responding with a three-goal performance against Montreal netminder Ken Dryden who faced 23 shots. It was all the sweeter for Jonathan considering how banged up he was for most of the season. "That guy has a shoulder so bad it popped out on him six times in one day,"[5] Cherry said of Jonathan.

Rosa stated that the Bruins "played with marvelous control of their emotions in an emotional game."[6] The raucous Boston Garden throng left a lasting impression on the veteran Boston scribe. "A crowd of 15,654—all friends of Gilles Gilbert and his teammates—roared through this game with shattering thunder again and again for Jonathan, for 'Zhil-Bare,' for every Bruin. Each ovation was earned—and relished."[7]

John Powers described the electric atmosphere of the crowd at Boston Garden. He wrote in the *Globe*, "They littered the Garden ice with working-class, underdog symbols—scalley caps and crushed beer cups—because it was a symbolic evening that cried out for them. How often does a full-blooded, two-fisted Tuscarora Indian, with a newly healed wrist, a bum shoulder, a sore tailbone, and a busted dental plate send a Boston-Montreal Cup series to a seventh game with a hat-trick?"[8]

Jonathan paid a price for his offensive prowess, however: After scoring his second goal at 7:23 of the third period, he went crashing into the goal post and lost two teeth. Montreal defenseman Gilles Lupien belted Jonathan from behind, but he remained upright long enough to bang home Boston's fourth goal which seemed to completely deflate the Habs. The hard shove by Lupien sent Jonathan headlong into the Habs' net—after the puck had crossed the line. "I was in the net, the puck was in the net, and I hit my shoulder on the post," Jonathan said afterward. "It doesn't hurt as much when the puck is in the goal." As for netting a hat-trick, Jonathan modestly stated, "The puck just seemed to be bouncing for me."[9]

"I told you they wouldn't beat us three [series] in a row," Cherry said, somewhat prematurely, to a herd of reporters after the game. "Now we go there and the pressure is on them."[10]

Powers' *Globe* colleague concurred. "The crowd stood up and applauded until tingles ran up your spine," Francis Rosa wrote. "Your spine did an encore at the noise after Gilbert's saves as the second period ran down. The pressure on your ears became unbearable when Jonathan got two third-period goals."[11]

The cheers were not restricted to Boston Garden. At Fenway Park, where the Red Sox were hosting the California Angels, when it was announced that the Bruins were leading the Canadiens 4–2, the baseball crowd erupted with a loud roar. When it learned the Bruins had expanded their lead to 5–2, the Red Sox fans gave the Bruins a standing ovation. Those were probably the only happy moments at Fenway Park on May 8 as the visiting Angels thumped the home side 10–2.

It was hard-nosed, typical Bruins hockey at its best. Rosa wrote that the Bruins "played with such poise, doing exactly what they had to do, never once panicking in the face of Montreal's attack, sporadic as it was."[12] Ernie Roberts reported, "[Don] Marcotte and Bobby Schmautz followed Lafleur and Shutt around like shadows."[13] Marcotte was so thorough in his task that he was often tailing Lafleur right to the gate of the Montreal bench.

"We were intimidated out there," Mario Tremblay admitted. "I don't know why, but we were."[14] The Habs' loss meant that Montreal had failed to win a game in Boston during the entire 1978–79 season, having tied both regular-season games at the Garden. The last season in which Montreal had not won a game in Boston was 1942–43 when they managed just one tie in eight regular-season and playoff games.

Writing in the *New York Times*, Deane McGowen declared, "Wayne Cashman, the captain of the Boston Bruins, had said before the game, 'It will be do-or-die for us at home.' The Bruins chose to do tonight in the Boston Garden and walloped the Montreal Canadiens, 5–2, tying their Stanley Cup semifinal at three games apiece."[15]

Cashman was indeed one of the big doers for Boston. He scored what would prove to be the game winner at 16:30 of the second period with heavy traffic in front of Dryden. Don Marcotte scored the other Boston goal. Larry Robinson and Pierre Mondou got the two Montreal tallies. Montreal led briefly 1–0 when Robinson beat Gilles Gilbert on a tip-in at 8:05 of the first period. The Habs' edge did not last long as Jonathan replied two minutes later with a tip-in of his own. In all four goals were scored in a space of four minutes. Don Marcotte gave the Bruins a 2–1 lead when his blast from the top of the faceoff circle went in the net off Dryden's glove. Mondou tied the game just 27 seconds later on a backhand shot that found a space between Gilbert's pads.

Although the Bruins had control of the game most of the time, the score was tied at 2–2 going into the second period. Undaunted, the Bruins took the lead on Cashman's second-period marker—a Brad Park shot that bounced in off his body as he was screening Dryden. The Bruins salted it away in the third period with two more tallies from Jonathan. Gilbert was not beaten again, only allowing the two Montreal goals on 27 shots. The delighted home crowd roared through the third period. *Hockey Night in Canada*'s Dick Irvin claimed it was the loudest he had ever heard a Boston Garden crowd cheer. (In 1943, Irvin's father, the late Dick Irvin, Sr., was the last Montreal coach to lose a playoff series to Boston.)

Clearly the result of Game #6 was unexpected among Montreal hockey reporters. "Ouch! Pesky Bruins Tie Series" read the front-page headline in the *Montreal Gazette*. In the accompanying story, Glenn Cole said the Bruins were thoroughly deserving of the win. He wrote, "The Bruins were in control for most of the game with the type of game they are famous for, the bumping, grinding style."[16]

Frank Orr of the *Toronto Star* accurately pointed out,

> For the first time since their domination of the NHL began in the 1975–76 season, the Montreal Canadiens find themselves backed into a small corner in the Stanley Cup playoffs. Thursday night at the Montreal Forum, the Canadiens will play their first match in that stretch of excellence in which they could be eliminated.
>
> The Canadiens have needed as many as six games in only two of ten previous playoff series. Now the plucky Bruins, with a solid 5–2 victory at Boston Garden last night, have evened the series at 3–3 to send it to one game.

"We'll just go to Montreal, shoot the works for 60 minutes, try to attack them because they attack us, and see what happens," said Bruin coach Don Cherry. "There's no reason why we can't get five more goals up there on Thursday night. The pressure is all on them now."

"We played 80 games to get the home–ice edge in the playoffs—and now we need it," said Habs winger Bob Gainey, repeating what he had stated after Game #4. "But any time a series goes to a seventh game, anything can happen."

Orr's earlier prediction of the Bruins dying in Game #6 was proven wrong. He now gave Boston a real shot at winning Game #7. He wrote, "The Bruins have rebounded with their best game of the series to push it to the limit. They outplayed the Canadiens in just about every area last evening, a performance that lifts their confidence."[17]

"The first four games of the series were tight and any one of them could have gone either way," said Bruin winger Terry O'Reilly. "Then the Canadiens won a convincing victory. We took one the same way, so that makes things pretty even for the seventh game. We're going to Montreal this time believing we have a very good chance of winning the game and going to the finals. I'd say the pressure is on the Canadiens now because they were supposed to beat us out. We're still the underdogs, but that's a role we enjoy."[18]

Orr described the Habs as "a glum, silent group as they dressed ultra-quickly and fled from Boston on a chartered plane."[19]

Ken Dryden lamented the way the game unfolded directly in front of his crease. "A lot of those [Boston] goals were avoidable," he told Will McDonough of the *Boston Globe*. "We gave up the puck in our own end and we let them put a lot of men in front of our net. Anytime you let a lot of men in front of the net, you are bound to give up goals."[20]

Montreal coach Scotty Bowman praised the Bruins' fighting spirit. "Give the Bruins credit," he said. "They had their backs to the wall and they came up with a big effort, forcing us to make mistakes. Now it's up to our team to do the same thing to them on Thursday. It was really a one-goal game for two periods, then they came up with a big third period."[21]

Orr wrote that the big surprise of the game was the unlikely scorer of a hat-trick—Stan Jonathan. "The Bruins had been counting on one of their dormant big shooters producing a strong game to give them some offensive zing. They got a big game—but from one of their grinders, winger Stan Jonathan who scored three goals. Although he scored 27 goals in the 1977–78 season, Jonathan is more renowned for his excellence in fisticuffs than in goal production. He had a miserable 1978–79 because of injuries, including a broken thumb that kept him out of the lineup for most of the second half."[22] John Powers called Jonathan "a skating hospital ward" and "a bull terrier on two legs"[23] in his report in the May 9 *Boston Globe*.

Jonathan, 23, credited sheer good fortune for his big night—easily the greatest game in his NHL career. "I was just lucky, I guess, being in the right place at the right time to get those three goals," said Jonathan. "The puck just seemed to be bouncing for me. I always seemed to be in the right place. It's one of those nights a hockey player will remember all his life, but the real story was the way our whole team refused to concede anything to the Canadiens. After they beat us [in Montreal] badly on Saturday, I think there were more than a few people who figured we were dead. But this club has so much guts that we just got it together and went right after them."[24]

Cherry had taken Jonathan out of Boston's lineup for the last five games of the regular season to give his tender wrist and assorted other wounds more time to heal in advance of the play-offs. The move had been a wise one.

"What more can I say about him?" Cherry said of Jonathan. "Except that I hung Blue's picture over where he sits. That's the highest praise I can give him."[25]

Orr continued his coverage. "The Bruins had assorted men who deserved the limelight," he wrote.

Don Cherry's favorite player from the 1978–79 Bruins, Stan Jonathan was the undeniable hero of Game #6 versus Montreal, scoring a decisive hat-trick in the game that leveled the series 3–3. Most fans, however, seldom remember that feat. Instead, Jonathan is the Bruin player most closely associated with the too-many-men debacle in Game #7.

"Goalie Gilles Gilbert delivered his fourth consecutive superb game since taking over the Bruins' net from Gerry Cheevers in Game #3. Brad Park played with his usual excellence on defense, but he had two splendid helpmates in Mike Milbury and Rick Smith."[26] Gilbert was named the game's first star—an honor he had copped after each Bruins win in the semifinal.

"In the fifth game we allowed the Canadiens to get the jump on us at the start, so the key here was to do a little jumping of our own," Cherry said in analyzing the contest. "We were a little looser than we wanted to be in the first period, but we tightened down well in the second period when the Canadiens have killed us in the games they've won. For once we won the second period with the only goal and that got us over a big hurdle."[27]

Orr was thoroughly impressed with Stan Jonathan—not just for his goal-scoring outburst in Game #6, but for his overall resilience. Orr made Jonathan the subject of a large sidebar story. It said, in part,

Gilles Gilbert flanked by superstars Phil Esposito and Bobby Orr. This photo was taken circa 1974 when Gilbert emerged as the successor to Gerry Cheevers in the Boston goal after Cheevers jumped to the World Hockey Association. When Cheevers returned to the Bruins in 1976, Gilbert's role on the team became less and less important. When the 1979 playoffs began, Gilbert was almost a forgotten man.

Stan Jonathan's body is really a mess. He wears one hand tightly taped to protect a weak thumb that was broken early in this NHL season and caused the Bruin winger to miss nearly half of it. His shoulder makes funny noises when he moves his arm. Last night his tailbone ached after a collision with a goal post, and two teeth were chipped off.

But Jonathan claimed he felt no aches or pains. After all, he had scored three goals in the Bruins' 5–2 win over the Montreal Canadiens to even the Stanley Cup semifinal at 3–3 and send it to a seventh game...[28]

The Bruins did not dress John Wensink for Game #6. Rookie Al Secord, a tough customer himself but far less likely to get into penalty trouble, was inserted in Wensink's place. Montreal played Game #6 without the services of Doug Risebrough who was out with a broken nose. He was expected to miss Game #7 as well.

When Boston assumed a three-goal lead in the third period, the Habs basically threw in the towel. Montreal coach Scotty Bowman withdrew his top guns—Lafleur, Shutt, Robinson, Savard and Lemaire—for the final seven minutes of the game to save their strength for Game #7 and remove the risk of injury. Don Cherry completely agreed with the move. "That's just smart hockey. Those guys carry a big load. Why would the Canadiens want to tire them out?"[29]

Wayne Cashman coolly expressed what every confident Boston fan was now thinking about Montreal having to host a deciding seventh game. "I have to think there might be pressure on them."[30]

When the final buzzer sounded, several zealous Bruin fans jumped onto the Boston Garden ice surface to congratulate the players—and especially Don Cherry. "One excited well-wisher plucked the handkerchief from Cherry's pocket, presumably as a keepsake. "The no-good so-and-so!" Cherry muttered to reporters, feigning outrage. "It really makes me mad. It matched my tie. Now I know how Elvis Presley felt."[31]

Still, the odds seemed to be stacked against Boston winning Game #7 in Montreal if history was to have any influence on the outcome. Since Don Cherry had replaced Bep Guidolin as the Bruins' coach in 1974, Boston had managed just one win and one tie in 12 regular-season games at the Forum. In the Stanley Cup playoffs, Cherry's Bruins were 0–8 on Montreal ice. The last time Boston had won a playoff game in Montreal was April 11, 1971—the year of the infamous quarterfinal collapse. That year Tom Johnson was Boston's coach, having taken the reins of the defending Cup-champion Bruins after Harry Sinden bolted over a contract dispute. In 1979 Johnson was employed as Sinden's right-hand man, one who dutifully reported everything and anything to his boss that smacked of disrespect. He was not a welcome presence around Cherry and his tight-knit Lunch-Pail bunch.

Always the showman, in the dying moments of Game #6, with the hometown rooters worked up to a frenzy, Cherry took a moment to wave to the Boston Garden faithful. He knew if things did not go the Bruins' way in the Montreal Forum two nights later, this was, in all likelihood, his last home game as coach of the Boston Bruins.

Meanwhile Montreal coach Scotty Bowman was miffed that Cherry seemed to be operating outside some boundaries that the NHL had established for every coach prior to the 1979 playoffs—especially for the two coaches butting heads in this epic semifinal. "Scotty Bowman feels that Cherry has violated the NHL's order against criticizing officials,"[32] reported Frank Orr. "Before the playoffs started, the league ordered all coaches to cease and desist from knocking the officials. In last year's final between the Bruins and the Canadiens, Bowman and Cherry staged a can-you-top-this competition in the baiting of refs, which earned each man a $1,000 fine."[33]

"They said there would be a $10,000 fine [this year] for discussing the officials,"

Bowman said. "Well, Cherry has had some comments on them and I haven't said anything yet."[34]

Bowman had annoyed Cherry by creating video montages for the officials to show how many Bruin penalties they had missed or overlooked so far. Cherry went a step further by stating that the NHL would prefer that Montreal advance to the finals against either the Islanders or the Rangers. That comment earned Cherry a personal telephone call from NHL president John Ziegler, who was just in his second season in charge. Ziegler diplomatically began by complimenting Cherry on his publicity-attracting antics and statements, but bluntly warned him not to insinuate the series was in any way fixed.

Both teams got surprisingly good news from Madison Square Garden. On the same night that Boston leveled their semifinal with Montreal at three games apiece, the New York Rangers completed a huge upset of the top-seeded New York Islanders. Steve Marantz of the *Boston Globe* wrote, "The regular-season champion Islanders went desultory to defeat, an uninspired unemotional team to the end. For the second straight year they are the NHL's playoff flop."[35] The Rangers surprised even themselves by winning the series in six games, largely due to the superb play of goalie John Davidson and the renaissance of Phil Esposito. "This is so sweet my teeth are rotting,"[36] declared Don Murdoch who scored the Rangers' first goal of the game. Murdoch had missed the first 40 games of the season after incurring a highly publicized suspension for cocaine possession.

When asked if he thought the Islanders hadn't taken the Rangers seriously, a cocky Ron Greschner replied, "They will—tomorrow."[37]

Ranger winger Don Maloney stated to reporters, "No one in his right mind would have picked us to be in the Stanley Cup finals when these playoffs started."[38] He was probably right. The Rangers became the first team in the five-year history of the NHL's double-seeding playoff format to advance to the final without the luxury of having a first-round bye as a regular-season divisional champion. It was only the second time since 1950 that the Rangers had gotten to the Cup final. Earlier in the series, Ed Westfall, who had played on the Bruins' Cup-winning teams in 1970 and 1972, and was playing his last NHL season with the Islanders before retiring, was asked what the difference was between the championship Bruins teams of the early 1970s and the not-quite-there Islanders of the late 1970s. His answer was succinct: "Bobby Orr."[39]

The Rangers were a hot team, no doubt. Davidson's goals-against average through three playoff rounds was a miserly 1.70. Phil Esposito seemed rejuvenated at age 37. The New Yorkers had beaten the Los Angeles Kings in two straight games in the preliminary round of the playoffs. In their quarterfinal they had ousted the Philadelphia Flyers four games to one. Now they had surprisingly upended the Islanders, largely considered by knowledgeable hockey people to be a far better team on paper than the Rangers were. "Can we continue this way? Why not?" declared a jubilant Davidson. "I'm in a groove now. I'm not the kind of guy to just stop."[40]

Nevertheless, there was an unspoken but understood common knowledge by both the Boston Bruins and Montreal Canadiens: The Habs-Bruins semifinal had become the defacto Stanley Cup championship series. In fact, Bob Miller openly said it: "I think whoever wins [Thursday's] game is going to win the Stanley Cup,"[41] he told Glenn Cole of the *Montreal Gazette*. The Habs-Bruins winner also would hold home-ice advantage during the final. With the stakes now at their highest level, Game #7 now took on an even greater level of significance.

The defeated Canadiens faced the expected questions from the media before heading for Logan Airport and their charter flight back to Montreal—and to uncharted territory for most of them. "What's the pressure going to be like in that seventh game back at the Forum?"

"I can't tell you," answered Ken Dryden. I've never been in a seventh game in Montreal."[42] Apart from Yvan Cournoyer who was sidelined with an injury, none of the 1978–79 Habs ever had. The last time a seventh game of any playoff series had been contested at the Forum was in the 1965 Stanley Cup final. That was Cournoyer's rookie season. Montreal easily defeated Chicago that night, 4–0.

"That's right," concurred Bob Gainey. "I've never played in a seventh game with this team."[43]

One person would be on the ice for Game #7 who was also on the ice in Game #7 of the 1965 Cup final: linesman John D'Amico.

Some Montreal writers were finding it hard to believe that their favored Habs were being pressed to the limit by the unglamorous, lunch-pail Bruins. Al Strachan of the *Montreal Gazette* even noted that the Bruins had the top dog as Scotty Bowman's attempt to lessen Blue's spotlight was not working.

> The Canadiens hate to be outdone in any segment of the game. But they haven't been able to match the notoriety received by Don Cherry's famed bull terrier, Blue.
>
> Scotty Bowman pointed out with a grin the other day that his dog, Waldo, has actually flown on a team charter, something that Blue has never done.
>
> In fact, when Bowman was in St. Louis, Waldo flew to Montreal, took the train to Toronto, and took another charter to St. Louis.
>
> And Waldo is certainly a better-looking dog than Blue who may be one of the world's ugliest creatures. Waldo is a white German Shepherd.
>
> But until Waldo gets his picture in *Sports Illustrated* like Blue did, we're not impressed.[44]

Since the NHL expansion era began in 1967–68, Boston's record when facing elimination in the playoffs was poor. They had won just three times with the ax hovering over their heads—a total that included their Game #6 win in this series. Nine times they had failed to come up with the necessary win to survive. Only once had the Bruins won a series when facing elimination (a 1976 quarterfinal versus Los Angeles). Still, the momentum in this see-saw series appeared to have shifted back to Boston. The date for Game #7—May 10—seemed to be a positive omen for the Bruins, falling on the ninth anniversary of Bobby Orr's famous Stanley Cup-winning goal.

One thing was beyond doubt to Bruin fans as they contentedly retired to their beds on the evening of Tuesday, May 8: If Boston did win Game #7 two nights hence at the Montreal Forum, Stan Jonathan's heroics in Game #6 would most certainly earn him a cherished and permanent place in Bruins' lore.

Game #6

First Period
1. Montreal—Robinson (Mondou, Lafleur) 8:05;
2. Boston—Jonathan (Doak, O'Reilly) 10:02;
3. Boston—Marcotte (Ratelle, Schmautz) 12:21;
4. Montreal—Mondou (Lambert, Dryden) 12:48.

Second Period
5. Boston—Cashman (Park, O'Reilly) 16:30.

Third Period
6. Boston—Jonathan (Miller, Smith) 7:23;
7. Boston—Jonathan (Cashman, Milbury) 15:24.

16

None Bigger
The Hype for the Final Game

"The two teams haven't exactly labored in vain in this series. The entertainment has been excellent. The revenue has been good. But they have accomplished nothing in the first six games. They're no further ahead than they were two weeks ago tonight. But tonight is the hour of decision…"
—*Hockey Night in Canada*'s Danny Gallivan,
moments before the opening faceoff of Game 7

"[A seventh game] is like playing in overtime. I think probably anything can happen."

—Larry Robinson

Even with the Stanley Cup final upcoming, the biggest game of the 1978–79 NHL season was definitely going to be played on the night of Thursday, May 10 at the Montreal Forum when the Bruins and Habs dramatically collided in Game #7 of their semifinal series. There was no bigger game. Everyone knew it. It was probably the biggest NHL game since the Canadiens faced off against the Chicago Blackwaks nearly eight years earlier in Game #7 of the 1971 Cup final.

Everything was on the line. Compelling questions abounded: Could the favored, three-time defending Cup champions subdue their pesky Lunch Pail Gang challengers who seemed unwilling to fold? Which team and which players would crack under pressure? Could the Bruins retain their momentum from Game #6 and finally discard the heavy baggage of history? Would it be Don Cherry's last game? Could he inspire one more Herculean effort from his charges? Would it be Scotty Bowman's last game? Had the Habs finally been pushed to their physical and emotional limit? How would the game be refereed? What would be the deciding factor? Everything seemed completely aligned for a memorable hockey game.

In the 17 previous playoff series between Boston and Montreal dating back to 1929, only three had progressed to a single, winner-take-all game—a statistic that surprised some reporters when they were alerted to it. Montreal had won a best-of-five semifinal series in 1931 on an overtime goal by George Mantha at the Forum in Game #5. (George's brother, Sylvio, is the answer to a great trivia question: He scored the first NHL goal at Boston Garden in 1928 when the Habs spoiled the very first Opening Night there.) In 1952 there was groggy Rocket Richard returning from a concussion to score the series-winner against Sugar Jim Henry, also in the semis and also at the Forum. The third occasion was the Habs' monumental 1971 quarterfinal upset in which the final game was played at Boston Garden. Montreal won that game, 4–2. Four Bruins on the 1978–79 team (Gerry Cheevers, Rick Smith, Don Marcotte and Wayne Cashman) had played in that disappointing 1971 contest. Jacques Lemaire, Guy Lapointe, Ken Dryden and Serge Savard were the four remaining active Canadiens from their 1971 Stanley Cup team. (Yvan Cournoyer was technically a fifth holdover, but he had played just 15 games for the Habs during the 1978–79 regular season and none in the playoffs due to a bad back. Cournoyer did not know it yet, but his NHL career was over after 16 seasons and 968 games.)

Hyperbole was not need to get any hockey fan revved up for Game #7, but it came anyway, of course, in great waves.

Bruin beat writer Leigh Montville believed the Montreal Forum to be the biggest obstacle that Boston would have to overcome mentally to win the deciding game. In a May 10 *Globe* article titled "Winning in the Forum—Toughest Job of All," Montville wrote,

> The big box of a building on Ste. Catharine's Street again is the cruel plate of glass in the bake shop window.
>
> Everything the Boston Bruins have always wanted is on one side. The Bruins again are on the other side. All they have to do [to be the favorites in the Cup final] is to just reach out…
>
> Only the Montreal Forum stands in front of them. Only the Forum and the Montreal Canadiens and tradition, history, hard-boiled statistics, and the fact [that] the Bruins never can win here.
>
> "Anything can happen," is the watchword of coach Don Cherry. "In one game—a puck can bounce, a goaltender can have a bad night. A lot of things can happen."

Frank Orr of the *Toronto Star* interviewed Don Marcotte to get the veteran Bruin forward's take on which team should feel more pressured going into climactic Game #7. Marcotte pointed to the Habs without hesitation. Under the headline "Bruin Advises Habs to Worry," Orr recorded Marcotte's sentiments:

> "If I were a Canadien, I'd be concerned about this game," [Don] Marcotte said. "They're a great team and were heavily favored to beat us with little trouble on their way to the final. We played well enough to win one of the first two games in their rink, then [we] beat them three times in ours. They know we're no pushovers."
>
> "In the seventh game we have nothing to lose. We weren't supposed to be there in the first place. I'd say the Canadiens' backs [are] against the wall. We were in that position at home. [We] pulled it off. For once it's nice to see the Canadiens in that spot."[1]

John Ahern of the *Globe* preferred to focus on a markedly different and peripheral angle about Game 7 in his May 10 article. He recognized that Boston goalie Gilles Gilbert was becoming a sentimental folk hero within the province Quebec because of his play, his French-Canadian ancestry, and his compelling underdog story. Ahern wrote,

> The populace of [Montreal] has a new hero today and it creates quite a quandary.
>
> The new hero … does not play for the Canadiens. Gilles Gilbert plays for Boston. How does a fan who sings *O Canada* only in French root against one of his own?
>
> Gilles is a native son. If he were [regarded] as the enemy when this series began, his performances have endeared him to his emotional kin.
>
> These same compatriots have embraced another Bruin—a brave from the Tuscarora tribe, Stan Jonathan.
>
> Jonathan was the hero of Game #6, and if Stanley is not exactly Parisienne, he's not Anglo-Saxon, either. The [Quebec] separatist movement is multi-pronged.

The uncertainty about Don Cherry's future status with the Bruins was predictably a common target for journalists. In a May 10 *Globe* piece titled "Cherry Doubts He'll Return," John Ahern noted,

Don Cherry made it perfectly clear: There is little chance [he will return] as coach of the Boston Bruins next season.

"This goes beyond money now," he said. "I have been ignored for three months. I haven't been asked or consulted about anything. I don't care about the money now. It's deeper than that."

Cherry has become a public figure [in Boston]. He communicates with the fan, the dog lover, the man on the street. His tactics are not orthodox; he has fun on the job and he doesn't take himself too seriously. However, he is very serious about … his players, whom he backs to the hilt.

"These guys are good enough to win everything. I want it for them. It would be nice for me too. But … there's not much chance I'll be back."

Frank Orr of the *Toronto Star* told his readers that Don Cherry's days in Boston were over regardless of how the semifinal or final turned out. In an article titled "I'm Leaving Boston' Cherry Re-Asserts" Orr declared,

Coach Don Cherry said yesterday that he definitely will not be with the [Bruins] next season, no matter what happens in tonight's seventh game.

Cherry's contract … runs out on June 1. He feels his record … has earned him a salary in excess of $100,000. The Bruins have offered $80,000. That appears to be the limit.

With the expansion draft [coming], some guys will be moving too. "[This] could be the closest many of them will get to a Stanley Cup. [Many] players and coaches have whole careers without getting to the seventh game of the semifinals," Cherry stated.

In a May 10 piece titled "Cherry's Cheery Way Keeps Bruins Flying," Tim Burke of the *Montreal Gazette* praised the Bruins and Cherry in particular. Burke noted,

Year after year, the Boston Bruins are still hanging in there in May, digging, scratching and struggling valiantly against a team superior in every aspect of hockey save, perhaps, desire.

The Bruins are probably the least talented of the six top teams in the NHL. But they compensate for their shortcomings with a super abundance of spirit and a wholesome "let's give it our best shot" attitude.

It seems incredible that the Bruins are going to let Cherry go after the playoffs. If ever a man reflected the hockey soul of Boston, it's Cherry.

A *Canadian Press* story that ran without a byline in the May 10 *Calgary Herald* preferred to focus on history as a way of predicting the outcome of Game #7. It said,

The Bruins have lost all 14 games they have played on Montreal ice since their last victory here, a 4–3 decision on October 30, 1976. In that total are six regular-season games, two games in the 1977 final, three games in the 1978 final and three games in the current series.

On the other hand, the Canadiens can be beaten in a seventh game on home ice. The Toronto Maple Leafs did it in the deciding game of a 1964 semifinal series, winning 3–1 on Dave Keon's three goals.

Referee Bob Myers, who had been selected by the NHL to officiate Game #7, admitted to feeling pressure before such an important contest. He told the Associated Press, "Sure, the tension is strong—much more than people think. Like the players, we're tense. The worst thing is that we have to stay on the defensive. We have to be ready but not too ready. The worst thing for a referee is to be tense before a game. You can easily get unnerved."[2]

Boston's Game #6 hero, Stan Jonathan, was focused on how the series was positively impacting his huge but close-knit family on the outskirts of Brantford, Ontario. He told the *Boston Globe*, "Back on the Reservation, my family (mother, father, grandmother, grandfather, nine sisters, and four brothers) will be watching and cheering. I want to be good for my mother. She has a heart condition, and if I play good [sic], she could be much better."

17

Game 7

Too Many Men

"Perhaps there have been better, more exciting hockey matches played than the one the Canadiens and Bruins produced last evening, but no one on hand could remember one. The high-strung, see-saw match, conducted at an ultra-swift pace, was the game at its thrilling best."

—Frank Orr, *Toronto Star*

"I'll go out on a limb and say that this game between the Bruins, one of the gutsiest teams ever to come down the pike, and the Canadiens, proud heirs to one of the great mystiques in the history of professional sports, will be recalled as long as the people who witnessed it are still among the quick."

—Tim Burke, *Montreal Gazette*

Starting with their first postseason meeting on March 19, 1929, to their most recent clash on May 14, 2014, the Boston Bruins and Montreal Canadiens have played 177 playoff games versus one another. (Consistent with their regular-season superiority, Montreal also holds a 106–71 lead over Boston in overall victories.) Of all those contests, by far the most talked-about game is Game #7 of their 1979 Stanley Cup semifinal. It was an exciting, well played, dramatic hockey game that featured numerous talking points and several plot twists. It also encapsulated the immense frustration that the Bruins' players, coaches, management and fans have felt for decades over their team's infuriating inability to upend the Habs in the playoffs and win critical games at the Montreal Forum.

Game #7 started out as a wide-open affair, with numerous end-to-end rushes by both Boston and Montreal. However, there were few good scoring chances in the early part of the first period as both teams' defensive units routinely stifled their opponents' attacks. Most of the shots on goal came from long range. Montreal seemed the tighter of the two teams. In the *Hockey Night in Canada* booth, analyst Lou Nanne accurately opined that the Habs seemed both tense and hesitant in the opening period.

The first two power play opportunities in the game uncharacteristically went to the Bruins. The first man-advantage situation went for naught, but Boston capitalized on the subsequent one. Rick Middleton put Boston ahead at 10:09 on a goal in which both he and Wayne Cashman were left alone in front of Ken Dryden. Middleton slid the puck into the right corner of the net. Dryden was slow getting back into position after he and Cashman became entangled in front of the goal crease. Dryden briefly complained to referee Bob Myers that the goal should have been disallowed because of the contact, but Myers was having none of it. Boston led 1–0. Cheers from a contingent of Boston fans could be heard clearly above the general silence in the Forum. Not long afterward, Stan Jonathan, the scoring hero of Game #6, had a partial breakaway and pulled Dryden out of position, but Serge Savard was close enough to the action to skate into the goal crease and stop the puck with his chest.

Montreal tied the score at 14:19 on a power play goal of their own while Bob Miller was sitting out a minor penalty. Jacques Lemaire scored on a wild scramble in front of Gilles Gilbert who had made an initial save, but he was unable to get to his feet. Lemaire, positioned near the left side of Gilbert's crease, backhanded the puck between Rick Smith's legs and into the net. Smith was on his knees trying to make a save. Late in the opening period Yvon Lambert was checked hard into the end boards by Mike Milbury. It was a clean play. The helmetless Lambert banged his head heavily on the glass and crumpled to the ice. He was groggy but was able to get to the Montreal bench on his own power once the play had stopped. Lambert would return to the game.

The first period ended with the game tied 1–1. Despite allowing one goal, Gilbert was the star of the game at that point. He made several excellent stops. (*HNIC*'s Danny Gallivan described one Gilbert save as "larcenous."[1]) As the two teams left the ice, a surprising amount of boos could be heard from the Forum faithful. Nervousness was prevailing as the Habs were not putting away the pesky Bruins as easily as expected.

Beginning the second period with confidence, the Bruins got an early goal. Wayne Cashman scored at the 0:27 mark. It was a typical Cherry-era Bruins goal: Jean Ratelle won the puck in the right corner behind the Montreal net. He fed a pass to Rick Middleton who was also behind the net on the left side. Middleton made another behind-the-net pass to Cashman. Dryden clearly did not anticipate that manoeuver. Cashman quickly moved in front of the net and backhanded the puck between Dryden's pads as the Montreal goalie reacted too late to stop Boston's captain. Boston retook the lead, 2–1.

The remainder of the second period featured "tremendous action,"[2] as *HNIC*'s Dick Irvin noted. Both teams had good scoring chances but Dryden and Gilbert were stalwarts. "This Gilbert is something else!"[3] declared Gallivan after Boston's goalie made two acrobatic saves. With about four minutes remaining in the period, Stan Jonathan appeared to have Dryden hopelessly out of position for the second time in the game, but instead of taking a long shot at an open net, he hesitated and looked to pass the puck to an available teammate in a better position. There was none—and the opportunity was lost.

The Bruins did not dwell on their misfortune for very long. Shortly after Jonathan's chance had been squandered, Wayne Cashman notched his second goal of the period at 16:12 on a beautiful play. Jean Ratelle stripped Guy Lapointe of the puck behind Montreal's net. Cashman picked up the puck, came out from behind Dryden looking to make a pass. When he saw no teammate open, Cashman continued skating out front. He whirled around and fired a sharp wrist shot into the top left corner of the net. Dryden seemed lost on the play and was likely distracted by Rick Middleton and Steve Shutt who were entangled in front of him. Boston led 3–1. The Bruins could have upped their lead to 4–1, but Peter McNab and Jean Ratelle were both denied in front of Dryden on good chances. Lapointe slid to block a Middleton attempt from the slot.

"Since the Bruins have gotten the two-goal lead, they've taken over this game," Lou Nanne stated to CBC's television audience. "They seem to smell victory. They sense the kill. They're going after it. They're like a tiger after its prey."[4] Danny Gallivan stated the obvious: "The Bruins are playing with a lot of enthusiasm."[5]

Many of the Montreal-based media figured Game #7 belonged to the feisty visitors. Tim Burke of the *Montreal Gazette* wrote, "The Canadiens were written off after the second period last night, scorned in a seething press lounge for their apparent reluctance to mix it up with the resolute Bruins. There wasn't a commentator in the lot who gave them a hope of ever coming back from being down 3–1 at that stage." Burke continued, "The Bruins had dominated them in those first 40 minutes, checking them mercilessly and running roughshod over the Canadiens in their own end. On the occasions the Canadiens did break through the excellent umbrella Boston established at their own blue line, Gilles Gilbert, the pride of St. Esprit, Quebec, pulled off some of the most sensational saves I have ever seen."[6] Recalling the game more than 15 years later, Jacques Lemaire concurred. "We were in trouble," he said. "Boston had us in big trouble. They were controlling the game."[7]

Five minutes into the third period Boston was still the team that was pressing forward, getting the better opportunities to score. Rick Middleton had a terrific chance to score on a wraparound play but could not lift the puck over the sprawling Dryden. Shortly thereafter, on a Montreal counterattack, Guy Lafleur turned the momentum of the game with one of his typical individual efforts. Moving swiftly across the blue line on the right wing, Lafleur sped by Al Sims and carried the puck around the Boston net. As he emerged in front of the net to Gilbert's right, Lafleur connected with a perfect pass to Mark Napier who beat the Boston goalie with a quick, low snap shot. The Bruins' lead had been halved to 3–2 at the 6:10 mark of the third period.

The dormant patrons at the Forum sprung back to life. "It's been a pretty quiet Forum crowd since Cashman's goal early in the second period," noted Dick Irvin, "but this place has erupted."[8]

"It's a bedlam place to be in,"[9] Lou Nanne agreed.

"A pall of gloom had started to envelop the Forum," Danny Gallivan reiterated, "but that goal by Napier has brought [the Montreal fans] back in a lively fashion."[10]

Following Napier's goal, the Bruins were besieged by the Canadiens. The continuous pressure resulted in a key penalty against Dick Redmond. Jacques Lemaire was rushing alone with the puck along the left side of the ice inside the Boston blue line. Redmond got his stick up too high around Lemaire's upper chest and shoulders for Bob Myers' liking. He whistled the play down and sent Redmond to the penalty box for two minutes for hooking. Redmond had only accrued 21 penalty minutes all season—and none in the playoffs—before the infraction against Lemaire. "The Bruins are livid!"[11] shouted Danny Gallivan.

Three things irked the visitors about Myers' penalty call: Jean Ratelle—and only Ratelle—had been sent to the penalty box earlier in the period for retaliating to an elbow to the head delivered by Bob Gainey. (Ratelle, a two-time Lady Byng Trophy winner, had picked up just six minor penalties in the entire season.) Boston managed to successfully kill that Montreal power play. Secondly, before the Ratelle penalty, Myers had been letting numerous borderline infractions by both teams go without penalizing them, so the two Boston penalties in quick succession before and after Napier's goal seemed to reinforce the Bruins' preconceived idea that Myers would not call the game fairly, at least from their standpoint. Finally, the Bruins also strongly suspected that Lemaire had greatly embellished the play by toppling to the ice too easily. Recalling the game 35 years later, Michael Farber of *Sports Illustrated* wrote, "Dick Redmond hooked Jacques Lemaire who, operatically, collapsed like the tubercular Mimi in the final act of *La Bohème*."[12]

Mild-mannered Jean Ratelle was irate. He furiously argued the call with Myers to no avail, of course. On the Boston bench, Don Cherry showed his displeasure by dramatically bowing to all and sundry—especially targeting Myers and the hostile Forum crowd. (Cherry's brazen theatrics are still regularly shown to this day as part of the opening montage to his "Coach's Corner" segment on *HNIC*.)

With Montreal applying sustained pressure, Guy Lapointe scored on the power play on a low screen shot from well inside the blue line. Brad Park had lost his stick on the play, further handicapping Boston's attempt to defend the Montreal man-advantage. Again Lafleur made the key pass. Coming out from behind the Boston net, he deftly fed the puck to Lapointe. Serge Savard's large presence in front of Gilbert gave the Bruins' goalie no view of Lapointe's slapshot that whizzed by him into the lower right corner of the net. The score was now level at 3–3 and the noise inside the Forum was deafening. The time of the goal was 8:16. In a little more than two minutes of playing time, the complexion of Game #7 had completely changed.

Montreal was applying most of the pressure for the next seven minutes but suffered a significant setback when Guy Lapointe was forced to exit the game with a wrenched knee with 4:43 left in the third period after a tussle with Rick Middleton behind the Boston net. Middleton executed something akin to a gut-wrench suplex on Lapointe who remained prostrate on the ice for several minutes. A stretcher was summoned. He was diagnosed with torn knee ligaments. Lapointe's untimely departure left the Habs with only three front-line defensemen.

That development seemed to enliven the Bruins. In a rare third-period attack on Dryden, the Bruins capitalized. Middleton again had a wraparound chance and this time it paid off. He picked up a loose puck behind the Canadiens' net and moved in front of Dryden. Middleton did not get anything close to full power behind his backhand shot, but it was just strong enough to slither under Dryden's right pad and into the net. Dryden looked awkward and unsure of himself on the play. It was reminiscent of Cashman's goal that had made the score 2–1 early in the second period. It was hardly a thing of beauty, but with 3:59 left in regulation time, the Bruins had retaken the lead they had squandered earlier in the period. "It should have been the victory,"[13] Francis Rosa would later write in his report for the *Boston Globe*. Guy Lafleur concurred. "It's the kind of goal that gets the guys down,"[14] he said. Leigh Montville of the *Globe* would later describe Middleton's goal—his second of the game—as "the final tease, the final prelude to heartbreak."[15]

Thirty-three years later in his autobiography, Brad Park recalled that a historic Bruins victory over Montreal seemed almost certain at that point. "We had them," he wrote. "A one-goal lead with less than four minutes to play. We had them, finally!"[16]

Following Middleton's clutch go-ahead goal, the play proceeded without a whistle for about 90 seconds. Boston was attempting to nullify any Montreal offensive thrusts before they really began—and were generally succeeding. The Bruins were deftly intercepting Montreal passes in the neutral zone and clearing them back into Montreal's end. Then, as Montreal began another rush toward the Bruins' zone, there was a clamor in the crowd. The *HNIC* coverage shows silhouettes of several Habs fans rising out of their seats and pointing excitedly toward the Bruins' bench area. Another Montreal attack into the Boston zone was broken up by Brad Park and a whistle was heard away from the play. There was a moment of confusion. Most of the players had no idea why the play had been stopped. Linesman John D'Amico had blown his whistle with 2:34 remaining in the third period. Boston had too many men on the ice. It was the fifth time Boston would be shorthanded in the game. Montreal had been shorthanded three times.

"It wasn't debatable," Brian Engblom said nearly 30 years later in an NHL Network interview. "There were seven Bruins on the ice. None was within 20 feet of the bench. It was a monumental screw-up."[17]

"I did not see it," recalled *HNIC*'s Dick Irvin in 1994. "I was walking down through the garage of the Forum to our studio. "Leo Monahan, a Boston writer [for the *Herald*

American], turned to me and said, 'I think the Bruins just received a penalty.' Yes, they had."[18]

Even with the Bruins holding a one-goal lead with under three minutes to play, the waterworks were freely flowing in and around the Boston bench. The sense that the too-many-men penalty was an ominous, disastrous turn of events was palpable. Appearing stoic, Cherry looked for signs of strength nearby to bolster his own confidence in a time of crisis. He did not find many. Cherry's teenage son, Timothy, who was officially listed as an assistant trainer, was crying. Jovial longtime Boston trainer John (Frosty) Forristal—who had seen just about everything in Bruins hockey since 1963 and always seemed to have a smile on his face—was crying. Cherry also recalls quickly glimpsing two burly Bruins fans who were sitting near Boston's bench. They were both crying too. This did not bode well for the visitors. *Hockey Night in Canada's* first pictures of the Boston bench after the penalty had been called showed two Bruins—Bob Miller and Stan Jonathan—on the ice but tiredly leaning over the boards.

One the reverse side of the coin, the fortuitous break was a reprieve for Montreal. "That penalty was what we needed to get us going," Scotty Bowman said afterward. "I thought we were snakebit when Middleton scored."[19]

Jacques Lemaire, who was 154 seconds away from retirement if the Bruins could maintain their lead, knew it was the key moment in the game. He recalled, "When they got that penalty, I knew we were going to score."[20] Guy Lafleur concurred. He said the Boston penalty had the effect of revitalizing the Habs.

As the bench penalty was being sorted out—Peter McNab was sent to the box by Cherry to serve the two-minute infraction—Scotty Bowman called a timeout on the Montreal bench to rest his troops for a last-ditch assault on Gilbert. This was a rare tactical occurrence in 1978–79. It was the first season that the timeout rule existed. Coaches had seldom utilized it simply because they had no experience using it. Serge Savard relayed a message from Bowman to goaltender Ken Dryden, no doubt telling him when he could expect to be pulled for an extra attacker, if needed. Bowman sent out five future Hall of Famers to operate the Montreal power play: Savard, Larry Robinson, Lemaire, Bob Gainey and Lafleur, of course. It was high drama: The entire series—and likely the 1979 Stanley Cup—hinged on what would happen during the next two minutes. Cherry would write in his autobiography that the Canadiens "looked like a pride of lions about to jump a wildebeest."[21]

The initial faceoff took place between the red line and the Bruins' blue line. The Canadiens advanced the puck into the Boston zone, but the Bruins managed to gain control. Dick Redmond tried to shoot the puck down the ice. He whiffed on the first attempt but was successful on the second. A second Montreal foray into the Bruins' end put even more pressure on the visitors. Boston got a temporary reprieve when Redmond slid into the side boards and pinned the puck for a faceoff. The Forum's clock showed 1:06 remaining in the Bruins' bench penalty and 1:40 left in the third period. Dryden remained in the Montreal net but was ready to head to his bench when summoned.

Don Cherry smartly took his timeout to rest his beleaguered defensemen. The Canadiens on the ice went into a huddle with Bowman to discuss strategy. In the *HNIC* broadcast booth, Danny Gallivan presciently said, "Well, there you have the entire season wrapped up in that scene: They're getting together to plan an attack that will give them the goal to keep their hockey lives going for this year."[22]

The faceoff was in the Boston zone to the right of Gilbert. Brad Park got the puck from the draw but became entangled with teammate Dick Redmond. Park fanned on his attempt to propel the puck around the Boston net. However, Park recovered it seconds later from an errant Serge Savard pass that dangerously deflected off Lemaire's skate right in front of Gilbert. Park calmly took two strides forward and decisively cleared the puck down the ice into the Montreal zone. "Fifty-five seconds left in the penalty … a minute twenty-seven seconds left in regulation time,"[23] Gallivan said to CBC's television audience as Guy Lafleur retreated to Montreal's end of the ice to gather the puck from Ken Dryden.

Lafleur picked up the puck and made a tight 360-degree turn to the right of Dryden. This manoeuver bought him some key separation room from Don Marcotte who was supposed to stay as close to Lafleur as possible at every moment. Marcotte hesitated for just a moment as Lafleur spun, but that split second allowed Steve Shutt to get between him and Lafleur. As Marcotte tried to pursue Lafleur, Serge Savard also subtly provided himself as an impediment to Marcotte's chase.

"Lafleur … coming out rather gingerly on that right side,"[24] said Gallivan.

Freed from the shadow of the pesky Marcotte, Lafleur advanced the puck over his own blue line and hit Jacques Lemaire with a pass along the right boards at the Boston blue line. Lemaire carried the puck to about the middle of the faceoff circle to the left of Gilbert and dropped a return pass to Lafleur who was advancing at full speed.

"He gives it to Lemaire … back to Lafleur…" continued Gallivan.

Lafleur wound up and blasted the puck at the Boston net.

"He scores!!!"[25]

In recalling the game 35 years later *SI*'s Farber called Lafleur's famous drive "the Hammer of Thor."[26] It zipped past the right of Gilbert—who fell backward with his arms spread apart as if he had been struck by a gunshot blast. As loud a roar as ever came from the old Montreal Forum was emitted from the overflow crowd when the red light came on. With 1:14 remaining, Game #7 was tied 4–4.

Lafleur's goal was a virtual carbon copy of the one he had scored in Boston Garden one week earlier in Game #4, taken from slightly farther away, perhaps 40 feet from the Boston net. It traveled with the same fearsome velocity and again beat Gilbert to his right. The shot in Game #7 was lower than his Game #4 shot, but there was also less room for error. To score from where Lafleur did, his shot had to be perfect. It was. Scotty Bowman called it "a hundred-to-one shot."[27]

Brad Park gave attached even longer odds to it. "The slapshot was one inch off the ice and one inch inside the post on Gillie's stick side," Park marveled in *Straight Shooter*, his 2012 autobiography. "This was a one-in-1,000 shot!"[28] Lafleur's teammate Mark Napier claimed, "That shot was so hard it hydroplaned, hitting the ice and skipping over the pad. I don't know any goalie then or now who would have stopped it."[29]

Nevertheless, some observers blame Gilbert for not stopping Lafleur's slapshot. A close, slow-motion examination of the *HNIC* replay shows that his goalie stick was off the ice and he was trying to stop the perfectly aimed shot by kicking out his right skate. None of Gilbert's teammates faulted him, however—especially after the barrage of Montreal shots he had already stopped in the first 58 minutes of the game.

"That was one hell of a shot," Terry O'Reilly admiringly said in an interview with the NHL Network 30 years afterward. "Most times when someone scores from that distance you think the goalie should have stopped it. We didn't call it a bad goal—not when the shot is that hard and it's just inside the goal post."[30] Lafleur agreed that Gilbert should be absolved of blame. "He didn't have time to move," Lafleur insisted. "I caught him deep in the goal."[31] It was Lafleur's eighth goal of the 1979 playoffs and his 50th career playoff goal.

"This has got to be heart-breaking for the Boston Bruins," Gallivan noted as *HNIC* showed multiple replays of Lafleur's goal from various angles. "The first two games of the series in here they played very well, and everything went against them late in the games. They lost both. Here tonight they saw a 3–1 lead wiped out. The came back, took the lead, and a bench penalty—of all things—caused the loss of the lead again."[32]

Scotty Bowman sent Lafleur back on the ice for the next faceoff. Both teams now suffered from the yips as the Forum's clock approached triple zeroes. From the faceoff at center ice, the puck was shot deep into the Montreal zone. Dryden, playing the puck behind his net, sloppily gave it away to Wayne Cashman, but there was no Bruin in front of the Montreal net to knock home his hopeful pass. Just moments later, Lafleur, on a swift counterattack, moved the puck over the red line and unloaded another booming drive from outside the Boston blue line. Gilbert barely reacted as the puck sailed by him, but it was off target and flew inches wide of the right goalpost. When the siren sounded to end the third period, Danny Gallivan noted with a large dose of understatement, "This has been a highly interesting and entertaining hockey game."[33]

In the visitors' dressing room, Cherry tried to raise his charges' sagging spirits. Employing a cagy bit of psychology, Cherry asked his tired and disappointed Bruins one basic question: "When we were down two games to none in this series, if I could have said to you, 'Would you be happy to go into overtime in the seventh game?' What would you have said?"[34] The answer for the underdog Bruins was obviously yes.

The atmosphere heading into overtime in Game #7 was markedly different than it was in Game #4 a week earlier in Boston. Despite Cherry's best effort to restore the Bruins' confidence, the tone for defeat had firmly been set. "The momentum had certainly changed," said Terry O'Reilly, with mixed metaphors. "With their history of pulling it out and our history of shooting ourselves in the foot versus Montreal—we were skating on pins and needles."[35]

The best chances in the early part of the overtime period went Boston's way. Don Marcotte had an open shot from the slot, but Dryden stopped him cold. Middleton and Terry O'Reilly had good opportunities as well. (O'Reilly had been playing with a badly damaged left elbow since the Pittsburgh series, but the injury was kept quiet.) Later, a pass from Peter McNab intended for Marcotte right in front of Dryden partially skipped over the blade of Marcotte's stick, causing him to shank the puck wide of the Montreal net. On the counter rush by the Canadiens, Gilbert made yet another spectacular save on a deflection by Jacques Lemaire who was position right in front of the goal crease. It appeared the puck was about to trickle over the goal line, but the Boston netminder, on the verge of exhaustion, reached back to grab it to preserve the tie score.

The decisive moment of the overtime actually began on a Rick Middleton rush. Cashman fed him a pass from inside the Boston blue line. Middleton, with no teammate supporting his attack, carried the puck over the Montreal blue line and tried to pass the puck to himself through Serge Savard's legs. The manoeuver failed. Savard pushed Middleton off the puck and Montreal quickly switched to offensive mode.

Savard found Réjean Houle—who, in Game #7, was making his first appearance of the series—in the neutral zone with a quick pass. Houle deftly redirected the puck to Mario Tremblay on the right wing. Boston's Al Sims—playing his last shift as a Bruin—forced Tremblay to the right boards, but allowed Tremblay barely enough room to make a cross-ice pass in front of the Boston net. The puck was delivered perfectly to a charging Yvon Lambert, who had stealthily moved behind Brad Park, to the right of Gilbert. "The pass was too far ahead to poke-check,"[36] Gilbert later said. [Author's note: This is a debatable statement. Tremblay's pass seemed well within Gilbert's reach—just a couple of feet in front of the goal crease—had he attempted to intercept it with his stick.] Park only got a fleeting glimpse of Lambert as he moved into the ideal position to receive Tremblay's feed. ("It was Hockey 101," Terry O'Reilly would recall. "Charge towards the net."[37]) Lambert—who had been thwarted twice before in Game #7 on similar plays—had half the net as a gaping target. He redirected the puck along the ice into the goal before Gilbert could move across his crease.

Several months later in an interview with Jim Proudfoot of the *Toronto Star*, Brad Park explained there was miscommunication between himself and Gilbert. "Hockey is a game of inches. When Lambert drives wide on my partner, Al Sims, I am heading back to the net with Lambert. Tremblay is almost at the goal line when he makes a goal-mouth pass. I see the puck going through the top of the crease and I hesitated as I thought Gilbert would tip it. Gillie figured I would tip it. The hesitation allowed the puck to reach Lambert as I uttered the infamous line, 'Oh, @#$%.'"[38]

The time of the goal was 9:33. It was the 52nd shot Gilbert had faced in nearly 70 minutes of intense action—and he had no chance whatsoever of stopping it once it got to Lambert. The Forum crowd went berserk. The winning goal marked the only time that the Canadiens were ahead in Game #7. Montreal had ousted Boston in the playoffs yet again. It was all so familiar to the visitors and their fans. But this one hurt more than any other—perhaps more than all the other defeats combined, including 1971.

As the Habs were celebrating their overtime win in a corner of the Forum's ice, Danny Gallivan commented, "The Boston Bruins can hold their heads very, very high. They were just outstanding."[39] His broadcast partner, Lou Nanne, agreed. "They were every bit as worthy of winning this game as the Montreal Canadiens," he said. "They can be very proud."[40]

Glenn Cole, a Habs beat writer for the *Montreal Gazette*, had become impressed with the Bruins—as had many of the media who had not followed them very closely all season. Cole wrote, "It's an old cliché, but it was too bad that someone had to lose."[41]

Well-earned and accurate plaudits they were, but they were hardly a substitute for victory—a victory that was well within the Bruins' grasp but had elusively slipped away. It was the first Boston-Montreal playoff series in the rivalry's long history in which the home team had won every game. It was also the second time in Bruins history that they had won all their home games in a season's playoffs yet failed to win the Stanley Cup. The only other instance occurred in 1936—before any of the 1978–79 Bruins had been born—when the team played just one postseason game at Boston Garden. In 1979 they had five playoff home dates.

When the brutally harsh reality of defeat had sunk in, Don Cherry's hardscrabble, tough-as-nails, lunch-bucket Bruins were reduced to tears in the visitors' dressing room. "And in one corner Gerry Cheevers tried not to cry. He did not succeed," wrote the eloquent Leigh Montville in the May 11 edition of the *Boston Globe*. "His eyes moved from one player to another in the concrete bunker of a dressing room, from Wayne Cashman to Gilles Gilbert to whomever happened to be passing, from player to player, friend to friend, and the heartbreak just tore him apart. The tears formed naturally in the corners of the goaltender's eyes."[42]

"I want to cry for every one of them," Cheevers ruefully told Montville. "Each guy I see makes me want to start crying all over again. I just feel so sorry for all of them. They tried so hard. I've never seen a team try so hard…"[43]

"How do you measure the sadness of it all?" Montville rhetorically continued. "Surely not in grand terms like life and death, street-corner accidents and malignant diseases, but on a gut level how do you measure it? The sight of all those guys, their nostrils wide open for two weeks now, their eyeballs cutting through the smoke over the ice like headlights, everybody diving and falling and stepping up a level in ability by simply trying. What had it won here in the end? Nothing. You had to cry a little bit. You couldn't stop."[44]

Much like the Confederates at Gettysburg, the Boston Bruins had just suffered a cat-astrophic defeat when victory appeared to be at hand. The result of the battle was obvious, but one had to admire the sheer courage of the vanquished no matter where one's allegiances fell.

"Oh, the Bruins had them—almost. Twice they had them ... almost. And each time Montreal wriggled its way out of the noose. The trap door that opened was under the Bru-ins," wrote Francis Rosa in his report for the *Boston Globe*. He continued, "Gilbert was the story in defeat. No goalie could ever play better. No alien goalie ever received a bigger ova-tion from the Forum fans for being named #1 star."[45]

In an Associated Press story that ran in the *Milwaukee Journal* without a byline, Gilbert sadly stated afterward, "As far as I am concerned, this game was for the Stanley Cup." Not surprisingly, the article described the Bruins' dressing room as "gloomy."[46]

Some Bruins wanted to comment on what had transpired but they could not find the appropriate words—or any words, in some cases. "There will be nothing out of me," Brad Park glumly told a gathering of reporters. "There is nothing I can say. I feel too bad."[47]

A French-language TV crew cautiously approached Wayne Cashman for some postgame comments. "Mind if we ask you a view questions?" said the interviewer, not quite sure how the grim and solemn Bruin was going to react.

"You can ask them," Cashman calmly replied. "But I'm sure I don't have the answers."[48] Later Cashman uttered one of the most poignant quotes to ever come out of a hockey player's mouth: "What bothers me is that my 13-year-old son was watching this game," the veteran Boston captain sadly said. "I tell him that hard work always pays off. What do I tell him now?"[49]

Leigh Montville conceded the Bruins had largely been the authors of their own demise.

> To be sure the Bruins helped croak themselves. They had the 3–1 lead at the end of two periods. They had the 4–3 lead with only three minutes to go in the game. They were the ones who botched, who somehow wound up with two centers on the ice at one time, seven men altogether, to be whis-tled for a penalty and set up Guy Lafleur's tying goal with only 1:14 left. To be sure, they botched a few times, surrendering three power-play goals, but really.... REALLY! They somehow deserved bet-ter. There are other things to say, but why bother? Why try? It's an absolute pits of an end here at the Forum.[50]

There were numerous images of the Bruins' defeat that would have been apt for any news-paper or magazine. The *Boston Globe* chose to run a close-up photo of Gilles Gilbert—who had fearlessly faced 52 Montreal shots and had stopped 47. In the end, the 52nd shot was all that really mattered. Gilbert was seated alone on the Boston bench after the game, waiting to be called onto the ice to be recognized as the game's first star. He had a detached, faraway look in his eyes—the type one sees in photographs of shell-shocked soldiers from the First World War.

The next day's *Montreal Gazette's* front page was adorned with a rather bland photo of Gilbert and Dryden shaking hands. On the front page of the next day's *Toronto Star* there was a small teaser photo in the top corner. It had been snapped at Boston's Logan Airport shortly after the Bruins' charter flight had touched down in the wee hours of Friday, May 11. It showed a distraught Terry O'Reilly—arguably Boston's toughest player—weeping on his wife's shoulder. It encapsulated the emotional enormity attached to this cruel defeat.

Within the *Star*'s sports section were huge photos of Wayne Cashman and Gilles Gilbert, each man displaying the same empty look of shock and abject sadness and disappointment.

"That was the most shots I've faced since I was a peewee,"[51] Gilbert admitted to reporters. He had been both brilliant and acrobatic. He had helped preserve, at least temporarily, the three leads the Bruins had held at various junctures during the memorable game. As Rosa noted, Gilbert was named first star of the game by *Hockey Night in Canada*. He got a huge ovation from the Forum crowd who clearly recognized a heroic effort when they saw one. It was a hollow consolation prize for Boston's goalie to be sure. Gilbert agreed. "It wasn't enough. We didn't win." Rosa agreed. "[It is] the same old bottom line,"[52] he sadly wrote.

"What else could he have done?" Montville commented about Gilbert. "What else? There were some saves that he made that were total inspiration, total reflex, totally out of his or anyone else's mind. What else could he do?"[53] Francis Rosa opined, "[Gilbert] stands as the single biggest reason why the Montreal-Boston semifinal series was memorable. He played goal for the last five games as no goalie has played against Montreal in many years."[54]

"They were terrific, these Bruins. They were absolutely terrific," Montville insisted. "How many times did they win this game? How many times did they lose it? How high, how close had they climbed, not just in this series but in three years of bit-by-bit work against the Canadiens to reach this final point, this final … disappointment."[55]

Then Montville hit the nail on the head—asking the one ripping question that was responsible for all the tears and anguish among the Bruins and their fans wherever they happened to be: "How hard would they have to work to get back here again? Could they ever get back here again?"[56]

The headline atop the sports section in the *Calgary Herald* blared, "Shattering Experience for Glass-Slipper Bruins." Lambert's goal had also shattered the hearts of Boston hockey fans too numerous to count. In a brief *Hockey Night in Canada* feature in 2012 celebrating the 60th anniversary of that iconic Canadian sports program, several "great moments" are shown accompanied by fans' reminiscences of them. After the Lafleur goal is shown, Canadian musician Gordon Downie, the lead singer for The Tragically Hip, stated his starkest hockey memory occurred at age 15. He vividly recalled waking up his little brother—who was too young to stay up on a school night in Newfoundland to watch the whole game—to tell him that their favorite team had lost yet again in the playoffs to the Montreal Canadiens, and the awful circumstances surrounding the defeat. "He wouldn't stop crying," Downie remembered. "He kept asking, 'Why, Gord? Why?'"[57]

A headline in the *Lewiston* (Maine) *Daily Sun* shouted, "Canadiens Escape Bruins in OT, Reach Finals." Yvon Lambert concurred with the idea that the Habs had been gifted the tying goal, but he spared little sympathy for the vanquished Bruins afterward. "They took a stupid penalty," he said. "I don't know what happened, but a team with their experience shouldn't be making a mistake like that in the playoffs."[58] Scotty Bowman had a little bit more compassion in his comments. "The Bruins are like us. We interchange lines a lot," he said. "We're vulnerable to [a bench penalty] like that. Seventy-five percent of the time it happens when one player thinks a teammate is coming off the ice."[59]

There were people within the Bruins' camp who blamed the officials. Cherry—the good ship's captain that he always aspired to be—took full responsibility for the fatal line change blunder, but he still thought Boston got the short end of the stick in the overall penalty department from Bob Myers. "I could sense something was going to happen with the officiating. It always does up here," he lamented. "They get away with murder. It's always that way. What were the power plays in the game … five for them and two for us?"[60] [Author's note: The actual ratio was 5:3.]

Cherry continued his beefs with Myers, "It started with that terrible call against Ratelle. I could sense then that we were going to get it."[61]

Boston general-manager Harry Sinden went a step further and opined, somewhat irrationally, that the too-many-men-on-the-ice infraction should have been overlooked by John D'Amico given the circumstances. "You just don't make that call in that situation," he fumed after the game. "If we had an extra man on the ice, he didn't interfere with the play—and if he didn't, the call shouldn't have been made. Never. Not in the final minutes of a seventh game."[62]

What was unquestionable is that the too-many-men penalty was—and still is—the single most infamous blunder in Boston sports history. Given the well-earned reputation that Boston's pro sports teams have for snatching defeat from the jaws of victory, that designation is significant. In recalling the game 35 years later, Michael Farber of *Sports Illustrated* upped the ante, calling the infraction "the most significant penalty in the history of major sports in North America."[63] Indeed, it is difficult to come up with more than a handful that could justifiably be mentioned in the same breath.

Certainly there had been cruel championship disappointments in the past in Boston—and more to come in the not-too-distant future. Seven months earlier the Red Sox had squandered an enormous July lead in the American League East and lost the division title to the hated New York Yankees on Bucky Dent's home run. That was a long and painful process, however; there was no single, distinct moment of collapse. The only comparable incident where one official's call dramatically affected a Boston sports team in such a negative way was referee Ben Dreith's dubious flag for roughing the passer against Ray (Sugar Bear) Hamilton on a third-and-18 play late in an AFC divisional playoff game—a contentious penalty that derailed the 1976 New England Patriots' drive to Super Bowl XI. Replays showed that Hamilton barely touched Oakland quarterback Ken Stabler. Stabler himself readily admitted the penalty was unwarranted. Dreith's ruling caused the Patriots to completely unravel. The Raiders parlayed their good fortune into a game-winning drive. That call, by any reasonable standard, was just plain bad; it was a costly official's blunder for which nobody on the Pats could be blamed. (The NFL deliberately did not schedule Dreith to work another Patriots game for 11 years. Even today, as a nonagenarian, Dreith still maintains his roughing-the-passer call four decades ago was correct.)

The Bruins, on the other hand, were clearly the architects of their own downfall at the Forum on May 10, 1979—just as Leigh Montville declared they were in his report for the *Boston Globe*. John D'Amico certainly got the call right. It was an inglorious and heartbreaking end to an otherwise heroic hockey season for the Boston Bruins. It was also a difficult reality for the team's passionate fans to accept. Not long after Game #7, a cartoon in the *Globe* showed an agitated Boston sports fan lying on a psychiatrist's couch muttering, "Roughing the passer! Bucky Dent! Too many men!"

Game #7

First Period
1. Boston—Middleton (Redmond, Cashman) 10:09 ppg;
2. Montreal—Lemaire (Savard, Lapointe) 14:19 ppg

Second Period
3. Boston—Cashman (Middleton, Ratelle) 0:27;
4. Boston—Cashman (Ratelle, Middleton) 16:12

Third Period
5. Montreal—Napier (Lafleur, Tremblay) 6:10;
6. Montreal—Lapointe (Lafleur, Gainey) 8:16 ppg;
7. Boston—Middleton (Ratelle, Sims) 16:01;
8. Montreal—Lafleur (Lemaire) 18:46 ppg

Overtime
9. Montreal—Lambert (Tremblay, Houle) 9:33

Shots on Goal
Boston: 10–5–12–3 = 30 (on Dryden)
Montreal 15–12–17–8 = 52 (on Gilbert)
Attendance at Montreal Forum: 17,453

18

The Immediate Aftermath

> "We had had Boston's number for a number of years. They played well. They
> outplayed us in many games that we won."
> —Montreal's Brian Engblom in a 2008 interview with the NHL Network

A clearly agitated and disappointed Don Cherry unabashedly spoke his mind in a media scrum in a corridor following his team's heartbreaking 5–4 loss in Game #7. Here is his colorful verbal exchange with a bevy of reporters:

CHERRY: When's it going to end? You could just see when it was 3–1…. One little mistake—just waiting when it was 3–1. When is it going to end?

REPORTER #1: I guess a fellow like Rick Middleton really wanted to play badly against the Rangers.

CHERRY: Well, yeah. [Cherry gives the reporter a quizzical look.]

REPORTER #1: If you'd have won you'd be playing the Rangers…

CHERRY: If my aunt had nuts she'd be my uncle! What kind of a question is that?

REPORTER #2: Don, you've seen a lot of games of hockey. How would you rate this one, the seventh game of a Stanley Cup series?

CHERRY: You guys will have to rate it. I'm too disappointed. I think it was a horseshit game that we lose like that. Geez, that was a tough one, I tell you. I don't think I'll have a much tougher loss than that—overtime, seventh game, going into the finals. Boy, what more can happen? What more can happen?

REPORTER #3: How about a prediction on the final?

CHERRY: It's like asking me what I want—syph or gonorrhea. What do I care?

The day after Game #7, Will McDonough of the *Globe* found a sullen Don Cherry at his home in North Andover, as expected. Cherry was futilely trying to digest and accept how close he and his Bruins had come to pulling off the great upset—only to lose it from their grasp so cruelly. Cherry, understandably, wanted to be far away from hockey—for a brief time, anyway. McDonough wrote,

Don Cherry stayed home [Friday], still trying to find a way to swallow Thursday's bitter overtime loss in Montreal.

"I don't see how I can be any more disappointed than I am right now," Cherry said. "I came home after the game and couldn't sleep. I just sat on the porch trying to think everything over."

Cherry continued, "The TV [networks] asked me to be an analyst for the finals, but I told them I couldn't do it. I just couldn't stand to watch the finals, thinking we should be playing. It would be too much for me."

Ernie Roberts of the *Globe* firmly believed that Don Cherry and his Bruins had no reason whatsoever to hang their heads after Game #7, saying they had fallen into the category of beaten but not disgraced. In the May 12 *Globe* he cheerfully wrote, "The incredible effort in Montreal Thursday night restored the Bruins to the popularity peak in New England they last enjoyed in the early '70s. It seems incomprehensible that Boston management can't sense this public affection for Don Cherry and won't take the necessary steps to retain him as coach. Lord help his successor, trying to equal Don's charisma and record..."

Other sports journalists were more pragmatic in their assessment of why the May 10 game was likely Cherry's last behind the Boston bench. Carl Fletcher of the *Cambridge* (Ontario) *Reporter* wrote,

> When the Boston Bruins expired Thursday in overtime, the man they call Grapes went with them—but hardly quietly.
>
> Don Cherry's five-year run as leader of the Lunch Pail Gang from Boston is over. They were less than two minutes from eliminating the Montreal Canadiens, but that didn't influence Cherry's future. He was unemployed—almost by his own choice—even if the Bruins had won.
>
> Cherry makes an estimated $45,000 [per season], wants $100,000, but the Bruins refuse to go beyond $80,000. So Cherry and a dog named Blue will move on to entertain us elsewhere.
>
> A verbal, explosive needler, Cherry deserves much of the credit for Boston's success in the last three years. Unfortunately they kept running into the Canadiens every May.

Terry O'Reilly was not the typically dominant player in the playoffs as he was in the regular season for the Bruins. Walter Frost of the *Globe* explained why in the May 25 edition: "Bruins' Terry O'Reilly will have surgery on Tuesday to remove bone chips from his left elbow. He injured the elbow in the Pittsburgh quarterfinal Stanley Cup series. During the Montreal semifinal, the elbow puffed to the size of a baseball."

Plaudits for the vanquished Bruins (and Cherry in particular) came from the Montreal beat writers too. In a May 11 *Montreal Gazette* piece, Al Strachan kindly wrote of Cherry's thoroughly professional postgame demeanor,

> A tired and obviously shaken Don Cherry still held his head high.
>
> Resplendent in a blue suede jacket and a light green vest and trousers, he climbed upon a chair a few minutes after his Bruins had gone down to a heartbreaking defeat. "I feel like crying, I really do. Not for me but for [the players]."
>
> "I'm as proud of my players as Scotty Bowman is of his."
>
> It's a shame to see it happen to an honest, hard-working guy like Cherry. He has done a tremendous job with his team and has received no thanks from his employers. And yet, here he was, moments after an excruciatingly painful loss, talking to reporters who don't make things any easier.
>
> Yet he did it with a lot of class.

Leigh Montville, in a May 13 *Globe* article, focused on the emotional impact that Game #7 had on Bruin fans with a series of rhetorical questions:

> Has there ever been a team that tried harder than the Bruins? Has there ever been a team that came closer? Has there ever been a more wonderful succession of teases than the ones the Bruins pulled off? How many games could they have won in this series? Six of the seven? How many times could they have won the last game?
>
> Think about it. Would there have been as much to talk about if the Bruins had won? Think about it.

Of course Game #7's high drama was worthy of a *Boston Globe* editorial. It was titled "Is the Almighty a Canadiens Fan?"

> For once, it does not seem even slightly trite to say that in defeat the Boston Bruins have gained great dignity and stature. They drove a truly great team, the Montreal Canadiens, right to the edge. In terms of spirit, the Bruins won. But they were denied the triumph of access to the Stanley Cup by a combination of events that, for the players, must have been crushing. For many of the rest of us, it was the realization of the inevitable—yet another Canadien victory...
>
> For all the players who fought so hard and came up with ashes we say: "Well done!"

Francis Rosa pleasantly discovered that Ken Dryden was genuinely sympathetic toward his beaten foes from Boston—especially fellow goaltender Gilles Gilbert. Rosa wrote in the May 12 *Globe*,

> He was the blind spot, Gilles Gilbert. He was … well … the malingerer? That was implicit in so many things coach Don Cherry said about the Bruins' goalie all season long.
>
> Today he stands as the single biggest reason the Montreal-Boston semifinal series was memorable. He played goal for the last five games as no goalie has played against Montreal in many years.
>
> "I feel sorry for him," said Ken Dryden. "That's the greatest goaltending the Bruins have had against us for three years, and I feel sorry for Jean Ratelle and Wayne Cashman and Terry O'Reilly who played such a great series."

By May 13 Rosa had dug deeply enough and found a something akin to a silver lining around the Bruins' lingering dark and gloomy cloud for their disappointed fans to consider. It probably did not make them feel any better about Game #7's outcome. Nevertheless, Rosa cheerfully noted that the formerly big, bad Boston Bruins had been suddenly transformed before the professional hockey world into sympathetic figures because of their valiant effort in defeat. He wrote,

> Isn't it beautiful? Boston, New England, and most of the hockey world (Montreal excepted) has turned the Bruins into some kind of heroes. In defeat? In defeat!
>
> Ever since David slew Goliath, the underdog has been everyman's kin. In the world of sport, David doesn't always win the battle but he wins everyone's hearts.

19

Who Even Remembers the 1979 Stanley Cup Final?

"In all deference to the New York Rangers, I think we had the Stanley Cup taken away from us Thursday night in Montreal. There is no doubt in my mind if we beat the Canadiens, no one could stop us from taking the Cup."
—Harry Sinden, quoted in the May 12 *Boston Globe*

Anticlimax: (noun) an event or conclusion that is far less important, powerful, or striking than expected.
—Dictionary.com

After two excellent semifinal series, the 1979 Stanley Cup finals were undoubtedly an anticlimax. The Habs-Bruins semifinal had been the real NHL championship series in everything but name. How often can something similar be said of a championship series in any of the major professional team sports? Yet, as soon as Yvon Lambert redirected Mario Tremblay's pass past Gilles Gilbert in Game #7, it was a foregone conclusion that the Montreal Canadiens would defeat the New York Rangers in the Cup final—and they did. So compelling was the Bruins-Habs semifinal series that many people who were alive and following hockey at the time misremember it as actually being the 1979 Stanley Cup final. Similarly, so steeped in NHL lore is the too-many-men blunder that scores of younger fans who do not remember the 1979 playoffs, or who were born after May 10, 1979, wrongly assume the Bruins and Habs met in the final—not the semis.

The Stanley Cup final was supposed to begin on Saturday, May 12, at the Montreal Forum. Thoroughly exhausted by their semifinal series with Boston, the Canadiens requested the opening game of the series be played a day later. Such was the clout the Habs had with the NHL, their wish was granted. (Don Cherry may have been right when he once cynically stated, "If it's good for the Montreal Canadiens, it's good for the NHL!") However, Sunday, May 13, presented a two-pronged dilemma: a broadcasting problem in Canada and a logistical problem at the Montreal Forum. A federal election campaign was in full swing—and on Sunday night CBC would be televising a candidate's debate. Further complicating matters was the Memorial Cup tournament to decide Canada's national junior hockey champions was taking place in Quebec. The Montreal Forum was supposed to host the final, which was scheduled for 2 p.m. on Sunday. The initial solution was to move the junior game to 11 a.m., play the Habs-Rangers opener at 4 o'clock in the afternoon—and let Pierre Trudeau, Joe Clark and Ed Broadbent have prime time to state their election platforms and argue with one another. The Memorial Cup organizers were displeased, to say the least, and simply moved the final on very short notice to Verdun, Quebec. (Even with those changes, CBC said—perhaps "warned" is a better word—that if the Montreal-New York game went into a long overtime, the network would cut away from *Hockey Night in Canada* precisely at 8 p.m. to televise the candidates' debate!) Times have certainly changed since 1979: It is difficult to imagine the NHL today moving the date of Game #1 of the Stanley Cup finals unless a major calamity was interfering with the teams' ability to play the contest as scheduled. Switching the venue for the prestigious Memorial Cup final on such short notice is equally unthinkable.

To many people's surprise, the Habs played listlessly and lost Game #1 to the Rangers 4–1 as the extra day of rest still had not completely rejuvenated Montreal from their mentally and physically exhausting seven-game semifinal versus Boston. Ken Dryden was yanked from the game and replaced by seldom-used backup goalie Michel (Bunny) Larocque with 10 minutes left in the third period—marking the first time Dryden had to endure such an indignity in the 108 playoff games he had started for the Habs. "We were a little bit flat," admitted Larry Robinson. "We weren't going as well as we should have as a whole."[1] Conversely, the Rangers played very well. One of their goals was a shorthanded tally by Dave Maloney. It was the sixth time in the 1979 playoffs the Rangers had scored a goal while killing a penalty—a new NHL record.

However, Montreal quickly found their typical excellent form in Game #2 and easily crushed the Rangers 6–2 two nights later to level the series. "Last night belonged to Ken Dryden,"[2] wrote Francis Rosa, who was covering the series for the *Boston Globe* despite the Bruins' absence from the championship festivities. It certainly did not start out that way. In fact, Dryden was supposed to be taking the night off. Between Game #1 and Game #2, Dryden had told the media he was considering broadening his hockey experiences by playing the 1979–80 season in the Soviet Union. Witty newspaper men cackled that Dryden—who had allowed 13 goals in the Habs' last three playoff games—was being forcibly exiled to Siberia.

Rattled and worried that Dryden's shaky performance in Game #1 would linger into the next contest, Scotty Bowman benched him for Game #2 and tabbed Larocque to be Montreal's starting goalie. It would have been Larocque's first playoff start since 1974. However, in a strange turn of events about 20 minutes before the opening faceoff, Larocque was injured in the Habs' pregame warm-up and Dryden took his place. Rosa described what occurred:

> Larocque was hit on the forehead with a 50-foot Doug Risebrough slapshot. It cracked his helmet. Larocque was sent to Montreal General Hospital where he was held overnight. Dryden took a few shots and was pressed into action.
> Dryden stood there. The Forum crowd booed him. His mind swirled. He fought back, mentally. The game hadn't even started.
> One minute into the game the New York Rangers had scored on their first shot at Dryden. The crowd booed.
> Before the night was over the crowd had stopped booing him and was cheering him and the Canadiens who had come back from a 2–0 deficit to win a 6–2 game and even the Stanley Cup finals at one game each.[3]

Dryden's strong performance in Game #2 was the turning point in the series. The next two games, played in New York City, were also Hab wins, by scores of 4–1 and 4–3.

If the 1979 Cup final is remembered at all, it was mostly for the extraordinarily odd conclusion of Game #4. Montreal had to score twice in overtime to win because their first "goal" in the extra period was not seen by either the goal judge Ken Elhart (who normally worked games at Chicago Stadium) or referee Andy van Hellemond. Judging by the buzz that went through the flabbergasted crowd at Madison Square Garden, they were perhaps the only two men in the entire building who did not think a game-winning Montreal goal had been scored.

Here is what happened: Larry Robinson unloaded a terrific slapshot from the Ranger blue line that sailed over goalie John Davidson's right shoulder. Television replays clearly show the puck going under the crossbar, bulging the taut twine at the top of the net, and then flying back out. The Habs were livid when the red light did not go on and van Hellemond—widely acknowledged as the NHL's best referee in the spring of 1979—did not signal a goal. Play continued for nearly a full minute before an offside stopped the action. "I saw the net move," Scotty Bowman calmly said afterward. "But if the goal judge doesn't switch on the light, the play continues."[4] Larry Robinson concurred. "You could see it went in cleanly," he told Glenn Cole of the *Montreal Gazette*. "It was human error."

"We won. That's the main thing," Robinson further declared. "When you have a close play like that, what usually happens is the other team comes back and scores. It's kind of frightening to think about a thing like that."

Montreal pled their case to van Hellemond after the whistle, but the use of video review to determine if a puck had entered the net was still many years away from being available as an officiating tool. Undaunted, just 25 seconds after play resumed, Montreal's Serge Savard scored a goal—one that actually counted—on a low backhand that Davidson clearly should have stopped. "I think Davidson was expecting me to pass the puck,"[5] Savard opined.

"Thanks, Serge," Robinson joked afterward. "That's the first 5–3 overtime game in Stanley Cup history."[6]

The Rangers were done. Everyone knew it. If they could not with either Game #3 or #4 at Madison Square Garden—especially with the enormous break they had gotten on the missed goal—what chance did they have going back to the Forum with Montreal just one win away from another inevitable Stanley Cup?

Now there was no doubt the hockey gods were shining on the Habs—and there was equally no doubt what would happen when the two teams returned to Montreal for Game #5 with the Canadiens holding a firm 3–1 series lead. Game #5 was more of a coronation than a contest. Montreal won easily, 4–1, to capture their fourth Stanley Cup in succession and their 22nd in a team history so long that it predates the NHL. Prime minister Pierre Trudeau, who was not much of a sports fan and would soon be ousted from office, was on hand. Against the laws of probability, he even snagged a wayward puck that flew into the crowd. It seemed all so predestined and inevitable.

The unexpected loss in Game #1 actually made the Cup win more satisfying for Habs fans as the trophy was won at the Forum for the first time since 1968. The six Stanley Cups the Canadiens had won between 1968 and 1979 had all been clinched on the road. By way of comparison, in 1979 Boston had won a total of five Stanley Cups in their 55-year history. The New York Rangers had won just three in 53 years of trying. Neither of those two teams was particularly choosy about where they won their Stanley Cups.

Francis Rosa summarized in the next day's *Globe*, "This was the Stanley Cup the New York Islanders thought they were going to win. This is the Stanley Cup the Boston Bruins should have won. This is the Stanley Cup New York Rangers thought they were destined to win. This is the Stanley Cup the Montreal Canadiens won."[7]

The Cup presentation also concluded the last NHL games ever played by Ken Dryden and Jacques Lemaire. Dryden was only 31 years old. To no one's great surprise, injured captain Yvan Cournoyer also retired shortly thereafter. This was his tenth Stanley Cup, equaling Jean Béliveau's total. Henri Richard, the Rocket's kid brother, has a record 11 Cup wins as a player.

It was Scotty Bowman's last game as coach of the Montreal Canadiens too. He became disgruntled when he was not offered the job as the team's general-manager when Sam Pollock retired in 1978. Bowman left the Habs with five Stanley Cups on his résumé. His 419 wins with Montreal ranks him second, behind only Toe Blake who coached the Habs to eight Stanley Cups in 13 seasons.

Bowman accepted an offer to be both coach and general-manager of the Buffalo Sabres. (According to Don Cherry's autobiography, Bowman asked him to come to Buffalo as his assistant with the understanding that he'd take over the role as Sabres head coach after one year. Cherry declined.) It was a dual position Bowman would hold until being relieved of his duties 12 games into the 1986–87 season. He was hardly through with hockey, though. Stops in Pittsburgh and Detroit as upper management would garner Bowman four more Stanley Cups in the 1990s before he finally retired.

Bowman's relationship with his Montreal players was the polar opposite of Don Cherry's with his Bruins: Bowman was largely unpopular with his Habs. Years later Steve Shutt famously said of Bowman, "You hated him 364 days of the year—and on the 365th you got your Stanley Cup ring."[8] Popularity among Bowman's underlings mattered little, however. In a 1998 article, *Sports Illustrated* declared Bowman to be the best coach ever in any of North America's four major professional sports—ranking him ahead of Casey Stengel, Vince Lombardi, Red Auerbach, and others. *SI* noted that no other coach had been as successful with as many teams or as many generations of athletes. Bowman's ability to adapt to both the conditions of a particular game and to changing times was remarkable given his demanding, authoritarian nature. "He started coaching guys who had summer jobs and crew cuts, and now he's coaching guys with Ferraris, earrings, blond streaks and agents,"[9] commented Brendan Shanahan, who played won three Stanley Cups with Bowman in Detroit.

Years later when Bowman and Cherry were at a function together, the old rivals engaged in some good-natured small talk. Bowman could not help but playfully needle Cherry about the disparity in Stanley Cups each man had won behind the bench. "If I have another son, I'll name him Stanley," declared Bowman. Cherry thought about Bowman's statement for a moment and replied, "Well, when I have my baby boy, I'm gonna name him Finals."[10]

The end of the 1978–79 season marked the end of an NHL era. The professional hockey landscape was changing. Four WHA teams—the Winnipeg Jets, Quebec Nordiques, Edmonton Oilers and New England Whalers—would be absorbed into the NHL. (New England's team, at the insistence of the Boston Bruins, was forced to change its name to the Hartford Whalers.) With 21 teams in the NHL in 1979–80 and more to come, meaningful battles between Original Six rivals in both the regular season and the playoffs would become rarer. (There has only been one Original Six matchup in the Stanley Cup final since 1979: Boston versus Chicago in 2013.) With the passage of time, the Bruins-Habs playoff encounters from the 1970s would justifiably become the stuff of fond nostalgia for hockey buffs.

20

The End of the
Don Cherry Era in Boston

"The basic idea is that a coach who does his job and then some, who produces a winner, controls his players, fills the seats and captivates the media, is doomed to go because he's become more important than upper management, which hired him to do just that in the first place."
—Tim Horgan of the *Boston Herald* trying to make sense of the Bruins' management's decision to part ways with Don Cherry

"I loved the guys. They loved me. Hey, nothing goes on forever."
—Don Cherry

With Boston's elimination in the 1979 Stanley playoffs official, it was only a matter of time before the tenuous relationship between Cherry and his employers would be resolved one way or the other. Few people expected Cherry to return. A column by Will McDonough in the May 18 *Boston Globe* was titled "This Town's Not Big Enough for Cherry, Sinden." Both parties—who were supposed to be observing a "cooling off period"—were now upset that the other was misrepresenting Cherry's earnings and taking pot shots at each other via the willing and insatiable Boston media. Cherry claimed his playoff money should not count as part of his salary because it was paid to him by the NHL rather than the Bruins. Harry Sinden retorted, "He wouldn't get playoff money if he were coaching Colorado this year, would he?"[1] McDonough's article accurately summed up the impasse: "There's no question the two men can't work together again. One or the other has to go, but they both like it here."[2]

As late as May 21 there was still a faint hope that Don Cherry would return as the coach of the Boston Bruins for the 1979–80 season. That Monday evening Cherry and Harry Sinden met at a Chinese restaurant in Woburn, MA to at least try to resolve their personal differences. The eatery was not exactly the twosome's first choice to hold such an important summit; it was actually the fourth. Cherry and Sinden were supposed to meet at a quiet coffee shop at a Holiday Inn at 9 p.m. only to discover that the hotel was hosting a disco-dancing contest that night. The clamor from the ballroom made any sort of quiet discussion impossible. They tried two other nearby gathering spots only to find the first one was filled to capacity and the second was closed. A nearly empty Chinese restaurant was selected almost by default, but it seemed to be an ideal setting. Cherry and Sinden moved to a distant corner for even greater privacy. Anonymity was not achieved, however. Their waiter quickly recognized the famous coach of the Boston Bruins and excitedly yelled out his name.

Cherry and Sinden were both diplomatic about what occurred during their meeting. "Even if I don't come back, I'd feel much better about leaving after getting together with Harry,"[3] he said. "We're friends again and it feels good. We had a nice meeting." Sinden concurred. "We thought it would be good to get together and square things away between ourselves. I think that was accomplished. I think both of us are relieved to be back on a friendly basis again."[4]

Earlier that Sunday both men had joined Bruins president Paul A. Mooney for a more serious discussion about Cherry's future. It was held at Boston's Algonquin Club. The pow-wow lasted two hours and everyone's grievances were aired. "I would call it a meeting where some progress was achieved, but the situation was not resolved."[5] Mooney coolly told Will McDonough of the *Boston Globe*. Another final meeting was scheduled for midweek.

Cherry's contract with the Bruins would expire on June 1, 1979. Despite widespread calls in the Boston media for cooler heads to prevail, there was zero chance that Cherry and the Bruins' management were going to bury the hatchet. "I've got a hunch," wrote Joe Fitzgerald in the *Boston Herald*, "that Harry's mind was made up the first time Cherry told a joke and got a laugh. From the moment Cherry walked on to center stage at the Garden, Sinden became a forgotten man, and his resentment has been festering for a long, long time."[6] Cherry expressed similar feelings in his autobiography. He wrote, "I loved the members of the media, and the feeling, judging by the attention I was getting, was mutual. The more press I got, the angrier Harry got."[7]

Cherry's leaving Boston has often wrongly been described as a firing. In his autobiography, Cherry insisted he voluntarily walked away from the Bruins after refusing the team's final offer on Thursday, May 24. That made it irrevocably official: The most consistently successful coach in Bruins history—a man who trailed only Art Ross and Milt Schmidt in regular-season coaching wins for Boston—was allowed to walk out the door and sign with the highest bidder. Will McDonough sadly wrote, "Thus, Don Cherry, perhaps the most popular Bruins coach ever, and a man who had won four straight divisional titles, ended the romance he had with this city."[8]

The *Boston Globe* reported that once Cherry's departure was finalized, the sports department received several telephone calls from upset Bruins fans—but nowhere near the volume that were anticipated. "Maybe it's because the rumors of Don Cherry leaving dragged on for so long, but the reaction of hockey fans has not materialized into an emotional frenzy," suggested Neil Singelais. "The majority of those who did call were solidly behind Cherry. It was obvious that Cherry, who always made himself available to the press and to sports talk shows, had proved to be his own best public-relations man."[9]

Although the newspaper was not deluged with phone calls, there were still numerous Cherry fans and allies who willingly expressed their displeasure at the developments via the *Globe*. Singelais dutifully reported a handful of their comments:

- Kevin Vahey of Cambridge, Massachusetts, a Bruin season-ticket holder for eight years, was one of those harboring nasty thoughts about the Bruins' organization. "Those bums are idiots," he shouted in frustration.
- Mary Glynn of Norwood, Massachusetts, said her only regret was the Bruins "didn't give Harry Sinden his release."
- Danny Venture of Brighton, Massachusetts, felt that "Cherry had to look out for himself."
- Nicky Sontoro, a high school student from East Boston, defended Cherry as "a good coach. He's one of the best things that has ever hit Boston."[10]

Shortly thereafter Cherry hired an agent to represent him in contract negotiations with any NHL team that inquired about his services. It was Alan Eagleson, the president of the NHL Players Association. He was best known in Boston as the lawyer who had represented Bobby Orr. "I've never had an agent before, but I've got one now," said Cherry. "I told him what I'd like to have. I'm going to let him do my talking."[11] Eagleson, told the *Globe*, "I think if the players can make an average of $100,000 per year, an outstanding coach like Don Cherry should be worth more than that."[12]

Cherry got a substantial raise—reputedly $150,000 per season for five years plus performance bonuses—when he took over the woeful Colorado Rockies shortly thereafter. (Cherry later claimed the amount was actually "$125,000 per season for a multi-year period" plus incentives.) The Toronto Maple Leafs, Buffalo Sabres, Atlanta Flames, and the newly admitted Hartford Whalers had all shown interest in acquiring Cherry's services, but the Rockies' offer was the most attractive but not necessarily the most lucrative. "My first reaction was to go to Buffalo, get into Boston's division, and win," Cherry told Terry Frei of the *Globe*. "But I've got a feeling for Denver. I just seem to like the players here. This team didn't quit. For some reason they would play the Bruins better in Boston Garden than at home. They beat us the last game in Boston [4–2 on February 27]. You'd have thought they won the Stanley Cup."[13] Cherry also said he liked the city of Denver, its surrounding area, and the challenge of attempting to turn around a bottom-rung team that went 15–53–12 in 1978–79 under two different coaches, Pat Kelly and Aldo Guidolin. (Aldo was the cousin of Bep Guidolin, whom Cherry succeeded in Boston.)

Cherry's contract was personally guaranteed by Rockies owner Arthur Imperatore even if the team, which was on shaky financial footing, happened to fold. It was a legitimate concern. The Rockies were formerly the Kansas City Scouts. They had entered the NHL as an expansion franchise in 1974–75 along with the Washington Capitals. After two dismal and financially disastrous seasons in Missouri, the team was hastily shifted to Denver where their fortunes did not improve all that much. In 1978–79 the Rockies were last in the league in both points and attendance. The average home crowd was about 6,000. (How bad was Colorado's home attendance? On February 20, the Bruins defeated the Rockies 5–3 in Denver before a meager crowd of 5,748. According to John Ahern of the *Globe*, that was the smallest crowd to see the Bruins play an NHL game since they moved from tiny Boston Arena to Boston Garden in 1928.) Imperatore was a New Jersey trucking magnate who had already sought the league's permission to move the team to the Meadowlands, but his request was denied.

After signing his deal with the Rockies, Cherry returned to Boston on May 31 to prepare to uproot his family one more time. Even as an ex-Bruins coach, Cherry was still newsworthy in Boston. His friends in the media were already missing him. (Ray Fitzgerald wondered in one of his columns if Cherry would teach Blue how to ski in Colorado.) Cherry ended up holding an impromptu press conference at Logan Airport. News of Cherry's hiring had an immediate impact on ticket sales in Denver. "They sold 2,000 season tickets and six boxes while I was out there," Cherry happily told Steve Marantz of the *Globe*. "One guy called up [to order tickets] and they told him to call back tomorrow. They were too busy."[14] Cherry told the media he had already begun shopping for western attire to augment his famous wardrobe. He also handed out stickers bearing the Rockies' logo to anyone who approached him in the terminal.

When it became a certainty the Cherry era in Boston was definitely over, several Bruin players descended upon their ex-coach's home in North Andover for an impromptu farewell gathering. It was as if there had been a death in the family. Neighbors began to bring containers of food to the Cherry home. (One reporter saw Blue stick her nose into a platter of fried clams!) Brad Park—who wasn't speaking to his coach early in the season—assumed the task of answering the numerous telephone calls from well-wishers. Bobby Schmautz sadly told a reporter, "The Bruins have made a big mistake. Not only have I lost my coach, I've also lost my best friend."[15] Some months later Schmautz fondly recalled, "We had 11 20-goal scorers one year. We weren't a team of stars. We were a team of hard-working guys, guys who worked together. [Cherry] made better hockey players out of all of us."[16]

Mike Milbury concurred with the overwhelming sadness of the occasion. "Oh boy," he told Francis Rosa. "It's not the loss of a coach but a team member. Why am I talking as if he's dead?" Milbury continued, "It's going to set us back. I don't feel happy about it. He was great to me personally. He's the man responsible for giving me every opportunity to play for the Bruins. If it wasn't for Don, I wouldn't have had the chance to prove myself. He saw something in me that maybe others didn't or wouldn't see. [It's] the same with Stan Jonathan, John Wensink and Rick Middleton. It's going to be rough."[17] Terry O'Reilly shared similar sentiments. "[Cherry] brought out the team factor more than any coach I've known," he said. "He didn't dwell on fundamentals. Each individual was only part of the team. As a result, we were the most team-oriented club in hockey."[18]

Francis Rosa summarized, "Boston had to lose a personality, a dynastic and successful man. It was Cherry. He loved having his Bruins called 'The Lunch Pail Gang.' What Cherry did was make the Bruins believe in him and themselves. And every workingman related to him and them. The Bruins will replace Cherry's job, not the man."[19]

In a May 25 Globe article titled, "He Stuck to his Guns," Will McDonough attempted to define Cherry in terms f famous military leaders:

> At the beginning of the series with the Montreal Canadiens, Don Cherry, a devotee of military history, decided to launch into a book about General Erwin Rommel.
>
> Two quick losses in the Forum and Rommel, the brilliant German general of World War II, went back on the shelf. Out came on Lord Nelson, the distinguished British naval commander who thrived on battles and controversy.
>
> "I am a lot like Nelson," said Cherry. "He was his own man, and the most important people to him were the sailors who worked and battled for him. He called them his 'band of brothers.' That's what I call my players. We're a band of brothers."

Cartoonist Paul Szep of the *Boston Globe* captured the sentiment of most Bruin fans perfectly: He drew a forlorn-looking Blue wearing a Bruins cap with his nose pitifully pointing downward. The caption beneath it said, "Cheer up, Blue, your old man did super."[20]

In an amusing May 31 *Globe* article, Leigh Montville pointed out that both Cherry and Chuck Fairbanks, the former New England Patriots coach, were practically neighbors. Fairbanks was now quite content to have left the Hub to become the head football coach of the University of Colorado. Montville suggested that Fairbanks and Cherry could hold a reunion of successful coaches who had been forced out of Boston.

Cherry's replacement was 49-year-old Fred Creighton, who was signed by the Bruins in early July to a three-year contract. His hiring put an end to the numerous rumors that were circulating in Boston sports circles about who the team's new coach might be. (The names of Roger Neilson, Scotty Bowman, Harry Sinden, and even ex-Bruins Phil Esposito and Ed Johnston were bandied about for a time.) Frequently described in the media as a "teaching coach," Creighton had solid NHL experience, having recently been dismissed after four moderately successful years with the Atlanta Flames. He was just the second coach in Flames history, having replaced Bernie Geoffrion in 1975. Under Creighton the Flames had risen from a hapless expansion team to one that at least made the Stanley Cup playoffs—but also one that never advanced past the first round. Atlanta's upset loss to Toronto in the preliminary round of the playoffs in two straight games sealed Creighton's doom in Dixie.

Before Creighton was officially hired by the Bruins, he told Fran Rosa via a telephone interview from his home, "I'm very much interested in coaching Boston. I like the intensity with which the Bruins played. There's no doubt that Don Cherry did a great job with them. He's a tough act to follow. I like the atmosphere in Boston. It's sort of a happy medium between Atlanta and Montreal. You're in the limelight and there's great interest, but it doesn't engulf you the way it does in Montreal."[21]

Replacing Cherry was indeed going to be an unenviable task for Creighton. In the July 2 edition of the *Boston Globe*, Ray Fitzgerald penned a hilarious column titled, "Some Friendly Advice on How to Coach the Bruins" in which he offered the new coach some foolproof pointers on how to prosper in Boston. In the preamble, Fitzgerald stated, "The players liked Cherry because he was one of them, which is precisely why he isn't around Causeway Street anymore. There was player criticism when he was dumped, so the new coach won't exactly be coming into a warm and enthusiastic dressing room."[22]

Fitzgerald introduced his list by stating the obvious: "The team has an age problem, a goalie problem and a defensive problem. But Creighton's biggest problem will simply be succeeding Don Cherry." Fitzgerald then proffered numerous helpful hints.

- Buy a dog.
- Place the dog's photo in a prominent spot on your desk.
- On dull news days, quote the dog.
- Remind everyone about once a week that referees have three sets of rules—a rigid one for the Bruins, a relaxed one for Les Canadiens, and a normal one for all the other teams.
- Appear on talk shows a lot.
- Give your phone number to any newsman who asks for it.
- Bench players who stray from their assigned roles.
- Tell the media this is a workingman's team, not a group of individual stars.
- Throw a fit when none of your working men make the All-Star team.
- Practise in the mirror until you've perfected "exasperated look" to be used whenever a Bruin gets a borderline penalty.
- Make thinly veiled references to front-office stupidity.
- Be available always to media, pull no punches, and avoid clichés used by 99 percent of coaches in all sports.
- Get a charge out of life.[23]

The season began well for the new man behind the Bruins' bench. On Opening Night at Boston Garden on October 11, 1979, the new-look Bruins easily beat the Winnipeg Jets—one of the four WHA teams absorbed by the NHL—by a 4–0 score. Gilles Gilbert recorded his first shutout in two years. Bob Miller scored after just 40 seconds. Much-heralded rookie defenseman Raymond Bourque got the fourth Bruin goal. (That same night Don Cherry made his coaching debut in Denver. His Colorado Rockies sloppily squandered a 3–0 third-period lead and had to settle for a 3–3 tie with St. Louis.)

Yet Creighton did not last one season as Boston's coach. Following an ugly 7–3 loss in Minnesota on March 19, after 73 games he was suddenly dismissed by general-manager Harry Sinden in a move that took the hockey world completely by surprise. Although the Bruins were in a minor slump in March (having compiled a 1–2–4 record in their past seven games), they still had a very acceptable 40–20–13 record, fourth-best in the 21-team NHL. (In Cherry's final season in Boston, after 73 games the Bruins had an almost identical record: 40–21–12.) Sinden explained the difficult decision to fire Creighton, made in conjunction with assistant general-manager Tom Johnson and club president Paul A. Mooney, to the *Boston Globe*:

> It was murder. We felt, after some deliberation over the last two weeks, that the team was not responding in areas in which we have been traditionally strong. These are areas that can be directly attributed to an attitude or an emotional approach to the game. We felt my making the move now we can get back to that approach.
>
> Creighton is a man we liked and respected. We have been aware of this situation for a couple of months. Ignoring the problem would not solve it. It wasn't going to go away.[24]

The bottom line was this: Creighton had not connected with the Bruin players. He did not pick up where Cherry had left off. Creighton's coaching style and persona were dramatically different than his flamboyant predecessor's. Creighton was deemed to have been a bad fit in Boston—and he probably was, despite the Bruins being 20 games over .500 in the 73 games he coached.

Sinden himself replaced Creighton as interim coach and led the Bruins to six wins in their final seven games—the only loss coming at the hands of the Montreal Canadiens at the Forum. It was Sinden's first NHL coaching job since he led the Bruins to the Stanley Cup in 1970.

Boston ended the season with 105 points—five more than they had posted in Don Cherry's last season—but the Bruins failed to top the Adams Division for the first time since 1975, finishing five points behind a very solid Buffalo Sabres team—a team coached by Scotty Bowman. (Regular season championships were now trivial. With the NHL playoffs expanded to include 16 of the league's 21 teams, finishing first no longer was rewarded with a bye.) Boston, seeded fourth, barely squeaked past the 13th-seeded Pittsburgh Penguins in the expanded best-of-five opening round of the Stanley Cup playoffs, taking the full five games to oust the improved Pens. They then lost to the New York Islanders—the NHL's emerging powerhouse—in the quarterfinals in five games. Three of them required overtime. Despite finishing the regular season 14 points in arrears of Boston, the fifth-seeded Islanders went on to win their first of four straight Stanley Cups in 1980—ousting the top two seeds (Buffalo and Philadelphia) in the semis and final respectively. Thus, in each of the four seasons from 1976–77 through 1979–80, Boston was defeated in the playoffs by the eventual Stanley Cup champion.

Montreal also surprisingly changed coaches before the 1979–80 season concluded—even faster than Boston did. Bernie (Boom Boom) Geoffrion, who had the unenviable task of replacing Scotty Bowman, did not even make it to New Year's Day. He stepped down after just 30 games. The Canadiens had a 15–9–6 record. Officially it was due to a recurring stomach ailment, which was partially true. (Geoffrion's first NHL coaching gig, with the New York Rangers in 1968, ended similarly when he developed ulcers.) In reality, the old-school Geoffrion, a Hab star from their glory days of the 1950s and 1960s, could not relate to modern players. Geoffrion resigned after an intense six-hour meeting with Irving Grundman following a 4–1 loss to the New York Islanders on December 11. He was shocked by the lackadaisical attitude of many Habs who openly defied curfews and accepted defeat too easily. "I'm sick and tired of them," Geoffrion angrily told the *Montreal Gazette*. "They're not acting like professional athletes. Why should I get sick over a bunch of guys who won't listen to me? I had a dream to coach this team. The dream is a nightmare now."[25]

Montreal summoned former coach Claude Ruel to replace Geoffrion. Ruel had guided the Habs to their first post-expansion Cup in 1968. He lost his first four games, but led Montreal to a 32–11–7 record in the Canadiens' remaining 50 contests of 1979–80, but the Habs' pursuit of a fifth straight Stanley Cup came up well short. Like the Bruins, the third-seeded Canadiens were upended in a quarterfinal, outplayed by the surprising Minnesota North Stars. Minnesota won three games at the Forum—including Game #7—an astonishing feat. The Montreal dynasty was suddenly over. Since 1980 the New York Islanders, Edmonton, Pittsburgh and Detroit have all produced NHL dynasties, or something close to them, but Montreal has not. Since their 1979 triumph, the once-mighty Canadiens have won just two Stanley Cups (in 1986 and 1993)—only one more than Boston has.

Gerry Cheevers hung up his goaltender's equipment following the 1979–80 season and took over as Bruins coach in 1980–81. He held the position for nearly as long as Don Cherry had. He was dismissed with 24 games to go in the 1984–85 season. As in 1980, Harry Sinden took over the Bruins' coaching duties for the remainder of the regular season and the 1985 playoffs.

A few days after being fired, Creighton told John Ahern of the *Globe* from his home in Marietta, GA that his termination had absolutely stupefied him. "I never gave [the possibility of dismissal] a thought. I had no reason to give it a thought. Even when Harry called me I had no idea what he had in mind. It was a shock. I'm still in shock."[26]

A year later Sinden said, "Firing Fred was the hardest thing I ever had to do. But there was a stirring on the team. Fred may have been right, that he never really became one of them. He's reserved. His philosophy is applying strategy. He was never hell for leather."[27]

Brad Park, who did not play his first game of the 1979–80 season until late January because of his recurring knee issues, said in his 2012 autobiography that Creighton's personality worked against him. "Fred was much quieter than Grapes was," he wrote, "and he was having trouble understanding the chemistry of the team he inherited."[28]

John Ahern had his own theory as to why the ax suddenly fell on Creighton: "What it came down to was the job Creighton had to fill. He had to follow Don Cherry, a controversial figure who had the love and respect of the players. Creighton is a low-key type, a different man entirely from Cherry. He was respected as a hockey man, but he was not close to the team. He wasn't one of the guys. That's not his style."[29]

So how did Don Cherry react to the surprising news from Boston? Bob Duffy of the *Globe* put it this way:

> The situation provided the perfect forum for Cherry's eloquent bluster. Hadn't his old nemesis, Sinden, panicked? Hadn't his replacement, Creighton, proved inadequate? But the man who rode out of Boston Garden in a blaze of acrimony last May 24 refused to indulge the impulse to claim vindication.
>
> "It would be a great story, wouldn't it?" he said from Denver. "I could come out and blast 'em. I've got nothing to lose. But I have no intention of gloating. My only reaction is one of sadness.
>
> "I'm sorry for Fred. I knew him pretty good [sic]. He's a good coach. From what I'd heard around the league, [the Bruins] weren't playing with the same intensity, but they've still got a lot of points."

Cherry did indulge in a tiny bit of self-aggrandizement. He noted, "I knew anyone coming in [after me] would have a tough time. It was a unique situation. Those guys all loved one another, and I loved all those guys. It's tough for someone else to step into a situation like that."

Cherry also defended and complimented Sinden's judgment in handling Boston's personnel matters. "I know Harry," he said. "When he thinks something's wrong, he moves. He doesn't hesitate. He goes ahead and does what he feels he has to. The man's got guts."

Despite coaching in a different NHL city, Cherry still expressed a strong kinship with his former team. "I'm sad because my boys are in trouble," he said. "I just hope they can work it out."[30]

Creighton's 73 games as the Bruins' bench boss was his last NHL coaching gig. He became disillusioned with hockey and took a job as a men's clothing salesman. "My whole hockey career had been an upward graph," Creighton said in a 1981 *New York Times* interview after he had returned to hockey as the coach and general-manager of the minor-league Indianapolis Checkers. "Then I lost two jobs in the space of a year. I was shook up [sic]. You wonder what's happening to you. I knew exactly why I lost the job in Atlanta—the [team's failure in the] playoffs. In Boston the players didn't know where I stood. Was I a Bruin or not? I told the players, 'This doesn't come overnight."[31] Creighton operated a pizza franchise after leaving pro hockey. He died on September 28, 2011, at the age of 81, from complications related to Alzheimer's disease. Seemingly forgotten in the Hub, there was no mention of his passing in the *Globe*.

Cherry also had a short stint in Colorado, lasting just one season because he ran afoul of team management there too because of his maverick ways and a nasty feud with Rockies general-manager Ray Miron. In announcing Cherry's dismissal, Rockies president Armand Pohan said, "As a teacher of younger players, Don's approach has failed to produce results."[32] Cherry scoffed at Pohan's statement. "I'm happy I wasn't around for the crucifixion," he sarcastically noted, "because I would have been blamed for that."[33]

Similar to what had happened in Boston a year earlier, hockey fans in Colorado were overwhelmingly behind Cherry. A poll conducted by the *Rocky Mountain News* showed an overwhelming majority of respondents (3,025 out of 3,083) wanted Cherry to stay as the Rockies' coach. The numbers reflected two unscientific call-in polls that a local television station in Denver ran. Cherry told Leigh Montville of the *Globe*, "The first poll—Should Don Cherry Be Fired, Yes or No?—the results were something like 89–5 in my favor. The next poll was 93–1." Cherry joked, "I'll get that guy! I got those other four; I'll get this last one too."[34] Public opinion did not matter, though. A headline in the May 21, 1980, *Boston Globe* read "Same Old Tune: Fans Love Cherry, Bosses Don't." Cherry also told Montville that the 1980 Stanley Cup finals featuring the New York Islanders and Philadelphia Flyers was dull because it was missing the Habs and him. Montville relished reconnecting with the outspoken, colorful ex-coach of the Bruins. He wrote of Cherry's squabbles with the Rockies' management, "In the day-to-day, year-to-year, turbulent existence of this man, this is just a normal occurrence. He is always going to be fighting with somebody about something, isn't he? He is a man of passion and ego. He is a man who wants to do it his way. The spotlight is his. The show is his, must be his, no matter who put up the money. He is Billy Martin. He is Earl Weaver. He is George Allen. He is Bobby Knight. He is … Don Cherry."[35]

One of Cherry's few highlights as Colorado's coach occurred on Sunday, December 2, 1979. That night Cherry's Rockies were visiting Boston Garden for the first time—and won in an upset, 5–3. In the days leading up to the Colorado-Boston game, Cherry told the Boston media that he was very much looking forward to seeing his old supporters again. "It'll be nice to see all the fans there," he stated. "I used to shake a million hands [in the Garden corridors]. Toward the end it was almost like I knew everybody."[36]

Cherry, of course, made the most of his return to his old stomping grounds. Clad in a shimmering, three-piece red velvet suit, Cherry deliberately took a roundabout route to the visitors' bench so he could emerge dramatically from under the stands. When Cherry appeared, the crowd, predictably, went wild. According to an editorial in the next day's

Globe—yes, Cherry's return to the Hub merited a *Boston Globe* editorial—Cherry "looked like Santa Claus after a touch-up by Fredericks of Hollywood."[37]

Boston led the Rockies 2–0 after the first period, but Colorado rallied, inspired the battle cry of some veteran players to "win this one for Grapes." With 53 seconds left to play, with the Rockies holding a 4–2 lead and the Bruins mounting serious pressure, Cherry smartly called a timeout to rest his beleaguered defense corps. During the lull in the action, a young fan leaned into the visitors' bench and asked Cherry for an autograph. Cherry, of course, obliged. Then dozens of fans asked for autographs. Cherry did his best to oblige them too. Someone threw a bunch of plastic grapes on the Garden ice as a tribute to the Bruins ex-coach. Cherry displayed the discarded faux fruit high above his head for all to see. The crowd went nuts.

Francis Rosa, who had reveled in covering Cherry's Bruins for the *Globe* and savored his return to Boston, declared the goings-on during the timeout to be outrageous. The story inaccurately circulated around the NHL that Cherry had called the timeout for the sole purpose of signing autographs. ("I wish I *had* thought of that," Cherry has said several times. "It would have been a great idea.") In the home team's dressing room, the defeated Creighton wryly commented, "I hope my homecoming to Atlanta will be just as sweet."[38] The Rockies' players presented Cherry with the game puck as a souvenir. In Colorado's four games versus Boston in 1979–80, Cherry's troops played above their heads. They managed a win, a tie, and two losses.

The 1979–80 Rockies managed one win against three losses versus Montreal—but the lone victory was a 7–5 triumph at the Montreal Forum exactly a week after Cherry's ballyhooed return to Boston. (It was Bernie Geoffrion's next-to-last game as the Habs' coach.) Colorado scored five goals in the third period to gain the win. Interestingly, Cherry's return to the Forum for the first time since the too-many-men debacle merited no special mention in the *Montreal Gazette*. The *Boston Globe* did not think it was particularly newsworthy, either. It only printed the game's box score with no accompanying story. Cherry must have wondered why that rare win at the Forum could not have happened seven months earlier. Cherry—who has one of the highest winning percentages in NHL history—compiled an absolutely dismal career coaching record in games versus the Habs at the Forum: two wins, 20 losses, and one tie.

Despite the occasional bright spots for Cherry that season in games in Boston and Montreal, the lowly Rockies lost 48 games in 1979–80—seven more regular-season losses than Cherry's Bruins absorbed in the final *two* seasons he coached in Boston. Finishing with the worst record in the NHL, Colorado failed to qualify for the postseason, of course. Shortly thereafter Cherry was hired by *Hockey Night in Canada* to provide analysis during the 1980 Stanley Cup playoffs. The following year *HNIC* put the unemployed Cherry in the broadcasting booth as a full-time analyst, but his bias toward both the Boston Bruins and, oddly, the Toronto Maple Leafs was just too blatant. Not knowing quite what to do with the engaging and colorful Cherry, *HNIC* created something called "Coach's Corner" as an intermission feature. Originally Cherry used the prerecorded spots to give hockey tips to youngsters, using NHL game video as a teaching tool. Soon, however, the segment broadened to a live open forum where Cherry happily expressed his off-the-cuff opinions on everything hockey—and beyond. It quickly became must-see TV in Canada. In 2017, it still is.

21

Who Was to Blame?

"Don Cherry is still a legend at the Forum. It's 11 p.m., coach—do you know where Stan Jonathan is?"

—Leigh Montville, in a *Boston Globe* piece prior to the 1990 Montreal-Boston playoff series, reflecting on various Bruin postseason disappointments and catastrophes versus the Habs

"Six men on the ice. Sixty men on the ice. How many men on the ice? The story has become legend, the number swollen in less than a decade. Who was the extra man on the ice? Terry O'Reilly? Mike Milbury? Stan Jonathan? Don Marcotte? All of the above? Any of the above? Who loses a game, a series, because of too many men on the ice?"

—Leigh Montville, in his April 25, 1988, *Sports Illustrated* article title "No Gain, Just Pain"

By definition, when a hockey team is penalized for too many men on the ice, it is a minor "bench" penalty. In 1979 it was NHL Rule 18; today it is rule 74. It is a team transgression; no individual player is specifically held accountable. Anyone can serve the two-minute penalty. On May 10, 1979, the Boston Bruins became the hockey team most famously guilty of this violation. Never before or since has a bench penalty so greatly contributed to the outcome of which team would win the Stanley Cup. Perhaps it never will again. (Proving that history—no matter how bizarre—does repeat itself, another too-many-men penalty derailed Boston in the seventh game of a playoff series versus Philadelphia in 2010.)

To his everlasting credit, Don Cherry took the blame for the catastrophic blunder and never wavered about it. He was the coach. He was in charge of the Bruins' line changes. Thus, he reasoned, it was his fault. Typical of his love of naval history, Cherry likened himself to a captain of a warship who had blundered under enemy fire. "On my gravestone it will read 'Here lies the coach who had too many men on the ice,'"[1] Cherry has said numerous times with a chuckle. Still, in serious interviews nearly four decades after the fact, it is patently clear that the circumstances of the Bruins' loss to Montreal in Game #7 still weigh mightily on him.

In the grand scheme of things, Cherry is correct. But this particular penalty was brought upon by the Bruins' relentless shadowing of Guy Lafleur. Whenever and wherever the kingpin of Montreal's offense stepped onto the ice, he was to be followed closely by Don Marcotte, the Bruins' version of Bob Gainey—a fanatical forechecking specialist.

Marcotte's primary task in Game #7 was to keep within an arm's length of Lafleur even if The Flower went to the bathroom, Cherry later joked. As regulation time in Game #7 wound down to five, four, and three minutes left on the Forum's clock, Scotty Bowman was only giving Lafleur short respites on the bench. Bowman was double-shifting and triple-shifting his best player, hoping he could be the decisive man on the ice. Once the Bruins regained the lead on Rick Middleton's wrap-around goal with 3:59 remaining, Lafleur became a virtual fixture on the ice for the Canadiens. Thus it became a more complicated situation for the Bruins to maintain their normal lines while trying to keep Marcotte on the ice too. It was almost inevitable there would be a miscommunication that would lead to too few or too many Bruins on the ice. With 2:34 left in the third period, 41-year-old linesman John D'Amico rightly blew his whistle.

Here's what Cherry told the *Boston Globe* just before his return to the Garden as Colorado's coach:

> I could go nuts thinking about it. We were a minute and 14 seconds away from winning the Stanley Cup.
>
> I've never told anybody what happened, but it was something that wouldn't happen again in a hundred years. Lafleur went through three line changes. Marcotte's orders were to stay on as long as Lafleur did. The left wingers got confused. Then when Marcotte came off, one guy got confused and jumped on. For 80 games this guy had turned to me and asked "Who's up?"—but he was so excited—we all were—that he didn't say it.[2]

Cherry admitted that he had foreseen the possibility of such a penalty because the noise in the Forum often drowned out his instructions to the players. "Before the game we had talked about what we could to avoid a too-many-men call," Cherry noted, "but it happened anyway."[3]

What actually occurred has been a matter of debate for nearly four decades. Some people claim the Bruins had too many men on the ice for as long as 30 seconds. That is an absurd notion. Although the television replays from *Hockey Night in Canada* do not show the exact moment of when the Bruins suddenly had six skaters on the ice, the excited Hab fans at the Forum only clamored for a penalty to be called for about five or six seconds before play was blown dead. (The May 12, 1979, *Boston Globe* carried a feature article titled "The Aftermath: The Play" that dealt entirely with the too-many-men call. According to writer Will McDonough, a study of the TV38 videotapes showed the Bruins had an extra man on the ice for exactly 12 seconds.) *HNIC* commentator Danny Gallivan was completely oblivious to what was going on. He wrongly thought the play had been whistled for Mark Napier being offside at the Boston blue line despite numerous fans in the crowd standing and pointing toward the Bruins' bench. It was analyst Lou Nanne (the Minnesota North Stars' general manager) who first realized what had happened. It was he who informed millions of engrossed television viewers that Boston was getting a too-many-men-on-the-ice penalty. Gallivan then stated the obvious: "It is a terribly inopportune time for the Boston Bruins to pick up a penalty of that nature and that magnitude."[4]

The announcers for Boston's TV38 were initially oblivious too. Neither play-by-play man Fred Cusick nor analyst Johnny Peirson saw what happened at the Bruins' bench in those crucial few seconds. "You follow the puck," explained Cusick to the *Globe* a week after the game. "If you're looking for a sixth-man violation, then you don't see the puck."[5] Furthermore, given the overhang of the visitors' television booth at the Forum, it was nearly impossible for Cusick and Peirson to see the area near the Bruins' bench.

In his autobiography, Brad Park remembered the circumstances this way. "I jumped over the boards and headed for the puck when the whistle went. I was confused. Someone said too many men, and I quickly counted defensemen to make sure my signals were correct. There were only two of us."[6]

Cusick and Peirson both came under fire for their "editorializing" about the officials even though a close examination of the TV38 replays showed the Bruins clearly had too many men on the ice for approximately nine seconds. [Author's note: That length of time was cited by *Globe* TV critic Jack Craig.]

"I can't tell you how long Johnny and I have been coming to the Forum and have seen the ways they find to beat you," Cusick noted, not clearly specifying whether "they" referred to the Canadiens or the officials. "Maybe that was a factor in our reactions. The question comes down to whether the violation was a flagrant one."[7] Peirson, who played for the Bruins for 13 seasons from 1946 to 1958, concurred. "I did not say there had not been a violation," he explained. "My point was that [the call] was inappropriate given the circumstances. Given the same situation, I would say it all over again."[8] During the intermission before overtime, neither Cusick nor Peirson dwelled on the fateful bench penalty that directly led to Lafleur's tying goal. They agreed to drop the subject.

Jack Craig strongly accused Cusick of abandoning objectivity as the time wound down in the third period. "Cusick seemed to root more and more [for the Bruins] as the prospects grew for an upset,"[9] Craig opined.

There are a few absolute certainties surrounding what happened in the key moments preceding the critical call. Don Marcotte was clearly not on the ice, so the confusion centered on which Bruin was to replace him. D'Amico, a veteran of 15 NHL seasons, was among the first to know there was a problem. Numerous Bruins were hollering at the six skaters for somebody in a black uniform—absolutely anybody—to get off the ice. D'Amico was within earshot of the shouting. About the only penalty an NHL linesman was empowered to call in 1978–79 was too many men on the ice. All other penalties had to be called by the lone referee. D'Amico certainly did not want to call that violation at that point in the game unless it was egregious. It was. According to some sources, including several Bruins, D'Amico gave the visitors every chance to correct the problem, even to the point of screaming at a wayward Bruin to get back to his bench. Instead the extra man pursued the puck. D'Amico sadly looked at Cherry, shrugged as if to say "What choice do I have?" and made the call he was obligated to make. Thirty-eight-year-old Bob Myers, in his 12th season as an NHL referee, had not noticed the problem. He asked D'Amico if he was completely certain that Boston had too many men on the ice. D'Amico responded affirmatively.

The Bruins only mildly disputed the call. Brad Park can be seen from a distance on *HNIC*'s coverage calmly and resignedly discussing the situation near center ice with both D'Amico and fellow linesman Ron Finn. According to Park's recollection, D'Amico told him Boston had too many men on the ice for about 20 seconds. (The situation was a case of déjà vu for both Park and D'Amico. Five years earlier, D'Amico had been a linesman in Game #7 of a Flyers-Rangers semifinal. Late in the third period, with the visiting Rangers trailing 4–3, D'Amico called New York for too many men on the ice when they attempted to pull goalie Ed Giacomin for a sixth attacker. D'Amico ruled that the Rangers' extra skater came onto the ice well before Giacomin had gotten near the visitors' bench. The penalty effectively squelched any real possibility of a New York comeback. NBC's telecast did not show whether or not D'Amico's call was correct, but it did show Park among a bevy of vexed Rangers arguing with the linesman.)

How could the Bruins really dispute D'Amico's call? Cherry, who had been extremely agitated over every penalty call against Boston throughout the game, had no outward reaction to the bench penalty. He knew what had went wrong and why the Bruins would be a man short with 2:34 left in the third period. Cherry claims that the confusion on the Boston bench was so thorough that he had to physically restrain two other Bruins from jumping onto the ice before D'Amico blew his whistle. "Would it have mattered if I hadn't stopped them?"[10] Cherry rhetorically asked years later. Upon his departure from the Bruins, Cherry told the Logansport (Indiana) *Pharos-Tribune*, "Just think, if I had three arms I'd be wearing a Stanley Cup ring right now. We'd have beaten the Rangers too, you know."[11] (Ranger goalie John Davidson, who also ended up as a hockey broadcaster, disagrees. In the 2017 Sportsnet documentary *Names on the Cup*, Davidson said, "I tell Grapes the too-many-men-on-the-ice penalty cost *us* the Cup because we would have beaten Boston.")

A slow-motion examination of the *HNIC* telecast of the critical seconds before D'Amico's whistle is blown shows the six Boston skaters on the ice were Brad Park, Bob Miller, Mike Milbury, Terry O'Reilly, Rick Middleton, and Stan Jonathan. (Those were the six mentioned in the *Globe*'s story.) Don Marcotte is conspicuously absent, confirming the high level of disarray at the Boston bench. According to Cherry's account, Marcotte was straddling the boards.

The Bruins themselves were quick to exonerate D'Amico. "He saw it," said Gerry Cheevers, whose only job that night as Gilles Gilbert's backup was to open the door at the left end of Boston's bench. "He tried to give us a chance but he had to make the call."[12]

Harry Sinden, who was initially livid about D'Amico's call, had his opinion changed by one of the six Bruin skaters on the ice. "When the game was over I was still ranting and raving," Sinden admitted. "Mike Milbury came over and told me that we had an extra man on the ice for a good 15 to 20 seconds. At the end of the game I thought [D'Amico] was wrong, but he made the right call."[13]

While D'Amico was given a pass by the Bruins, referee Bob Myers was not granted the same immunity from criticism. "All the Bruins felt that Myers fell apart in the third period, something Cherry had feared earlier in the day and had discussed with writers at about 1 p.m.," McDonough wrote.

Cherry had said seven hours before game time, "If Myers lets the players play the game we have a good chance. If he starts giving Montreal power plays and four-on-fours, we can't win."

When the game ended, the prophetic Cherry expressed his frustrations with Myers: "In the early part of the third period he let three or four Montreal penalties go uncalled. I thought that was fine; he's not going to call anything, no matter what happens this period. That's the way it should be. Then he started with that terrible call against Jean Ratelle after Bob Gainey elbowed him. I could sense we were going to get it."[14]

Including the subsequent penalty from the too-many-men-on-the-ice debacle, Montreal had three power plays in the third period. Boston had zero.

Wayne Cashman uttered similar sentiments. "Every time we'd get a lead here, we'd come up shorthanded and they would get back in it," he noted. "We get ahead, we get a penalty, and they come back."[15]

In his autobiography published three years after the infamous penalty, Cherry vowed he would never reveal the identity of the player who wrongly jumped onto the ice. He did not want to further embarrass someone who already felt terrible about making the mistake of all mistakes. The guilty party, Cherry said, was in tears as he skated back to the Boston bench. (In a 2014 interview for the *Sports Illustrated* mini-documentary on Game #7, Cherry revealed the guilty party was a forward.)

Thom Sears wrote in 2012, "More than three decades later, Cherry's acceptance of the blame still stands; in the spirit of winning as a team and losing as a team, neither he nor any member of the Bruins have ever publicly speculated which team member may have been at fault."[16]

Cherry and his players did not need to identify who was at fault as others were more than willing to do so:

- In the 1980s Don Cherry hosted a syndicated sports interview show set in a faux pub. It was called *Don Cherry's Grapevine*. One episode's guest was Guy Lafleur. (To his credit, Cherry had absolutely no qualms about having members of those dastardly multiple-Cup-winning Habs teams on his program. Cherry had great respect for them and their talents. He considered several of them to be friends.) At one juncture in the program, Lafleur began talking about his memories of Game #7 in 1979 and matter-of-factly identified Stan Jonathan as the extra Bruin who jumped onto the ice. Strangely, Lafleur's comment was not edited from the broadcast even though one would assume that Cherry had considerable control over which parts of interviews made it into his show and which parts were culled.
- On May 12, 1979, the *Montreal Gazette* carried an amusing human-interest story about a Bruin fan in that city who lost a bet to a friend when Montreal won Game #7. There was no cash on the line, just personal dignity. Because his Bruins lost, Alain Laflamme had to crawl on his hands and knees two blocks to a favorite pub while being led on a dog leash by his buddy, Yvan Plante, a Habs fan. Plante carried a large placard, written in French, that read "Jonathan battu par Lambert"—which translates to "Jonathan defeated by Lambert." Was Plante's use of Jonathan's name a mere coincidence? It's unlikely.
- By the mid–1990s the goat horns had been firmly affixed to the unfortunate skull of Stan Jonathan—the same Stan Jonathan who had had the game of his life two nights earlier in Game #6 when he joyously scored a hat-trick and lost two teeth in the process. A *Sports Illustrated* feature article published in 2014 and the aforementioned *SI* documentary video about Game #7 state in no uncertain terms that Jonathan was the illegal sixth Bruins skater. This claim went undisputed.
- In a 2012 book about famous playoff overtime goals titled *Next Goal Wins*, author Liam Maguire wrote, "Jean Ratelle noticed there were six Bruins skaters on the ice, and he climbed back over the boards before the referee could catch the error. But an overanxious Stan Jonathan raced onto the ice and checked Mark Napier and this time the ref [sic] made the call."[17]

Fast forward to the evening of Tuesday, September 26, 1995. Boston Garden is about to be shut down and demolished after 67 NHL seasons because it had become horribly antiquated. Before moving to their larger, posh new digs to begin the 1995–96 season, the Bruins rightly decide to give their longtime home on Causeway Street an enormous going-away bash. It is billed as the Garden's "Last Hurrah." Although it is only a preseason game, the Montreal Canadiens are fittingly invited to be the last visiting team to play there. It completes the circle: The Habs had been the first visiting team in the building back in 1928. Every Boston Bruins fan with any sense of history wants to be present at the Garden on this night for what a Canadian Press correspondent irreverently called "an occasion where former Bruin greats, almost-greats, and no-so-greats were honored."[18]

Lucky ticketholders are pleasantly surprised when they are greeted at the turnstiles by A-list Bruins alumni. (*"Hi, I'm Phil Esposito. Thanks for coming out tonight."*) The hockey game is secondary to the ceremonies that will occur after its conclusion and at halftime. (Yep, the game, won by Boston 3–0, was played in two 25-minute halves.) Future Bruins general-manager Don Sweeney scored the last goal at the Garden. The Bruins' organization does everything right. Greats from their Original Six–like rivals are feted during the extended halftime break. Johnny Bower, Stan Mikita, Frank Mahovlich, Jean Béliveau, Maurice Richard and Emile Francis are all greeted warmly by the knowledgeable Boston fans who know and remember talent when they see it. Each man is given a souvenir of the occasion. Nobody thinks of booing retired linesman John D'Amico—who, in 1995, was the NHL's supervisor of officials—when he is introduced as a league VIP. The dignified halftime ceremony oozes class and respect, but the grand finale immediately after the game is what everyone has come to see.

The climactic event of the gala is when the surviving Bruins whose numbers are retired return to the ice for a final time. In a scene reminiscent of January 9, 1979, when the #4 jersey was hoisted to the rafters, the Garden crowd goes absolutely bonkers, of course, when 47-year-old Bobby Orr—who could pass for 35—is fittingly the last Bruin alumnus introduced. ("Our next guest is the greatest player in the history of the National Hockey League…"[19] began 76-year-old emcee Fred Cusick before completely being drowned out by a deafening roar.) But the most telling moments to fans of the 1978–79 Bruins occur in the 30 minutes preceding Orr's entrance. It was when the lesser Bruin alumni are summoned onto the ice in alphabetical order—wearing retro jerseys corresponding to their eras—for one last bow and final skate around the Boston Garden ice if they so choose.

The fourth man presented (behind Don Awrey, Leo Boivin and Gerry Cheevers) is 61-year-old Don Cherry. Cusick and Bob Wilson, the familiar voices of Bruins hockey for decades, share the emcee duties. They alternate introductions for each alumnus. Cusick reads Cherry's brief intro: "Our next guest coached the Bruins from 1974–75 to '78-'79. He won the Jack Adams Trophy as the league's top coach in 1976—the only Bruins coach to have been honored with that award. Please welcome Don Cherry!"[20]

It was the first time that Cherry had represented the Bruins in any sort of official capacity at Boston Garden since Game #6 of the 1979 Boston-Montreal semifinal. In the 16 years since 1979, Cherry had become a living legend in Canada for his "Coach's Corner" segments on *Hockey Night in Canada.* The career minor-league defenseman who had once supplemented his hockey income in the offseason by doing menial labor for $2 an hour had made himself a millionaire … by simply being Don Cherry, the outspoken, take-no-prisoners, straight-shooter who had endeared himself to the Boston media and Bruin fans in the late 1970s. His celebrity status in Canada is staggering. Year after year polls indicate that Cherry is the most recognizable person in the country—ranking ahead of both Wayne Gretzky and prime minister Jean Chrétien in 1995.

Upon hearing Cusick say Cherry's name, the crowd roars. Cherry surprises observers by briefly embracing old adversary Harry Sinden who was stationed on the ice to present all the honored attendees with crystal mementoes of the night. The ovation Cherry gets is long, sustained and heartfelt. Clad in a typically gaudy red tartan jacket and a necktie adorned with the Bruins logo and a likeness of Blue, Cherry milks his few moments in the limelight for every second he can. Forget the whiteness of Cherry's thinning hair and the middle-age wrinkles on his face. To fans old enough to remember the 1970s, it is as if it were early May in 1979 and the Boston Bruins are still the everyman's NHL team. For a few moments Cherry again is 45 years old and his lovable, lunch-pail retreads are going to be conquering hockey heroes this time for sure. Cherry, absolutely beaming, is in his glory. One expects him at any moment to make some outrageous, off-the-cuff remark in defense of himself and his beloved Bruins, or make some reference to Blue or Lord Nelson. He opens his arms to take in the delighted crowd's affection. He bows. He blows them kisses.

He gives them two thumbs-up as he walks on the red carpet and they become even louder. He bows again. The present-day Bruins seated on the home team's bench applaud too and widely smile at the scene. Even Sinden gets a kick out of it; he cannot suppress a chuckle and a huge grin. No one present on this night blames Cherry for the catastrophic bench penalty on May 10, 1979, that is for certain. It is just a tremendous thank-you for a run of five excellent, fun years when the Bruins were routinely the second-best team in the NHL. During the game WSBK's Sean McDonough interviewed Cherry and unabashedly referred to him as the most popular Bruin' coach ever. After the game he succinctly labeled Cherry's appearance to be a triumphant return. It was indeed.

Not long afterward 40-year-old Stan Jonathan is introduced between Tom Johnson and Gord Kluzak. He too gets a long, warm reception—noticeably lengthier and more enthusiastic than what was given to the more skillful teammates of his era: Don Marcotte, Jean Ratelle, Brad Park, and Rick Middleton. Bruin fans are generally well versed in their team's history which features far more heartbreaks than triumphs. Most fans in the stuffy, creaky Boston Garden that night probably know—or at least strongly suspect—that Jonathan was the man whose enthusiasm carried him onto the ice when he should not have been there. It does not matter one iota. Guilty or not, Jonathan is not assigned any blame. He senses this too and smiles warmly at the unconditional love he gets. What happened at the Montreal Forum 16 years and four months before has no bearing whatsoever on this wonderful night of nostalgia and celebration.

22

April 26, 1988

Liberation Day for Bruin Fans

"Here they are. Again? The Montreal Canadiens. The uniforms have not changed. The people have not changed. Nothing has changed. Nothing ever changes. There is another Stanley Cup playoff series at hand—the Boston Bruins tangling again with these marauders in bleu, blanc et rouge ... and anyone who lives in Boston knows what the result will be."

—Leigh Montville of *Sports Illustrated*, in an article titled "No Gain, Just Pain," written prior to the Bruins-Canadiens 1988 Adams Division final

"1943: Last Bruins' Breakthrough: World War II was Still Raging; the Boston Celts Were a Soccer Team; and the Bruins Beat Montreal in the Playoffs. There Have Been No World Wars or Bruin Repeats Since."

—*Boston Globe* headline, April 22, 1988

It does not appear in red letters on any calendar, but Liberation Day for the Boston Bruins and their loyal fans finally arrived on Tuesday, April 26, 1988. Long overdue, it came two weeks shy of the ninth anniversary of the too-many-men-on-the-ice game.

Professional hockey had changed in the interim. In 1979 hardly any players wore helmets. In 1988 practically everyone did, as did most referees. Goal creases were now rectangles within semicircles. NHL teams now had multiple coaches; the idea of a head coach not having at least one assistant seemed quaint and inefficient. There were now 21 NHL teams instead of 17. The league's double-seeded playoff format where any team could play any other team was long gone—having been replaced in 1982 by intra-divisional playoffs. The Boston Bruins were still a fixture in the Adams Division with the Buffalo Sabres, but the three other teams alongside them were now the Quebec Nordiques, the Hartford Whalers and the Montreal Canadiens. (Of course, with Boston and Montreal vying in the same division, the new playoff format greatly increased the chances of a Bruins-Habs series each spring.)

Some things stayed the same though: The game itself was pretty much unchanged. The Bruins and Canadiens both retained their ancient home buildings from the 1920s although their ages and shortcomings were beginning to show. The boards and ice surfaces in NHL arenas still remained free from advertisements, and there were still just three on-ice officials assigned to an NHL game. Oh, yes: Entering the 1988 Adams Division final the Boston Bruins still had not beaten the Montreal Canadiens in a Stanley Cup playoff series since the Second World War.

In 1988 an inflated number of 16 teams qualified for the Stanley Cup playoffs. That meant the long regular season served but one purpose in the five-team Adams Division—to eliminate only the bottom team. The other four each qualified for the playoffs. It was the fifth consecutive season that featured a Boston-Montreal playoff series. In the previous four seasons the Bruins and Montreal Canadiens faced off in the first round of the play-offs—the round officially called the "divisional semifinals." In each of those four years the Habs won, of course. They won without Ken Dryden, Yvan Cournoyer, Scotty Bowman, and Jacques Lemaire. They even won without Roger Doucet's passionate singing. (Doucet died from a brain tumor at age 62 in July 1981. Doucet's wife, Geraldine, succeeded him as the Forum's anthem warbler.) Didn't the Canadiens always win? Certainly…

In 1984—the first spring Boston and Montreal met in the playoffs since their epic 1979 encounter—the Bruins were overwhelming favorites, having accrued the best record in their conference during the regular season with 104 points. Boston had gone 6–0–1 in their final seven games to finish atop the Adams Division. Conversely, Montreal had listlessly lost their last six regular-season games and were 29 points in arrears of the Bruins in the final standings.

But, as in 1930 and 1971, the wheels fell off for the mighty Bruins once the playoffs began. Boston swiftly dropped the best-of-five series to Montreal in three straight games. They scored an anemic two goals in the entire series—both by Tom Fergus—in losing 2–1, 3–1 and 5–0. During the regular season Boston averaged 4.2 goals per game. In one game versus the Habs in November, Boston scored ten goals. Yet history had cruelly repeated itself. An unheralded Montreal goaltender named Steve Penney stole the Bruins' thunder, just as Rogie Vachon, Ken Dryden and George Hainsworth had done in past springs. Penney's emergence may have been the most remarkable of all. He had played in just four regular-season games in 1983–84—and had lost all four. "It takes the luster out of finishing first," declared Gerry Cheevers, now the Bruins' coach, who possessed a tremendous grasp of the obvious. "We were soundly defeated."[1]

(Penney would record three shutouts in the 1984 playoffs and be credited with nine victories as Montreal surprisingly advanced to the Wales Conference final. Penney played 54 games for Montreal the following season. That was his apex. He would only appear in 91 total NHL games for the Habs and Winnipeg spread over five mediocre seasons. He lost the majority of them. By the spring of 1988, Penney's NHL career was over.)

It was somehow fitting that Jacques Lemaire—the Montreal forward who had scored the Stanley Cup-winning goal against Cheevers in 1977—was now coaching the Canadiens. Lemaire had taken the helm of the stumbling Habs with 17 games left on Montreal's sched-ule. Francis Rosa of the *Boston Globe* asked the same bitter question Bruin fans in 1971 did: "What does it profit a team to win first place and lose in the first [playoff] series?"[2]

In 1985, the Adams Division standings were reversed from the previous season. The Bruins, despite uncharacteristically finishing fourth with only 82 points, took the favored Habs to the absolute brink, losing three games to two. The loss in Game #5 was a 1–0 defeat at the Forum. The winning goal came on a Montreal counterattack, with just 51 seconds left on the clock, from the stick of Mats Naslund. The Bruins had outplayed Montreal for most of the game and had clearly carried the play for most of the third period. On April 10 Boston had won Game #1 at the Forum 5–3. It was Boston's first playoff win in that house of horrors since 1971. Yet still the Habs won the series. "We should have won," noted Boston goalie Doug Keans after Game #5, "But one shot made the difference. Hockey isn't fair."[3] Michael Madden of the *Boston Globe*, in a piece titled "A Familiar Way to End the Season," wrote, "Speak of fate, but these Bruins would like to inquire about justice."[4]

In 1986, the last time the NHL had best-of-five series to open the playoffs, Montreal swept the Bruins by scores of 3–1, 3–2, and 4–3. "Some time in the next century someone will look at the *Hockey Book of Records* and be startled by the number of times Montreal has beaten the Boston Bruins in playoff games,"[5] glumly wrote Francis Rosa in the *Boston Globe* after the final defeat. "I don't believe there's a jinx," declared Boston's Steve Kasper, who had succeeded Don Marcotte as the Bruins' best forechecking forward. "We had a few more breakdowns than they did. That's why they won."[6]

The following April, in 1987, in a best-of-seven opening round, Montreal again inflicted a humiliating sweep on the Bruins by scores of 6–2, 4–3, 5–4, and 4–2. It marked the 18th straight time that Montreal had beaten Boston in a playoff series—a record of utter post-season dominance unmatched anywhere in North American professional sports. "Montreal had the edge in every department," Harry Sinden conceded. "In some cases it's just a slight edge, but put them all together and they add up."[7] The *Globe*'s Francis Rosa relayed a quip he heard a Montreal hockey writer utter: "Maybe if Montreal had a basketball team Boston could win."[8] It seemed like there would be no end to hockey's version of Sisyphus' ordeal.

By the spring of 1988, 1943 seemed like eons ago—even though there were still many Bruins alive and kicking from the last Boston team to beat the Habs in the playoffs. Some of the 1943 Bruins had difficulty recalling details, however. When asked about it, goaltender Frank Brimsek, age 72, had no recollection whatsoever of the 1943 Boston-Montreal playoff series despite playing every minute of every Bruins game that season. "I can't remember it," Brimsek admitted to John Powers of the *Globe*. "It was a long time ago. It's a little too far back."[9]

Others had keener memories. Bep Guidolin, who preceded Don Cherry as Boston's coach, made the 1942–43 Bruins as a mere 16-year-old when NHL rosters were decimated by wartime manpower demands. He recalled, "It wasn't a big hurrah for us to beat Montreal. We knew we could do it."[10] Indeed, Boston's playoff triumph over Montreal was expected. In 1942–43 the Habs were a .500 team that had barely squeaked into the playoffs one point ahead of the Chicago Blackhawks. Remarkably, the Canadiens had not won a single post-season series since winning the Stanley Cup in 1931.

Ab DeMarco—whose son played three games for the 1978–79 Bruins—notched the overtime goal in Game #5 of the 1943 semis that sent the Bruins into the Stanley Cup final versus Detroit. The decisive goal was a typical Bruins tally: Dit Clapper fired the puck into the corner of the Montreal zone. Guidolin got to it first. He was roughed up by three Habs but still managed to center the puck to DeMarco in the slot who beat Montreal goalie Paul Bibeault with a rising shot. "I didn't hesitate. I picked a high spot and just drove it." DeMarco recalled the bedlam that overtook Boston Garden once the red light flashed. "The roof fell in. Everyone was going crazy, throwing hats and coats. I thought people would jump from the balcony."[11] In the victorious dressing room coach Art Ross, who had seen his favored Bruins lose in playoff upsets to the Canadiens in both 1930 and 1931 amidst questionable officiating, declared, "Well, it's about time we beat those bastards—and we beat them fair and square."[12] Conversely, Montreal coach Dick Irvin was griping to reporters. He deemed Boston's triumph to be lucky.

In 1988 Boston and Montreal managed to avoid each other in the opening round of the Adams Division playoffs as the Habs finished in first place with 103 points and the Bruins came in a strong second with 94. Montreal knocked off the Hartford Whalers in the first round. Boston got by Buffalo in six games to win a Stanley Cup playoff series for the first time since 1983. Thus, what was turning out to be the annual Boston-Montreal playoff clash would send one team to the Prince of Wales Conference final.

The opening game, on Monday, April 18, was a stinker as far as the Bruins were concerned. Fortunately for most of their fans, few saw very much of Montreal's easy 5–2 win. A major electrical failure just outside the Forum prevented most of the game from being broadcast. On *Hockey Night in Canada*, Don Cherry bluntly stated that Bruin fans ought to be thankful for the unexpected power outage as it spared them from viewing their team's awful showing. Strangely, the next power outage in the series had nothing to do with transformers and kilowatts; it had to do with the Montreal Canadiens.

On April 20 Boston won Game #2 at the Forum by a 4–3 score, ending a nine-game playoff losing streak to Montreal. The tide was turning.

By happenstance, Cherry was present at Boston Garden for the next two games as a member of *Hockey Night in Canada*. Previously *HNIC* had exercised a measure of diplomacy by not sending Cherry to Boston in order to avoid any possible trouble with Bruins management. Paul A. Mooney, the former president of the Bruins—who was no longer with the team in 1988—had once stated the only way Cherry would get into Boston Garden again would be if he bought a ticket. In fact, when Cherry began working on *Hockey Night in Canada*, Mooney telephoned the show's producer, Ralph Mellanby, to issue a warning: "When Cherry was in Boston he thought he was Lord Nelson." Mellanby replied, "That's okay. Since Cherry's been here he thinks he's running the CBC."[13]

Cherry, of course, attracted gawkers and autograph-seekers at Boston Garden, but he was extremely gracious in his comments about his former employers. He said he felt no bitterness toward the Bruins' management—especially with Mooney out of the picture. Furthermore, he declared Harry Sinden to be the best general-manager in the NHL, citing his acquisition of Cam Neely as evidence. Sinden was considerably less gracious. Upon hearing Cherry's compliment, Sinden said it would have meant more had it come from Sam Pollock.

Cherry's presence perhaps had a positive effect on the Bruins. Games #3 and #4 were won by Boston 3–1 and 2–0 as Boston's French-Canadian goaltender Réjean (Reggie) Lemelin starred. Suddenly, the Bruins were leading the punchless Habs three games to one in a Stanley Cup playoff series for the first time since the historic spring of 1943. A headline in the April 25 *Globe* declared, "Bruins Turn the Tables: Canadiens Grope for Explanations for their Unfamiliar Position." Montreal forward Guy Carbonneau, exhibiting a sense of arrogant entitlement, had trouble accepting where the series stood. "We're not in a position we like," the disbelieving Hab told the *Globe*'s Kevin Paul Dupont. "Against Boston we're used to being ahead 2–1 or 3–1."[14]

Game #5 was back at the Forum on April 26. Boston won easily 4–1 to wrap up the series, but no one in a Bruin uniform, in the team's executive box, or even among the hopeful Boston media permitted himself the luxury of being the slightest bit comfortable until the final siren echoed through the rapidly dwindling Forum crowd. The same, of course, could be said of any knowledgeable Bruin fan watching on television or listening to a radio broadcast somewhere. Most had been down this road before. History told them to expect some god-awful, series-altering occurrence. Leigh Montville—who had written a terrific, tongue-in-cheek, pre-series piece for *Sports Illustrated* advising Bruin fans not to watch the Adams Division final because he presumed the series' outcome would be the same as the previous 18—was especially concerned that something horrible would manifest to stop Boston from winning even this one-sided game. As the minutes ebbed away, Montville admitted he envisioned all sorts of crazy scenarios that might prevent the milestone Boston triumph. He wrote in the *Globe*, "Was Rocket Richard going to come out of the stands … to right all these injustices in the third period? Was Jean Béliveau going to …

leave the press box and bring some cohesion and dignity to the Canadiens' operation? Guy Lafleur. Where was Guy Lafleur? Ken Dryden. Steve Penney. Gump Worsley. All the gods of the Forum. Where were they? What would happen? Too many men on the ice? Don't say that. Don't be that cruel."[15]

But there was no catastrophe, no bad bounce, no stupid penalty, no questionable officiating, no unfathomable choke, or no supernal interference to stop the Bruins' overdue triumph. Mercifully the third period sped by. At times several minutes ran off the clock between whistles. Still some Bruins perceived the Forum's clock was running too slowly— or not at all. Keith Crowder, an eight-year Boston veteran, told Montville he'd experienced time standing still. "I looked up at the clock when there was about 30 seconds left. It was like the clock wouldn't move. It was like the ice would open up … or something." He concluded, "This was a huge monkey off our backs." Montville's article was accurately titled "Forty-Five Years of Dues are Paid."

Fran Rosa, still covering the Bruins for the *Globe* at age 68, was thrilled to be finally reporting a Boston playoff series victory over the Habs. He giddily wrote,

> Guess what happened at the Forum last night. Stan Jonathan, wherever you are. And Don Cherry. Guess what happened.
>
> Those magnificent Bruins with their skates barely touching the ice, with a tunnel-vision purpose that wouldn't be deflected, and with their hearts bigger than the moon, took their fans to another planet last night.
>
> They defeated the Montreal Canadiens, 4–1, in the process telling everyone, "If there ever was a jinx, you can take it and…"

Cam Neely and Steve Kasper each scored twice in the convincing Bruin triumph. (In a juicy bit of irony, Kasper was born in Saint-Lambert, Quebec, a suburb of Montreal.) Neely's second goal—a breakaway early in the third period on a counterattack—went against the run of play. It came after Montreal had applied sustained, enormous pressure on the Bruins who refused to crack. The fourth goal was fatal to the Habs, but there were nearly 16 minutes remaining for Boston to kill. They did so efficiently and superbly. The weight of history seemed to be no burden.

Dave Newell was the referee. It was Dave Newell who—precisely nine years earlier in the same arena—had widely been perceived in Boston as the villain of Game #1 in 1979 for disallowing Rick Middleton's apparent tying goal and for bizarrely not awarding the Bruins a penalty shot when Serge Savard handled the puck in Montreal's goal crease.

The Bruins had won two games in a Stanley Cup playoff series in Montreal for only the second time. The first time was a 1930 semifinal victory over the Montreal Maroons— the other expansion team that entered the NHL along with the Bruins in 1924–25. The Maroons went bankrupt in 1938.

The victorious Boston coach was 36-year-old Terry O'Reilly, the most noteworthy grinder in Don Cherry's crew from a decade earlier. Having retired as a player after the 1984–85 season, O'Reilly had been on the losing end of six Boston-Montreal playoff series. (Five as a player and one as a coach.) It was his pitiful, pain-wracked, agony-of-defeat face, crying on his wife's shoulder that appeared on the front page of the May 11, 1979, *Toronto Star*. Heck, O'Reilly was one of the six Bruin skaters who was on the ice when John D'Amico whistled too many men. At the historic moment of victory, O'Reilly spryly vaulted over the boards to celebrate. He practically danced off the Forum ice in unrestrained joy with an enormous smile on his face.

The reaction of the Bruin players depended upon their length of service to the team. Montville realized this immediately. "There was an equation here that roughly equated pain to joy," the scribe penned. "How many years had you followed this long series of toil and travail? How much time had you spent pounding your head into that Forum wall? That was how good that you felt now that the pounding—45 years and 18 Stanley Cup series since 1943—had ended."

Thirty-four-year-old Rick (Nifty) Middleton, in his twelfth year a Bruin, was typical of the battle-scarred graybeards on Boston's roster—but he was the only one who had played in the 1979 semifinal. (The Habs retained two veterans from 1978–79: Bob Gainey, age 34; and Larry Robinson, age 36.) "I'm in a daze," Middleton stated. "This is the happiest moment of my life. I really don't know what to do to celebrate. I feel so good. I'm standing here and I don't know what to do."[16] Nine years earlier Middleton had scored the wraparound goal at 16:01 of the third period of Game #7 which, at the time, appeared to be the series-winner. With Montreal finally vanquished, Middleton's mission in his hockey life was complete. Nifty would retire at the end of the 1987–88 season.

General-manager Harry Sinden was the longest-suffering person within the Bruins' leadership group. "Look around at these kids in the dressing room," Sinden noted. "They don't have any particular pleasure. They could have beaten any team out there tonight. They're just happy to have won. It's the people who've been here for a while. Me, I'm the constant in this thing. I'm overjoyed—and so are all of those people who've been sitting in their living rooms, watching, for all those years."[17]

Sinden said he was pleasantly surprised by the reaction and behavior of the Montreal fans who had resolutely stuck around to the bitter end. Many sought him out to offer congratulations. "The [Montreal fans] were actually very nice. A lot of them shook my hand. It was kind of neat. They would kind of give it to me in all those other years. It's funny: I don't think you know about other teams' fans until you see them after their team loses. I'd never seen them lose here, so I never knew."[18] On *Hockey Night in Canada*'s postgame show, Don Cherry, clearly delighted by the outcome, was all smiles and sunshine. In his giddy happiness, Cherry incorrectly chopped two years off the Bruins' playoff losing streak versus Montreal, inaccurately claiming the drought had been a mere 43 years instead of 45.

The longest-suffering "Bruin" in the Forum that night never once wore a team uniform or served in any sort of management capacity. It was NESN play-by-play man Fred Cusick who had been with the team since 1952. Cusick, age 69, had been present for 16 of the Bruins' 18 consecutive playoff setbacks at the hands of the Habs either on television or radio, from the five-game defeat in the 1953 Stanley Cup final to the sweep loss in the first round in 1987. He and NESN analyst Derek Sanderson—who had lost three playoff series to the Canadiens as a player—got to call the historic game for the folks watching in New England. Cusick seemed to report the four Bruin goals that night with extra zeal, but he was remarkably calm and subdued as the final minute ticked off the clock. "Forty seconds left. The long drought has ended,"[19] he professionally reported without a trace of emotion. Sanderson, however, gleefully noted, "How sweet it is! I never got to see this as a player, but boy, it's sweet as a broadcaster! The Boston Bruins are one happy bunch."[20] Danny Gallivan did not have to endure the indignity of broadcasting a Montreal loss to Boston in a playoff series, having retired from *HNIC* four years earlier.

The Bruins did not win the Stanley Cup in 1988. They beat the New Jersey Devils in the Wales Conference final in a seven-game series that featured a wildcat officials strike just before Game #4. The triumph earned the team its first trip to the Stanley Cup final since 1978 when Cherry, Cheevers, Ratelle, Park, McNab, Sheppard, Schmautz—and O'Reilly and Middleton—were the toast of the Hub. Boston was no match for the powerful Edmonton Oilers in the championship series. (Edmonton won in a strange four-game sweep—one that took about 4⅔ games. A power failure terminated and nullified Game #4 at aging Boston Garden late in the second period.) In the grand scheme of things, though, Boston's loss to Edmonton was a minor inconvenience. To most Bruin fans, their team had won a greater prize in 1988 with their deserved victory over Montreal in the Adams Division final: Sisyphus had finally managed to roll his gigantic boulder to the summit of that enormous, seemingly insurmountable hill.

Epilogue

"Somewhere in the world there is a defeat for everyone. Some are destroyed by defeat, and some made small and mean by victory. Greatness lives in one who triumphs equally over defeat and victory."

—John Steinbeck

The years have been kind to the 1978–79 Boston Bruins. Until Gary Doak's death on March 25, 2017, every player who donned a Bruins uniform that dramatic season—along with the team's coach and general-manager—was still alive. Only a handful of peripheral figures had passed away.

Trainer John (Frosty) Forristal, who battled alcoholism late in his life, succumbed to brain cancer on May 30, 1995, at the young age of 51. (Bobby Orr compassionately shared his home with Forristal to make his final weeks comfortable. Orr also served as a pallbearer at Forristal's funeral. It was widely attended by Bruin alumni who fondly recalled his total dedication to the players.) Forristal, at age 19 in 1963, had just been discharged from a short stint in the U.S. Marine Corps. He was hired as the Bruins' stick boy for $90 a week after his mother alerted him to the job opening. He worked his way up to being a "co-trainer" with Dan Canney—which meant for 20 years they did everything from sharpening the Bruins' skates and washing and mending their sweaters and socks to finding a place for the team to eat and enjoy adult beverages after a game. Forristal also stitched wounds and provided physical treatment to his Bruins to the best of his abilities despite having no medical training whatsoever. Forristal's *Boston Globe* obituary (in which his surname was spelled with two L's) called him "a Gleasonesque character with the perpetual smile and appetite for life who could keep them stitched—and keep them in stitches. His eyes spoke of mischief."[1] Forristal was the only American member of Team Canada 1972 that famously battled the USSR in eight memorable contests, having been personally selected as the squad's trainer by coach Harry Sinden. In the series-deciding game in Moscow, when all hell threatened to break loose, Forristal, clad in a bright red Team Canada jumpsuit, was seen by millions of television viewers thrusting both middle fingers toward the arena's VIP box where Leonid Brezhnev and other Soviet bigwigs were seated.

Dan Canney, who was listed as the Bruins' "head trainer" from 1962 to 1985, passed away suddenly on January 22, 2017, in Charlestown, Massachusetts, at the age of 84. He left behind Peg, his wife of 60 years.

Team president Paul A. Mooney went to an early grave in 2000 at age 59, a victim of cancer. He became president of the Bruins and Boston Garden in October 1975 when the team and the arena were purchased by Sportsystems. He retained his dual position for 12 years until retiring in 1987. During his tenure, he strongly opposed the 1979 NHL-WHA merger. He also dismissed longtime organist John Kiley over a petty dispute. Mooney was constantly at odds with Don Cherry during the 1978–79 season. (It was not a coincidence that Cherry did not make any trips to Boston for his *Hockey Night in Canada* duties until after Mooney had left the Bruins.) On the positive side, Mooney was very prominent in making sure that Boston forward Normand Léveillé, the team's top draft selection in 1981, was properly cared for after a cerebral aneurysm in 1982 put the 19-year-old forward in a coma for three weeks and left him unable to walk.

Longtime Bruin television and radio broadcasters Fred Cusick and Bob Wilson have also passed. Both enjoyed long lives. The modest Cusick, who had been honored in 1988 with the Lester Patrick Award for his contributions to hockey in the United States, was 90 when he died on September 15, 2009. "His ego would fit in a thimble,"[2] said Johnny Peirson, Cusick's broadcast partner for 18 seasons, in a 1994 interview. (Peirson, age 92, was still alive in August 2017.) Cusick had called Bruin games for 45 seasons when he retired in 1997. Wilson was 85 at the time of his death on January 15, 2015. Fittingly the Bruins' television broadcast booth at TD Garden has been named after Cusick while the home radio booth has been named in honor of Wilson.

M. Weldon Haire, the smooth-voiced Boston Garden public-address announcer with the aristocratic-sounding name, died on August 9, 1982, at age 65 "after a long illness," according to his *Globe* obituary. Haire started as the Boston Celtics' P.A. man in 1949 and kept that job until 1980. He replaced Bruins P.A. announcer Frank Fallon—who passed away suddenly on November 29, 1973—and held that position until his own death. Working the Garden's microphone for both the Celtics and the Bruins was only a sideline for the busy Haire, a Second World War veteran. He was a teacher, a basketball coach, and he owned an independent insurance agency for 30 years. In what was left of his precious spare time, Haire wrote for the *Lowell Sun* and served as sports editor of the *Chelmsford Weekly News*.

Assistant general-manager Tom Johnson—Harry Sinden's faithful deputy—died in November 2007 of heart failure at the age of 79 at his Falmouth, MA home while stacking firewood. He won six Stanley Cups in eight seasons as a Hall-of-Fame defenseman with Montreal in the 1950s. In 1958–59 he won the Norris Trophy as the NHL's best defenseman, ending teammate Doug Harvey's run of four straight awards. Johnson also played for the Bruins for two seasons (1963–64 and 1964–65) to conclude a very impressive career. He is probably most famous for coaching the 1970–71 Bruins who rampaged through the regular season only to lose to Montreal in a shocking quarterfinal playoff upset. Johnson did, however, coach the Bruins to the Stanley Cup in 1971–72. His 142–43–23 record in not quite three full seasons as Boston's coach gives him the honor of having the best winning percentage by far (.738) of not just any coach in Bruins history, but of any NHL coach with a minimum 200 games on his résumé. (By comparison, Scotty Bowman's winning percentage is a distant .657.) In February 1973 Johnson surprisingly moved from behind the Boston bench to a new role as assistant general-manager to Harry Sinden. Upon hearing of Johnson's death, Sinden kindly said, "If we are all allowed an ultimate friend, mentor, confidant, and teacher, Tom Johnson was all of those to me."[3] After the 1978–79 season, Johnson served as the Bruins' vice president until his retirement in 1998.

Organist John Kiley—who began his entertainment career at age 15 by providing musical accompaniment in a silent-movie theater—died on July 15, 1993, at age 80. He entertained hockey and basketball fans at Boston Garden from 1941 to 1984 and baseball fans at Fenway Park from 1953 until 1989—and even earlier at Braves Field when Boston still had a National League club. Kiley often chose his musical selections with whimsical humor. On steamy days at Fenway, Kiley liked to "cool off" the ballpark's patrons with *White Christmas*. His *Boston Globe* obituary, written by Bob Ryan, lovingly described him as "a bit of a ham."[4] Curiously, a song popularized by Maurice Chevalier titled *Paree* became Kiley's upbeat signature tune for the Bruins, which he played at every opportunity. (Why *Paree*? According to hockey historian Stan Fischler, the tune was popular in Europe when the Bruins made an overseas trip in the late 1920s. Considering that Kiley began working for the Bruins more than a decade later, Fischler's explanation is questionable.) The 71-year-old Kiley was ridiculously dismissed from his longstanding job at Boston Garden in 1984 by president Paul Mooney in a dispute over a parking spot! Upon Kiley's voluntary retirement in 1989, the Red Sox chose not to get a new organist for Fenway Park, instead opting for trendier recorded pop music. Upon hearing that news, Kiley conceded with a touch of melancholy, "You have to give the public what they want."[5]

Lest we forget Blue, Don Cherry's beloved bull terrier, the omnipresent four-legged symbol of Bruindom in the late 1970s. She was humanely put down in 1989 at the age of 15. Her death merited news coverage in several Canadian newspapers—especially the *Toronto Sun* which to this day revels in anything associated with Cherry. In the mid–1980s Cherry and Blue did a series of Canadian TV commercials for Bridgestone Tires—one of which had Blue decked out in a black tie and top hat! Cherry claimed in a 1989 *Boston Globe* interview with Leigh Montville that Budweiser's Spuds MacKenzie was a clear rip-off of his pet. "The English bull terrier has been around for 150 years. In all that time only one other had done a commercial. What do you think?"[6] Since the death of the original Blue, Cherry has owned other white bull terriers—each of which he also named Blue. The crest of the OHL's Niagara Ice Dogs features a fierce-looking cartoon dog called Bones. It was modeled after the original Blue's image when the team was located in Mississauga and Cherry was a part owner of the club.

Many of the eloquent *Boston Globe* sports journalists who covered the Bruins' exploits that memorable season are gone. In fact, John Ahern, Tom Fitzgerald and Ray Fitzgerald all sadly died within a span of 15 months in the early 1980s—an enormous three-pronged blow to Boston's newspaper community and to everyone who appreciated fine sports journalism. (Tom Fitzgerald—a personal favorite of Don Cherry—had retired from the Globe staff in 1977, so he did not cover the 1978–79 Bruins.) Will McDonough suffered a fatal heart attack in 2003 at the age of 67. His son, Sean, is a nationally known, versatile voice in sports broadcasting.

Ernie Roberts, who edited the *Boston Globe*'s sports section and wrote a popular weekend column, died on March 23, 2009, at age 88. Colleagues Dan Shaughnessy and Bob Ryan claimed Roberts was largely responsible for assembling the team of writers that made the *Globe*'s sports section so impressive. He started at the *Globe* as a co-op student in 1947 and stayed there until retiring in 1983. Roberts quietly preferred intercollegiate athletics over pro sports, so much so that for the first half of the 1960s he also served as Dartmouth College's sports information director. Beginning in June 1974 Roberts began each of his 394 Saturday *Globe* columns with a cheery "Good morning!" and then a description of what he or a certain sports personality might be having for breakfast. It was a silly gimmick, but Roberts' readers liked it. His final column ended with, "Adieu, folks. Don't burn the toast."[7]

Francis Rosa outlived his same-generation colleagues by far, passing away on January 4, 2012, of lung and cardiac ailments at age 91. He deserves special mention. The dapper Rosa was probably the most respected Boston hockey writer ever. Rosa's lengthy obituary in the *Boston Globe*, written by Bryan Marquard, recalled an incident during the 1972

Stanley Cup final. The Bruins had just beaten the New York Rangers to take a three-games-to-one lead in the series. The downcast Rangers refused to talk to any Boston reporters—with the lone exception of the gentlemanly Rosa. "Player after player opened up [to him] in interviews," the obit claimed, "perhaps because like all athletes, they knew that if they spoke to Mr. Rosa their thoughts and words would grace the next day's newspaper."[8] Harry Sinden said of Rosa, "He became one of the family. In those days we didn't seem to have the wall that's between some of the writers and the teams today. I went to dinner with him many times on the road. I thought of him as a good friend."[9] His obituary in the *Globe* further described Rosa as a "generous reporter [who] filled thousands of stories with quotes throughout his career, allowing the musings of college and professional athletes to illuminate the games they played."

Boston Garden itself no longer exists, a casualty of modernization and a demolition crew's wrecking ball in 1998—three years after hosting its last Bruins' home game. During the 1978–79 season the arena's shortcomings were so worrisome that a March 25 *Boston Globe* editorial warned, "Boston could well lose one of its major sports franchises to another city, or to its suburbs, within the next few years. That possibility becomes almost a certainty the longer the city asks the Bruins and the Celtics to perform in the antiquated Boston Garden and still compete with teams playing in far larger, far more attractive settings."[10] Constructed primarily as a boxing venue, Boston Garden served as the Bruins' home from 1928 to 1995. It was cramped, obsolete, and it lacked luxuries, but it was a huge part of Bruins lore. More importantly, it was an intimidating part of the Bruins' collective persona. "The angle of the seats seemingly had the fans looming over the ice. The roar of the crowd created claustrophobic thoughts in the visitors' minds,"[11] Fred Cusick wrote in his autobiography. Fans were tantalizingly close to the action. In contrast, it has been estimated that three-quarters of the seats at TD Garden—the building that was erected as a modern replacement—would not fit inside cozy Boston Garden. The Bruins' new home was constructed a mere 18 inches from where Boston Garden once stood on Causeway Street. The acreage where Boston Garden once stood is now a parking lot. In the first two decades of TD Garden's existence it had three different corporate names. In the 67 seasons the Bruins called Boston Garden home, it had just one. On a YouTube video showing a 1978 Bruins-Habs playoff game, two posters lamented the loss of their beloved hockey venue. One commented, "[It was] the best place to see a hockey game … so intense. The crowd was sitting almost over the ice." Another wrote, "TD Garden is like a funeral home compared to the real Boston Garden."[12]

As was mentioned in this book's preface, in researching the portions that primarily focus on the Bruins, I happily rediscovered why it had been such a joy to follow this remarkable team as a teenager: The 1978–79 Boston Bruins were a fun and thoroughly likeable group! The season-long narrative of the gritty, workmanlike Bruins facing battle after battle in their uphill, quixotic quest for the elusive Stanley Cup—be it the on-ice struggles versus the seemingly invincible Habs, overcoming injuries and illnesses, coping with the underhanded decisions of dastardly referees, or handling the villains in the team's front office—is what made them such a beloved bunch to me. No doubt thousands of Bruin fans would concur. The fact that their final game was lost under cruelly heartbreaking circumstances only makes their legacy more endearing to their followers.

The sum of those 1978–79 Boston Bruins was greater than the individual parts. The Montreal Canadiens were the superior team on paper, of course. In the end, their overall edge in talent mattered. Nevertheless, those Bruins possessed an intangible something that made them consistent winners in the Don Cherry era—just not Stanley Cup champions.

They were a team of men: an eclectic coterie comprised of sheer class and dignity (Jean Ratelle); bluster, bombast and a confident swagger (Don Cherry); frenzied energy (Terry O'Reilly and John Wensink); intelligence, (Peter McNab and Dick Redmond); panache (Rick Middleton); veteran smarts (Gerry Cheevers, Rick Smith, Don Marcotte, and Gary Doak); youthful enthusiasm (Mike Milbury, Al Sims, Al Secord and Bob Miller); timely heroes (Gilles Gilbert); and remarkable guts (Brad Park, Wayne Cashman and Stan Jonathan).

Yes, they were a stellar group of men. Unfortunately, on the infamous night of Thursday, May 10, 1979, at the Montreal Forum, there were just too many men.

Appendix A
Boston's Key Personnel, 1978–79

*The age stated is how old each person would have been on his birthday in 1979.

Blue, age 5*

"Tough as nails … best dog in the world. After those bull terriers—they're so strong and confident—all other dogs are downhill."[1] That was Don Cherry's description of his favorite breed of dog. He was specifically describing his beloved Blue, the most famous canine in hockey history.

Blue is the only female on this list. Including the coach's pet as one of the 1978–79 Boston Bruins may seem odd, but it is difficult not to place Blue on the team's roster based on the vast amount of news coverage she got during the Don Cherry era. Cherry's bull terrier (and alter-ego) became a local celebrity because Cherry made constant references to her. John Powers of the *Boston Globe* deemed Blue to be "the most symbolic bull terrier since George Patton's."[2]

Cherry kiddingly told reporters that Blue occasionally helped him decide which goalie to start in a big game, a comment that displeased general-manager Harry Sinden who saw no humor in it. According to an anecdote that appears in one of Cherry's books, Blue's fame began when the *Globe's* Tom Fitzgerald asked him which goalie would be starting versus the New York Rangers. Cherry responded as a joke, "Blue told me to start Cheevers."[3] That night, Cherry recalled, Gerry Cheevers recorded a shutout. [Author's note: Cherry's memory is faulty here. Not once in the Cherry era did the Bruins inflict a shutout on the Rangers.] Regardless of the accuracy of the details, Boston's hockey writers began expecting Cherry to confer with Blue regarding goaltender assignments.

References to Blue, of course, were incorporated into many of Cherry's speeches to his team as examples of toughness and loyalty that he wanted the Bruins to emulate. One time when Blue was present at Boston Garden to be included in the Bruins' official team photo, all the players had already taken their positions near center ice. Trainer Frosty Forristal approached the ice with Blue from a distant gate used by the Zamboni driver. Cherry called for Blue, but she balked at going onto the Garden's ice surface to join him. The players started kidding Cherry about his famously tough dog being afraid to walk on the ice. However, Blue opted for a different route: She made her way through the corridors to an open gate much closer to where the team had assembled—and merrily joined Cherry and his Bruins. "Blue was just being smart," Cherry recalled years later. "She found a way to make a shorter trip across the ice."[4]

Being compared to Blue was the highest honor Cherry could bestow upon any individual. Journalist George Plimpton—who, at age 50, famously played goal for Boston for five hectic minutes of a 1977 preseason game—noted in his book *Open Net*, "Cherry had a near-symbiotic relationship with his dog. I never met Blue while I was with the Bruins, but the dog was an overriding presence in [the Bruins' training] camp in Fitchburg, and especially in Boston."[5]

"I don't teach her any tricks," Cherry insisted. "Blue doesn't 'sit.' I don't want anyone to tell my dog to sit. In fact, I had an awful argument with a friend. I never talked to her for a year because she kept yelling at my dog to sit."[6]

Cherry became infuriated once when he was approached to enter Blue in an ugly dog contest. In the end, because the event was a charity fund-raiser, Cherry agreed to let Blue participate—as a judge, not as a participant.

Blue and her master hated to be separated from each other for long. Thus Cherry was reluctant to venture far if it meant Blue had to be put in a kennel. When he and Rose were given a complimentary 14-day holiday package in Hawaii, he spent almost every moment fretting about his absent dog. "Here we were in beautiful Hawaii," recalled Rose, "and Don said it was the most miserable two weeks of his life. He never left the hotel room."[7] After that disastrous outing, Cherry was never voluntarily away from Blue for such a long period again.

The May 25, 1979, edition of the *Boston Globe* contained a letter from John A.M. Rowe, an irked reader from Cambridge, MA. Rowe was outraged that the Boston terrier breed had recently been declared the official state dog of Massachusetts. He thought the honor should have gone specifically to Blue because of her "true Boston character."[8]

Just before the 1979 Boston-Montreal playoff series began, Blue was the subject of a *Globe* feature. In it Cherry discussed Blue's impact on the Bruins. "We do a lot of kidding about it," he admitted, "but look at Stanley Jonathan, John Wensink, Terry O'Reilly, Rick Middleton, Bobby Miller, Bobby Schmautz, the whole bunch of them. They all have a little bull terrier in them or it's no use playing on our team."[9]

"Blue has become a symbol that has transcended dogdom," John Powers declared. "Channel 38 uses her for promos."[10]

Blue's fame, of course, expanded well beyond the greater Boston area. To Cherry's horror, fans of other NHL teams began insulting his beloved pooch in an attempt to unnerve the Boston coach and the Bruins as a whole. Late in his tenure as Bruins coach Cherry lamented, "The last time we were in Buffalo there were two 60-foot signs disparaging Blue. Two 60-footers! Nobody gets those signs."[11] When Ranger fans obscene chants at Cherry failed to produce any reaction from the coach, the Madison Square Garden crowd turned to verbally denouncing Blue. "Imagine that. Seventeen thousand fans going after a man's dog…,"[12] Cherry recalled with a sigh.

Cherry claimed Blue's favorite song was Stevie Wonder's *You are the Sunshine of My Life*—a tune that still makes him teary long after Blue departed the earthly world in 1989. Blue lived to the advanced age of 15, making her a centenarian in dog years.

Wayne Cashman, age 34

Wayne Cashman was the captain of the 1978–79 Bruins—and deservedly so. Not only was he a natural leader, Cashman represented the transition between the powerhouse Esposito-Orr era in Boston and the grind-them-to-death, Lunch Pail A.C. years of the late 1970s. Cashman's toughness—combined with an ability to score frequently—was an enormously positive factor during both eras.

"He was definitely one of the two or three best left wingers I've ever seen," Gerry Cheevers said of Cashman. "He was undoubtedly the greatest corner man the game has ever seen."[13] Cheevers was talking about Cashman's unrivalled ability to retrieve loose pucks from the left corner in the opposition's end of the ice and feed them to whichever Bruin was awaiting a pass in front of the net. "Just throw the puck into my corner, get in the slot, and I'll get it back to you,"[14] was the simple instruction Cashman gave Phil Esposito the season Espo notched his record-shattering 76 goals. Possessing such a dedicated work ethic, Cashman easily transitioned in to the Cherry-era Bruins.

Cashman had a certain controlled meanness about him that did not go unnoticed in the rest of the NHL. Opponents who glimpsed Cashman pursuing them into a corner of the rink in pursuit of a loose puck were known to flinch, noticeably slow down, or stop skating altogether. "When Wayne Cashman dies, it would only be too fitting if he were buried in the corner of the cemetery,"[15] wrote blogger Joe Pelletier. Cashman would also quickly take matters into his own hands if anyone dared to run at Bobby Orr or Phil Esposito. "In the age of the Big Bad Bruins, Wayne was the biggest and the baddest,"[16] opined Pelletier. Cashman knew his own reputation well. During the 1972 Canada-Soviet series, Cashman addressed his teammates before Game #2 in Toronto after they had shockingly lost the first game 7–3 in Montreal. "You just play your game tonight," he told them. "I'll be the big, bad Bruin."[17] Cashman's physical play severely rattled the Soviets as Canada won 4–1.

In 2015, hockey writer Rick Cole brought together three former NHL referees—Bruce Hood, Bryan Lewis and Ron Wicks—and collectively interviewed them on a myriad of topics. All three agreed on a few things: the two-referee system is an improvement; video replay to assist officials is progress; Bobby Orr was the greatest player of all time; and Wayne Cashman was the toughest NHLer to deal with. Wicks opined, "You had to watch a guy like Cashman. He was a pretty good fighter but he was a little bit on the edge. [Wicks rotated a finger at the side of his head to indicate that Cashman was crazy.] And if somebody got him going … look out! I remember one night a player in Atlanta took a run at Bobby Orr, and Bobby had just been in for about his eighth knee operation. Cashman had him against the boards. He spun his stick and said, 'You try that again and I'll take both your eyes out one at a time.' And on the way out he says, 'And I might take a referee too.'"[18]

Before he succeeded Johnny Bucyk as the Bruins' captain, Cashman was merely quiet but determined. With the added responsibility on his shoulders, Cashman opened up more and became a team cheerleader when the captain's "C" was sewn onto his jersey. "Back in the days of Esposito and Orr, Cash was a follower," recalled general-manager Harry Sinden. "Now he's a helluva leader on the ice and in the dressing room."[19] Part of Cashman's leadership was to play with discomfort as an example to his teammates. Despite enduring intense back pain that required traction in a Boston hospital between home games of the Habs-Bruins semifinal in 1979, the gutsy Cashman was the most reliable Bruins offensive player in that series. A bad back was not the only ailment Cashman endured in 1978–79. Toward the end of March, Cashman was afflicted with a painful full-body rash, so irritating that he could not sit or lie comfortably. "I haven't slept for three nights,"[20] Cashman ruefully told the *Boston Globe*. The Hub's media called it "the Cash rash."

When Cashman retired at the end of the 1982–83 season, he had spent his entire career as a Boston Bruin. His NHL career had started with one game in 1964–65—which made Cashman the last active NHLer who could claim to have played in the Original Six era. In one fan poll, Cashman was voted the greatest Bruin player who spent his entire NHL career with Boston. It was a quirky honor, but Cashman finished ahead of both Milt Schmidt and Dit Clapper in the voting—two all-time great Bruins who have had their numbers retired.

Cashman was probably the most noteworthy Bruin who was absent from "the Last Hurrah"—the memorable September night in 1995 when Boston Garden hosted its final hockey game and the Bruins feted their alumni. The explanation was simple: Cashman does not like ceremonies.

Although he seemed like a humorless beast to opposing players, Cashman had a definite wild and crazy side that was well known to all the Bruins once they got to know him. Cashman once broke his foot swinging from a chandelier. It was Cashman who cut the anthem singer's microphone cord before a key Boston playoff game in Los Angeles in 1977. Perhaps the most amusing off-ice incident involving Cashman was the time he was arrested in a case of mistaken identity for a bank robbery suspect. Taken to a holding cell, Cashman was told he was entitled to make one telephone call—which he did. A little while later a delivery boy showed up at the police station. "Chinese food for Mr. Cashman," he said.

Gerry Cheevers, age 39

Forever known as Boston's "money goalie"—a winner when it counted most—Gerry (Cheesey) Cheevers could be described with plentiful adjectives: funny, calm, business-like, professional, crazy, hard-working, thoughtful and goofy. All of them were accurate assessments of the Bruins' longtime, reliable netminder.

Despite performing in numerous high-pressure games, Cheevers always impressed coach Don Cherry with his stoicism. "Cheevers' idea is that it's only a game," Cherry noted. "He's not going to make himself sick over it."[21] Leigh Montville wrote in a *Boston Globe* piece, "Gerry Cheevers was a visible rendering of the pilot's calm voice as the aircraft hit just a bit of turbulence over Schenectady."[22] During the 1979 Habs-Bruins semifinal, Montville opined, "Give me Bob Gainey's heart when I'm starting to build a perfect hockey player. Give me Larry Robinson's size. Give me [Guy] Lafleur's moves. Give me Cheevers' disposition."[23]

Cheevers began as a bare-faced goalie in the NHL's Original Six era; a Boston-Toronto game from 1966 on YouTube shows Cheevers playing with no mask. He donned one shortly thereafter. As a conspicuous salute to his wisdom, Cheevers began adorning his plain white mask with magic-marker stitches to show what his face might have looked like had he not been wearing it. The idea came from Boston trainer Frosty Forristal. Cheevers' "stitched mask" became the most recognizable in hockey; it also started the enduring culture of goalie-mask art.

Twice a Stanley Cup champion with Boston, the 1971–72 season was Cheevers' best. He played in 32 consecutive games without suffering a defeat (24 wins and eight ties). By the 1978–79 season, Cheevers was a grizzled veteran, but he was still a top-notch NHL netminder despite his advancing age. "When the money is on the line, the Bruins haven't had a better goalie in the past 50 years,"[24] said defenseman Gary Doak. Cheevers' solid play versus Pittsburgh in a 2–1 win in Game #3 of the quarterfinals—when he was summoned on short notice to replace the suddenly ill Gilles Gilbert—was perhaps his finest moment of 1978–79.

Although Cheevers was utterly fearless in big games, he sometimes deferred to self-preservation in less important situations. Once, late in a game the Bruins were winning handily versus Chicago, Cheevers literally fled from the Boston goal crease when the Black-hawks' Cliff Koroll wound up from very short range to blast a spinning puck toward the Boston goal. The puck whizzed into the center of the abandoned Boston net. When defenseman Brad Park gave his goalie a quizzical look, Cheevers was quick with an honest reply: "That could have hit me!"[25]

Don Cherry, age 45

When Don (Grapes) Cherry assumed the coaching position for Boston Bruins in 1974, few people had ever heard of him. By his 80th birthday in 2014, there was scarcely a hockey fan in North America who did not know who Don Cherry was, especially in Canada.

Cherry was behind the bench when a very good Bruins team unexpectedly lost in the opening round of the 1975 Stanley Cup playoffs to the Chicago Blackhawks in a best-of-three opening-round series. In his remaining four years at the helm of the Bruins, Cherry's team would never again be surprised by an inferior team in the playoffs.

When Bobby Orr and Phil Esposito were no longer part of the Bruins' roster, Cherry transformed the team into his "lunch pail" group—an assemblage of players who worked hard every shift and were the ultimate NHL team in the truest sense of the word.

In 1975–76, Cherry won the Jack Adams Memorial Trophy as the NHL's Coach of the Year. It would be 22 years before another Bruins coach was so honored. "Of course it's a tremendous compliment," Cherry modestly told Tom Fitzgerald of the *Boston Globe*, "but a man has to keep a sense of perspective. I'm not a believer in coaches being geniuses. If the excuse for having a losing team is not having the horses, the same thing applies the other way. A coach doesn't get anywhere without the right players and the right kind of players."[26]

Being named Coach of the Year undoubtedly was a major factor in Cherry's appointment to the coaching staff of Team Canada for the 1976 Canada Cup tournament that September. Cherry worked alongside veterans Scotty Bowman, Bobby Kromm and Al MacNeil. Cherry's sage advice was responsible for Darryl Sittler's overtime goal against Czechoslovakia in the final. Cherry noticed that Czech goalie Vladimir Dzurilla moved far out of his net to challenge shooters. Cherry rightly figured that Dzurilla could be pulled out of position on a fake shot—and the shooter would be able to move around him and have an open net. Cherry relayed his theory to the Canadian players before the overtime period began. That's precisely how Sittler scored the winning goal.

Despite the camaraderie Cherry shared with his troops, he could be harsh with his players. Peter McNab recalled an incident when Cherry berated him as "the worst player in the goddamn universe."[27] The analytical McNab's first thought was, "It doesn't get much worse than that. It's a pretty big universe. There has to be some hockey player somewhere worse than I am!" Another time Rick Middleton reported to training camp overweight so Cherry began calling him Porky Pig. Nevertheless, Middleton adored Cherry. "Don Cherry taught me how to play the game,"[28] Middleton insisted.

The Boston media—and media personnel far beyond the Hub—loved Cherry from the first moment he took charge of the Bruins. Cherry regaled them with amusing anecdotes from his nomadic years as a minor-league defenseman, and he could always be counted on to say something interesting and controversial to fill column space on slow news days—an invaluable resource much appreciated by hockey writers. It was this frankness and natural gift for stirring the pot that has made Cherry such a captivating television personality in Canada. Cherry welcomed publicity and made a point of getting to know all the Boston-based hockey reporters. He had no qualms about sharing his unlisted telephone number in case they wanted his opinion on anything at a moment's notice.

Cherry's popularity extended to hockey writers in other cities who discovered that he was the best interview in the NHL because of his bluntness. Tim Burke of the *Montreal Gazette* wrote, "Cherry's most refreshing feature is his unalloyed honesty. His syntax is from the docks and his menu from a greasy spoon and he is proud of it. Always accessible, full of imagination and ribald humor, Cherry is a newspaperman's delight."[29] Similarly, during the 1979 playoffs, Eddie MacCabe of the *Ottawa Citizen* declared Cherry to be "surely the most enjoyable character in the NHL."[30]

Cherry famously battled the NHL and the Bruins' front office in the Boston media for pretty much the duration of his colorful five-year tenure in Boston. His dazzling, self-styled wardrobes and attention-seeking, over-the-top behavior aside, Cherry was a frequent winner behind Boston's bench.

Although he was a traditionalist, Cherry was among the first NHL coaches to embrace the common-sense notion of using videotape technology as an instructional aid. He also created video highlight packages to boost his Bruins' individual and collective egos. It was all designed to make the Bruins greater believers in themselves. "Cherry sees champagne even though the labels say beer,"[31] John Ahern wrote in the *Globe*.

In his final four seasons in Boston, Cherry's team impressively finished first in the Adams Division every year. Twice Boston reached the Stanley Cup final. Twice more they were eliminated in the semifinals. A model of consistent excellence, the Bruins' longest regular-season losing streak during Cherry's 400 games with Boston was a mere three games. When the Bruins did mildly slump under Cherry's leadership, it was newsworthy. In a January 18, 1979, *Globe* story, Fran Rosa noted, "Boston sports fans, who hardly noticed the Bruins winning game after game, have now discovered the Bruins because they are losing game after game. It takes three straight defeats to start the questions."[32]

About the only people in Boston eager to see Cherry leave after the 1978–79 season were the Bruins' upper management. Even including his one-season stint as coach of the lowly Colorado Rockies the year after he left Boston, Cherry attained 250 regular-season victories faster than any coach in NHL history. Cherry, in many ways, was the familiar face of the Boston Bruins of the late 1970s. St. Louis coach Barclay Plager concurred. He told the *Globe* before a Blues-Bruins game, "[The Bruins] are Don Cherry's personality through and through. They always come out with thunder whether they're playing in Boston or on the road. That means they'll be working hard. To beat them you have to work harder."[33]

Gary Doak, age 33

"Doak has been around here a long time," wrote John Ahern in a November 7, 1978, *Boston Globe* piece on the Bruins, "and he's less conspicuous than a kid who might have checked in for a tryout yesterday. Doak isn't spectacular, nor does he make mistakes. Fans notice only the players in those categories."[34]

Ahern's remark was wholly accurate. Gary Doak was never a headline-maker nor a major offensive threat—he only scored 23 goals in 789 regular-season NHL games—but he was an absolutely fearless stay-at-home defenseman who earned the respect of teammates and foes alike. He seldom hesitated to sprawl on the ice to block shots. Constantly inviting injury, Doak was sidelined frequently with an assortment of ailments resulting from his reckless abandon.

Doak's career began with Detroit where he played four games for the Red Wings in 1965–66. The Bruins picked him up in a trade in February 1966 and he stayed with Boston through their 1970 Stanley Cup triumph. "He doesn't rush like Bobby Orr," Harry Sinden said of Doak at the time, "but defensively he takes a back seat to nobody on our squad."[35] Doak's profile in the Hockey Hall of Fame's player database labels him "a stay-at-home blueliner who tattooed impressions of his shoulders and elbows on any opponent who came within range."[36]

Doak had a nomadic existence in the NHL in the early 1970s. The Bruins lost Doak in the 1970 expansion draft when he was plucked from their roster by the Vancouver Canucks. A valued veteran who was given plenty of ice team, Doak played 77 games for the Canucks in 1970–71, the highest seasonal total in his career. He did not stay in Vancouver long. Six games into the following season Doak was shipped to the New York Rangers as part of a five-player transaction. Often playing alongside Brad Park, his team lost to Boston in the 1972 Cup final. Two weeks after the season ended, Doak was involved in another trade where he returned to Detroit. In 1973–74 he headed back to Boston—in a trade for Garnet (Ace) Bailey—and stayed on the Bruins' roster for eight more seasons to conclude his solid NHL career. After retiring as a player, Doak was a Bruins assistant coach under Gerry Cheevers from 1981 to 1985. Doak also served as coach of the University of Massachusetts team from 1985 to 1987. Proud of his long association with the Bruins, Doak continued to represent the team all his life. He seldom missed an alumni event.

"Gary was the type of player who never let up," Gerry Cheevers recalled. "He had that rambunctious style of play that kept him going even if he was risking injury."[37] Doak was absent from the Bruins late in the 1978–79 regular season with both chest and shoulder injuries. Late in the season he was summoned to his hometown of Goderich, Ontario to tend to his ailing father, thus reducing his games-played total even further.

Years later Sinden spoke fondly of Doak and his unheralded contributions to the team's overall success. The general-manager noted, "As much as any player, Gary exemplified the attitude surrounding the Bruin teams of the 1970s."[38]

Don Cherry was a big supporter too. He thought Doak was playing the finest hockey of his career in 1978–79. "I'm being fair to the other [defensemen] when I say that he's been something else," Cherry insisted. "He's been super—nothing short of that."[39]

Upon Doak's death from cancer on March 25, 2017, at age 71, Bruins president Cam Neely told the *Boston Herald*, "It's a sad day for the Bruins' organization. [Doak] did so much with the organization after he retired. He hung around. He was always available for charity events for the alumni. Just a sad day."

Dwight Foster, age 22

Rookie Dwight Foster found his first full year with the Boston Bruins to be a trying experience in which he did nearly as much spectating as playing.

His first taste of the NHL in 1977–78 was cut short after 14 games because of a knee injury that required surgery. The youthful forward got into 44 regular-season games in 1978–79, scoring 11 goals. He also appeared in all 11 of Boston's playoff games that season. However, his rawness made coach Don Cherry somewhat leery of playing him in critical situations. The best example of this is that Foster's ice time in Game #7 versus Montreal consisted of exactly three seconds—comprising a faceoff to conclude the final moments of regulation time.

Curiously, a columnist for the *Kitchener-Waterloo Record* reported that Foster was relieved that Boston did not advance to the 1979 Stanley Cup final. Foster said two more weeks of hockey would have delayed his wedding plans and interfered with the radiator business he had just established in Kitchener, Ontario—the city where he had played junior hockey superbly for four seasons.

Foster led the Ontario Hockey League in scoring in his last junior season with 60 goals and 83 assists. He still holds four significant Kitchener Rangers team records: Most goals in a game (5), most assists in a season (83), most points in a season (143), and most points in a career (382). The three seasonal marks were all set in 1976–77. Those stats made him highly regarded. Foster was selected 16th overall by the Bruins in the 1977 amateur draft.

Foster never came close to replicating his junior hockey offensive totals in the NHL, however. His best goal-scoring campaign came in 1980–81—his last year with the Bruins before his rights were traded to Colorado—when he notched 24 scores. In fact, Foster's Wikipedia entry describes him as "a strong defensive forward with marginal offensive ability."[40]

Gilles Gilbert, age 28

After playing in just 23 games in 1978–79—just slightly more than lightly regarded third-string netminder Jim Pettie—Boston backup goalie Gilles Gilbert was definitely a fringe player with the Bruins when the Boston-Montreal semifinal began. He was supposed to play in Game #3 of Boston's quarterfinal versus Pittsburgh, but a sudden attack of hives sidelined him and Gerry Cheevers once again was between the pipes for the Bruins. Gilbert's time with the Bruins seemed to be over.

However, in an effort to shake up the team, Don Cherry played one of his frequent hunches by starting Gilbert in Game #3 versus Montreal. Boston won and Gilbert was selected as the game's first star. Cheevers, the elder of the two Boston goalies by ten years, was suddenly Gilbert's backup for the rest of the series and did not play after Game #2.

Gilbert's NHL career started with the Minnesota North Stars. He played 44 games for them between 1971 and 1973. (In one of those contests, Gilbert allowed one of the most picturesque goals in Bruins history: It's the one where Bobby Orr is roughly slammed down to the ice by North Star defenseman Fred Barrett but still makes a perfect pass to Johnny Bucyk while lying flat on his back. Bucyk then skillfully backhands the puck past a startled and sprawling Gilbert for a goal. It may have been the greatest assist of all time.)

After Boston's Stanley Cup triumph in 1972, the Bruins' goaltending was in disarray. Gerry Cheevers had jumped to the World Hockey Association. The Bruins' goalie of the future, Dan Bouchard, was lost to the Atlanta Flames in the expansion draft that same year. Ed Johnston was well past his prime. Undoubtedly, weak goaltending kept Boston from advancing past the first round of the Stanley Cup playoffs in 1973. Harry Sinden dealt Fred Stanfield to the North Stars for Gilbert prior to the 1973–74 season. Gilbert quickly became the Bruins' most reliable goalie as Boston returned to the Stanley Cup final after a one-year hiatus. Gilbert practically matched Philadelphia's Bernie Parent—the Conn Smythe Trophy winner—save for save in the series.

When Don Cherry became Boston's coach the following season, Gilbert and Cherry immediately clashed. Cherry perceived that Gilbert was distracted, self-centered, and not wholly committed to the team. Cherry's opinion of Gilbert never really improved over the years, even though Gilbert won 17 straight games during the 1975–76 season. (He may have been the only Bruin player who truly disliked Cherry. Had Cherry not left the Bruins after 1978–79, Gilbert would have almost certainly found a new team for 1979–80.) Gilbert and teammate Gerry Cheevers reputedly did not get along, either. Ray Fitzgerald, in an April 3 *Boston Globe* article about Cheevers, noted that Boston's two best goalies were "not exactly soulmates."[41]

Nevertheless, Gilbert was outstanding in the five playoff games he played against the Canadiens in the spring of 1979. He was named the first star in four of them—including Game #7. Boston could have easily lost that contest by five or six goals had it not been for

Gilbert's acrobatic and excellent work in the Bruins' net. The Habs fired 105 shots at the Bruins net—52 of which were on target. On a Montreal Canadiens fan website, a blogger named Andrew Berkshire, who examined Game #7 in extreme detail, commented, "Call it lucky if you want, and his technique doesn't stand up, but this game should go down as one of the best goaltender performances ever. The caliber of shooters [Gilbert] was facing combined with pure shot volume should have made this a rout."[42]

"I think I ruined his career," Guy Lafleur candidly said of Gilbert in 2012. "When I scored that tying goal on him in 1979 and we ended up beating the Bruins in the semifinals, Gilles was a good goalie. Unfortunately for him, after that tying goal, he didn't go too far."[43] In 1988 Harry Sinden said, "I remember that seventh game [in 1979], watching Gilles Gilbert. He played a great game, and I remember thinking, 'Well, we're set in goal for the next 10 years.' The next year he couldn't stop a thing."[44] As it turned out, Gilbert only spent one more season with Boston before ending up in Detroit for three mediocre campaigns with the Red Wings. His pro hockey career ended at age 34.

Stan Jonathan, age 24

"Stan reminded me of my pet dog, Blue," Don Cherry proclaimed in his autobiography. "They're both small but enormously tough. I liked Stanley so much that I took a beautiful painting of Blue from home and had it hung directly on top of Jonathan's locker."[45]

Such was the admiration that coach Don Cherry had for his scrappy, 24-year-old battling forward form the Six Nations Reserve near Brantford, Ontario. Stan (Bulldog) Jonathan was described as a "chunky Indian"[46] by John Ahern in the pre-political-correctness era of the *Boston Globe*. Cherry could relate to Jonathan on many levels. He had been raised in a family of 14 children. "With a family as large as mine, we had to have rules," Jonathan noted. "Hard work was one of them. If you wanted something bad enough, you had to work for it."[47]

His father had a good-paying but perilous job, working on the steel beams at high-rise construction sites. For four summers, beginning at age 16, Stan followed his father's footsteps. "I was scared the first couple of times I went up," he recalled, "but I learned it wasn't all that dangerous if you followed safety precautions. It's a lot like hockey; if you get careless you can get hurt."[48]

Bruins blogger Joe Pelletier referred to Jonathan as "a human bowling ball"[49] who may have been the best fighter on a pound-for pound basis the NHL ever saw. Jonathan was just 5-foot-8 and 175 pounds but he was a dynamo who could score. Jonathan caught Cherry's attention when he went to see Doug Halward play in a junior game. The Bruins selected Jonathan in the fifth round of the 1975 amateur draft. In 1975–76 he led the International Hockey League in playoff scoring while playing for the Dayton Gems. The next year he was in Boston's lineup where he immediately became a fan favorite—a spot he solidified by soundly thrashing Chicago tough guy Keith Magnuson. Jonathan scored on a high percentage of his shots, getting 17 goals in just 71 shots (23.9 percent) in his rookie season with the Bruins. The next year his percentage was almost identical, but this time he scored 27 times for the Bruins. He was one of 11 Bruins who attained the 20-goal mark that season. Four decades later it remains an NHL record for most players on one team in one season to reach that milestone. "I don't think that record will ever be broken," Jonathan predicted in a 2014 video interview with the *Boston Herald*. "I just can't see it happening the way hockey is played today."[50]

Jonathan is perhaps best remembered by casual fans for a brutal melee he had with

Montreal's Pierre Bouchard six minutes into Game #4 of the 1978 Stanley Cup finals. Fireworks were assured when Montreal sent out its corps of enforcers to confront the Boston threesome of Terry O'Reilly, John Wensink and Jonathan. (The carnage is available on YouTube.) Giving away six inches in height and anywhere from 40 to 60 pounds to his adversary, Jonathan bludgeoned the bigger Hab into a bloody pulp after a series of right-handed blows and one climactic left. Bouchard crumpled to the ice with a broken cheekbone. By the time the final punch was thrown, Boston Garden's ice surface and linesman John D'Amico were both liberally splattered with Bouchard's blood.

A broken wrist sustained in a 4–4 tie versus Buffalo on November 12, 1978, sidelined Jonathan for more than half of the 1978–79 regular season, but he returned for the Stanley Cup playoffs even though his wounded limb had not totally healed properly.

Don Marcotte, age 32

"If Don Marcotte could have jumped in my pants, he would have jumped in my pants."[51] That was Guy Lafleur's description of Boston's best defensive forward. Lafleur made the amusing, hyperbolic remark in a 2012 interview with the *Vancouver Province* when he was asked to name the best checker he ever faced in the NHL. Without hesitation, he picked Don Marcotte. Lafleur is not alone in his praise of the tenacious Bruin. Don Cherry once opined that it was "criminal" that Marcotte never once won the Frank Selke Trophy as the league's best defensive forward. Marcotte's biography in the Hockey Hall of Fame's database describes him as "mixing his one part talent and skill with his nine parts of heart, desire and hustle to render himself indispensible...."[52] Although Marcotte's teammates were irked following the 1977–78 season when Marcotte finished a distant third in the voting, typical of his selfless nature, Marcotte never complained about not winning the Selke Trophy. "I never gave it any thought," he said. "I got my reward by tying up some good scorer or scoring myself."[53]

Marcotte, a French-Canadian from Victoriaville, QC, specialized in neutralizing the opposition's big scoring threat with his uncanny pursuit skills. Few have ever done it as well as Marcotte did for 865 games in an NHL career spent entirely with Boston that spanned from 1965 through 1982.

Marcotte caught on with the Bruins as a regular in January 1970 when he was 22 years old—just in time for the team's first Stanley Cup championship in 29 years. He was often paired with Derek Sanderson and Ed Westfall to form Boston's enormously effective "checking line"—a unit that did a fabulous, workmanlike job but was routinely overlooked in the glamorous and high-scoring Orr-Esposito era. The following season, 1970–71, the defensive minded Marcotte scored just 15 goals for the Bruins, but six of them came when Boston was playing shorthanded.

The first NHL opponent Marcotte was assigned to "shadow" was Chicago sniper Bobby Hull. He did so successfully—earning himself the permanent role as the man Boston coaches assigned to disrupt the opponents' superstar. While some forwards might consider such defensive play to be drudgery, Marcotte thrived on the challenge and the intangible rewards that came with it. "Every goal I take away from a player on the other team is as good as one I might have scored myself,"[54] he said in a March 1982 interview with the *Christian Science Monitor*.

Terry O'Reilly believed that focus was the key to Marcotte's tremendous success as a shadow. "Donnie has tremendous concentration. He never takes his eye off his winger and he never stops skating."[55]

"Nobody knows the fundamentals of the game better than Don," insisted Don Cherry. "If you were going to send a hockey player to Mars, it would be Marcotte. They could watch him play and manufacture perfect players. He skates, checks, and gets his share of goals. That's the perfect hockey player."[56] Cherry always had one piece of advice for any Boston rookie: "Are you watching Marcotte? I want you to study him every second, both on the ice and off."[57]

Marcotte's abilities were well known in NHL circles—especially his forechecking prowess. Accordingly, he was selected to be part of Team NHL that played the Soviet Union's national team in the three-game Challenge Cup series in February 1979.

Being a checking forward did not mean Marcotte forgot about scoring. He collected 268 goals in his distinguished NHL career. Seven times he notched at least 20 goals in a season.

Peter McNab, age 27

When Phil Esposito was suddenly traded away from Boston in November 1975, the Bruins lost someone who had a truly dominating presence in the slot—for about seven months. In came Peter McNab, who was acquired from Buffalo in a June 1976 off deal that sent flashy but underachieving André Savard to the Sabres. McNab adapted nicely to his new surroundings. He had a huge impact as a Bruin center, averaging about 80 points per season in the seven years he spent in Boston. McNab might be the most underappreciated Bruins star in recent memory.

"He never got the credit he deserved," insisted teammate Rick Middleton. "He was a big guy [6-foot-3, 210 pounds] and not the fleetest of skaters, so they were always picking on him. They were never satisfied with his game. Here's a guy who scored 40 goals. They should have been happy with him."[58]

"They" were Don Cherry and Harry Sinden, who seldom agreed on much, but they did concur that McNab could improve upon his overall skill set—a lot. Sinden once loudly criticized McNab by saying his checking had "not improved one iota."[59] Cherry heard Sinden's remark—as did just about every Bruin—and Boston's coach began negatively referring to one of his most reliable scorers as "One Iota." Despite the harsh riding he seemed to constantly get from his bosses, McNab loved his years as a Bruin in the Cherry era, especially the players' camaraderie.

McNab was always a serious threat to score because he practiced firing pucks into the net from the slot by the hundreds. The result was a deadly, quick release that consistently beat one NHL goalie after another. The season the Bruins had 11 players who notched 20 goals or more (1977–78), McNab led the team with 41. McNab explained why he worked on his goal-scoring touch so much. "These guys are in the corners getting the crap kicked out of them," he bluntly said. "They're going to pass me the puck. I'd better be ready to shoot it."[60]

Historian Matt Kalman correctly points out, "McNab might not have followed Esposito into the Hall of Fame, but he filled his predecessor's role perfectly for only one less season. That's something that should earn him tons of credit in Bruins' history."[61]

Rick Middleton, age 26

"Game after game he demonstrated stick-handling and skating talents that brought fans out of their seats."[62] That's what longtime Bruins broadcaster Fred Cusick had to say about Rick (Nifty) Middleton in his memoirs. Coach Don Cherry was similarly impressed, telling the *Boston Globe* early in the 1978–79 season, "Middleton is the talk of the NHL. His potential is unlimited."[63] In a 1981 *Sports Illustrated* article titled "There's No One So Shifty as Nifty," Brad Park said, "I've seen them all, and Nifty's the best one-on-one player in hockey. Give Nifty the puck and 90 percent of the time he'll turn the other guy inside out."[64]

The 5'11", 170-pound Middleton was the closest thing that the grinding Boston Bruins had to a dazzling goal-scorer in the late 1970s and into the next decade. Middleton, a feared sniper in junior hockey, was a first-round draft selection by the New York Rangers in 1974. However, Middleton seemed somewhat lost in New York City. His two seasons on Broadway surprisingly saw him record negative plus-minus stats for a team in decline. "When I first got to the NHL in New York," Middleton recalled in a 2009 interview, "all they wanted me to do was score. I'd try to go down the ice and beat everybody. That was hazardous to my health. I ended up getting my teeth knocked out and breaking my leg in the same week in my rookie year."[65]

"Rick Middleton was a floater until he came to the Bruins," wrote Al Strachan of the *Montreal Gazette* during the 1979 playoffs. "Now he works: He skates hard and even blocks shots. Instead of spending his career as a typical NHL fringe player, he has become a valuable two-way forward."[66]

The Bruins saw Middleton's true potential, though, and were only too happy to acquire him before the 1976–77 campaign in exchange for a rapidly fading Ken Hodge in one of the most lopsided trades in Boston history. Hodge played slightly more than one full season as a Ranger. Conversely, Middleton productively blossomed into Boston's major scoring threat until his retirement n 1988.

Middleton liked the change of scenery and adapted quickly to Boston. He made an auspicious splash, impressively scoring a hat-trick in his Bruin debut on October 7, 1976, versus Minnesota. "The first-nighters at the Garden may have caught the debut of a rising young star," Fran Rosa accurately predicted in the next day's *Boston Globe*. "His name is Rick Middleton. His age is 22. His number is 16. Remember all three for he is a scorer."[67]

"There's no more exciting player in hockey than Middleton," Don Cherry told the *Globe* in January 1979. "Every time he gets the puck I think he's going to score."[68] His nickname Nifty came from his frequent dekes. Middleton readily admitted he almost always relied on finesse to beat goalies because he did not possess a hard shot.

Middleton was indeed a natural goal-scorer, but he also excelled as a penalty-killer—a rare combination that came to fruition when coach Don Cherry urged him to work on the defensive aspects of his game that he had neglected for most of his formative hockey years. Midway through the 1978–79 season, Middleton was among Boston's most reliable checkers. "Now during a tight game, I make sure Middleton is on the ice during the last minute for his defensive skills," Cherry told the *Globe*'s John Ahern. "That's the highest compliment I can pay him."[69]

Still, Middleton's most underappreciated asset was his remarkable ability to stay out of the penalty box. Only once in his terrific, 14-year NHL career did Middleton's seasonal penalty-minute total exceed 20. Six times it was below 10.

Middleton developed numerous facets to his game under Cherry's tutelage. He could even be counted upon to be a "grinder" if necessary. During a 4–2 win versus Colorado on December 21, 1978, Middleton picked up three assists by vigorously digging the puck out of the corner to set up each goal. Francis Rosa declared in the *Globe* that "Middleton spent so much time along the boards he has splinters coming out of his ears."[70] During the Bruins'

1983 seven-game playoff series versus Buffalo, Middleton compiled 19 assists—an NHL record.

Still, Middleton is mostly remembered for scoring clutch goals, quite a few of them of the thrilling variety. A goal Middleton scored versus Montreal in the 1978 Stanley Cup finals was especially picturesque. Bruins historian Matt Kalman declared Nifty's career "makes you wonder why YouTube wasn't invented decades earlier in order to display the spectacular highlights Middleton produced almost every night."[71] The *Globe* ran a glowing feature on Middleton on March 7, 1979, penned by Ernie Roberts. Its title was "Middleton Deal: Bruins Got a Stinger ... Rangers Got Stung." He never failed to post a positive plus-minus total in each of the 12 seasons he spent in a Boston Bruin uniform. In his last season with New York, Middleton was an awful minus-38. His exclusion from the Hall of Fame is perplexing.

A groin injury suffered in March made Middleton somewhat questionable going into the 1979 Stanley Cup playoffs, but he rose to the occasion. He played in all 11 Bruins postseason games and scored 12 points.

Mike Milbury, age 27

Mike Milbury, a native of Walpole, Massachusetts, went undrafted after playing collegiate hockey at Colgate University. Luckily for him, John Hoff, a friend of Don Cherry, remembered how well Milbury had played defense in NCAA games, so he was added almost as an afterthought to the Bruins' ranks—the 61st player on a 60-man roster. His journey to the NHL was unlikely. He first put on a pair of skates as a 13-year-old—very late in life for most aspiring hockey players.

Following his NHL debut game in 1976, Cherry lambasted Milbury for playing "too soft." On Milbury's first shift in his next game he flattened Toronto's Pat Boutette with a clean, devastating body check. He became a Cherry favorite from that point onward. "He worked so hard and fought for everything he got out of his career," Cherry said of Milbury. "He turned into a really good defensive defenseman with some good offensive skills. Anytime there was anything that needed to be done on the ice, he did it."[72] Terry O'Reilly agreed, "[Milbury] was a good teammate and very analytical. He would do whatever needed to give us a spark."[73]

In 1978–79 Milbury was in his third full NHL season. He was in a strange and unique position among the Bruin players: He often traveled in the same car with coach Don Cherry because they lived nearby one another in suburban North Andover, Massachusetts. "It was a little bit uncomfortable showing up at the rink with the coach driving me," Milbury recalled. "[Cherry] would practise his pregame speeches on me during the trip to the arena. I knew exactly what to expect when he delivered them to the team. I was never surprised."[74]

One would think the other Bruins would have resented Milbury for being something akin to a "coach's pet" as Cherry's carpool buddy, but that was not the case. Milbury's strong work ethic overcame any unspoken concerns or criticisms his fellow Bruins may have had. "You respected Mike because you knew his path to the NHL was not an easy one,"[75] Peter McNab said.

Bob Miller, age 23

Perhaps the least heralded of all the mainstays of the 1978–79 Bruins, center Bob Miller was a second-year player who appeared in 77 of Boston's 80 regular-season games and collected 15 goals and 33 assists. He was valuable to the Bruins because he avoided the serious injuries that befell so many of his teammates. Don Cherry usually played Miller on a line between wingers Bobby Schmautz and Don Marcotte.

Born in Billerica, Massachusetts, Miller played for the University of New Hampshire and earned a spot on the U.S. team that competed at the 1976 Winter Olympics in Innsbruck, Austria. (The squad recorded two wins and three losses to finish fifth of six nations in the tournament's "A" Pool. Miller's most memorable experience in Austria had nothing to do with hockey. He happened to enter a tavern just as a wild fight broke out. "It was like a saloon brawl in a western movie. Chairs were flying everywhere,"[76] Miller remembered. He suffered a gash on his cheek and was briefly placed under arrest by the local police.) Miller also represented his country at the 1981 Canada Cup and at the IIHF World Championship tournaments in both 1981 and 1982.

In his rookie season, Miller—whom his teammates dubbed Harpo because his mop of curly hair—was one of the 11 Bruins to record 20 goals in 1977–78. In a profile by Leslie Visser that appeared in the *Boston Globe* in November 1978, Miller was called a complete and wonderful surprise by Don Cherry.

In the late 1970s U.S.-born players were curiosities in the NHL, but they were starting to grow in numbers. In 1978–79, Americans accounted for one-eighth of the NHL's players. None were on Team NHL, however—the league all-stars who confronted the Soviet Union national team in February 1979. (In fact, Visser's *Globe* story was titled: "Bob Miller: An American Makes Good in Pro Hockey.") Miller was praised by Boston scout John Carlton thusly: "Bob thinks like a Canadian. He's adapted to the pros easier than any American I've ever seen."[77]

The Cherry–like Bruins were never known for being fleet of foot, so Miller's terrific speed was a welcome asset to the team. Cherry hyperbolically gushed early in the season that Miller might be the NHL's fastest skater. He was Boston's fourth-round pick in the 1976 amateur draft. Statistically, Miller's career plateaued in 1978–79; he never quite lived up to the Bruins' long-term expectations. By February 1981 he had been traded to the Colorado Rockies.

Dennis O'Brien, age 30

By 1978–79 Dennis O'Brien was at the tail end of a wildly nomadic NHL career that began with the Minnesota North Stars in 1970–71. The left-shooting defenseman was best known as the answer to a hockey trivia question as he remarkably played for four different NHL teams during the 1977–78 season: Minnesota, Cleveland, Colorado, and Boston. Luckily, Boston was O'Brien's last stop on his hectic travel itinerary that season. The Bruins, of course, reached the Stanley Cup final in 1978 while his other three teams failed to qualify for the playoffs. O'Brien played in 14 of Boston's 15 playoff games that spring.

He was more known for his toughness than his scoring touch. O'Brien recorded more than 1,000 career penalty minutes in 592 NHL games but only scored 31 goals. O'Brien played 64 games for Boston in 1978–79 in his last full year in the NHL largely because the Bruins' defensive corps was heavily beset by injuries all season. He was basically perceived as a reliable, long-term substitute defenseman—and nothing more. However, with the Bruins' full roster enjoying a rare period of complete health heading into the 1979 postseason, O'Brien was abruptly shuttled aside by Don Cherry in favor of his first-stringers. He saw no action whatsoever during the Stanley Cup playoffs. At one point in the season Francis Rosa of the *Boston Globe* sympathetically called O'Brien "the man who [sic] nobody appreciates."[78]

O'Brien was central in a comical incident in Bruins history. There was mass confusion one game when both teams decided to make wholesale player changes on the fly. For a moment only O'Brien and the two goaltenders were on the ice. Despite having the entire ice surface to himself, O'Brien, who had the puck inside the Boston blue line, steadfastly obeyed Cherry's edict that his defensemen—with the lone exception of Brad Park—were not permitted to rush the puck out of their zone or pass it along the middle of the ice surface; they had to fire it off the boards or the glass. O'Brien, a creature of habit, did just that. The puck ricocheted high off the glass and nearly struck referee John McCauley on the head. The flummoxed and angry official asked O'Brien why he would do such a thing when there was no opponent pressuring him. O'Brien honestly replied, "If Grapes wants it off the glass, Grapes gets it off the glass."[79]

In the summer of 1979 O'Brien was left unprotected by the Bruins before the special expansion draft to re-stock the four surviving WHA teams about to enter the NHL. He was selected by none of them. Clearly O'Brien's career was nearing an inglorious end. After appearing in just three games for Boston during the 1979–80 season, the Bruins cut O'Brien and he vanished from pro hockey.

Terry O'Reilly, age 28

Scotty Bowman called him "the catalyst that every team needs."[80] Minnesota's general-manager Lou Nanne said he was "the one player I'd love to have on my team."[81] Bobby Orr thought he should have won the Hart Trophy in 1978 because he was, in his opinion, the most valuable player to his team. "He should be the league MVP," Orr said. "I look at the [box scores] every day, and I always see his name there, getting an assist or scoring a goal, and I know all the other things he does."[82] Who was the subject of those flattering comments? It was energetic Terry O'Reilly.

Arguably the most popular player on the Boston Bruins during the late 1970s was right winger Terry O'Reilly. He was absolutely a perfect fit for Don Cherry's gritty, "lunch pail" gang. O'Reilly would never win any awards for being graceful or elusive on the ice, but he epitomized the grinding work ethic that made the Bruins such a successful outfit year after year. Never afraid to go into the corners and fight for the puck, O'Reilly was often found near the top of both the team's scoring and penalty-minute stats. During Game #7 versus Montreal, *Hockey Night in Canada's* Danny Gallivan admiringly referred to O'Reilly as "indefatigable."[83]

From a distance, O'Reilly seemed terribly ungainly and reckless, rarely completing a shift in which he was not sprawled on the ice or awkwardly entangled with an opponent somewhere along the boards in close pursuit of the puck. A January 12, 1979, *Boston Globe* editorial praised O'Reilly as a "once-clumsy enforcer who has polished his skills to become an all-around player."[84]

Because of O'Reilly's unique buzzing style, Phil Esposito playfully nicknamed him "Taz"—an allusion to the out-of-control Tasmanian Devil from the Warner Bros. cartoons. However, the scrappy O'Reilly was incredibly effective at winning close-engagement battles and creating turnovers at the other team's end of the ice. With his zealous, damn-the-torpedoes, everyman approach to his profession—combined with having the most Irish of surnames—how could O'Reilly not become an overwhelming favorite among Boston hockey fans? Years later linemate Peter McNab highly said of him, "I always felt that if in my career a Stanley Cup wasn't going to be in the cards, the hockey gods gave me the next best thing: I got to play with Terry O'Reilly. There was a fire within him that just never went out in either a game or a practice."[85] After the 1978–79 season, Francis Rosa of the *Boston Globe* firmly declared O'Reilly to be the Bruins' best player—high praise, indeed.

Despite his rugged and reckless style, O'Reilly managed to play in all 80 regular-season games and each of Boston's 11 playoff games in 1978–79. Only Jean Ratelle—who was exempted from most practices—matched O'Reilly's double feat of endurance and healthiness. (O'Reilly probably should have missed the majority of Boston's playoff games in 1979. Sometime during the Pittsburgh quarterfinal, he injured his left elbow. During the Montreal series, it became grotesquely swollen—but he played anyway, with the media completely oblivious to his pain and discomfort. Two weeks after the series ended O'Reilly underwent surgery to have several bone chips removed.)

O'Reilly's off-ice interests included chess, antiques, and making stained-glass windows—gentle pastimes one would not likely associate with one of the toughest characters in Bruins history. Despite getting into numerous scuffles in his career, he seldom talked about his fights with reporters. When asked about them by the media, O'Reilly would generally redirect the discussions back to the game itself.

Following the ceremonies to conclude the final game at Boston Garden in 1995, O'Reilly, Stan Jonathan and Fern Flaman took the opportunity to pose for a unique group photo in a very appropriate place: the home team's penalty box.

Brad Park, age 31

Brad Park had the misfortune of being the second-best defenseman in the NHL for many years—but he did not see it that way. Years afterward, Park graciously remarked, "I saw no reason to be upset because I was rated second to Bobby Orr. After all, Orr not only was the top defenseman in the game but he was considered the best player ever to put on a pair of skates. There was nothing insulting about being rated number-two to such a superstar."[86]

Park was a 20-year-old when he made his NHL debut for the New York Rangers on November 30, 1968. It occurred at Boston Garden. Park got an assist in the Rangers' 4–1 win. Park's first goal also came against the Bruins. It was the ninth Ranger goal in a 9–0 shellacking of Boston at Madison Square Garden on February 23, 1969.

Overshadowed by the flashier Orr in the early 1970s (Orr and Park were both born in 1948) and to a lesser degree Montreal's Larry Robinson and the Islanders' Denis Potvin later in the decade, Park was a more-than-capable marquee blueliner who flourished when he came to the Bruins from the Rangers in November 1975 along with Jean Ratelle in exchange for Phil Esposito and Carol Vadnais. Park was as shocked by the blockbuster trade as anyone else. He was the Rangers' captain at the time—but the previous two Rangers who had worn the "C" (Bob Nevin and Vic Hadfield) had also been traded during their captaincies. "I had no inkling at all of such a trade," Park recalled years later. "From what I understand, neither did Ratelle or Esposito."[87] Park was 27 at the time of the trade and, according to his Wikipedia biography, was perceived by the New York media and Ranger fans as "overpaid, overweight and over the hill."[88]

After seven-plus seasons as a Ranger, Park's move to Boston was somewhat perilous because in 1971 he had co-written a book titled *Play the Man* that was highly critical of the Bruins' style of hockey. Park broadly classified the entire Bruins roster as "animals" and specifically took verbal shots at Phil Esposito, Ted Green and John McKenzie. Furthermore, Park blasted Boston Garden as "a zoo" and described Bruin fans as "maniacal." He went on to describe the arena as "grubby." Park unkindly wrote, "Without a doubt it's the worst rink in the NHL. It's old and shabby and always looks as though it could use another coat of paint and at least two more vacuum cleanings."[89] Such remarks did not go unnoticed by the locals in Beantown. For a while Park was accorded special police protection whenever the Rangers had to make a road trip to Boston. (At the 1972 All-Star Game in Minnesota, there was palpable tension in the East Division's dressing room between Park and Orr, Esposito and McKenzie who were teammates for one night. Nevertheless, Park assisted on McKenzie's goal in the East's 3–2 win.)

Park's biographer, Thom Sears, described the impact of *Play the Man*: "In the end, it wasn't so much what Brad had said that was the problem—after all, many other players agreed with his candid assessments. The problem was he put his comments into print rather than leaving them on the ice, as was the normal code of conduct for NHLers."[90]

"My first instinct was to refuse to go," Park recalled about his 1975 trade to Boston, "but that didn't last long. I knew I had responsibilities both as a family man and as a professional."[91]

All was quickly forgiven, though, as Park quickly filled a sizable chunk of the void left by Bobby Orr's departure after the 1975–76 season. In fact, Park had been on the Bruins' radar for a while as Orr's knee troubles became progressively worse and his forced retirement seemed near. As a Bruin, Park was instructed by Don Cherry to focus on the defensive aspects of hockey first and not try to win games all by himself, as was the case when he played in New York.

Park was especially motivated to do well against his old team whenever the Bruins clashed with the Rangers. "All the so-called knowledgeable hockey people were saying that New York got the best of the deal, so I just had to go out and show the Boston people that they got the best of it."[92] Hockey historian Brian McFarlane absolutely agreed. "I think the trade to Boston revitalized Park,"[93] he said.

Park was appalled by how shabbily his old fans in New York acted toward him when he played for Boston at Madison Square Garden, but it made his transition into a Bruin all the easier. "When I went back to New York, I got booed every time I touched the puck. Every time!" Park remembered with disgust decades after the trade. "I busted my ass for eight years and that's the reception I got. The first time Espo returned to Boston he got a standing ovation."[94] Nevertheless, Park was ranked by ESPN as the 11th-greatest New York Ranger of all time. A similar 2010 poll by bleacherreport.com placed Park in the tenth spot.

In his own quiet way, Park became the linchpin of the Cherry-era Bruins. Seldom making costly errors, he was an invaluable commodity, routinely exceeding 40 minutes of ice time per game even though he was often beset by serious knee injuries. During the 1978–79 season, Park's physical troubles were so persistent that it was not until late February that he could go through an entire game without his bad right knee grotesquely swelling up. Reporters seldom saw Park in the Bruins' dressing room after a game without an ice pack. "By 1978," Park recalled in his autobiography, "I had the last cartilage removed in my knee and I was only 30 years old. My knees were bone on bone."[95]

"Brad seemed to have bad knees forever," said longtime teammate Jean Ratelle. "No other defenseman in the history of the league could play defense in his own end and do the things that he did with knees like that."[96]

Park was a steadying influence on both the Boston power play and penalty-killing units. When he was absent from the lineup, the Bruins were without a certain element of intelligent game control. When Park was in their lineup, however, they were at least a match for any other team in the NHL—and better than almost all of them. His slapshot from the blue line was as hard and accurate as anyone's. Park is likely the best defenseman in NHL history never to have won the Norris Trophy. He finished runner-up to Bobby Orr four times. (Park finished second in the voting in two other seasons after Orr retired.) Park candidly admitted he tried to model his style of play after Orr based on watching highlights of Boston's fabulous #4 in action.

Park was also an excellent interview subject who responded to journalists' questions with thoughtfulness, intelligence, insight and a ready wit—a combination that always pleased the sophisticated Bruins beat writers and their readers. Park even fed Don Cherry an occasional zinger to use in his interviews. After one particularly lopsided Boston victory over Minnesota, Park leaned into Cherry's office to offer this pithy quip: "Tell [the reporters] it was an up-and-down game. When they got up, we knocked 'em down!"[97]

Jim Pettie, age 26

Goaltender Jim Pettie may be best remembered by hard-core hockey fans for his unusual nickname: Seaweed. He acquired it because his hair became distinctly stringy when he perspired. (The condition was hereditary; his father was nicknamed Kelp for the same reason.) Pettie embraced the moniker: he had it stenciled across his mask. Pettie played one game in goal for the Bruins in 1976–77, one game in 1977–78, and 19 games in 1978–79—and that was the extent of his spotty NHL career.

The lone game Pettie played in the 1976–77 season came on December 1 versus Chicago. It was a big one: It was Boston's first game where Bobby Orr was on the opposing team. When Pettie got the startling news from Don Cherry that he would be facing the famous ex-Bruin, his face turned ashen and his eyes bugged out of his head, causing the rest of the Bruins to erupt in laughter. Pettie managed to put his fears—and a touch of nausea caused by nervousness—aside and defeated the Blackhawks, 5–3.

A feisty netminder, one season in the minors Pettie accrued 145 minutes in penalties! (In his brief NHL career he picked up 13 PIM—a high total for a goalie who played so few games.) He did not get much work in Boston because he was well below Gerry Cheevers and Gilles Gilbert on the talent level. Nevertheless, Pettie played superbly against Montreal in Boston's 3–1 loss in the Forum on January 27. Pettie also recorded one shutout in 1978–79. It came on March 3 in a wild 5–0 home win versus the Minnesota North Stars—the game where Don Cherry was ejected by referee Gregg Madill. "Pettie looked like Glenn Hall out there, blocking shots and getting to his feet quickly," Cherry proudly stated afterward. Pettie also recorded a win versus the New York Rangers before a typical hostile Madison Square Garden crowd. His net minding that night again received rave reviews from reporters.

Pettie achieved his highest degree of fame for merely being a roommate. He shared hotel accommodations with "participatory journalist" George Plimpton during the 1977–78 preseason, the year the esteemed 50-year-old writer played goal for the Bruins for five terrifying minutes of an exhibition game versus the Philadelphia Flyers. (The Bruins insisted Plimpton sign a waiver absolving the team of any liability in case he were injured or killed in the stunt!) Accordingly, Pettie got plenty of ink in *Open Net*, Plimpton's acclaimed book about his hockey adventure.

Pettie also created headlines with a truly bizarre hotel-room incident. He and onetime Bruin Darryl Edestrand were roommates while playing for the minor-league Rochester Americans in the AHL during the 1977–78 season. One evening, Pettie was relaxing in a hot bath while Edestrand was sleeping in the buff on a bed. Somehow six local police officers and the hotel's night manager wrongly entered the quiet hockey players' room in response to a complaint about noise coming from a wild party. Pettie and Edestrand took offense at their tranquility being disturbed. Tempers flared. A scuffle broke out between the miffed twosome and the local constabulary. The result was a truly eye-catching newspaper headline the following day: "Nude Hockey Players Assault Cops."

Jean Ratelle, age 39

"Jean is a fantastic gentleman. It's an honor to just know the man, let alone be on the ice with him."[98] That's what Rick Smith told reporters after he had assisted on Jean Ratelle's overtime goal in Game #4 versus Montreal.

Ratelle was easily the most elegant of Boston's rugged lunch-pail bunch. He was also the team's elder statesman, being two months older than Gerry Cheevers. Ratelle, whose first NHL game occurred as a junior call-up in 1960, had already enjoyed a great career as a New York Ranger before his tenure in Boston. He had been part of the Rangers' potent GAG (Goal a Game) Line with Rod Gilbert and Vic Hadfield. In 1971–72 all three finished in the top five scorers in the NHL. It looked like Ratelle was going to win the NHL scoring title that season, but he lost 15 games to injury late in the campaign and was overtaken by Phil Esposito. Nevertheless Ratelle's 109 points established a Rangers scoring record that lasted until Jaromir Jagr broke it 34 years later.

Ratelle, a forward with a tremendously valuable knack for scoring timely goals, had come to Boston along with Brad Park and Joe Zanussi in the famous November 7, 1975, trade that sent superstar sniper Phil Esposito and defensive stalwart Carol Vadnais to the New York Rangers. Tom Fitzgerald of the *Boston Globe* called it "the most startling trade in hockey history."[99] It probably was. In the end, all three marquee players ended up liking their new homes. "As it turned out, it was a great move for me and my family to be traded to Boston," Ratelle said upon his retirement. "If Bobby Orr hadn't been injured, we would have won a Stanley Cup or two."[100]

Ratelle was a tricky offensive player in a subtle way. He would have opposing defensemen completely perplexed with his body language whenever he carried the puck over the blue line. If they believed he was going to pass the puck, he would smoothly skate right by them to the net. If they did not commit to him, he would slide a perfect, feather-like pass to a teammate. "Who wouldn't want to play on a line with Jean Ratelle?" Stan Jonathan fondly asked years later.[101] Ratelle also excelled in winning key faceoffs. The bigger the draw, the more likely Ratelle would be dispatched by Don Cherry to take it.

Ratelle exuded class and dignity and often drew favorable comparisons to the esteemed Jean Béliveau—a high compliment for any hockey player, especially one of French-Canadian descent. Accordingly, he became a protected and beloved figure of wisdom and experience in the Bruins' dressing room. No mercy would be shown to any Boston opponent who dared take liberties with the stately Ratelle. (Ratelle had just one fight in his entire hockey career—as a junior with the Guelph Biltmores in the late 1950s. According to Bruin lore, when his Boston teammates found out about the scuffle some 20 years after it occurred, they sincerely asked him, "Do you want us to get him for you, Ratty?")

As he approached the end of his Hall-of-Fame career in 1979, Ratelle was given special permission by Don Cherry to skip most of the team's practices to preserve his energy for games. The strategy paid off marvelously as Ratelle became a clutch scorer and a reliable, quiet leader for the Bruins. Cherry claimed he could never bring himself to criticize Ratelle because he looked like a priest—and because there was usually very little about Ratelle's smart, stylish and successful style of hockey to criticize anyway. He was also one of the few Bruins who managed to stay healthy throughout the season. He played in all 91 of Boston's regular-season and playoff games in 1978–79.

By his retirement following the 1980–81 campaign, Ratelle had scored 20 goals or more in a season 14 different times. Altogether he notched 491 NHL goals. Although he looked placid and peaceful on the outside, Ratelle was a fierce, team-oriented competitor. During the Montreal series in 1979, Ratelle was first to complain to the officials if he thought the Bruins were being wronged on penalty calls. Long after his retirement, he was asked what his most satisfying NHL season was. Ratelle thoughtfully pondered the question for a few moments and then responded, "My team worked very hard every year ... but I never won the Stanley Cup. For that reason, I can't look back and say that any one year was really satisfying. In the end, we lost."[102]

The dignified Ratelle possessed a terrifically wry sense of humor and occasionally delighted the Bruins' beat writers with amusing quips. After a Boston 5–3 victory over the Cleveland Barons in 1978 in which Ratelle's line combined for a remarkable 13 points, Ratelle deadpanned, "Well, somebody has to do the dirty work."[103]

Dick Redmond, age 30

A newcomer to the Bruins in 1978–79, the introverted Dick Redmond spent most of his first season in a Boston uniform trying to prove his worth to Don Cherry and struggling to adjust to the Bruins' system. The older brother of Mickey Redmond (who twice had recorded 50-goal seasons for Detroit), Dick was at a disadvantage from the moment he arrived in Boston: He came from the Atlanta Flames in the summer of 1978 in a three-way deal that saw the popular Gregg Sheppard traded to Pittsburgh.

Redmond failed to impress Cherry early in the 1978–79 season with either his hockey or his personal habits. At one practice Cherry saw mysterious brown splotches on the ice and quickly found the source: Redmond was spitting tobacco juice. Cherry quickly informed his new defenseman, "You've got 30 seconds to get rid of that tobacco or I'll knock it down your throat with my fist!"[104]

Not especially physical in his defensive play—he was seldom penalized, accruing just 21 penalty minutes in 64 games in 1978–79—Redmond did not seem to fit the typical Bruin mold for what a defenseman ought to be. Early in the season Redmond would sometimes go half a period without getting a shift. However, by the end of the season, Redmond had found his niche as a key multi-role player for Boston. In an April 21, 1979, article in the *Boston Globe*, Francis Rosa wrote, "The Bruins have a fifth defenseman. Cherry considers [Redmond] an all-purpose player, using him as a point man on the power play, as a forward on penalty killing, and, if necessary, as a left winger for defensive purposes."[105]

Redmond loved the varied responsibilities that were foisted upon him under Cherry. "I love killing penalties. It's great fun," declared Redmond. "I like the challenge of taking faceoffs. I like it when the coach puts me in at left wing. He has confidence in me and it makes me feel awfully good. He's great that way."[106]

Cherry, who had been Redmond's biggest critic at the start of the season, was openly singing his praises by the time the playoffs started. As early as January Cherry was showering Redmond with wonderful plaudits. "Redmond is my greatest accomplishment," Cherry stated. "He was more maligned than any other player who has come to the Bruins in my five years here. Now he's one of our most valuable players. I wish we had him in the last two [Stanley Cup] finals. We might have won the Cup with him. I mean that."[107] A headline in the *Boston Globe* before Game #1 of the 1979 playoff series versus Montreal echoed what Cherry had been declaring. It read, "Bruins look to Redmond as their key."

Bobby Schmautz, age 34

Bobby Schmautz was a late-blooming right winger who reached his pinnacle as a member of the Boston Bruins. His NHL career began in the Original Six era with Chicago, but he was mostly a journeyman minor-league player until he was signed by the expansion Vancouver Canucks in 1970. Acquired by the Bruins midway through the 1973–74 season, Schmautz flourished when Don Cherry took the reins of the team. He became a consistent 20-goal scorer and a personal favorite of his coach. Schmautz scored exactly 20 goals in 65 games for Boston in 1978–79, plus two more in the playoffs. Schmautz experienced back problems late in the season that caused him to miss five games in a row.

Years later in a compilation of hockey anecdotes, Cherry described Schmautz as "absolutely ruthless. When he didn't have a good scoring opportunity, he'd 'waste one.' He'd shoot it right at the goalie's head as hard as he could. He'd ring it off the goalie's mask. Then the next shot would be right along the ice for a goal. He was a scary guy, but I loved him."[108]

One poster on a hockey blog comically declared that "Schmautzie could put the puck in the balcony from the top of the crease. He had a great but unpredictable shot."[109]

On the negative side, the 5'9" Schmautz earned a reputation as a player who was quite handy with his hockey stick—but not only for the noble purposes of shooting or passing the puck. Schmautz called his stick "the great equalizer"[110] that made up for what he lacked in physical stature. Cherry often hinted that Schmautz was a dirty player without actually saying it. Opponents disparagingly referred to him as "Dr. Hook."—a nickname that Schmautz happily embraced.

Paul Stewart, who played in the NHL and WHA and later embarked on a very successful officiating career in the NHL, was highly critical of Schmautz. Stewart stated in an eloquent 2014 blog entry that Schmautz was just one of only two players whom he had encountered in his long tenure in professional hockey whose hand he would refuse to shake to this day. The lingering disrespect festered because of a series of nasty on-ice incidents when Schmautz played for Colorado and Stewart was a Quebec Nordique.

When Don Cherry left the Bruins for Colorado at the end of the 1978–79 season, it was the beginning of the end for Schmautz in Boston. Under new coach Fred Creighton, Schmautz's role on the Bruins was greatly reduced. He basically signed his own death warrant as a Bruin after Cherry's Rockies beat Boston on December 2. Schmautz bluntly told reporters that the Bruins had been outcoached.

Schmautz was traded to the Edmonton Oilers eight days later for Dan Newman—who never played a game for Boston. Two months later the Oilers shipped Schmautz to Colorado in exchange for Don Ashby where he happily rejoined Cherry as a member of the Rockies.

Al Secord, age 21

Al Secord was absolutely the most impactful rookie on the Bruins' roster in 1978–79. He was a tough customer from his first game onward. In 71 games, Secord, a left winger, scored 16 goals and amassed 125 penalty minutes for Boston. When Don Cherry learned that Stan Jonathan would be sidelined with a broken wrist for most of the season, the Boston coach optimistically opined that Secord could capably fill Jonathan's role as the Bruins' toughest hombre whenever necessary.

The following season Secord upped his goal total to 23; his penalty-minute tally rose to 170. Eighteen games into the 1980–81 season, Secord had failed to score a goal, so he was hastily dealt to Chicago for defenseman Mike O'Connell. While the Bruins gained a solid and reliable defender in O'Connell, with the advantage of hindsight the trade seemed to be panicky and premature from a Boston standpoint. Secord scored 54 goals for the Blackhawks in 1982–83—the sixth-best goal total in the NHL that season. Blogger Joe Pelletier wrote, "[Secord] took over from Bobby Hull as the Blackhawks' 50-goal scorer. At the same time he took over from Keith Magnuson as the Hawks' enforcer and heart and soul. It sounds almost like a perfect combination for a hockey player."[111]

After enjoying an excellent NHL career in which he scored 273 goals in 12 seasons, Secord embarked on a dramatic lifestyle change: He became a qualified commercial pilot and flew passenger planes for American Airlines.

Al Sims, age 26

The player on the 1978–79 Bruins who caused the most dissention between Don Cherry and Harry Sinden was defenseman Al Sims. Sims had been with the Bruins on and off since 1973–74, shuttling to and from Boston and their top farm team in Rochester, New York, after playing two full seasons on the blue line alongside Bobby Orr. "It has been suggested that Sims buy a house in Albany, partway between Boston and Rochester,"[112] wrote John Ahern in a feature *Boston Globe* piece about Sims in February 1979 when Sims seemed to have made his way onto the Bruins as a permanent fixture. Sims consistently demonstrated a strong work ethic. Naturally, Cherry thought highly of him—a feeling shared by most of his Bruin teammates. Sinden, for some unknown reason, however, was less enamored with his young defenseman.

After playing a particularly excellent game versus the St. Louis Blues in October, Sims told the *Boston Globe*, "I want to make this team. I'll do anything. Don [Cherry] tells me to pretend I'm going back to Rochester tomorrow just to keep me loose. My confidence is growing."[113]

Sims' stats seem to back up Cherry's favorable opinion of him. Sims played 67 games in 1978–79 and finished plus-22 in the plus-minus category. Throughout the season he proved to be a valuable man on the blue line, especially when injuries began to take a heavy toll on Boston's defensive corps. Furthermore, Sims shared the team's annual Eddie Shore Award as a co-winner with Rick Middleton—a trophy given to the Bruin judged to be the team's most valuable player in its home games.

Nevertheless, at the conclusion of the season, Sinden opted to leave Sims unprotected when the NHL held its special draft to stock the four WHA teams that would join the NHL for the 1979–80 season. Sims was claimed by the Hartford Whalers. "I never expected to find Al Sims there at the time we got him," said a pleasantly surprised Jack Kelley, the Whalers' general-manager. "We felt really fortunate to get him."[114] Sims was a reliable defenseman in the two years he spent in Hartford. He only missed four of 160 games.

Harry Sinden, age 47

Rightly or wrongly, Boston general-manager Harry Sinden—along with president Paul A. Mooney—was portrayed as a Bruins in-house villain in 1978–79 by the Boston media, largely because of his refusal or inability to get along with flamboyant and popular coach Don Cherry.

Putting aside that very public feud, Sinden had a long record of assembling contending and Cup-winning teams in Boston. From 1959–60 to 1966–67, the Bruins were a perennially hapless lot, missing the playoffs in each of those eight seasons. The following 29 seasons Boston qualified for postseason play every year—an NHL record that even Montreal has never matched. Most of those campaigns were under Sinden's watch. He coached Boston to the Stanley Cup in 1969–70. Sinden surprisingly left the Bruins because he was unhappy with his salary. After a two-year hiatus from the NHL—in which he absorbed a financial hit in the construction business and coached Team Canada 1972 to victory in the famous Summit Series against the Soviet Union—he returned to Boston as upper management, succeeding the esteemed Milt Schmidt as the team's general-manager. "It's a bit ironic," wrote Bruins historian Matt Kalman. "The man who left the organization over a $5,000 dispute after leading the Bruins to the Stanley Cup in 1970 returned to the club as its general-manager, and for more than 30 years, built a reputation as a penny-pincher."[115] Sinden's reputation for parsimony was something that he did not boast about, but he did not deny it either. "I watch over [the team's money] as though it were even better than my own," he once said. "I'm not the guy who's about to give the store away."[116]

Although he was frugal with the team's expenditures, Sinden was quite liberal in moving players in and out of Boston to make the club as complete and competitive as possible year after year. Anyone was fair game for a trade under Sinden's dutiful watch. It was Sinden who had the guts to trade Phil Esposito (and Carol Vadnais) to the New York Rangers in exchange for Jean Ratelle and Brad Park. The move proved in the long run to be very sound as it revitalized a sagging Bruins team and put them on solid footing for the remainder of the 1970s. Sinden also pulled the strings to acquire Rick Middleton from the New York Rangers and, more than a decade later, Cam Neely from the Vancouver Canucks. Both superstars came to Boston for next to nothing. Although he is generally held in low esteem by Bruins fans for his perceived miserly ways, the sullen Sinden was as passionate as anybody connected with the Bruins about Boston's heroic attempt to unseat Montreal in 1979. He wanted Boston to win too—that was undeniable. Years after Don Cherry was deposed as Boston's coach, even he admitted that Sinden was excellent at acquiring key personnel for the Bruins year after year.

Rick Smith, age 31

Much like Gary Doak, in 1978–79 Rick Smith was enjoying a return to the Bruins after a lengthy hiatus.

Smith was a second-year NHLer with Boston when the Bruins won the Stanley Cup in 1969–70. The reliable defenseman had the misfortune of being traded from Boston to the terrible California Seals near the end of the 1971–72 season in a deal that brought another defenseman, Carol Vadnais, to the Bruins. Thus Smith missed a second Stanley Cup in Boston that spring. After jumping to the WHA's Minnesota Fighting Saints when the rival pro league began in 1972, he returned to the NHL with the St. Louis Blues in 1976. Smith played just 18 games for the Blues before ending up back in Boston in a trade the Blues made for little-used Bruin Joe Zanussi.

Smith experienced a renaissance with the Bruins. One of Don Cherry's favorites because of his defense-first mentality on the blue line—Smith never scored more than nine goals in any single NHL season—he played in 65 games in 1978–79 and in all 11 of the Bruins' playoff games that year. He was also a tough customer. During a hard-fought game in Chicago, Smith badly wrenched his knee after being checked heavily into the boards.

He simply yanked it back into place and did not miss a shift—although he confessed afterward that the dislocated joint was a little bit sore. Overall, Smith was a valuable but rather unheralded Bruin for most of the Don Cherry era.

Mike Walton, age 34

Mike (Shaky) Walton, who had played on the Bruins' Stanley Cup team in 1971–72, was "a reclamation project" in 1978–79, according to Don Cherry. The mercurial Walton had one of the more interesting personalities in hockey history. Twice he walked out on the Toronto Maple Leafs which led to his trade to Boston in 1971. In 1975 Walton did the same thing as a member of the Minnesota Fighting Saints of the WHA, quitting the team during a game and driving away from the arena still clad in his uniform. Any team that signed Walton risked a potential attitude problem.

Walton played for three NHL teams in 1978–79. The Bruins were his second stop. They acquired him after he had been released by the St. Louis Blues. He appeared in 14 games for Boston. He notched four goals and two assists before the Bruins let him go. He finished the 1978–79 season with the Chicago Blackhawks. He played one season in West Germany in 1979–80 to conclude his pro career.

Walton had been an important offensive cog in the Bobby Orr–like Bruins. He and Orr roomed together on road trips and jointly operated a summer sports camp in Orillia, Ontario. Small for a center—he was 5'10"—Walton made up for his lack of stature with blazing speed and excellent puck-handling skills. He scored 28 goals for the Bruins in the 1971–72 season. Two years later, as a member of the Minnesota Fighting Saints in 1973–74, he led the WHA in scoring with 57 goals and 117 points.

A bizarre accident in early 1973 nearly ended Walton's hockey career. At a St. Louis hotel where the Bruins were staying before their January 4 game versus the Blues, Walton stumbled and fell headlong through a plate-glass door in his room, severely cutting himself. (Specifics of the incident vary. Boston coach Tom Johnson told the Associated Press, "Mike stepped out onto the balcony for a breath of fresh air. As he started back into the room he tripped on the screen."[117] Later accounts claimed Walton was engaging in horseplay and crashed through the door while trying to avoid being soaked by a bucket of water!) Walton lost five pints of blood in the gory mishap. For a while his life was imperiled. More than 200 stitches were needed to close multiple gashes on Walton's legs and chin. Nevertheless, he made a complete recovery. Walton missed about a quarter of the Bruins' games that season, but still managed to score 25 goals in 56 games.

Upon his retirement from hockey, Walton became a real estate agent. Several of his clients were current and former NHL players.

John Wensink, age 26

John Wensink is remembered mostly for being the Bruins' most reliable and spirited battler. In his final season of junior hockey with the Cornwall Royals, the feisty Wensink amassed a whopping 242 penalty minutes.

With an unkempt, bushy hairstyle, the six-foot, 200-pound Wensink resembled "a Hell's Angel on ice skates," according to one Bruin historian. "When I think back he was hairy; he was scary; he was intimidating. He looked like the craziest guy in the movie *Slapshot*,"[118] declared another. Often forgotten is that Wensink had a very good offensive year for Boston in 1978–79, scoring 28 goals—and compiling 106 penalty minutes. His goal total was the third best on the Bruins. He surprisingly outscored Terry O'Reilly, Wayne Cashman and Jean Ratelle. Only Don Cherry was not amazed at Wensink's unexpected offensive contributions to the team. Before the season even started, Cherry Told Francis Rosa that Wensink had greatly broadened his overall skill set. Linemate Bobby Schmautz concurred. He claimed Wensink's performance in the Bruins' exhibition schedule showed he was vastly over the previous season.

Despite his newly discovered scoring touch, Wensink could still be the ruthless competitor that he was advertised to be. In Boston's 5–2 home win over Buffalo on November 23, Wensink caught Buffalo rookie Larry Playfair moving the puck behind his net with his head down. A perfectly timed shoulder check to the head—absolutely legal in 1978–79—knocked the careless Sabre cold and sent him to Massachusetts General Hospital. It was Playfair's first shift in the NHL.

Wensink is most famous for a memorable incident versus the Minnesota North Stars on December 1, 1977, at Boston Garden. After badly pummeling Alex Pirus, the Stars' supposed enforcer, Wensink skated to within a few feet of the visitors' bench and audaciously beckoned with his arms extended for anyone and everyone to dare mix it up with him. "Wensink came over to challenge the entire Minnesota team!" declared Bruins TV broadcaster Fred Cusick. Wensink got no takers. He concluded his performance by skating off the ice, while twice contemptuously waving his right hand in disgust at the unresponsive North Stars. Wensink was assessed 27 minutes in penalties for his antics—including a 10-minute misconduct for the dramatic bench-challenge. After the game, Wensink told Francis Rosa of the *Globe*, "You notice I stayed far enough away from the bench so they couldn't pull me onto it. I'm smart. Besides, I'm glad no one took the challenge. I was too tired." Thirty years later, in an ESPN interview, a chagrined Wensink recalled the incident and offered no explanation for it other than an adrenalin rush.

Of course, Wensink's volatility was inherently risky. Don Cherry opted not to dress him for three of the seven games versus Montreal in the 1979 playoffs despite Wensink's newly acquired goal-scoring proclivity. He was deemed too likely to collect undisciplined penalties.

Originally drafted by St. Louis in 1973–74, Wensink played just three games for the Blues before being dispatched to the minor leagues for an extended period. He re-emerged in the NHL as a Bruin late in the 1976–77 season. Wensink spent four productive seasons with Boston and spent a year each with the Quebec Nordiques, Colorado Rockies and New Jersey Devils before calling it a career at the end of the 1982–83 campaign.

Like many NHL's enforcers, Wensink preferred peaceful times off the ice. His favorite hobby was hand-crafting exquisite doll houses.

Appendix B
Statistics and Game Results

"Age" is how old each player was on February 1, 1979. Abbreviations: A—Assists; EV—Even Strength Goals; Exp—Experience (years played in NHL before 1978–79 season; R=rookie); G—Goals Scored; GA—Goals Against; GAA—Goals Against Average; GP—Games Played; GS—Games Started; GW—Game-Winning Goals; MIN—Minutes Played; Opp—Opponent Goals Scored; PIM—Penalties in Minutes; PTS—Points; S/C—Shoots; SH—Short-Handed Goals; SO—Shutouts; Summary— Point Total (G=goals, A=assists; P=points); T—Tie; Tm—Team Goals Scored; T/O— Ties Plus Overtime/Shootout Losses

1978–79 Boston Bruins' Roster and Regular-Season Player Statistics

#	Player	Pos	Age	Ht	Wt	S/C	Exp	Birth Date	Summary
7	Bill Bennett	LW	25	6–5	235	L/–	R	May 31, 1953	1 G, 4 A, 5 P
12	Wayne Cashman (C)	LW	33	6–1	208	R/–	12	June 24, 1945	27 G, 40 A, 67 P
30	Gerry Cheevers	G	38	5–11	185	–/L	11	December 7, 1940	23–9–10, 3.16 GAA
19	Ab DeMarco	D	29	6–0	170	R/–	8	February 27, 1949	0 G, 0 A, 0 P
25	Gary Doak	D	32	5–11	175	R/–	13	February 26, 1946	6 G, 11 A, 17 P
27	Dwight Foster	C	21	5–10	190	R/–	1	April 2, 1957	11 G, 13 A, 24 P
1	Gilles Gilbert	G	29	6–1	175	–/L	9	March 31, 1949	12–8–2, 3.54 GAA
17	Stan Jonathan	LW	23	5–8	175	L/–	3	September 5, 1955	6 G, 9 A, 15 P
21	Don Marcotte	LW	31	5–11	183	L/–	11	April 15, 1947	20 G, 27 A, 47 P
8	Peter McNab	C	26	6–3	210	L/–	5	May 8, 1952	35 G, 45 A, 80 P
16	Rick Middleton	RW	25	5–11	170	R/–	4	December 4, 1953	38 G, 48 A, 86 P
26	Mike Milbury	D	26	6–1	200	L/–	3	June 17, 1952	1 G, 34 A, 35 P
14	Bob Miller	C	22	5–11	180	L/–	1	September 28, 1956	15 G, 33 A, 48 P
19	Graeme Nicolson	D	21	6–0	185	R/–	R	January 13, 1958	0 G, 0 A, 0 P
28	Dennis O'Brien	D	29	6–0	195	L/–	8	June 10, 1949	2 G, 8 A, 10 P
24	Terry O'Reilly	RW	27	6–1	200	R/–	7	June 7, 1951	26 G, 51 A, 77 P
22	Brad Park	D	30	6–0	200	L/–	10	July 6, 1948	7 G, 32 A, 39 P
31	Jim Pettie	G	25	6–0	195	–/L	2	October 24, 1953	8–6–2, 3.59 GAA
10	Jean Ratelle	C	38	6–1	180	L/–	18	October 3, 1940	27 G, 45 A, 72 P
6	Dick Redmond	D	29	5–11	178	L/–	9	August 14, 1949	7 G, 26 A, 33 P
11	Bobby Schmautz	RW	33	5–9	172	R/–	10	March 28, 1945	20 G, 22 A, 42 P
20	Al Secord	LW	20	6–1	205	L/–	R	March 3, 1958	16 G, 7 A, 23 P
29	Al Sims	D	25	6–0	182	L/–	5	April 18, 1953	9 G, 20 A, 29 P
23	Rick Smith	D	30	5–11	190	L/–	8	June 29, 1948	7 G, 18 A, 25 P
19	Tom Songin	RW	25	6–3	195	R/–	R	December 20, 1953	3 G, 1 A, 4 P
27	Mike Walton	C	34	5–10	175	L/–	11	January 3, 1945	4 G, 2 A, 6 P
18	John Wensink	LW	25	6–0	200	L/–	3	April 1, 1953	28 G, 18 A, 46 P

1978–79 Boston Bruins' Regular-Season Goatending Statistics

Rk	Player	Pos	Age	GP	GS	W	L	T/O	GA	GAA	SO	MIN
1	Gerry Cheevers	G	38	43		23	9	10	132	3.16	1	2509
2	Gilles Gilbert	G	29	23		12	8	2	74	3.54	0	1254
3	Jim Pettie	G	25	19		8	6	2	62	3.59	1	1037
	TEAM TOTAL			80		43	23	14	268	3.35	2	4800

Boston Bruins Individual Playoff Statistics—1979

Rk	Player	Pos	Age	GP	G	A	PTS	+/-	PIM	EV	PP	SH	GW
1	Jean Ratelle	C	38	11	7	6	13		2	5	2	0	2
2	Rick Middleton	RW	25	11	4	8	12		0	2	2	0	1
3	Wayne Cashman	LW	33	10	4	5	9		8	3	1	0	1
4	Don Marcotte	LW	31	11	5	3	8		10	5	0	0	0
5	Peter McNab	C	26	11	5	3	8		0	5	0	0	0
6	Mike Milbury	D	26	11	1	7	8		7	1	0	0	1
7	Terry O'Reilly	RW	27	11	0	6	6		25	0	0	0	0
8	Stan Jonathan	LW	23	11	4	1	5		12	4	0	0	0
9	Brad Park	D	30	11	1	4	5		8	1	0	0	1
10	Bobby Schmautz	RW	33	11	2	2	4		6	1	1	0	0
11	Dwight Foster	C	21	11	1	3	4		0	1	0	0	0
12	Dick Redmond	D	29	11	1	3	4		2	0	0	1	0
13	Rick Smith	D	30	11	0	4	4		12	0	0	0	0
14	Bob Miller	C	22	11	1	1	2		8	1	0	0	1
15	Gary Doak	D	32	7	0	2	2		4	0	0	0	0
16	Al Sims	D	25	11	0	2	2		0	0	0	0	0
17	John Wensink	LW	25	8	0	1	1		19	0	0	0	0
18	Gerry Cheevers	G	38	6	0	0	0		0	0	0	0	0
19	Gilles Gilbert	G	29	5	0	0	0		0	0	0	0	0
20	Al Secord	LW	20	4	0	0	0		4	0	0	0	0
	TEAM TOTAL			11	36	61	97		127	29	6	1	7

Boston Bruins Individual Playoff Goaltending Statistics—1979

Rk	Player	Pos	Age	GP	GS	W	L	GA	GAA	SO	MIN
1	Gerry Cheevers	G	38	6	6	4	2	15	2.50	0	360
2	Gilles Gilbert	G	29	5	5	3	2	16	3.06	0	314
	TEAM TOTAL			11	11	7	4	31	2.76	0	674

Boston Bruins 1978–79 Game-by-Game Results: Regular Season

P	Date	Opponent	Tm	Opp	W	L	T	Streak
1	1978-10-12	Pittsburgh Penguins	W	8	2	1	0	0	W 1
2	1978-10-14	@ Pittsburgh Penguins	T	4	4	1	0	1	T 1
3	1978-10-15	Toronto Maple Leafs	W	4	2	2	0	1	W 1
4	1978-10-18	@ Los Angeles Kings	W	3	2	3	0	1	W 2
5	1978-10-20	@ Vancouver Canucks	W	5	1	4	0	1	W 3
6	1978-10-22	@ Chicago Black Hawks	L	5	6	4	1	1	L 1
7	1978-10-24	@ St. Louis Blues	W	7	2	5	1	1	W 1
8	1978-10-25	@ Minnesota North Stars	T	2	2	5	1	2	T 1
9	1978-10-28	@ Toronto Maple Leafs	W	5	3	6	1	2	W 1
10	1978-11-02	New York Islanders	W	4	1	7	1	2	W 2
11	1978-11-04	Philadelphia Flyers	L	3	7	7	2	2	L 1
12	1978-11-05	Montreal Canadiens	T	1	1	7	2	3	T 1
13	1978-11-09	Washington Capitals	W	6	2	8	2	3	W 1
14	1978-11-11	@ Detroit Red Wings	L	1	7	8	3	3	L 1

P	Date	Opponent		Tm	Opp	W	L	T	Streak
15	1978–11–12	@ Buffalo Sabres	T	4	4	8	3	4	T 1
16	1978–11–16	Toronto Maple Leafs	L	4	6	8	4	4	L 1
17	1978–11–17	@ Atlanta Flames	W	6	2	9	4	4	W 1
18	1978–11–19	St. Louis Blues	W	5	2	10	4	4	W 2
19	1978–11–23	Buffalo Sabres	W	5	2	11	4	4	W 3
20	1978–11–25	@ Washington Capitals	T	5	5	11	4	5	T 1
21	1978–11–26	Atlanta Flames	W	4	2	12	4	5	W 1
22	1978–11–30	@ Buffalo Sabres	W	4	3	13	4	5	W 2
23	1978–12–02	Philadelphia Flyers	W	5	3	14	4	5	W 3
24	1978–12–03	@ New York Rangers	W	3	2	15	4	5	W 4
25	1978–12–05	@ Toronto Maple Leafs	W	5	1	16	4	5	W 5
26	1978–12–07	Detroit Red Wings	W	6	5	17	4	5	W 6
27	1978–12–09	@ Philadelphia Flyers	L	2	9	17	5	5	L 1
28	1978–12–10	Minnesota North Stars	T	4	4	17	5	6	T 1
29	1978–12–12	Vancouver Canucks	W	7	3	18	5	6	W 1
30	1978–12–14	Washington Capitals	W	5	2	19	5	6	W 2
31	1978–12–16	New York Rangers	W	4	1	20	5	6	W 3
32	1978–12–17	@ New York Rangers	W	4	1	21	5	6	W 4
33	1978–12–21	Colorado Rockies	W	4	2	22	5	6	W 5
34	1978–12–23	Buffalo Sabres	W	6	4	23	5	6	W 6
35	1978–12–27	@ Toronto Maple Leafs	T	1	1	23	5	7	T 1
36	1978–12–30	@ Montreal Canadiens	L	1	6	23	6	7	L 1
37	1978–12–31	@ Buffalo Sabres	W	7	3	24	6	7	W 1
38	1979–01–03	@ Chicago Black Hawks	W	6	3	25	6	7	W 2
39	1979–01–05	@ Colorado Rockies	W	5	3	26	6	7	W 3
40	1979–01–06	@ Minnesota North Stars	W	5	2	27	6	7	W 4
41	1979–01–11	Minnesota North Stars	W	6	4	28	6	7	W 5
42	1979–01–13	@ Pittsburgh Penguins	L	3	5	28	7	7	L 1
43	1979–01–14	Los Angeles Kings	L	3	6	28	8	7	L 2
44	1979–01–16	@ St. Louis Blues	L	2	5	28	9	7	L 3
45	1979–01–18	St. Louis Blues	W	4	0	29	9	7	W 1
46	1979–01–20	Buffalo Sabres	L	1	2	29	10	7	L 1
47	1979–01–22	Atlanta Flames	W	3	1	30	10	7	W 1
48	1979–01–25	New York Islanders	L	2	4	30	11	7	L 1
49	1979–01–27	@ Montreal Canadiens	L	1	3	30	12	7	L 2
50	1979–01–28	Los Angeles Kings	L	3	5	30	13	7	L 3
51	1979–01–31	@ Chicago Black Hawks	T	2	2	30	13	8	T 1
52	1979–02–01	Chicago Black Hawks	W	6	1	31	13	8	W 1
53	1979–02–03	@ New York Islanders	T	4	4	31	13	9	T 1
54	1979–02–04	Vancouver Canucks	W	6	1	32	13	9	W 1
55	1979–02–14	@ New York Rangers	L	1	5	32	14	9	L 1
56	1979–02–15	@ Philadelphia Flyers	L	3	5	32	15	9	L 2
57	1979–02–17	@ Minnesota North Stars	T	3	3	32	15	10	T 1
58	1979–02–20	@ Colorado Rockies	W	5	3	33	15	10	W 1
59	1979–02–21	@ Los Angeles Kings	L	1	3	33	16	10	L 1
60	1979–02–24	@ Vancouver Canucks	W	4	3	34	16	10	W 1
61	1979–02–27	Colorado Rockies	L	2	4	34	17	10	L 1
62	1979–03–01	Philadelphia Flyers	T	4	4	34	17	11	T 1
63	1979–03–03	Minnesota North Stars	W	5	0	35	17	11	W 1
64	1979–03–04	@ Detroit Red Wings	W	6	4	36	17	11	W 2
65	1979–03–08	@ Atlanta Flames	L	5	7	36	18	11	L 1
66	1979–03–10	@ Minnesota North Stars	W	4	3	37	18	11	W 1
67	1979–03–11	New York Islanders	T	4	4	37	18	12	T 1
68	1979–03–13	@ New York Islanders	L	2	7	37	19	12	L 1
69	1979–03–15	New York Rangers	L	4	7	37	20	12	L 2
70	1979–03–17	Chicago Black Hawks	W	4	2	38	20	12	W 1
71	1979–03–19	Toronto Maple Leafs	W	4	3	39	20	12	W 2
72	1979–03–22	Pittsburgh Penguins	L	1	3	39	21	12	L 1
73	1979–03–24	Detroit Red Wings	W	5	2	40	21	12	W 1

P	Date	Opponent		Tm	Opp	W	L	T	Streak
74	1979-03-28	@ Buffalo Sabres	L	2	9	40	22	12	L 1
75	1979-03-29	Minnesota North Stars	W	7	4	41	22	12	W 1
76	1979-03-31	@ Washington Capitals	W	4	1	42	22	12	W 2
77	1979-04-01	Montreal Canadiens	T	3	3	42	22	13	T 1
78	1979-04-04	@ Toronto Maple Leafs	T	3	3	42	22	14	T 2
79	1979-04-05	Buffalo Sabres	L	3	9	42	23	14	L 1
80	1979-04-08	Toronto Maple Leafs	W	6	3	43	23	14	W 1

Boston Bruins 1979 Playoff Results
Quarterfinal (vs. Pittsburgh)

April 16	Pittsburgh 2 at Boston 6 (win)
April 18	Pittsburgh 3 at Boston 4 (win)
April 21	Boston 2 at Pittsburgh 1 (win)
April 22	Boston 4 at Pittsburgh 1 (win)

Semifinal (vs. Montreal)

April 26	Boston 2 at Montreal 4 (loss)
April 28	Boston 2 at Montreal 5 (loss)
May 1	Montreal 1 at Boston 2 (win)
May 3	Montreal 3 at Boston 4 (OT) (win)
May 5	Boston 1 at Montreal 5 (loss)
May 8	Montreal 2 at Boston 5 (win)
May 10	Boston 4 at Montreal 5 (OT) (loss)

Chapter Notes

Preface

1. Phil Pepe and Zander Hollander *The Book of Sports Lists* (Los Angeles: Pinnacle Books, 1979), 245.
2. Dick Irvin, re-broadcast of Game #7 of the 1979 Boston-Montreal semi-final series, NHL Network, 2008.
3. Brian Cazeneuve, "Three Little Words: Too Many Men," *Sports Illustrated* video feature, 2014.

Introduction

1. John J. Hallahan, "Bruins Win in League Opener," *Boston Globe*, December 2, 1924, 12.
2. John J. Hallahan, "Bruins Picked to Win," *Boston Globe*, April 1, 1930, 13.
3. *Ibid.*
4. *Ibid.*
5. John J. Hallahan, "Canadiens Repeat, Winning the Title," *Boston Globe*, April 4, 1930, 1.
6. Harold Kaese, "Short Series of Yesteryear Would Make Bruins' Fans Jittery," *Boston Globe*, April 14, 1971, 89.
7. Victor O. Jones, "Bruins Rally to Win, 5–4," *Boston Globe*, March 25, 1931, 1.
8. *Ibid.*
9. Victor O. Jones, "Canadiens Tie Up Series, Winning, 1–0," *Boston Globe*, March 27, 1931, 40.
10. Victor O. Jones, "Canadiens Make It Two Straight," *Boston Globe*, March 29, 1931, A1.
11. Victor O. Jones, "Bruins Win, 3–1, Tying Up Series," *Boston Globe*, March 31, 1931, 1.
12. Victor O. Jones, "Tongues Wag on Hockey Boners," *Boston Globe*, April 3, 1931, 41.
13. *Ibid.*
14. *Ibid.*
15. L.S.B. Shapiro, "Canadiens Triumph Over Bruins, 3–2, to Capture Series," *Montreal Gazette*, April 2, 1931, 20.
16. Leigh Montville, "No Gain, Just Pain," *Sports Illustrated* online archives, April 25, 1988.
17. Tom Fitzgerald, "Canadiens Score 2 in Third Period, Oust Bruins 3–1," *Boston Globe*, April 9, 1952, 11.
18. Leigh Montville, "No Gain, Just Pain," *Sports Illustrated* online archives, April 25, 1988.
19. Tom Fitzgerald, "Canadiens Win, 5–1; Bruins Out of Stanley Cup," *Boston Globe*, April 1, 1955, 38.
20. Tom Fitzgerald, "Bruins Seen as Threat for Cup Next Season," *Boston Globe*, April 18, 1957, 8.
21. Tom Fitzgerald, "Habs Beat Bruins 5–3," *Boston Globe*, April 21, 1958, 14.
22. Tom Fitzgerald, "B's Drop Finale to Leafs, 5–2," *Boston Globe*, April 3, 1967, 23.
23. Harold Kaese, "Bruins' Chance Appears Strong," *Boston Globe*, April 4, 1968, 45.
24. Kevin Walsh, "Sinden Puzzled by Bruins' Slump," *Boston Globe*, April 12, 1968, 28.
25. *Ibid.*
26. Tom Fitzgerald, "Espo (4), Bruins Crush Toronto in Wild Opener, 10–0; Orr Hurt," *Boston Globe*, April 3, 1969, 49.
27. Tom Fitzgerald, "Future Belongs to the Bruins," *Boston Globe*, April 27, 1969, 83.
28. *Ibid.*
29. *Ibid.*
30. *Ibid.*
31. *Ibid.*
32. *Ibid.*
33. Gary Ronberg, "Tea Party for Bobby's Bruins," *Sports Illustrated* online archives, May 4, 1970.
34. Jerry Nason, "None Laughing at Bruins Now," *Boston Globe*, May 3, 1970, 89.
35. Gary Ronberg, "Tea Party for Bobby's Bruins," *Sports Illustrated* online archives, May 4, 1970.
36. Bud Collins, "Bruins Lock Out 'Chicago Six,'" *Boston Globe*, April 24, 1970, 29.
37. Harold Kaese, "Short Series of Yesteryear Would Make Bruins' Fans Jittery," *Boston Globe*, April 4, 1971, 89.
38. *Ibid.*
39. Tom Fitzgerald, "Orr Loses Cool as Bruins Top Canadiens, 3–1," *Boston Globe*, April 8, 1971, 53.
40. Leigh Montville, "No Gain, Just Pain," *Sports Illustrated* online archives, April 25, 1988.
41. Tom Fitzgerald, "Canadiens' Onslaught Staggers Bruins, 7–5," *Boston Globe*, April 9, 1971, 21.
42. Harold Kaese, "Canadiens' Six-Goal Surge No More than a Grandiose Fluke," *Boston Globe*, April 11, 1971, 73.
43. *Ibid.*
44. Tom Fitzgerald, "Canadiens' Onslaught Staggers Bruins, 7–5," *Boston Globe*, April 9, 1971, 21.

45. Dan Diamond, *The Ultimate Prize: The Stanley Cup* (Kansas City: Andrews McMeel, 2003), 142.

46. Leigh Montville, "Bruins 'All Right Now,' Says Sanderson," *Boston Globe*, April 13, 1971, 25.

47. *Ibid.*

48. "Bruins Lose, 8–3, Forced to 7th Game," *Boston Globe*, April 16, 1971, 1.

49. "Canadiens Burst Bruins' Bubble, 4–2," *Boston Globe*, April 18, 1971, 1.

50. Harold Kaese, "Bruins' Plight: Inexcusable, but Self-Made, Well-Deserved," *Boston Globe*, April 18, 1971, 81.

51. Mark Mulvoy, "Brief Reign of the Lordly Bruins," *Sports Illustrated* online archives, April 26, 1971.

52. *Ibid.*

53. *Ibid.*

54. *Ibid.*

55. Leigh Montville, "No Gain, Just Pain," *Sports Illustrated* online archives, April 25, 1988.

56. "Bruins-Blues Quoteboard," *Boston Globe*, April 21, 1972, 38.

57. Tim Burke, "Bruins-Rangers: The Bitterness Continues," *Montreal Gazette*, May 13, 1972, 17.

58. *Ibid.*

59. Tim Burke, "Rangers Down One, but They're Happy," *Montreal Gazette*, May 1, 1972, 13.

60. Ted Blackman, "Francis Defied 'Hot Hand' on Day Orr Wasn't Ablaze," *Montreal Gazette*, May 1, 1972, 13.

61. Tim Burke, "Bruins-Rangers: The Bitterness Continues," *Montreal Gazette*, May 13, 1972, 17.

62. *Ibid.*

63. Tom Fitzgerald, "Orr Scores ... Cheevers Saves ... Cup's in Hand!" *Boston Globe*, May 12, 1972, 51.

64. Kevin Walsh, "Champs Seemed Able to Win When They Wanted," *Boston Globe*, May 12, 1972, 24.

65. Tom Fitzgerald, "New-Look Bruins Usher in Season Against Kings at Garden Tonight," *Boston Globe*, October 8, 1972, 72.

66. Tom Fitzgerald, "Bruins Succumb, 6–3, Surrender Stanley Cup," *Boston Globe*, April 11, 1973, 63.

Chapter 1

1. Don Cherry, *Straight Up & Personal* (Toronto: Anchor Canada, 2014), 186.

2. Don Cherry, *Don Cherry's Hockey Stories and Stuff* (Toronto: Anchor Canada, 2008), 50.

3. Bob Kinsley, "Cherry Signs Multiyear Pact as Bruins Coach," *Boston Globe*, June 14, 1974, 51.

4. Francis Rosa, "Don Cherry," *Boston Globe*, September 2, 1974, 84.

5. Ernie Roberts, "Boston's Own Dandy Don," *Boston Globe*, January 27, 1978, A4.

6. Eddie MacCabe, "Lucky 'Bleepers' Beat Bruins," *Ottawa Citizen*, April 27, 1979, 23.

7. Ernie Roberts, "Boston's Own Dandy Don," *Boston Globe*, January 27, 1978, A4.

8. *Ibid.*

9. Tom Fitzgerald, "Cherry Accepts Blame for Debacle," *Boston Globe*, October 11, 1974, 52.

10. *Ibid.*

11. Francis Rosa, "Espo, Brooks, Help Bruins Break Drought, Flyers, 4–1," *Boston Globe*, October 18, 1974, 47.

12. Matt Kalman, *100 Things Bruins Fans Should Know & Do Before They Die* (Chicago: Triumph Books, 2010), 100.

13. *Ibid.*

14. *Ibid.*, 101.

15. Tim Burke, "Cherry's Cheery Way Keeps Bruins Flying," *Montreal Gazette*, May 10, 1979, 59.

16. Matt Kalman, *100 Things Bruins Fans Should Know & Do Before They Die* (Chicago: Triumph Books, 2010), 100.

17. *Ibid.*, 102.

18. *Ibid.*

19. *Ibid.*, 101–102.

20. Kevin Shea, "Hockey Hall of Fame Spotlight: Brad Park," www.hhof.com, May 10, 2005.

21. Francis Rosa, "It Was a Question of Cherry's Style," *Boston Globe*, May 27, 1979, 30.

22. "Don Cherry," Don Cherry's Wikipedia biography page.

23. Francis Rosa, "It Was a Question of Cherry's Style," *Boston Globe*, May 27, 1979, 30.

Chapter 2

1. Will McDonough, "Same Coach, Same Strategy—But Cherry Pickers Are Silent Now," *Boston Globe*, May 4, 1977, 55.

2. Tom Fitzgerald, "Park et al. Tout Cheevers," *Boston Globe*, May 2, 1977, 20.

3. *Ibid.*

4. *Ibid.*

5. *Ibid.*

6. *Ibid.*

7. Will McDonough, "Flyers Planned to Make the Final, but Bruins Stole Their Script," *Boston Globe*, May 2, 1977, 20.

8. Francis Rosa, "Montreal Scared of Bruins?" *Boston Globe*, May 7, 1977, 17.

9. *Ibid.*

10. Thom Sears and Brad Park, *Straight Shooter: The Brad Park Story* (Mississauga, ON: John Wiley and Sons Canada, 2010), 72–73.

11. Francis Rosa, "Montreal Scared of Bruins?" *Boston Globe*, May 7, 1977, 17.

12. Tom Fitzgerald, "Bruins: Ready or Not?" *Boston Globe*, May 7, 1977, 21.

13. *Ibid.*

14. Alan Richman, "Cherry's Plaint Isn't Coming Across," *Boston Globe*, May 12, 1977, 29.

15. Will McDonough, "Ref Robbed Us—Cherry," *Boston Globe*, May 11, 1977, 54.

16. Peter Gammons, "They Ruined the Bruins," *Sports Illustrated*, May 23, 1977, 26.

17. Will McDonough, "Bruins Are Left Awestruck," *Boston Globe*, May 13, 1977, 52.

18. *Ibid.*

19. Ernie Roberts, "Starr Envies Patriot Draft," *Boston Globe*, May 14, 1977, 17.

20. Francis Rosa, "Canadiens Sweep Cup, Top Bruins in OT, 2–1," *Boston Globe*, May 15, 1977, 87.

21. *Ibid.*

22. Alan Richman, "Canadiens' One Regret: Clincher Not at Home," *Boston Globe*, May 15, 1977, 94.

23. *Ibid.*

24. Peter Gammons, "They Ruined the Bruins," *Sports Illustrated*, May 23, 1977, 26.

25. Alan Richman, "Canadiens' One Regret: Clincher Not at Home," *Boston Globe*, May 15, 1977, 94.

26. Ted Blackman, "Canadiens of '58 Were Better," *Montreal Gazette*, May 16, 1977, 16.

27. Francis Rosa, "Canadiens Sweep Cup, Top Bruins in OT, 2–1," *Boston Globe*, May 15, 1977, 87.

28. Tom Fitzgerald, "Cheevers Disappointed, but Unashamed," *Boston Globe*, May, 15, 1977, 95.

29. Francis Rosa, "Canadiens Have Winning in System—And What a System," *Boston Globe,* May 16, 1977, 24.

30. Tom Fitzgerald, "Cheevers Disappointed, but Unashamed," *Boston Globe*, May, 15, 1977, 95.

31. Tom Fitzgerald, "Wait Till Next Year? Bruins Planning Now," *Boston Globe*, May 16, 1977, 24.

Chapter 3

1. Francis Rosa, "Bruins' Three-Goal Third Sends Flyers Home, 6–3," *Boston Globe*, May 12, 1978, 25.

2. *Ibid.*

3. Brian McFarlane, *Hockey Night in Canada*'s broadcast of Game #5 of the 1978 Bruins-Flyers semi-final series, May 11, 1978.

4. Bill Clement, *Ibid.*

5. *Ibid.*

6. *Ibid.*

7. Bob Ryan, "Bruins' Could-Do-It Talk More than Bombast," *Boston Globe*, May 13, 1978, 22.

8. *Ibid.*

9. *Ibid.*

10. Bob Lobel, WBZ radio's coverage of Game #2 of the 1978 Stanley Cup finals, May 16, 1978.

11. Al Strachan and Lewis Harris, "Gallivan Watches on TV as Bruins Blank Canadiens," *Montreal Gazette*, May 19, 1978, 1.

12. *Ibid.*

13. *Ibid.*

14. Al Strachan, "Canadiens Trounced? Yes. That's the Name of the Game," *Montreal Gazette*, May 19, 1978, 17.

15. *Ibid.*

16. *Ibid.*

17. Francis Rosa, "Bruins Tie Series with 4–3 OT Win," *Boston Globe*, May 22, 1978, 25.

18. *Ibid.*

19. *Ibid.*

20. Mark Mulvoy, "Aiming to Set an Upset," *Sports Illustrated* online archives, May 29, 1978.

21. "Suddenly the Habs Are on the Run," *Kitchener-Waterloo* (ON) *Record*, May 22, 1978, B1.

22. Francis Rosa, "Fight Night in Canada: Bruins Lose 4–1," *Boston Globe*, May 24, 1978, 49.

23. *Ibid.*

24. Will McDonough, "Bruins Hardly Thrilled About Being Second Best," *Boston Globe*, May 26, 1978, 41.

25. Mark Mulvoy, "The Cup Runneth Ever," *Sports Illustrated* online archives, June 5, 1978.

26. *Ibid.*

27. *Ibid.*

28. Will McDonough, "Bruins Hardly Thrilled About Being Second Best," *Boston Globe*, May 26, 1978, 41.

29. Mark Mulvoy, "The Cup Runneth Ever," *Sports Illustrated* online archives, June 5, 1978.

30. Francis Rosa, "Tremblay Leads Canadiens to 4–1 Clincher Over Bruins," Boston Globe, May 26, 1978, 37.

31. Will McDonough, "Bruins Hardly Thrilled About Being Second Best," *Boston Globe*, May 26, 1978, 41.

32. *Ibid.*

Chapter 4

1. Zander Hollander, ed., *The Complete Handbook of Pro Hockey*, 1979 ed. (New York: Signet, 1978), 97–98.

2. Mark Mulvoy, "NHL 1978–79: Scouting Reports," *Sports Illustrated* online archives, October 23, 1978.

3. Francis Rosa, "McNab Moves Out of the Doghouse, Becomes a Top Dog," *Boston Globe*, March 26, 1978, 72.

4. Francis Rosa, "The Chase for the Cup," *Boston Globe*, October 6, 1978, A8.

5. *Ibid.*

6. *Ibid.*

7. *Ibid.*

8. Jim Proudfoot, *Pro Hockey NHL 75–76* (Markham, ON: Pocket Books, 1975), 160.

9. Francis Rosa, "Bruins Toss 'Dynamite' Line at Penguins," *Boston Globe*, October 12, 1978, 42.

10. Francis Rosa, "Bruins Swing into Season by Downing Penguins, 8–2," *Boston Globe*, October 13, 1978, 39.

11. Bob Whitley, "Same Old Penguins in Boston," *Pittsburgh Post-Gazette*, October 13, 1978, 11.

12. Francis Rosa, "Bruins Swing into Season by Downing Penguins, 8–2," *Boston Globe*, October 13, 1978, 39.

13. *Ibid.*

14. Fran Rosa, "Hospital Checks Park's Knee," *Boston Globe*, October 14, 1978, 24.

15. *Ibid.*

16. Steve Marantz, "Park Out 5–8 Weeks," *Boston Globe*, October 18, 1978, 24.

17. Francis Rosa, "Bruins Come Out Smoking, Send Blues Spawling, 7–2," *Boston Globe*, October 25, 1978, 61.

18. Francis Rosa, "It Was a Question of Cherry's Style," *Boston Globe*, May 27, 1979, 30.

19. Francis Rosa, "Cheevers Returning; Pettie, Demarco Go," *Boston Globe*, November 7, 1978, 72

20. Francis Rosa, "Penguins Tie Bruins, 4–4, with 30 Seconds to Play," *Boston Globe*, October 15, 1978, 54.

21. Francis Rosa, "Bruins Glide Early, Cruise Past Toronto, 4–2," *Boston Globe*, October 16, 1978, 29.

22. *Ibid.*

23. Peter Gammons, "Miller Scores the Winner as Bruins Trip Kings, 3–2," *Boston Globe*, October 19, 1978.

24. John Ahern, "Ballard High on Bruins," *Boston Globe*, November 1, 1978, 27.

25. Francis Rosa, "Bruins Come Out Smoking, Send Blues Sprawling, 7–2," *Boston Globe*, October 25, 1978, 61.

26. John Ahern, "Ballard High on Bruins," *Boston Globe*, November, 1 1978, 27.

Chapter 5

1. Francis Rosa, "Cherry, Westfall Joust," *Boston Globe*, November 3, 1978, 38.

2. *Ibid.*

3. *Ibid.*

4. Francis Rosa, "Canadiens Catch Bruins, 1–1," *Boston Globe*, November 6, 1978, 45.

5. *Ibid.*

6. *Ibid.*

7. *Ibid.*

8. *Ibid.*

9. *Ibid.*

10. Glenn Cole, "Houle Ties Up Bruins," *Montreal Gazette*, November 6, 1978, 35.

11. John Ahern, "Cherry Praises Doak," *Boston Globe*, November 8, 1978, 76.

12. Francis Rosa, "Demand Your Rights, Goalies," *Boston Globe*, November 26, 1978, 90.

13. *Ibid.*

14. Francis Rosa, "Middleton Loss Forces Shuffle," *Boston Globe*, November 27, 1978, 28.

15. Thom Sears and Brad Park, *Straight Shooter: The Brad Park Story* (Mississauga, ON: John Wiley & Sons Canada, 2012), 195.

16. Francis Rosa, "Bruins Dump Flames, 4–2, for Cherry's 200th Victory," *Boston Globe*, November 27, 1978, 27.

17. *Ibid.*

18. Don Cherry, *Don Cherry's Hockey Stories and Stuff* (Toronto: Anchor Canada, 2008), 217.

19. "Phillipoff Out for Five Weeks," *Boston Globe*, November 28, 1978, 33.

20. Francis Rosa, "For Bruins the Key Is Consistency," *Boston Globe*, December 10, 1978, 77.

21. *Ibid.*

22. Francis Rosa, "Marcotte Planned Goal," *Boston Globe*, December 18, 1978, 32.

23. Francis Rosa, "Fan Voting for All-Stars Miffs Cherry," *Boston Globe*, December 19, 1978, 34.

24. *Ibid.*

25. Francis Rosa, "Some Gift Ideas for the Pro," *Boston Globe*, December 24, 1978, 39.

26. *Ibid.*

27. Francis Rosa, "Injury No Barrier to Success," *Boston Globe*, December 23, 1978, 22.

28. Francis Rosa, "Cup 'Preview' Downplayed by Cherry," *Boston Globe*, December 30, 1978, 18.

29. *Ibid.*

30. Francis Rosa, "Cashman Get Bruins Back on Right Track, 7–3," *Boston Globe*, January 1, 1979, 71.

31. Peter Gammons, "Bruins Don't Capture Headlines—Just Victories," *Boston Globe*, December 27, 1978, 47.

Chapter 6

1. Francis Rosa, "Bruins Bagged by Airline," *Boston Globe*, January 4, 1979, 36.

2. John Powers, "No. 4 Hasn't Lost That Magic," *Boston Globe*, January 10, 1979, 1.

3. *Ibid.*

4. Tom Fitzgerald, "Orr Aids Bruins to 6–2 Opening Win Over Red Wings," *Boston Globe*, October 20, 1966, 53.

5. Tom Fitzgerald, TV38's coverage of Bruins-Soviet Wings exhibition game, January 9, 1979.

6. John Powers, "No. 4 Hasn't Lost That Magic," *Boston Globe*, January 10, 1979, 1.

7. Ray Fitzgerald, "Orr's Future? One Wonders," *Boston Globe*, November 30, 1975, 94.

8. Bobby Clarke, *Hockey: A People's History*, CBC Home Video, 2006.

9. Bobby Hull, *Ibid.*

10. George Plimpton, *Open Net* (New York: Penguin, 1987), 67.

11. Francis Rosa, "…And the Game: Russians Spoil the Party, 4–1," *Boston Globe*, January 10, 1979, 35.

12. *Ibid.*

13. Jerry Kirshenbaum, "The Wrath of Grapes," *Sports Illustrated* online archives, January 15, 1979.

14. *Ibid.*

15. *Ibid.*

16. Francis Rosa, "Bruins' Offer Disappointing to Cherry," *Boston Globe*, January 17, 1979, 21.

17. *Ibid.*

18. *Ibid.*

19. Don Cherry, *Don Cherry's Hockey Stories and Stuff* (Toronto: Anchor Canada, 2008), 150.

20. *Ibid.*, 115.

21. John Ahern, "Cherry Worrying," *Boston Globe*, January 11, 1979. 18.

22. Francis Rosa, "Canadiens Thwart Pettie in Forum, 3–1," *Boston Globe*, January 28, 1979, 41.

23. *Ibid.*

24. Glenn Cole, "Canadiens Pressed to Grab Win Despite Classy Tilt Against Bruins," *Montreal Gazette*, January 28, 1979, 29.

25. Dave Carter, "Cheevers Helps Mold Bruins' Rookie Goaler," *Montreal Gazette*, January 28, 1979, 29.

26. Francis Rosa, "Canadiens Thwart Pettie in Forum, 3–1," *Boston Globe*, January 28, 1979, 41.

27. Dave Carter, "Cheevers Helps Mold Bruins' Rookie Goaler," *Montreal Gazette*, January 28, 1979, 29.

28. Francis Rosa, "Canadiens Thwart Pettie in Forum, 3–1," *Boston Globe*, January 28, 1979, 41.

29. *Ibid.*

30. *Ibid.*

31. Francis Rosa, "Players Rap Referee Myers," *Boston Globe*, February 1, 1979, 34.

32. *Ibid.*

33. E.M. Swift, "Earning Their Stripes," *Sports Illustrated*, October 11, 1982, 44

34. Ernie Roberts, "Ol' Blue Was Bored," *Boston Globe*, February 10, 1979, 21.

35. John Ahern, "Cherry's Status Disturbs Players," *Boston Globe*, February 19, 1979, 33.

36. Francis Rosa, "Two Firsts—Shoutout for Pettie, 5–0; Ejection for Cherry," *Boston Globe*, March 4, 1979, 58.

37. *Ibid.*

38. *Ibid.*

39. Fred Cusick, TV38's broadcast of Boston-Minnesota game, March 3, 1979.

40. Francis Rosa, "Cheevers Makes Coaching Debut," *Boston Globe*, March 4, 1979, 58.

41. Francis Rosa, "Bruins, Islanders in 4–4 Tie," *Boston Globe*, March 12, 1979, 29.

42. *Ibid.*

43. *Ibid.*

44. *Ibid.*

45. Francis Rosa, "Espo's 4 Goals Ruin Bruins, 7–4," *Boston Globe*, March 16, 1979, 57.

46. Francis Rosa, "Bruins Capture Adams Title, 4–1," *Boston Globe*, April 1, 1979, 49.

47. *Ibid.*

48. Glenn Cole, "Langway's Goal Gives Canadiens Tie," *Montreal Gazette*, April 2, 1979, 27.

49. *Ibid.*

50. John Ahern, "Bruins Need Win for 3d Best Mark," *Boston Globe*, April 3, 1979, 39.

51. Glenn Cole, "Langway's Goal Gives Canadiens Tie," *Montreal Gazette*, April 2, 1979, 27.

52. Ray Fitzgerald, "Cheevers the Gerry of Old," *Boston Globe*, April 3, 1979, 37.

53. Francis Rosa, "Battered Bruins Can't Wait for Rest," *Boston Globe*, March 31, 1979, 23.

54. Francis Rosa, "Bruins Hit 100 Points with 6–3 Win," *Boston Globe*, April 9, 1979, 35.

55. *Ibid.*

56. *Ibid.*

57. Francis Rosa, "Battered Bruins Can't Wait for Rest," *Boston Globe*, March 31, 1979, 23.

58. Glenn Cole, "Wings Jolt Canadiens' Hopes," *Montreal Gazette*, April 9, 1979, 63.

59. Ed Simon, Canadian Press coverage of April 8, 1979, Islanders-Rangers game.

60. Don Cherry, *Grapes: A Vintage View of Hockey* (Scarborough, ON: Avon, 1982), 27.

Chapter 7

1. Francis Rosa, "Previewing the Playoffs," *Boston Globe*, April 8, 1979, 74.

2. William Nack, "Undaunted and Unhaunted," *Sports Illustrated*, April 16, 1979, 32.

3. *Ibid.*

4. *Ibid.*

5. Francis Rosa, "Time Heals Bruins' Wounds, All Hands Ready for Playoffs," *Boston Globe*, April 12, 1979, 55.

6. Glenn Cole, "Real Season Time Again," *Montreal Gazette*, April 10, 1979, 63.

Chapter 8

1. Francis Rosa, "Bruins, Beware: Penguins Are Peaking," *Boston Globe*, April 16, 1979, 38.

2. *Ibid.*

3. Steve Marantz, "Denis Herron," *Boston Globe*, April 22, 1979, 82.

4. Don Cherry, *Grapes: A Vintage View of Hockey* (Scarborough, ON: Avon, 1982), 5.

5. Francis Rosa, "Bruins, Beware: Penguins Are Peaking," *Boston Globe*, April 16, 1979, 38.

6. *Ibid.*

7. Francis Rosa, "Bruins Look Healthy, Show Penguins, 6–2," *Boston Globe*, April 17, 1979, 33.

8. *Ibid.*

9. John Ahern, "Bruins Say Penguins Can Be Better," *Boston Globe*, April 18, 1979, 26.

10. Bob Whitley, "Riled-Up Bruins Whip Penguins in Opener," *Pittsburgh Post-Gazette*, April 17, 1979, 15.

11. John Ahern, "Bruins Turn to Gilbert, Cherry Won't 'Open Up,'" *Boston Globe*, April 20, 37.

12. Bob Whitley, "Pirates, Penguins Come Up a Little Short," *Pittsburgh Post-Gazette*, April 19, 1979, 20.

13. Steve Marantz, "Herron Blames Referee for Two Bruins' Goals," *Boston Globe*, April 19, 1979, 51.

14. *Ibid.*

15. Don Cherry, *Grapes: A Vintage View of Hockey* (Scarborough, ON: Avon, 1982), 7.

16. John Ahern, "'Aching' Cheevers Rushes to Rescue," *Boston Globe*, April 22, 1979, 82.

17. *Ibid.*

18. Francis Rosa, "Bruins Take Another, 2–1, Need Another," *Boston Globe*, April 22, 1979, 77.

19. John Ahern, "'Aching' Cheevers Rushes to Rescue," *Boston Globe*, April 22, 1979, 82.

20. *Ibid.*

21. Francis Rosa, "Bruins Take Another, 2–1, Need Another," *Boston Globe*, April 22, 1979, 77.

22. Francis Rosa, "Bruins Wrap Up Penguins in Four, 4–1," *Boston Globe*, April 23, 1979, 33.

23. Bob Whitley, "Penguin Season Ends with a 4–1 Bruin Win," *Pittsburgh Post-Gazette*, April 23, 1979, 13.

24. Francis Rosa, "Bruins Wrap Up Penguins in Four, 4–1," *Boston Globe*, April 23, 1979, 33.

25. *Ibid.*

26. Associated Press report on Boston-Pittsburgh quarterfinal playoff game of April 22, 1979.

27. Canadian Press report on Montreal-Toronto quarterfinal playoff game of April 22, 1979.

28. *Ibid.*

29. Glenn Cole, "Canadiens Sweep Away Maple Leafs," *Montreal Gazette*, April 23, 1979, 49.

30. Associated Press "Stanley Cup Playoffs," *Pittsburgh Post-Gazette*, April 26, 1979, 13.

Chapter 9

1. Glenn Cole, "Jarvis Back in Gear for Bruins' Faceoff," *Montreal Gazette*, April 26, 1979, 56.

2. *Ibid.*

3. Al Strachan, "Playoff Predictions," *Montreal Gazette*, April 26, 1979, 57.

4. Francis Rosa, "Bruins Look to Redmond as Their Key," *Boston Globe*, April 26, 1979, 46.

5. *Ibid.*

6. *Ibid.*

7. *Ibid.*

8. *Ibid.*

9. John Ahern, "History Hardly on Bruins' Side," *Boston Globe*, April 25, 1979, 60.

10. Glenn Cole, "Playoff Predictions," *Montreal Gazette*, April 26, 1979, 57.

Chapter 10

1. Francis Rosa, "Canadiens Go 1 Up, Rule Bruins 4–2," *Boston Globe*, April 27, 1979, 57.

2. Frank Orr, "Bruins Are Beginning to Wonder If They Can Get a Break in Montreal," *Toronto Star*, April 27, 1979, B1.

3. *Ibid.*

4. *Ibid.*

5. *Ibid.*

6. *Ibid.*

7. *Ibid.*

8. *Ibid.*

9. *Ibid.*

10. Francis Rosa, "Canadiens Go 1 Up, Rule Bruins 4–2," *Boston Globe*, April 27, 1979, 57.

11. Leigh Montville, "Another Heartbreak," *Boston Globe*, April 27, 1979, 57.

12. *Ibid.*

13. Frank Orr, "Bruins Are Beginning to Wonder If They Can Get a Break in Montreal," *Toronto Star*, April 27, 1979, B1.

14. Eddie MacCabe, "Lucky 'Bleepers' Beat Bruins," *Ottawa Citizen*, April 27, 1979, 23.

15. Frank Orr, "Bruins Are Beginning to Wonder If They Can Get a Break in Montreal," *Toronto Star*, April 27, 1979, B1.

16. *Ibid.*

17. *Ibid.*

18. *Ibid.*

19. *Ibid.*

20. *Ibid.*

21. *Ibid.*

22. Glenn Cole, "Canadiens Hang on to Win," *Montreal Gazette*, April 27, 1979, 27.

23. *Ibid.*

24. *Ibid.*

25. *Ibid.*

26. Francis Rosa, "Canadiens Go 1 Up, Rule Bruins 4–2," *Boston Globe*, April 27, 1979, 57.

27. *Ibid.*

28. *Ibid.*

29. *Ibid.*

Chapter 11

1. Glenn Cole, "'Lucky' Canadiens Storm Back to Take 2–0 Series Lead to Boston," *Montreal Gazette*, April 30, 1979, 51.

2. Frank Orr, "Hab Power Pounces for 5–2 Win," *Toronto Star*, April 29, 1979, C1.

3. *Ibid.*

4. Glenn Cole, "'Lucky' Canadiens Storm Back to Take 2–0 Series Lead to Boston," *Montreal Gazette*, April 30, 1979, 51.

5. Frank Orr, "Hab Power Pounces for 5–2 Win," *Toronto Star*, April 29, 1979, C1.

6. Francis Rosa, "Canadiens Belt Bruins, 5–2, Go Two Up," *Boston Globe*, April 29, 1979, 45.

7. *Ibid.*

8. Frank Orr, "Hab Power Pounces for 5–2 Win," *Toronto Star*, April 29, 1979, C1.

9. Francis Rosa, "Canadiens Belt Bruins, 5–2, Go Two Up," *Boston Globe*, April 29, 1979, 45.

10. *Ibid.*

11. Frank Orr, "Hab Power Pounces for 5–2 Win," *Toronto Star*, April 29, 1979, C1.

12. *Ibid.*

13. Leigh Montville, "Visitor to Montreal Has Some Thoughts," *Boston Globe*, April 30, 1979, 29.

14. Frank Orr, "Hab Power Pounces for 5–2 Win," *Toronto Star*, April 29, 1979, C1.

15. Leigh Montville, "Visitor to Montreal Has Some Thoughts," *Boston Globe*, April 30, 1979, 29.

16. Glenn Cole, "'Lucky' Canadiens Storm Back to Take 2–0 Series Lead to Boston," *Montreal Gazette*, April 30, 1979, 51.

17. Francis Rosa, "Canadiens Belt Bruins, 5–2, Go Two Up," *Boston Globe*, April 29, 1979, 45.

18. Al Strachan, "Cherry Not Sweet with Gatecrasher," *Montreal Gazette*, April 30, 1979, 53.

Chapter 12

1. Francis Rosa, "Park's Late Sizzler Burns Canadiens," *Boston Globe*, May 2, 1979, 25.

2. *Ibid.*

3. Frank Orr, "Bruins Hit Top Gear but Habs in Park," *Toronto Star*, May 2, 1979, D1.

4. *Ibid.*

5. *Ibid.*

6. *Ibid.*

7. *Ibid.*

8. Glenn Cole, "Bruins Grind Out a Tough Win," *Montreal Gazette*, May 2, 1979, 17.

9. *Ibid.*

10. *Ibid.*

11. *Ibid.*

12. Thom Sears and Brad Park, *Straight Shooter: The Brad Park Story* (Mississauga, ON: John Wiley and Sons Canada, 2010), 107.

13. *Ibid.*

14. *Ibid.*

15. Frank Orr, "Bruins Hit Top Gear but Habs in Park," *Toronto Star*, May 2, 1979, D1.

16. *Ibid.*

17. *Ibid.*

18. *Ibid.*

19. *Ibid.*

20. *Ibid.*

21. *Ibid.*

22. *Ibid.*
23. *Ibid.*
24. *Ibid.*
25. *Ibid.*
26. Leigh Montville, "The Pain Can Wait," *Boston Globe*, May 3, 1979, 61.
27. Frank Orr, "Boston Notebook," *Toronto Star*, May 2, 1979, D2.
28. *Ibid.*
29. *Ibid.*

Chapter 13

1. Frank Orr, "Ratelle Deserved a Big Night," *Toronto Star*, May 4, 1979, B1.
2. *Ibid.*
3. *Ibid.*
4. *Ibid.*
5. *Ibid.*
6. *Ibid.*
7. *Ibid.*
8. *Ibid.*
9. Dick Irivin, *Hockey Night in Canada* broadcast of May 3, 1979 Boston-Montreal semi-final playoff game.
10. Frank Orr, "Ratelle Deserved a Big Night," *Toronto Star*, May 4, 1979, B1.
11. Ray Fitzgerald, "Canadiens Swarmed In—But Didn't Have Sting," *Boston Globe*, May 4, 1979, 53.
12. *Ibid.*
13. *Ibid.*
14. *Ibid.*
15. Ernie Roberts, "Delp's Sentiment Deserves Applause," *Boston Globe*, May 5, 1979, 22.
16. Ray Fitzgerald, "Canadiens Swarmed In—But Didn't Have Sting," *Boston Globe*, May 4, 1979, 53.
17. *Ibid.*
18. *Ibid.*
19. Frank Orr, "Ratelle Deserved a Big Night," *Toronto Star*, May 4, 1979, B1.
20. Ernie Roberts, "Thank God for Rattie—Cashman," *Boston Globe*, May 4, 1979, 54.
21. *Ibid.*
22. *Ibid.*
23. Al Strachan, "This Route's Not New for Canadiens," *Montreal Gazette*, May 4, 1979, 32.
24. *Ibid.*
25. *Ibid.*
26. *Ibid.*
27. Frank Orr, "Ratelle Deserved a Big Night," *Toronto Star*, May 4, 1979, B1.
28. *Ibid.*
29. *Ibid.*
30. *Ibid.*
31. *Ibid.*
32. *Ibid.*
33. *Ibid.*
34. Ernie Roberts, "Thank God for Rattie—Cashman," *Boston Globe*, May 4, 1979, 54.
35. Ernie Roberts, "Delp's Sentiment Deserves Applause," *Boston Globe*, May 5, 1979, 22.

36. Al Strachan, "Bruins Think Cherry Not Worth His Salary," *Montreal Gazette*, May 4, 1979, 31.
37. *Ibid.*

Chapter 14

1. Francis Rosa, "Fast-Starting Canadiens Top Bruins, 5–1," *Boston Globe*, May 6, 1979, 49.
2. *Ibid.*
3. *Ibid.*
4. Frank Orr, "History Provides the Edge for Habs," *Toronto Star*, May 7, 1979, B1.
5. Francis Rosa, "Fast-Starting Canadiens Top Bruins, 5–1," *Boston Globe*, May 6, 1979, 49.
6. *Ibid.*
7. *Ibid.*
8. Francis Rosa, "Fast-Starting Canadiens Top Bruins, 5–1," *Boston Globe*, May 6, 1979, 49.
9. *Ibid.*
10. Frank Orr, "History Provides the Edge for Habs," *Toronto Star*, May 7, 1979, B1.
11. *Ibid.*
12. *Ibid.*
13. *Ibid.*
14. *Ibid.*
15. *Ibid.*
16. *Ibid.*
17. *Ibid.*
18. *Ibid.*
19. Francis Rosa, "Fast-Starting Canadiens Top Bruins, 5–1," *Boston Globe*, May 6, 1979, 49.
20. *Ibid.*
21. Jim Coleman, "The Habs Took Their Cue from Doucet," *Calgary Herald*, May 7, 1979, D2.
22. *Ibid.*
23. *Ibid.*
24. Frank Orr, "History Provides the Edge for Habs," *Toronto Star*, May 7, 1979, B1
25. Jim Coleman, "The Habs Took Their Cue from Doucet," *Calgary Herald*, May 7, 1979, D2.

Chapter 15

1. Francis Rosa, "Bruins Take It to Montreal, 5–2," *Boston Globe*, May 9, 1979, 29.
2. *Canadian Press* archives, coverage of May 6, 1979, Montreal-Boston Stanley Cup semi-final game.
3. *Ibid.*
4. Ernie Roberts, "And Suddenly There Was One…," *Boston Globe*, May 9, 1979, 1.
5. *Ibid.*
6. Francis Rosa, "Bruins Take It to Montreal, 5–2," *Boston Globe*, May 9, 1979, 29.
7. *Ibid.*
8. John Powers, "A Skating Hospital Ward Named Jonathan Turns Tide," *Boston Globe*, May 9, 1979, 32.
9. *Ibid.*
10. *Ibid.*
11. Francis Rosa, "Bruins Take It to Montreal, 5–2," *Boston Globe*, May 9, 1979, 29.

12. *Ibid.*
13. Ernie Roberts, "And Suddenly There Was One…," *Boston Globe*, May 9, 1979, 1.
14. *Ibid.*
15. Deane McGowen, "Bruins Down Canadiens 5–2; Tie Series 3–3," *New York Times*, May 9, 1979, 9.
16. Glenn Cole, "Bruins Force a Seventh Game on Stan Jonathan's Hat Trick," *Montreal Gazette*, May 9, 1979, 65.
17. Frank Orr, "Canadiens in a Corner First Time in Years," *Toronto Star*, May 9, 1979, D1.
18. *Ibid.*
19. *Ibid.*
20. Will McDonough, "Canadiens Glad They're Homeward Bound," *Boston Globe*, May 9, 1979, 30.
21. Frank Orr, "Canadiens in a Corner First Time in Years," *Toronto Star*, May 9, 1979, D1.
22. *Ibid.*
23. John Powers, "A Skating Hospital Ward Named Jonathan Turns Tide," *Boston Globe*, May 9, 1979, 32.
24. Frank Orr, "Canadiens in a Corner First Time in Years," *Toronto Star*, May 9, 1979.
25. Ernie Roberts, "And Suddenly There Was One…," *Boston Globe*, May 9, 1979, 1.
26. Frank Orr, "Canadiens in a Corner First Time in Years," *Toronto Star*, May 9, 1979.
27. *Ibid.*
28. *Ibid.*
29. *Ibid.*
30. *Ibid.*
31. Al Strachan, "Handkerchief Gone but Cherry Lavishes in Boston Triumph," *Montreal Gazette*, May 9, 1979, 66.
32. *Ibid.*
33. *Ibid.*
34. *Ibid.*
35. Steve Marantz, "Amazin' Rangers Wrap It Up, 2–1," *Boston Globe*, May 9, 1979, 30.
36. *Ibid.*
37. *Ibid.*
38. *Canadian Press* archives, report on the Rangers-Islanders Stanley Cup semi-final game, May, 9, 1979.
39. *Ibid.*
40. Steve Marantz, "Amazin' Rangers Wrap It Up, 2–1," *Boston Globe*, May 9, 1979, 30.
41. Glenn Cole, "Bruins Force a Seventh Game on Stan Jonathan's Hat Trick," *Montreal Gazette*, May 9, 1979, 65.
42. Will McDonough, "Canadiens Glad They're Homeward Bound," *Boston Globe*, May 9, 1979, 30.
43. *Ibid.*
44. Al Strachan, "Even Cherry's Bull Terrier Blue Isn't Outdone," *Montreal Gazette*, May 9, 1979, 66.

Chapter 16

1. *Toronto Star*, May 10, 1979.
2. "NHL Playoffs: Canadiens, Bruins in Game 7," *Gettysburg* (PA) *Times* (AP), May 10, 1979, p. 21.

Chapter 17

1. Danny Gallivan, *Hockey Night in Canada* broadcast of the May 10, 1979 Boston-Montreal playoff semi-final game.
2. Dick Irvin, *Ibid.*
3. Danny Gallivan, *Ibid.*
4. Lou Nanne, *Ibid.*
5. Danny Gallivan, *Ibid.*
6. Tim Burke, "An Incredible Game Resurrected the Glory," *Montreal Gazette*, May 11, 1979.
7. Jacques Lemaire, "Three Little Words: Too Many Men," *Sports Illustrated* video feature, 2014.
8. Dick Irvin, *Hockey Night in Canada* broadcast of the May 10, 1979, Boston-Montreal playoff semi-final game.
9. Lou Nanne, *Ibid.*
10. Danny Gallivan, *Ibid.*
11. *Ibid.*
12. Michael Farber, "Too Many Men," *Sports Illustrated* online archives, May 12, 2014.
13. Francis Rosa, "Canadiens Win It in Overtime, 5–4," *Boston Globe*, May 11, 1979, 61.
14. *Ibid.*
15. Leigh Montville, "Bruins Fall in Overtime After Gilbert's Gymnastics," *Boston Globe*, May 11, 1979, 1.
16. Thom Sears and Brad Park, *Straight Shooter: The Brad Park Story* (Mississauga, ON: John Wiley and Sons Canada, 2010), 200.
17. Brian Engblom, NHL Network's re-broadcast of Game #7 of Montreal-Boston 1979 semi-final series, 2007.
18. Dick Irvin, *Hockey Night in Canada*'s re-broadcast of Game #7 of Montreal-Boston 1979 semi-final series, 1994.
19. Scotty Bowman, NHL Network's re-broadcast of Game #7 of Montreal-Boston 1979 semi-final series, 2007.
20. Jacques Lemaire, *Ibid.*
21. Don Cherry, *Grapes: A Vintage View of Hockey* (Scarborough, ON: Avon, 1982), 11.
22. Danny Gallivan, *Hockey Night in Canada* broadcast of the May 10, 1979, Boston-Montreal playoff semi-final game.
23. *Ibid.*
24. *Ibid.*
25. *Ibid.*
26. Michael Farber, "Too Many Men," *Sports Illustrated* online archives, May 12, 2014.
27. Scotty Bowman, NHL Network's re-broadcast of Game #7 of Montreal-Boston 1979 semi-final series, 2007.
28. Thom Sears and Brad Park, *Straight Shooter: The Brad Park Story* (Mississauga, ON: John Wiley and Sons Canada, - 2010), 201.
29. Mark Napier, NHL Network's re-broadcast of Game #7 of Montreal-Boston 1979 semi-final series, 2007.
30. Terry O'Reilly, NHL Network's re-broadcast of Game #7 of Montreal-Boston 1979 semi-final series, 2007.
31. Guy Lafleur, NHL Network's re-broadcast of Game #7 of Montreal-Boston 1979 semi-final series, 2007.

32. Danny Gallivan, *Hockey Night in Canada* broadcast of the May 10, 1979 Boston-Montreal playoff semifinal game.

33. *Ibid.*

34. Don Cherry, *Grapes: A Vintage View of Hockey* (Scarborough, ON: Avon, 1982), 13.

35. Terry O'Reilly, NHL Network's re-broadcast of Game #7 of Montreal-Boston 1979 semi-final series, 2007.

36. Thom Sears and Brad Park, *Straight Shooter: The Brad Park Story* (Mississauga, ON: John Wiley and Sons Canada, 2010), 202.

37. Terry O'Reilly, NHL Network's re-broadcast of Game #7 of Montreal-Boston 1979 semi-final series, 2007

38. Thom Sears and Brad Park, *Straight Shooter: The Brad Park Story* (Mississauga, ON: John Wiley and Sons Canada, 2010), 202.

39. Danny Gallivan, *Hockey Night in Canada* broadcast of the May 10, 1979, Boston-Montreal playoff semi-final game.

40. Lou Nanne, *Hockey Night in Canada* broadcast of the May 10, 1979, Boston-Montreal playoff semi-final game.

41. Glenn Cole, *Montreal Gazette*, "Canadiens into Finals," *Montreal Gazette*, May 11, 1979, 31.

42. Leigh Montville, "Bruins Fall in Overtime After Gilbert's Gymnastics," *Boston Globe*, May 11, 1979, 1.

43. *Ibid.*

44. *Ibid.*

45. Francis Rosa, "Canadiens Win It in Overtime, 5–4," *Boston Globe*, May 11, 1979, 61.

46. "Montreal Ousts Bruins in OT," *Milwaukee Journal*, May 11, 1979, 14.

47. Leigh Montville, "Bruins Fall in Overtime After Gilbert's Gymnastics," *Boston Globe*, May 11, 1979, 1.

48. *Ibid.*

49. *Ibid.*

50. *Ibid.*

51. Francis Rosa, "Canadiens Win It in Overtime, 5–4," *Boston Globe*, May 11, 1979, 61.

52. *Ibid.*

53. *Ibid.*

54. *Ibid.*

55. Leigh Montville, "Bruins Fall in Overtime After Gilbert's Gymnastics," *Boston Globe*, May 11, 1979, 1.

56. *Ibid.*

57. Gordon Downie, *Hockey Night in Canada* 60th anniversary retrospective clip, 2012.

58. Steve Marantz, "Losing 3–1, Bowman Thought All Was Lost," *Boston Globe*, May 11, 1979, 64.

59. *Ibid.*

60. Francis Rosa, "Canadiens Win It in Overtime, 5–4," *Boston Globe*, May 11, 1979, 61.

61. *Ibid.*

62. *Ibid.*

63. Michael Farber, "Too Many Men," *Sports Illustrated* online archives, May 12, 2014.

Chapter 19

1. Glenn Cole, "Rangers Stun Canadiens," *Montreal Gazette*, May 14, 1979, 17.

2. Francis Rosa, "Montreal Deflates Rangers," *Boston Globe*, May 16, 1979, 29.

3. *Ibid.*

4. Glenn Cole, "Canadiens One Victory Away from Another Stanley Cup," *Montreal Gazette*, May 21, 1979, 13.

5. *Ibid.*

6. *Ibid.*

7. Francis Rosa, "Canadiens Hoist the Cup Fourth Straight Year, 4–1," *Boston Globe*, May 22, 1979, 37.

8. Phil Schlenker, *Let's Talk Hockey: 50 Wonderful Debates* (Bloomington: iUniverse Books, 2009), 30.

9. "Scotty Bowman," jrank.org.

10. Don Cherry, *Don Cherry's Hockey Stories and Stuff* (Toronto: Anchor Canada, 2008), 129.

Chapter 20

1. Will McDonough, "This Town's Not Big Enough for Cherry, Sinden," *Boston Globe*, May 18, 1979, 57.

2. *Ibid.*

3. Will McDonough, "Cherry, Sinden Become Friends Again, But…," *Boston Globe*, May 22, 1979, 37.

4. *Ibid.*

5. *Ibid.*

6. Don Cherry, *Grapes: A Vintage View of Hockey* (Scarborough, ON: Avon, 1982), 42.

7. *Ibid.*

8. Will McDonough, "An Unrelenting Cherry Abandons Ship," *Boston Globe*, May 25, 1979, 49.

9. Neil Singelais, "…The Fans," *Boston Globe*, May 25, 1979, 52.

10. *Ibid.*

11. Will McDonough, "Cherry Hires an Agent—Name Is Eagleson," *Boston Globe*, May 29, 1979, 37.

12. *Ibid.*

13. Terry Frei, "Cherry Starts Down the Rockie (15–53–12) Road," *Boston Globe*, May 31, 1979, 50.

14. Steve Marantz, "Cherry: I'll Make It Go," *Boston Globe*, June 1, 1979, 51.

15. Don Cherry, *Grapes: A Vintage View of Hockey* (Scarborough, ON: Avon, 1982), 39.

16. *Ibid.*

17. Francis Rosa, "The Cherry Reaction: The Players … Disappointed but Not Surprised," *Boston Globe*, May 25, 1979, 52.

18. *Ibid.*

19. *Ibid.*

20. Don Cherry, *Grapes: A Vintage View of Hockey* (Scarborough, ON: Avon, 1982), illustration section.

21. Francis Rosa, "Creighton to Be Next Coach of Bruins," *Boston Globe*, June 29, 1979, 49.

22. Ray Fitzgerald, "Some Friendly Advice on How to Coach the Bruins," *Boston Globe* July 2, 1979, 32.

23. *Ibid.*

24. Francis Rosa, "Creighton Fired, Sinden Back (Until End of Season)," *Boston Globe*, May 26, 1980, S1.

25. Red Fisher, "Geoffrion Quits, Ruel Back Behind Canadiens' Bench," *Montreal Gazette*, December 13, 1979, 97.

26. John Ahern, "The Aftermath of the Firing … Creighton Silent—And Shocked," *Boston Globe*, March 24, 1980, S1.

27. Gerald Eskenazi, "Fred Creighton Is Back—But How Far?" *New York Times* online archives, July 12, 1981.

28. Thom Sears and Brad Park, *Straight Shooter: The Brad Park Story* (Mississauga, ON: John Wiley and Sons Canada, 2010), 217.

29. John Ahern, "The Aftermath of the Firing … Creighton Silent—And Shocked," *Boston Globe*, March 24, 1980, S1.

30. Bob Duffy, "The Reaction: Cherry Turns to Diplomacy," *Boston Globe*, March 23, 1980, S1.

31. Gerald Eskenazi, "Fred Creighton Is Back—But How Far?" *New York Times* online archives, July 12, 1981.

32. Neil Singelais, "Same Old Tune: Fans Love Cherry, Bosses Don't," *Boston Globe*, May 21, 1980, S1.

33. *Ibid.*

34. Leigh Montville, "He's Still Laughing," *Boston Globe*, May 16, 1980, S1.

35. *Ibid.*

36. Steve Marantz, "He's a More Mellow Cherry," *Boston Globe*, December 2, 1979, 49.

37. "The World According to Grapes," *Boston Globe* editorial, December 2, 1979, 14.

38. Francis Rosa, "It's Sweet for Cherry: Bruins Fall, 5–3," *Boston Globe*, December 3, 1979, 37.

Chapter 21

1. Don Cherry, "Three Little Words: Too Many Men," *Sports Illustrated* video feature, 2014.

2. Steve Marantz, "He's a More Mellow Cherry," *Boston Globe*, December 2, 1979, 49.

3. Will McDonough, "The Aftermath: The Play," *Boston Globe*, May 12, 1979, 21.

4. Danny Gallivan, *Hockey Night in Canada* broadcast of the May 10, 1979, Boston-Montreal playoff semi-final game.

5. Jack Craig, "Broadcasters Vocal on Penalty," *Boston Globe*, May 18, 1979, A16.

6. Thom Sears and Brad Park, *Straight Shooter: The Brad Park Story* (Mississauga, ON: John Wiley and Sons Canada, 2010), 201.

7. Jack Craig, "Broadcasters Vocal on Penalty," *Boston Globe*, May 18, 1979, A16.

8. *Ibid.*

9. *Ibid.*

10. Steve Marantz, "He's a More Mellow Cherry," *Boston Globe*, December 2, 1979, 49.

11. Thom Sears and Brad Park, *Straight Shooter: The Brad Park Story* (Mississauga, ON: John Wiley and Sons Canada, 2010), 202.

12. Will McDonough, "The Aftermath: The Play," *Boston Globe*, May 12, 1979, 21.

13. *Ibid.*

14. *Ibid.*

15. *Ibid.*

16. Thom Sears and Brad Park, *Straight Shooter: The Brad Park Story* (Mississauga, ON: John Wiley and Sons Canada, 2010), 201.

17. Liam Maguire, *Next Goal Wins* (Toronto: Random House Canada, 2012), 47.

18. *Canadian Press* archives, coverage of "The Last Hurrah" at Boston Garden, September 27, 1995.

19. Fred Cusick, NESN's coverage of "The Last Hurrah" (Montreal-Boston September 26, 1995, exhibition game).

20. *Ibid.*

Chapter 22

1. Francis Rosa, "Bruins Get Stonewalled; Canadiens Roll to Sweep of Series, 5–0," *Boston Globe*, April 8, 1984, S1.

2. *Ibid.*

3. Michael Madden, "A Familiar Way to End the Season," *Boston Globe*, April 17, 1985, 27.

4. *Ibid.*

5. Francis Rosa, "Familiar Canadiens Beat Tunes Out of Bruins, 4–3," *Boston Globe*, April 13, 1986, 55.

6. *Ibid.*

7. Francis Rosa, "What's Next for Bruins?" *Boston Globe*, April 14, 1987, 69.

8. *Ibid.*

9. John Powers, "1943: The Bruins' Last Breakthrough," *Boston Globe*, April 22, 1988, 47.

10. *Ibid.*

11. *Ibid.*

12. *Ibid.*

13. Don Cherry, *Don Cherry's Hockey Stories and Stuff* (Toronto: Anchor Canada, 2008), 143.

14. Kevin Paul Dupont, "Bruins Turn the Tables," *Boston Globe*, April 25, 1988, 52.

15. Leigh Montville, "Forty-Five Years of Dues Are Paid," *Boston Globe*, April 27, 1988, 83.

16. *Ibid.*

17. *Ibid.*

18. *Ibid.*

19. Fred Cusick, NESN's coverage of Montreal-Boston playoff game, April 26, 1988.

20. Derek Sanderson, *Ibid.*

Epilogue

1. Kevin Paul Dupont, "Frosty Took Great Care of the Bruins," *Boston Globe*, June 1, 1995, 74.

2. Stu Hackel, "The Voice of the Bruins," *Sports Illustrated* online archives, March 7, 1994.

3. Fluto Shinzawa, "Tom Johnson, 79, Hall of Fame Player, Coach of Bruins' Last Stanley Cup Title," *Boston Globe*, November 23, 2007, C19.

4. Bob Ryan, "Kiley Was a Three-Sport Star," *Boston Globe*, July 16, 1993, 27.

5. *Ibid.*

6. Leigh Montville, "Cherry Still at Home in Garden," *Boston Globe*, April 22, 1989, 38.

7. Bryan Marquard, "Ernie Roberts; Sports Editor Cultivated Writers for *Globe*," *Boston Globe*, March 24, 2009, B14.

8. Bryan Marquard, "Francis Rosa, Hockey Hall of Fame Sportswriter, 91," *Boston Globe* online obituary archives, January 8, 2012.

9. *Ibid.*

10. "Big-League Teams, Bush-League Arena," *Boston Globe* editorial, March 25, 1979, 86.

11. Fred Cusick, *Fred Cusick: Voice of the Bruins* (Champaign, IL: Sports Publishing, 2006), 2.

12. YouTube video, comment section, "1978 Stanley Cup Finals Montreal Canadiens @ Boston Bruins Overtime Part 2," posted May 22, 2011.

Appendix A

1. Ernie Roberts, "Boston's Own Dandy Don," *Boston Globe*, January 27, 1978, A4.

2. John Powers, "Dog Named Blue Is This Man's Best Friend," *Boston Globe*, April 15, 1979, 47.

3. *Ibid.*

4. *Ibid.*

5. George Plimpton, *Open Net* (New York: Penguin, 1987), 84.

6. Ernie Roberts, "Boston's Own Dandy Don," *Boston Globe*, January 27, 1978, A4.

7. *Ibid.*

8. John A.M. Rowe, "Wrong Dog," *Boston Globe* (letter to editor), May 25, 1979.

9. John Powers, "Dog Named Blue Is This Man's Best Friend," *Boston Globe*, April 15, 1979, 47.

10. *Ibid.*

11. *Ibid.*

12. *Ibid.*

13. Matt Kalman, *100 Things Bruins Fans Should Know & Do Before They Die* (Chicago: Triumph Books, 2011), 149.

14. *Ibid.*

15. Joe Pelletier, "Wayne Cashman," bruinslegends.blogspot

16. *Ibid.*

17. *Ibid.*

18. Rick Cole, "Black and White and ALWAYS Right," websports.ca, May 25, 2015.

19. Joe Pelletier, "Wayne Cashman," bruinslegends.blogspot.ca.

20. Francis Rosa, "Rash Bugs Cashman," *Boston Globe*, April 4, 1979, 46.

21. Matt Kalman, *100 Things Bruins Fans Should Know & Do Before They Die* (Chicago: Triumph Books, 2011), 76.

22. Leigh Montville, "It Worked Out Fine for Sinden," *Boston Globe*, April 27, 1988, 86.

23. Leigh Montville, "Visitor to Montreal Has Some Thoughts," *Boston Globe*, April 30, 1979, 29.

24. Matt Kalman, *100 Things Bruins Fans Should Know & Do Before They Die* (Chicago: Triumph Books, 2011), 77.

25. Brad Park, "Gerry Cheevers," *Legends of Hockey* (video documentary series).

26. Tom Fitzgerald, "A Wiser Don Cherry Talks About His Bruins," *Boston Globe*, May 9, 1976, 83.

27. Matt Kalman, *100 Things Bruins Fans Should Know & Do Before They Die* (Chicago: Triumph Books, 2011), 264.

28. Sports Legends New England, "Rick Middleton Episode," 2010.

29. Tim Burke, "Cherry's Cheery Way Keeps Bruins Flying," *Montreal Gazette*, May 10, 1979, 59.

30. Eddie MacCabe, "Lucky 'Bleepers' Beat the Bruins," *Ottawa Citizen*, April 27, 1979, 23.

31. John Ahern, "Maple Leafs In, Jonathan Out," *Boston Globe*, November 16, 1978, 51.

32. Francis Rosa, "Cherry: 'We're Mentally Fatigued,'" *Boston Globe*, January 18, 1979, 36.

33. *Ibid.*

34. John Ahern, "Cherry Praises Doak," *Boston Globe*, November 7, 1978, 76.

35. Joe Pelletier, "Greatest Hockey Legends: Gary Doak," bruinslegends.blogspot.ca.

36. "Gary Doak," Hockey Hall of Fame player database.

37. Joe Pelletier, "Greatest Hockey Legends: Gary Doak," bruinslegends.blogspot.ca.

38. *Ibid.*

39. John Ahern, "Cherry Praises Doak," *Boston Globe*, November 7, 1978, 76.

40. "Dwight Foster," wikipedia.org.

41. Ray Fitzgerald, "Cheevers the Gerry of Old," *Boston Globe*, April 3, 1979, 37.

42. Andrew Berkshire, "Revisiting Great Games: Boston vs. Montreal Game #7 of the 1978–79 Semifinal," habseyesontheprize.com, November 28, 2012.

43. Steve Ewen, "Guy Lafleur on Gilles Gilbert and Famed Blast for 1979 Playoff Goal: 'I Think I Ruined His Career,'" *The* (Vancouver) *Province* online archives, January 5, 2012.

44. Leigh Montville, "It Worked Out Fine for Sinden," *Boston Globe*, April 27, 1988, 86.

45. Don Cherry, *Grapes: A Vintage View of Hockey* (Scarborough, ON: Avon, 1982), 233.

46. John Ahern, "Maple Leafs In, Jonathan Out," *Boston Globe*, November 16, 1978, 51.

47. Joe Pelletier, "Stan Jonathan," Greatesthockeylegends.com.

48. *Ibid.*

49. *Ibid.*

50. Jen Royle, "Stan Jonathan," *Boston Herald Talk of the Town* video series, 2014.

51. Steve Ewen, "Guy Lafleur on Gilles Gilbert and Famed Blast for 1979 Playoff Goal: 'I Think I Ruined His Career,'" *The* (Vancouver) *Province* online archives, January 5, 2012.

52. "Don Michel Marcotte," Hockey Hall of Fame player database.

53. Andrew Berkshire, "Revisiting Great Games: Boston Vs. Montreal Game #7 of the 1978–79 Semifinal," habseyesontheprize.com, November 28, 2012.

54. Christopher Bowden, "Defensive Standout Don Marcotte Proves Two-Way Hockey Still Pays Off," *Christian Science Monitor* online archives, March 22, 1982.

55. *Ibid.*

56. *Ibid.*

57. *Ibid.*

58. Matt Kalman, *100 Things Bruins Fans Should Know & Do Before They Die* (Chicago: Triumph Books, 2011), 265–266.

59. *Ibid.*

60. *Ibid.*

61. *Ibid.*

62. Fred Cusick, *Fred Cusick: Voice of the Bruins* (Champaign, IL: Sports Publishing, 2006), 135.

63. Ernie Roberts, "Middleton Deal: Bruins Got a Stinger, Rangers Got Stung," *Boston Globe*, March 7, 1979, 61.

64. Mike DelNagro, "There's No One So Shifty as Nifty," *Sports Illustrated* online archives, March 30, 1981.

65. Sports Legends New England, "Rick Middleton Episode," 2010.

66. Al Strachan, "Bruins Insist They'll Be Tougher at Garden," *Montreal Gazette*, April 30, 1979, 53.

67. Francis Rosa, "Middleton's Three Get Bruins Going, 6–2," *Boston Globe*, October 8, 1976.

68. Francis Rosa, "Cherry Touts Middleton," *Boston Globe*, January 23, 1979, 76.

69. John Ahern, "Rick Middleton," *Boston Globe*, January 14, 1979, 62.

70. Francis Rosa, "Secord Back on Firing Line, Sparks Bruins, 4–2," *Boston Globe*, December 22, 1978, 24.

71. Matt Kalman, *100 Things Bruins Fans Should Know & Do Before They Die* (Chicago: Triumph Books, 2011), 175.

72. *Ibid.*, 191–194.

73. *Ibid.*

74. *Ibid.*

75. *Ibid.*

76. Lesley Visser, "Bob Miller: An American Makes Good in Pro Hockey," *Boston Globe*, November 25, 1978, 21.

77. *Ibid.*

78. Francis Rosa, "Walton Is In, Park Out," *Boston Globe*, December 9, 1978, 26.

79. Don Cherry, *Don Cherry's Hockey Stories and Stuff* (Toronto: Anchor Canada, 2008), 121–122.

80. Dick Irvin, *Hockey Night in Canada* broadcast of the May 10, 1979, Boston-Montreal playoff semi-final game.

81. Lou Nanne, *Hockey Night in Canada* broadcast of the May 10, 1979, Boston-Montreal playoff semi-final game.

82. Francis Rosa, "Orr's Song to O'Reilly: 'Ya Gotta Have Hart,'" *Boston Globe*, March 12, 1978.

83. Danny Gallivan, *Hockey Night in Canada* broadcast of the May 10, 1979, Boston-Montreal playoff semi-final game.

84. "Outclassed by the Soviets," *Boston Globe* editorial, January 12, 1979, 16.

85. Matt Kalman, *100 Things Bruins Fans Should Know & Do Before They Die* (Chicago: Triumph Books, 2011), 87.

86. Hockey Hall of Fame player database, "Pinnacle: Brad Park."

87. Hockey Hall of Fame player database, "Spotlight: Brad Park."

88. *Ibid.*

89. Matt Kalman, *100 Things Bruins Fans Should Know & Do Before They Die* (Chicago: Triumph Books, 2011), 155.

90. Thom Sears and Brad Park, *Straight Shooter: The Brad Park Story* (Mississauga, ON: John Wiley and Sons Canada, 2010), 174.

91. Hockey Hall of Fame player database, "Spotlight: Brad Park."

92. *Ibid.*

93. Brian McFarlane, *Legends of Hockey* (video documentary series), "Gerry Cheevers."

94. Hockey Hall of Fame player database, "Spotlight: Brad Park."

95. Thom Sears and Brad Park, *Straight Shooter: The Brad Park Story* (Mississauga, ON: John Wiley and Sons Canada, 2010), 198.

96. *Ibid.*, 179.

97. Francis Rosa, "Jonathan, Bruins Keep North Stars in Dark," *Boston Globe*, March 17, 1978, 34.

98. Frank Orr, "Ratelle Deserved a Big Night," *Toronto Star*, May 4, 1979, B1.

99. Tom Fitzgerald, "Park a Bruin, Espo a Ranger in Five-Man 'Shocker,'" *Boston Globe*, November 8, 1975, 1.

100. Hockey Hall of Fame player database, "Spotlight: Jean Ratelle."

101. Joe Pelletier, "Stan Jonathan," greatesthockeylegends.com.

102. Hockey Hall of Fame player database "Spotlight: Jean Ratelle."

103. Francis Rosa, "Mcnab Moves Out of the Doghouse, Becomes Top Dog," *Boston Globe*, March 26, 1978, 72.

104. Francis Rosa, "Bruins Look to Redmond as Their Key," *Boston Globe*, April 26, 1979, 46.

105. *Ibid.*

106. Francis Rosa, "Doak Back to Beef Up Bruins' Defense," *Boston Globe*, April 21, 1979, 26.

107. Francis Rosa, "Bruins Look to Redmond as Their Key," *Boston Globe*, April 26, 1979, 46.

108. Don Cherry, *Don Cherry's Hockey Stories and Stuff* (Toronto: Anchor Canada, 2008), 209.

109. "Number8," "Bobby Schmautz?" hfboards.hockeysfuture.com, March 12, 2013.

110. Don Cherry, *Grapes: A Vintage View of Hockey* (Scarborough, ON: Avon, 1982), 238.

111. Joe Pelletier, "Al Secord," greatesthockeylegends.com.

112. John Ahern, "Al Sims: His New Life with the Bruins Represents a Change for the Better," *Boston Globe*, February 11, 1979, 62.

113. Francis Rosa, "Bruins Come Out Smoking, Send Blues Sprawling, 7–2," *Boston Globe*, October 25, 1978, 61.

114. Francis Rosa, "Whalers Draft Sims; Winnipeg Reclaims Hull," *Boston Globe*, June 14, 1979, 54.

115. Matt Kalman, *100 Things Bruins Fans Should Know & Do Before They Die* (Chicago: Triumph Books, 2011), 41.

116. *Ibid.*

117. Associated Press archives, January 4, 1973.

118. *One Tough Guy*, ESPN Films, 2014.

Bibliography

Books

Cherry, Don, with Stan Fischler. *Grapes: A Vintage View of Hockey*. Scarborough, ON: Avon, 1982.

Cherry, Don, as told to Al Strachan. *Don Cherry's Hockey Stories and Stuff*. Toronto: Doubleday Canada, 2008.

Cherry, Don. *Straight Up and Personal: The World According to Grapes*. Toronto: Anchor Canada, 2014.

Cusick, Fred. *Fred Cusick: Voice of the Bruins*. Champaign, IL: Sports Publishing, 2006.

Diamond, Dan. *The Ultimate Prize: The Stanley Cup*. Kansas City: Andrews McMeel, 2003.

Gilbert, Rod, and Brad Park. *Playing Hockey the Professional Way*. New York: HarperCollins, 1972.

Hollander, Zander, ed. *The Complete Handbook of Pro Hockey*, 1979 ed. New York: Signet, 1978.

Kalman, Matt. *100 Things Bruins Fans Should Know Before They Die*. Chicago: Triumph, 2010.

Keene, Kerry. *Tales from the Boston Bruins Locker Room*. Champaign, IL: Sports Publishing, 2011.

Maguire, Liam. *Next Goal Wins*. Toronto: Random House Canada, 2012.

McFarlane, Brian. *The Lively World of Hockey*. New York: Signet, 1968.

Park, Brad, with Stan Fischler. *Play the Man*. New York: Dodd, Mead, 1971.

Plimpton, George. *Open Net*. New York: Penguin, 1987.

Proudfoot, Jim. *Pro Hockey NHL 75–76*. Markham, ON: Pocket, 1975.

Robson, Dan. *Quinn: The Life of a Hockey Legend*. Toronto: Penguin, 2015.

Sanderson, Derek. *Crossing the Line*. New York: HarperCollins eBooks, 2012.

Schlenker, Phil. *Let's Talk Hockey: 50 Wonderful Debates*. Bloomington: iUniverse, 2009.

Sears, Thom, and Brad Park. *Straight Shooter: The Brad Park Story*. Mississauga, ON: John Wiley & Sons Canada, 2012.

Newspapers (Microfilm and Online)

Bangor (ME) *Daily News*

Boston Globe

Calgary Herald

Cambridge (ON) *Reporter*

Indiana Evening Gazette

Kitchener-Waterloo (ON) *Record*

Lewiston (ME) *Daily Sun*

Logansport (IN) *Pharos-Tribune*

Lowell (MA) *Sun*

Milwaukee Journal

Montreal Gazette

Newport (RI) *Daily News*

New York Times

Ottawa Citizen

Pittsburgh Post-Gazette

The Sporting News

(Toronto) *Globe & Mail*

Toronto Star

Vancouver Province

Online Resources

Bleacherreport.com

Bobbyorr.com

Brittanica.com

Bruinslegends.blogspot.com

Bruins.NHL.com

Canada.com

Canadiens.NHL.com

Csmonitor.com

ESPN.com

Greatesthockeylegends.com

Hhof.com

Hockeybuzz.com

Hockeydb.com

Hockey-reference.com

Hockeysfuture.com

Jrank.org

NHL.com

NHLofficials.com

Si.com

Thehockeynews.com

Theprovince.com

Websports.ca

Yourememberthat.com

Youtube.com

Index